Women in Old Norse Society

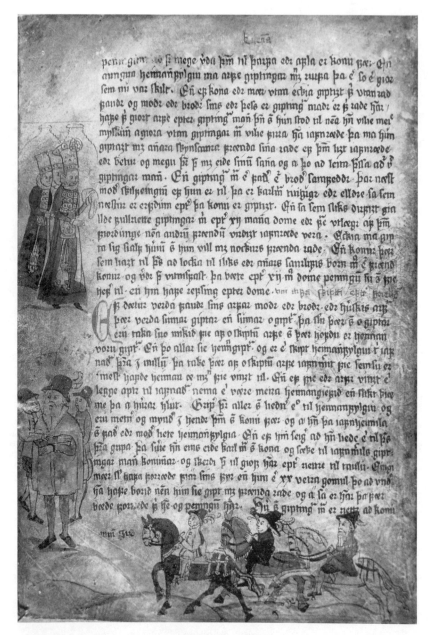

Illustration shows a bride urged forward to her wedding by two female relatives. The drawing is found in the margin of the marriage section in *Jónsbók* in the manuscript Reykjabók (MS. AM 345 fol. 38v) dating from circa 1600. Used by permission of Stofnun Árna Magnússonar in Reykjavík, Iceland.

WOMEN
IN
OLD NORSE
SOCIETY

Jenny Jochens

CORNELL UNIVERSITY PRESS
Ithaca and London

Publication of this book was aided by grants from
the Carlsberg Foundation and Towson State University.

First published 1995 by Cornell University Press.
First printing, Cornell Paperbacks, 1998.

Printed in the United States of America

Library of Congress Cataloging-in-Publication Data

Jochens, Jenny, 1928–
Women in Old Norse society / Jenny Jochens.
    p.   cm.
Includes bibliographical references and index.
ISBN 0-8014-3165-4 (alk. paper)
ISBN 0-8014-8520-7 (pbk.: alk. paper)
1. Women—History—Middle Ages, 500–1500.   2. Women—Norway—History.
3. Women—Iceland—History.   4. Old Norse literature—History and criticism.
5. Women in literature.   I. Title.
                HQ1147.A–Z.N8J63   1995
305.4'09'02—dc20   95-31506

Cornell University Press strives to utilize environmentally responsible suppliers
and materials to the fullest extent possible in the publishing of its books. Such
materials include vegetable-based, low-VOC inks and acid-free papers that are
also either recycled, totally chlorine-free, or partly composed of nonwood fibers.

Cloth printing 10 9 8 7 6 5 4 3 2
Paperback printing 10 9 8 7 6 5 4 3 2 1

To
Birgit Baldwin

Dearest Daughter, Best Friend, Esteemed Colleague
10 VIII 1960   17 VI 1988

Hver ván er, at ek muna vilja lifa við harm þenna?

veitk ófullt
ok opit standa
sonar skarð,
es mér sær of vann.
Egils saga, chapter 78

Contents

Contents

Preface

My work on women in the Old Norse tradition is the indirect result of my involvement in the Woman's Studies program at Towson State University.[1] In the mid-seventies I began to add courses on European women to the curriculum in the History Department and to participate in interdisciplinary courses with colleagues from the departments of literature, anthropology, psychology, and biology. A chief concern of women's history in its early days was to find, in the words of Natalie Davis, "women worthies," women who had made important contributions to the cultures of the past but had been forgotten by (male) historians. Applying this approach to my own teaching about women in the Middle Ages, I initially thought I had found a perfect candidate in the allegedly strong Norse Woman known from Eddic poetry and the family sagas (or sagas of Icelanders).[2] Thus Brynhildr and Guðrún became featured *vedettes* in my lecture repertoire and *Vǫlsunga saga* and *Laxdœla saga* were assigned as required reading.

By the time of my first sabbatical leave in 1977 I was prepared to abandon a previous project in medieval French history and to plunge into the saga world. This decision was spurred by an emerging suspicion that the saga "worthies" did not represent flesh-and-blood women from the pagan age in which they had been situated or from the Christian age of the saga writers themselves, but that they were images formed in men's imagination. As the methodology of women's studies gained sophistication, such representations were assigned to the study of gender, a concept that was not created until the mid-eighties. To pursue my suspicion, then, I needed not only to immerse myself in the entire Norse literary tradition but to acquire the evolving techniques of gender analysis.

I had chosen Old Norse as a minor elective at the University of Copenhagen, and when I first came to this country I rekindled my interest in the Norse world by reading sagas with Stefán Einarsson at the Johns Hopkins University. I now presumed to master all genres of the Norse literary corpus and to become acquainted with the massive secondary literature. As I began to publish my findings in articles, I little realized that it would take more than fifteen years before the sources would begin to release their secrets of female existence in the Germanic north.

In fact, the Norse material did not yield a uniform figure of a proud pagan woman but offered multifaceted portraits of imagined and real women, from pagan goddesses to Christian milkmaids, conjured in multiple combinations and permutations by inspired poets and gifted prose authors. Meanwhile, conscientious historians and legal experts had preserved precious information about women's everyday life of marriage and work in pagan and Christian settings.

Although women's own voices cannot be separated from this predominantly male chorus, the myriad of female figures generated by male authors do divide readily into two groups. The first group includes portraits of divine figures and heroic women of which the latter are based on perceptions and events in Continental Europe. These images were created by male poets and later elaborated by prose writers. The second group offers comparatively mundane descriptions of ordinary women in both pagan and Christian settings in Iceland and Norway; these pictures were constructed by thirteenth-century authors and historians from their observations of contemporary society and combined with oral tradition and deductions about the world of their pagan ancestors.

The boundary between the two groups is of course permeable, but the great wealth of these traditions makes it necessary for me to separate my work into two studies. A forthcoming study, titled *Old Norse Images of Women,* will treat the first group:[3] divine, mythic, and heroic women whose images were initially depicted by Latin authors in writing and articulated by Germanic singers in oral lays, now preserved only in Old Norse Eddic poetry and elaborated in saga narratives. The present book focuses specifically on Norway, especially Iceland, and the women whose lives are described primarily in the two genres known as the sagas of Icelanders and the contemporary sagas, further corroborated from the perspective supplied by the laws. Echoing Georges Duby, I "shall refrain from calling [these pictures] the 'real' (since mental representations have no less reality), but rather [I shall define them as reflecting] the tangible aspects of existence."[4] The forthcoming study of images will be directed to readers primarily interested in the female share in Germanic myth and poetry, whereas this book will appeal to scholars concerned with social issues of ancient and medieval Iceland and Norway, such as the transformation of pagan marriage under the influence of churchmen and the importance of women's work in a pastoral economy. The richness of the Old Norse tradition about women in the

Preface

Germanic-nordic* world will, however, become most fully apparent only after both books are examined.

Gender studies have evolved over the past twenty years to include not only men's images of women but also the study of family history and analysis of women's work in relation to men's. My own work reenacts this development. In a recapitulation of the first stage of women's history, I add a few "women worthies" to the roster of important figures from the nordic past. Although the analysis of images will withdraw these figures from the world of "real" women, as revealing male perceptions of "the others," they offer important clues to gender. To the domain of social and family history, long recognized as pertaining to women's history par excellence, my sources add valuable information about marriage, reproduction, infanticide, and work.[5]

In these two books, I attempt to do for Germanic Norse women what the Dane Vilhelm Grønbech did primarily for men in his monumental four volumes of *Vor Folkeæt i Oldtiden,* translated into English by William Worster and in part rewritten and revised by Grönbech in the two volumes of *The Culture of the Teutons.*[6]

Citations in Old Norse are kept to a minimum. Translations are always placed before the original and are my own, unless otherwise indicated. The Old Norse phrases are required when single words are to be closely analyzed and when appropriately corresponding terms are lacking in English. Full sentences in Old Norse have been provided occasionally to add clarification for specialists. In all cases it is my hope that the common base of Germanic languages will stimulate the pleasure of linguistic recognition in readers of English and German. Personal names are consistently rendered in normalized Old Norse nominative forms, even when well-known English equivalents exist. (Thus, I refer to Sigurðr and Guðrún, not Sigurd and Gudrun.) Where still extant, geographic names will be given in modern Icelandic. After a few pages readers unfamiliar with Icelandic letters should become accustomed to them; ð ("eth") is a voiced consonant pronounced as "th" in "mother"; its unvoiced counterpart þ is captured in the initial sound of the letter's own name "thorn"; ǫ is the normalizing way in which scholars render the later (and still current) ö; and ae and oe have been conflated in œ.

The completion of this book has required access to primary and secondary works, availability of time and institutional support, inspiration from colleagues and students, and sustenance from friends and family. My work could not have been done in Baltimore without the fine collection of *Islandica* in

---

*The word "nordic" will be consistently set in lower case.

the Milton S. Eisenhower Library of the Johns Hopkins University assembled by Stefán Einarsson during his long tenure in the English Department. I am grateful to the library for the generous borrowing privileges I have enjoyed. Unfortunately, the library has been forced to reduce Icelandic acquisitions since Stefán's return to Iceland in 1962, but I have been able to compensate by resorting to three major Icelandic collections, the Fiske Collection at Cornell University, the Arnamagnæan Institute at the University of Copenhagen, and Árnastofnun at the University of Iceland in Reykjavík. All three institutions have welcomed me with the greatest courtesy and helpfulness.

My own institution, Towson State University, has supported me generously with sabbatical leaves, semesters of reduced teaching loads, travel grants to present papers at conferences here and abroad, and a grant-in-aid toward publication. In 1981 I received a National Endowment for the Humanities Summer Stipend and in 1987–1988 a Fellowship for College Teachers. While I was working at the Arnamagnæan Institute in Copenhagen during a sabbatical leave in 1984, an apartment was made available to me by the Danish National Bank. I am grateful to the Carlsberg Foundation in Copenhagen for a grant toward publication.

My colleagues at Towson State University have patiently and cheerfully listened to first versions of many conference papers and articles, and they have been unstinting in their encouragement of my work. With vigor and enthusiasm my students have immersed themselves in the saga world and offered valuable comments, questions, and papers. I thank them all. My most significant professional contacts have occurred at meetings. The opportunity to present papers invariably resulted in constructive comments that provoked additional thinking and rewriting. Among these occasions, the most important have been the annual conferences of the Society for the Advancement of Scandinavian Study and the triennial International Saga Conferences. I wish to thank Theodore M. Andersson and the anonymous reader who read this manuscript for Cornell University Press and offered valuable criticism. Moving through the labyrinth from manuscript to book, my work has benefited from the expert guidance of Bernhard Kendler and the editorial staff at Cornell University Press. I am grateful to Barbara Dinneen for sympathetic and sensitive copyediting. I owe a debt of gratitude to Sverrir Tómasson and Davíð Erlingsson for having scrutinized my Old Norse citations.

My children, Peter, Ian, Birgit, and Christopher, and their spouses, have on numerous occasions provided hospitality and access to their university libraries. As grandchildren appeared, visits became more frequent but the time in the library shorter. I owe special thanks to Aris Fioretos, my daughter's friend, whose support, friendship, and inspiration during the last six years have been invaluable. My greatest debt is to my husband, John W. Baldwin.

Preface

He has patiently read and reread many versions of this book and helped me to clarify my thinking, sharpen my arguments, and improve my prose. By now he knows more about the Old Norse world than he ever wanted to and more than he thought possible when we first met in a seminar in medieval canon law in Paris forty years ago.

JENNY JOCHENS

Baltimore, Maryland

Women in Old Norse Society

Introduction

In the summer of the year 1000 the leaders of Iceland convened for the yearly meeting of their deliberative body, the so-called *alþingi*—by then a generation old.[1] They were faced with unrest stirred up by a vocal minority of Christians. This small group of Icelanders had accepted the new religion in the course of the two previous decades, either during travels abroad or while listening to persuasive missionaries sent to the island by the Norwegian king. That the new converts were zealous is indicated by the action of the alþingi; during the meeting of the previous year lawmakers had found it necessary to pass a regulation that obligated people to prosecute relatives—presumably Christians—who had blasphemed the old gods. The adherents of the new religion were now so numerous that armed struggle was barely avoided as pagans and Christians alike declared themselves outside the law in order to form a new society. Threatened by the dissolution of their community, the chieftains agreed that the pagan Þorgeirr, leader of the alþingi—his title was law speaker—should be commissioned to settle the issue. He delivered a speech in which he referred to recent warfare in Denmark and Norway provoked by resistance to the missionary efforts of local kings. To avoid replication of these conditions, he proposed "one law and one religion" for all of Iceland. The assembly promptly agreed and asked him to make the necessary legal changes. "Then it was declared to be law that all people should be Christians and receive baptism who were previously unbaptized in this land."[2] Thus, circa 1125, the historian Ari Þorgilsson related the conversion of Iceland, basing his account on reports from people whose close relatives had been present at the occasion only two or three generations earlier.[3] This event stood toward the end of the long, momentous process of the Germanic conversion to Christianity, begun by Ulfilas among the Ostrogoths at the close of the late fourth century and later punctuated by the dramatic conversions of Clovis, king of the Franks, in 496, Ethelbert, king of Kent, in 597, and Harald Bluetooth, king of Denmark, in about 950. The Icelandic story is remarkable for its peaceful resolution of a problem that had caused so much bloodshed elsewhere.

The conversion of Iceland raises the problem of the impact of Christianity on the female half of the human race. This, in fact, is one of the most controversial issues in women's history. One point of view argues that Christianity was deeply imbued from the beginning with Jewish and Roman patriarchy, which became intensified by an all-male clergy and resulted in misogyny as the most lasting and profound legacy of Christianity for women. An opposite argument claims that the Christian message was fundamentally a liberating force that included women as well, and although the original radicalism of Jesus on this issue, as on so many others, became diluted with time, women were better off during the Christian period and in Christian countries than they had been before and elsewhere.

Few would deny the close association between misogyny and Christianity, and hardly a Christian church today can claim innocence. The most cogent comparison is not between Christianity and modern secular society, however, but between the conditions of women in a Christian and a non-Christian country in a contemporary setting, or before and after the advent of the religion in a historical context. The latter comparison is facilitated by the extent to which literacy was present during the transformation.

In western Europe conversion overtook not only the literate Roman pagans but also the largely illiterate Germanic tribes. Pushed from the east by the Huns, they first entered the Roman Empire in the late fourth century. Both as converts and destroyers of the host society, they and their descendants faced the task of building a new Christian Europe on the debris of the old Christian Roman Empire. Within four centuries this new civilization was attacked and colonized by a new branch of the vast Germanic family, the vikings from the north, who were cousins of the first Continental tribes and like them illiterate and pagan. By the early decades of the new millennium, therefore, the Germanic-nordic peoples had journeyed and settled from the Vistula to Vínland and from Carthage to Iceland. In these *Völkerwanderungen* they influenced and were in turn themselves shaped by the cultures they invaded, as manifested most significantly in the conversion to Christianity.

At the moment of their first contact with Roman and Christian culture both the Continental Germans, including the Anglo-Saxons, and the nordic-Germanic tribes possessed rich cultural traditions that they had encoded orally in their own vernacular languages. They thus conveyed their values through laws intended for social organization and lays composed for educational and pleasurable listening. Much of this vernacular tradition was lost among the Continental tribes or, at best, like the Germanic law codes, transcribed into Latin. The ancient wandering and adventures had been preserved in pan-Germanic memory, but their *Geschichtsschreibung,* in the full Benjaminian sense of the word, was specifically in Old Norse, as Icelandic mythographers, poets, and historians committed to writing their common Germanic legacy, to which they supplied additional permutations from their northernmost outposts.[4] Whereas Continental Europe explored its classical roots in a movement known as "the Renaissance of the twelfth century," a century later Icelandic (and a few Norwegian) scholars were engaged in a comparable enterprise to revive their distant heritage. Their homelands, however, had lain outside the Roman Empire, and Christianity had approached them a half millennium later than on the Continent; their heritage was, therefore, not classical, but Germanic, and their "renaissance" not Christian, but pagan.

The process of converting the Germanic world continued for at least seven centuries, but the task of investigating pre-Christian Germanic society, including the image and social position of women, requires study of an even longer period. It encompasses the first observations from outsiders (such as the Roman Tacitus in the first century), the extensive corpus of Germanic legal codes, and fragments of poems and sparse epic texts—from the Continent as well as from the Anglo-Saxons—and it culminates in the rich northern legacy epitomized by Snorri Sturluson in the first half of the thirteenth century.

Sharing close cultural and linguistic affinities, these sources form a vast Germanic continuum that endured for over a millennium. The Old Norse writers of the thirteenth century bear the latest and fullest witness because of their identification with their Germanic pagan forebears. Interpreted with caution, they can testify to the poetry and mythology of early Germanic peoples on the Continent as well as to the culture of their more recent nordic relatives. This poetry and mythology presents divine female figures and identifies four images of human women: the warrior, the prophetess/sorceress, the revenger, and the inciter. Although the divine figures disappeared with the acceptance of Christianity, the human images survived for a millennium, not only in poetry but also in the prose of the heroic sagas and of the sagas of Icelanders. The poetic images, however, rarely permit us to discern the daily social existence of Germanic women on the Continent as well as in the north. The basic and ordinary problems pertaining to the lives of women, such as reproduction, marriage, and work, can be best examined by close reading of sagas.

This book is therefore based chiefly on three genres of prose narratives and the compilations of law.[5] The narratives consist of the sagas of Icelanders (Íslendingasǫgur), the kings' sagas (*konungasǫgur*), and the contemporary sagas (*samtíðarsǫgur*).[6] The first group, which includes such well-known stories as *Laxdœla saga* and *Gísla saga,* not to mention the indisputable masterpiece of *Njáls saga,* is set primarily in pagan times in Iceland. The second group deals largely with Norwegian royalty from mythical times to the mid–thirteenth century and thus encompasses both pagan and Christian eras. Best known is Snorri Sturluson's *Heimskringla* (Sphere of the Earth), which is also the most comprehensive. A single reign — that of King Hákon (1204–1263) — is treated by Snorri's nephew Sturla Þórðarson in *Hákonar saga Hákonarsonar.* The third category treats the Christian society of Iceland during the twelfth and thirteenth centuries; the most important representative of this group is the large compilation known as *Sturlunga saga,* where again the name of Sturla Þórðarson appears as the author of *Íslendinga saga,* the longest segment of the compilation. Norway and Iceland both produced extensive compilations of law. By the late ninth century, when the settlers left for Iceland, the mother country had already established several provincial laws, none of which has survived from this early date. The settlers used the oral version of one of them, the Borgarthing Law, as inspiration for their own legislation, but unlike the Norwegians, they wanted a single law applicable to the entire country. The result was *Grágás* (Grey Goose), the largest of all Germanic law codes, which contains elements antedating the arrival of Christianity.

The chief obstacle to delineating nordic society before the arrival of Christianity is that no Norse sources, neither literary nor legal, were committed to writing until the thirteenth century, when the authors themselves had become Christian. A geographic image can elucidate this complexity.[7] A striking feature of the majestic Icelandic landscape are the torrential rivers that carve white and black ribbons through vistas of mountains. The first settlers in Iceland designated a number of these rivers as "White River" (Hvítá).[8] What makes them appear white is not the foam of rapids but the opaqueness of the water. Emerging from beneath glaciers, the streams carry sediment, mud, gravel, and stones that, when reflected by the sun, create a milky-white sheen. In contrast, rivers that carry water off the surface of mountains are crystal clear. Not reflecting the light in the same manner, they appear as "black rivers."[9] I employ this distinction between and confluence of clear and white rivers to signify the mixture of pagan and Christian, native (Germanic and nordic) and imported, ancient and medieval contained in the Old Norse world. (These pairs of terms are used interchangeably throughout the book.) The pagan, native, or ancient features are represented in the clear streams, whereas the Christian, imported, or medieval elements emerge in the white rivers. To associate Christianity with white is not inappropriate, for its founder was known as White-Christ (Hvíta-Kristr) in Iceland.[10]

The first settlers also observed a third kind of stream, called "Mixed River," or "Mixture" (Blanda) for short, which channeled water from the two other sources. The difference between the density of each source—a feature that changes with the temperature and the amount of solutes present—retards the mixing of the two types of water. The Blanda therefore contains alternating bands of clear and opaque water distinguishable for some time and over a certain distance. I shall apply this image to the obstacle at hand. Since (with the exception of runes) writing arrived in the northern world with Christianity, we may picture the authors of all the written evidence as situated downstream on the Blanda after the confluence of the white with the clear. Receiving the two sources together, the writers attempted to separate them, mix them, or perform both operations in varying degrees. Because of the different densities of the waters, the two sources could be distinguished for a while. Analogously, the authors of the twelfth and thirteenth centuries could perceive a pagan world relatively free of Christian elements, though a certain degree of mediation from the new religion was unavoidable. Likewise, when they reported unselfconsciously on their contemporary Christian society, they included pagan sources as well. I try to identify the mixing performed by the medieval authors, knowingly or unknowingly, and to separate the two sources as far as possible.

This book draws its subject matter from Norway and Iceland during the period between the late ninth century, when pagan Norwegian colonists first settled in Iceland, and the middle of the thirteenth century, when in 1262 the colonists' Icelandic descendants were forced to accept the overlordship of the Norwegian crown.

Chapter 1 introduces both the Germanic-nordic and the pagan-Christian continuity by focusing on the thirteenth-century woman Guðný Bǫðvarsdóttir, mother of Snorri Sturluson, and her alleged ancestress, Guðrún Gjúkadóttir, the sister of the fifth-century Burgundian king Gundaharius.

The influence of Christianity on the lives of women is examined in the following two sections on marriage and reproduction (Chapters 2 and 3). Marital regulations in the north resembled those of the Continental tribes as enacted in the Germanic law codes. Despite churchmen's efforts to introduce Christian morality, pagan behavior in marriage and divorce, as well as male sexual conduct, continued virtually unchanged into Christian times. Churchmen may have had some success, however, in introducing the notion of female consent whereby a woman was permitted, if not to choose, at least to approve or reject the marital candidate. Not surprisingly, the meager information about lovemaking and birthing techniques reflects age-old patterns, but churchleaders did succeed in abolishing infanticide.

I examine leisure activities in Chapter 4. In this domain the two sexes were for the most part separated, for men enjoyed these nonproductive activities to a greater degree than women. The analysis of leisure provides an introduction to understanding women's remarkable contribution to the Icelandic economy.

Chapter 5 offers a gendered analysis of the work needed to maintain an

Icelandic farm in a way that provided for the entire family. Women's most important work was spinning and weaving. Homespun was used for every conceivable domestic purpose, not least of which was clothing the entire population from cradle to grave. Chapter 6 opens by illustrating this obvious use of the cloth and proceeds to examine the equally remarkable fact that lengths of this cloth became the standard of measurement for commercial exchange, employed in trading as well as in payment of taxes and fines. For several centuries homespun was the most important item of export; thus the island obtained grain, flour, and other necessities that could not be produced locally. Treating these problems from a woman's perspective, the chapter provides a gendered view of economic history.

The Conclusion recapitulates the underlying Germanic-nordic and pagan-Christian continuum. The authors of the sagas of Icelanders wanted to project back into pagan times the Christian program of sexual morality preached by church leaders in their own time (but not practiced by their contemporaries). A careful reading of all the evidence, however, reveals that the prevalence of concubinage, extramarital liaisons, arranged marriages, and divorce in the thirteenth century is less a willful neglect of the corresponding points in churchmen's program of monogamy, fidelity, consent, and indissolubility than a continuation of ancient practices cleverly disguised in the sagas of Icelanders. Two minor disruptions do appear in this continuum, one caused by ideology and the other by technology. The Christian program was not entirely neglected, for churchmen gained some influence in marital and sexual matters and were themselves forced increasingly to practice celibacy. Concerning the laity, churchmen gained a hearing on consent and incest regulations, and they became more involved in the marriage ceremony itself through the ritual of reading the banns before marriage and through the celebration of the wedding in front of the church, followed by a nuptial mass. Technological improvements appeared as medieval Icelanders perfected the exploitation of the few but unusual resources of the island.

An Appendix examines the origins and the interpretive questions raised by the written sources. To accommodate the reader who wishes to approach the subject of Old Norse women as quickly as possible, I have left these questions for the end. Seasoned scholars of Old Norse may consult this section to ascertain my stance on the sources. Readers seriously committed to women's history who lack training in Old Norse texts may wish to invest their time in this chapter before proceeding to the rest of the book. I include only those sources that best facilitate an examination of women's roles in Norse society; I don't pretend to offer a complete survey of Icelandic literature.

CHAPTER ONE

Guðný Bǫðvarsdóttir and Guðrún Gjúkadóttir: Nordic-Germanic Continuity

On 6 November 1221 Guðný Bǫðvarsdóttir died at her son's farm, Reykjaholt (presently Reykholt), in Borgarfjörður in southwest Iceland. A brief generation later (July 1255), the Germanic Guðrún Gjúkadóttir appeared in the dreams of Jóreiðr, a young Icelandic girl living at a farm in Miðjumdalr, about fifty miles from Reykholt. ¶Guðný was the mother of Snorri Sturluson, perhaps the most prominent Icelander ever. Through him and four other children, Guðný became the ancestress of a large clan, the Sturlung family, whose male members dominated Icelandic politics during the thirteenth century. Guðný herself could claim a venerable family tree that connected her with remote Norwegian ancestors, who, in turn, were grafted on to the legendary Germanic lineage exemplified in Sigurðr the Dragonslayer (*Fáfnisbani*), the first husband of Guðrún Gjúkadóttir.

Some of these genealogical links may be fanciful, but Guðný Bǫðvarsdóttir's own existence cannot be doubted. Guðrún Gjúkadóttir, by contrast, is more elusive. Her poetic image combines the historical features of an alleged sister of the Burgundian king Gundaharius (ON Gunnarr; he died in 437) with the contemporary figure Ildico, who was married to the Hunnish leader Attila and present at his death in 454. Ildico's name (compare Germanic Hildr as, for example, in Brynhildr) suggests Germanic origin. The wife of the Frankish Sigurðr (Siegfried), the Hunnish Atli (Attila), and the Ostrogothic Jǫrmunrekkr (Ermanaric), Guðrún was endowed with a long life in Germanic and Old Norse poetry, starting perhaps as early as the sixth century in (now lost) Germanic lays.[1] The oldest existing version of her story is found in the Eddic poem *Atlakviða*, recomposed in Norway in the late ninth century. As Jóreiðr's dreams suggest, she continued to haunt the artistic and popular imagination in the north until the end of the Middle Ages.

The figures of these two women, the Germanic Guðrún and the Icelandic Guðný, frame the picture of Old Norse literature in this attempt to understand the ancient Germanic world and its continuation in medieval Icelandic society. Despite changes introduced by Christianity, the Norse material—preserved and created in Guðný's thirteenth-century settled Iceland—constitutes a cultural continuum with Guðrún's fifth-century Germanic migrations. Connected through Sigurðr, the two women exemplify the Germanic-nordic continuity, and in this work they highlight in particular the transition from paganism to Christianity.

Guðný's death in 1221 is inscribed in most Icelandic annals.[2] Embedded in records of significant human and natural events both domestic and international—deaths of kings, consecrations of bishops, battles, royal marriages, as well as shipwrecks, earthquakes, and comets—the notice suggests that Guðný was an important person. It is therefore a disappointment to discover how little is actually known about her, at least compared to the wealth of information available on her husband and sons. A few passages in the panoramic work known as *Sturlunga saga*, the last self-portrayal of medieval Icelanders, suggest only the barest outlines of her life.[3]

In 1160, when Guðný was in her late teens or perhaps younger, she was married to Sturla Þórðarson, a man by then in his mid-forties and already the father of eight living children by several women, only one of whom had been his wife. Sturla's association the previous year with Guðný's father, Bǫðvarr, may have brought the young girl to his attention. The celebration of the wedding at Sturla's farm at Hvammur (recently rebuilt after a fire) indicates that Sturla was politically more powerful than his father-in-law.[4] In the course of her marriage Guðný gave birth to three boys and two girls.[5] Like their father and, in turn, their own sons, the three men became prominent national leaders. *Sturlunga saga* is therefore not only the story of this powerful family, but the account of the political life of Iceland during the century prior to the acceptance of the Norwegian king's overlordship in 1262.

Readers of the saga catch only glimpses of Guðný during her married life, as, for example, when she admonishes the men on the farm to get out of bed and help her husband during an attack (1171; 1:91), when she arranges a ring dance for the household and guests (1:89), and when she futilely tries to use an old family connection to her husband's advantage (1:98). When Sturla died in 1183 at the age of sixty-seven, Guðný stayed on at Hvammur with most of the children. Her oldest son was now eighteen.

Sturla had continued to womanize after his marriage, but we know nothing of Guðný's feelings about this behavior. After her husband's death she herself captured the attentions of a married man, Ari Þorgilsson. He came to Hvammur for frequent visits and "a great love" developed between them. A few years later they entrusted their respective farms to responsible people and traveled together to Norway, where Ari died in 1188 (1:229–31).

Now middle-aged and returning home, Guðný assumed the management of her farm. In 1191 she received a visit from Bjǫrn, one of her husband's illegitimate sons born during their marriage, and she journeyed with him and Sturla, another illegitimate son, and her own two older sons to a nearby bath (1:232). As the children married, her interest in her family extended to in-laws and grandchildren, as witnessed in 1199 by a dream that she reported concerning the health of her daughter-in-law Halldóra, then pregnant with her second child (1:236–37). Another grandchild was designated her foster son (1:303). Guðný probably raised this grandson herself, normal in a foster arrangement, and she made special provisions for him in her will.[6] She was well acquainted with the facts of fostering, for her husband had accepted Jón Loftsson's offer to raise their youngest son, Snorri. From the age of three until after his marriage, Snorri lived at Jón's estate at Oddi, a household dominated by rich cultural interests (1:113).[7] Because of Snorri's exceptional mind, Sturla's domestic decision had far-reaching consequences for the intellectual life of Iceland.[8]

Snorri's absence from home may explain why his mother extravagantly "squandered" (*eytt*) his paternal inheritance during her widowhood, thus leaving him apparently impecunious. His benefactor Jón died in 1197, but Snorri stayed at Oddi for a while longer, although it was clear that other arrangements had to be made. When his brother Þórðr negotiated a marriage for him with a rich woman, Herdís, his future seemed secure, but, like every groom, he still needed to supply the bride price (*mundr*). Making up for the spent inheritance, Guðný provided Snorri's "wife price" (*kvánarmundr*) from the land at Hvammur, and the wedding was celebrated there. Although it was rumored that Snorri was to share the farm with his mother, he returned to Oddi accompanied by his wife (1:237). A few years later the young couple took over his father-in-law's estate at Borg (1:240). Snorri had reason to be displeased with his mother's handling of his inheritance, but apparently she enjoyed the trust of her other sons, and eventually she regained Snorri's confidence as well. She later managed Þórðr's farms at Staðr and Eyri, and when Snorri went abroad in 1218, he placed his mother in charge of Reykholt, his favorite estate. She was then in her mid- or late seventies. When Snorri returned, she remained with him until her death in 1221.

Such are the meager facts of Guðný's life that can be culled from *Sturlunga saga*. A significant detail can be added, however, not from the contemporary sagas to which *Sturlunga saga* belongs, but from the sagas of Icelanders that allegedly depict the previous centuries.[9] The author of *Eyrbyggja saga* reports that Guðný was present when the bones of Snorri the Chieftain (*goði;* he died in 1031) and of his mother Þórdís Súrsdóttir were dug up from their first burial under a church built by Snorri *goði* himself and reinterred under a new church (*Erb* 4.65:183–84).[10] This "translation" likely took place after 1183, the year Guðný's husband died. Had Sturla been alive, his presence would have been expected, since he was a direct descendant from Snorri *goði* (they were separated by three male and two female links).[11] The two men had much in common. They were both more intellectually shrewd than physically powerful and, consequently, they obtained important positions through political maneuvers. Both men produced large families and died at the age of sixty-seven.[12]

Though perhaps aware of the similarities between Snorri *goði* and her husband, Guðný may have looked with more empathy on Þórdís's bones, which, she remarked, were black and singed. Born and bred in Iceland, the thirteenth-century Guðný observed, but was not directly involved in, her husband's and sons' large-scale political affairs. By contrast, according to *Gísla saga* and *Eyrbyggja saga,* the tenth-century Þórdís had been at the very center of her brothers' and husbands' activities, as I shall show, first in a settlement in Norway and later in the first establishment of a new family in Iceland.[13] Like Guðný during her widowhood, Þórdís was dependent on her son after her divorce and during her old age. She managed Snorri's estate at Helgafell and moved with him to the new farm in Sælingsdalstunga, where they were both to be buried.[14] Guðný most likely knew these details about Þórdís, for as a direct descendant in the male line from the first settlers, she would have taken interest in the older woman's life.[15]

More than two centuries separated Þórdís's burial from Guðný's viewing of her bones. The important question is not whether Guðný was present or even if the event ever occurred, but why the saga author chose to record it.[16] As a culmination to his complicated multi-generational story involving the emigration of several families from Norway and their settlement in Iceland, the author places Guðný Böðvarsdóttir, mother of the most prominent man in Iceland, at a ceremony honoring Snorri's forefather, likewise named Snorri, and his mother, Þórdís.[17] This choice exemplifies the purpose and importance of the sagas of Icelanders: they link contemporary society and the world of the first colonists; they were fashioned by authors who employed reliable contemporary information, relatively firm oral tradition, archaeological evidence, vague memories, and romantic imaginings to provide background, coherence, and identity to contemporary listeners and readers. Encompassing both history and literature, the sagas of Icelanders constitute a unique category among medieval vernacular writings.

An episode in the life of Þórdís, as told in *Gísla saga*, brings us in brief contact with Guðrún Gjúkadóttir, the other emblematic woman. The vignette is significant not only because it — like Jóreiðr's dream — highlights the presence of the sixth-century Germanic woman in the minds of Norwegian settlers and Icelandic colonists, but also because it calls attention to a problem that involved the most intimate aspects of women's lives in a kinship-based society. Þórdís's brother Gísli had killed or maimed several of her suitors when the family was still living in Norway, and in Iceland he proceeded to murder her first husband Þorgrímr (*Gí* 6.2:6–9, 16:53–54). Although Gísli's earlier homicides had been committed in order to protect both his sister's and the family's reputation, the pretext for Þorgrímr's murder was distinctly Gísli's own honor, because he suspected Þorgrímr of having killed Vésteinn, his (Gísli's) foster brother and brother-in-law. His culpability was not generally known, but Gísli was so confident of his sister's loyalty that he revealed his deed in a stanza that she overheard, understood, and later conveyed to her new husband Bǫrkr, Þorgrímr's brother, thus providing him with reason for revenge against Gísli (*Gí* 6.18:58; str. 11).[18] Told of Þórdís's betrayal by their brother, Gísli quoted another stanza in which he compared his sister unfavorably to Guðrún Gjúkadóttir, who had remained faithful to her brothers (*Gí* 6.19:62; str. 12).

Guðrún's name alone recalled to Icelandic listeners the story of the fifth-century Burgundian woman who by her own hands murdered her two sons to take revenge against her husband Atli, who had killed her two brothers. This classic version of the Continental Nibelung story is told in the oldest extant version, the Eddic poem *Atlakviða*, composed perhaps in the late ninth century in Norway. By the thirteenth century, when *Gísla saga* was written, however, Continental authors had already reworked the story in the *Nibelungenlied* and reversed the victims of revenge. Now Guðrún (here named Kriemhilt) encourages revenge on her brothers for their murder of her first husband Sigurðr (here named Siegfried). On the Continent women still responded to personal grievances according to the old Germanic method of inciting men to take revenge on their behalf. Societal changes, however, eventually privileged marriage over kinship, and women were able to substitute the murderer of husband for the killer of brothers as the object of the revenge to which they incited their male relatives.

The old version of the story was known in Iceland from the oldest Eddic poem, and though Gísli's two stanzas contain traces of later poetry, the saga author nonetheless reiterates the old kinship views.[19] Immediately after he recites the two stanzas, Gísli complains to his brother (in prose) that he has not deserved Þórdís's act, for he had placed his own life in jeopardy for her honor in the past. In other words, Gísli, a tenth-century Norwegian settler and poet, expected from his sister Þórdís the loyalty to kin that first had been credited to the fifth-century Germanic Guðrún. Furthermore, by the mid–thirteenth century, when the Icelandic prose author wrote his account, a woman was not yet allowed to replace the old kinship ties to a brother with allegiance to her spouse. Þórdís's siding with her husband at this moment shows, however, that Icelandic wives were beginning to let new marital affinity override older feelings of kin loyalty—though by no means completely. Þórdís herself later divorced her husband and severely wounded the man who had killed her brother (*Gí* 6.36:116).

In Þórdís, Guðný reached back in an almost tangible way to a colonist from Norway, a foremother of her own children. This model was not sufficient in a new country, however, and Icelandic authors searched at length for ancestors beyond the "landtaking men and women" (*landnámsmenn*) in the mother country of Norway. This quest is most evident in "The Book of Settlements" (*Landnámabók*), a compilation that records more than four hundred of the original settlers, as well as their ancestors and descendants. In Guðný's case the genealogist listed eleven Icelandic and ten Norwegian generations before reaching a mythological Svási, who sprang from the Dofri mountains.[20]

Given Iceland's continuing ties with Norway, it is not surprising that Icelanders emphasized their Norwegian connections. Not only do the lives of Þórdís and Guðný join the two countries, but branches of the family tree also reveal other close connections between the nordic and the larger Germanic worlds. Some genealogies grafted Icelandic and Norwegian ancestors onto expanding branches from the world outside the north, merged them with limbs that connected the human race to divinities, and eventually united them all to a universal trunk sprouting from Adam's loins.[21]

Further investigation of Guðný's ancestors also led the genealogist to Ragnarr Furry-Breeches (*loðbrók*), who had married Áslaug, alleged to be the daughter of Sigurðr the Dragonslayer (*Fáfnisbani*) and his first love Brynhildr.[22] Thus the elaborate genealogy created for Guðný made her the transmitter of this legacy to the Sturlung family.[23] The appeal of Ragnarr and his son by Áslaug, Sigurðr Snake-Eye, (*ormr-í-auga*) derives from the fact that the former was the vehicle for, and the latter the first human result of, a merger of nordic humanity with an exemplar of the famous Sigurðr lineage from the Germanic past. Through Ragnarr and his sons, the north of the ninth century merged with the literary version of a historic Germanic past dating to the fifth century, thus creating a glorious present for the nordic people and making possible a promising future from mixed Germanic-nordic stock. The marriage between Ragnarr and Áslaug, however, did more than provide human respectability for the nordic barbarians and infuse viking energy into Sigurðr's otherwise extinguished lineage. In addition to a glorious future through his daughter, the Germanic hero was endowed with a mythical past by being made a descendant of the chief god Óðinn himself.[24]

Perhaps the oldest of the many Icelandic genealogies concern the Sturlung family and they are preserved in two manuscripts of Snorri Sturluson's *Edda*.[25] Unfortunately, they do not refer to Guðný Bǫðvarsdóttir, but they do include her mother-in-law Vigdís and validate Guðný's own reproductive efforts by listing her children.[26] Guðný's absence is not surprising, for indeed only a few women are included in this reproducing mass of humanity that stretches back to Adam.[27] Observing daily their own navels, men (and women) are invariably reminded of their maternal connection; in Iceland, however, as elsewhere in medieval Europe, men constructed endless genealogical chains in which father engenders son, with only a grudging glance at a few of the women who were of necessity involved.[28] While affirming the power of patriarchy, these lists and images may also reflect male reproductive uncertainty and anxiety.[29] In any event, genealogists working on Guðný's ancestry in the thirteenth century clearly perceived many permutations of close kinship between contemporary Icelandic families and the Germanic past exemplified in Sigurðr, its most famous hero.

Sigurðr's first love was Brynhildr. When he unknowingly betrayed her and married Guðrún, Brynhildr decided on revenge and caused his death. This famous story, best known from Eddic poetry and the prose rendition in *Vǫlsunga saga*, would have been familiar to an Icelandic public. Nevertheless, when the theme of a similar love triangle was transferred to an Icelandic setting (in *Laxdœla saga*), the heroine was not named after Sigurðr's first love, Brynhildr, but after his wife Guðrún, who came to play an extraordinary role in the Norse imagination.[30] Judged by the frequency of the name Guðrún, she was an extremely popular figure both in literature and life. More prevalent in Iceland than in Norway, her name is found in an eleventh-century skaldic stanza.[31] She appears in fifteen of the seventeen poems and short narratives devoted to the Nibelung story in Codex Regius, the single manuscript containing the Eddic poetry. Furthermore, Guðrún or the derivative Guðríðr is affixed to almost sixty people in the sagas of Icelanders and almost forty in the Sturlung complex. The name was also very common among the ordinary people who appeared in charters and documents. When Bishop Árni gave instructions for emergency home baptisms and incorporated the baptismal formula in the so-called New Christian Law (1275), he used the Christian Jón and the (originally) pagan Guðrún as typical gender names.[32] More than 10 percent of the population carried the name in 1703, according to the first Icelandic census, and it remains the most common female name in contemporary Iceland.[33]

Guðrún's role in the Sigurðr legend may suggest an explanation for this popularity. Not fully delineated in the first half of the drama, Guðrún comes into her own in the second act. After Sigurðr's death she is married against her will to Atli, the Hunnish leader. Wishing to obtain the riches of his brothers-in-law, Atli invites them for a visit, and, although warned by their sister, they accept. When Atli is unable to make the brothers divulge the hiding place of the Nibelung gold, he kills them. In revenge, Guðrún murders the two sons she bore Atli and later stabs Atli himself to death. *Atlakviða,* possibly the oldest poem in the Sigurðr legend, describes these events in remarkable detail.[34] The strong appeal to the nordic imagination of close ties between a woman and her natal family may, then, explain the popularity of Guðrún's name. Moreover, it was the father's privilege to name his child. I am not suggesting that every father who named his daughter Guðrún wished the heroine's morbid fate upon his own offspring, but a milder image of the family loyalty conjured up by Guðrún's name was a legacy that many men could wish for their daughters, especially during infancy and childhood, before involvement with other families materialized. Meanwhile, the model of the woman who remained loyal to her native kin was still in fashion in the mid–thirteenth century when the author of *Gísla saga,* used it to characterize Þórdís.

Guðrún was not merely fixed in the consciousness of Icelanders by role and name, but also by her pagan persona. *Bárðar saga Snæfellsáss,* a late saga, probably from the middle of the fourteenth century, that hovers on the border between the sagas of Icelanders and the heroic sagas, reports that Helga Bárðardóttir spent the last years of her life either hiding in nature or lodging secretly with other people. At one point a mysterious woman who rooms with Þóroddr and his son is said to be Guðrún Gjúkadóttir although, in fact, it is Helga (*Brð* 13.7:123). It is impossible to tell whether the rumor of Guðrún Gjúkadóttir's presence arose in popular consciousness or simply occurred to the author, although a degree of the former undoubtedly was necessary for the latter.[35] That Guðrún remained a familiar figure in the minds of ordinary Icelanders is more clear from Jóreiðr's dream (*St* 1:519–22). In July 1255, after a dreadful year of endless calamities and battles following the infamous burning of Flugumýrr, a young girl named Jóreiðr Hermundardóttir has a dream during mass.[36] Meeting an impressive-looking woman who has arrived on horseback from the north, Jóreiðr inquires about the fate of the men who were involved in the disasters and questions the purpose of their actions, especially of the burning. Speaking in verse, the woman answers that the men intend to restore paganism to the entire country. At this response Jóreiðr woke up. Dreaming about the same woman on two later occasions, she repeats her question. In the last dream the woman reveals that she is Guðrún Gjúkadóttir. To Jóreiðr's frightened query as to the purpose of pagan people in Iceland, Guðrún responds: "It should not be of any concern to you whether I am Christian or heathen, because I am a friend to my friend" (*Engu skal þik þat skipta . . . hvárt ek em kristin eða heiðin, en vinr em ek vinar míns; St* 1:521). Reassured, Jóreiðr continues her inquiry into the future fate of prominent Icelandic leaders. In a final installment Jóreiðr once again encounters Guðrún, who now demonstrates her previous assertion by punishing a man who had behaved most ignominiously at the burning of Flugumýrr.

The Christian Jóreiðr's fear of the pagan Guðrún Gjúkadóttir alerts us to an undeniable tension between the old and the new religion. Little is known of women's reaction to the decision to accept Christianity, but *Laxdœla saga* does preserve an intriguing detail. Guðrún Ósvífrsdóttir, an Icelandic name-sake of Guðrún Gjúkadóttir of almost equal fame, is the heroine of *Laxdœla saga*, and one of the most memorable women from the pagan setting of the sagas of Icelanders. Born about 970, she had just entered her third marriage when Christianity was accepted and therefore was probably not present at the alþingi. There is no direct reference to Guðrún's conversion, but at her estate at Helgafell—where she lived with her father and sons after her third hus-band's death—she erected a church in which she later buried her father (*Lx* 5.66:196).[37] After the death of her fourth husband, in circa 1026, she became deeply religious (*trúkona mikil*): she was the first woman to learn the psalter in Iceland, and she spent hours praying in her church. A dream of her grand-daughter Herdís (whom Guðrún was fostering) revealed that under the exact spot where Guðrún knelt regularly, an ancient sibyl or sorceress (*vǫlva*) was buried. (Such a site was known as a *vǫluleiði*.) In the dream the sibyl com-plained that the prayers disturbed her. Guðrún complied by having the bones dug up and removed, together with the sibyl's brooch (*kinga*) and large magi-cal wand (*seiðstafr mikill; Lx* 5.76:223-24), the normal accoutrements of a pagan sorceress. Although this passage uncovers tension between the ancient and the new faith, it also suggests that the author could pass easily from aspects of his own Christian religion to details of the old pagan cult.[38]

Indications of tension notwithstanding, Iceland accepted Christianity with remarkable ease, compared to the other nordic countries. The alþingi made a voluntary political decision to convert; everybody was to be baptized immedi-ately, and infant baptism was instituted to assure the compliance of future gen-erations. Nonetheless, the pagan Guðrún Gjúkadóttir lived on in the popular Icelandic imagination to such a degree that she would appear spontaneously and frequently in the dreams of a sixteen-year-old girl and assure her young nordic sister that whether pagan or Christian she was "a friend to my friend."[39] This vignette is emblematic of the search for Icelandic women and their roles in the Old Norse literary, historical, and legal tradition. The tension between the old and the new religion articulated by the Christian granddaughter of Guðrún Ósvífrsdóttir in the early eleventh century, on the one hand, and, on the other, the friendly reassurance that the older pagan Guðrún expressed at this time evoke both a pagan-Christian conflict and a Germanic-nordic conti-nuity in this world of the "two friends." They raise also the well-worn themes of continuity and change. If these categories were applied to Norwegian and Icelandic men during the half millennium covered by our sources, the theme of change would undoubtedly predominate. When the distinctions are applied to women such as Guðrún Gjúkadóttir, Þórdís Súrsdóttir, Guðrún Ósvífrsdóttir, and Guðný Bǫðvarsdóttir, however, continuity is more striking.

CHAPTER TWO

Marriage

THE PAGAN-CHRISTIAN CONFLICT

Marriage offers a particularly clear illustration of Christianity's influence on the lives of women. Germanic marriage was basically a commercial contract, the so-called marriage by purchase (*Kaufehe*), arranged between the groom and the father of the bride. Christians introduced new ideas into the north, among them the doctrine of consent. Having borrowed the general concept from Roman law, churchmen applied it especially to women, and female consent became one of the hallmarks of Christian marriage.[1] Self-determination in marriage thus became an integral part of the Western tradition, in contrast, for example, to Asiatic cultures where, even now, both men and women enter marriages arranged by their families. In the West, the quaint custom of the father giving the bride away remains as the only vestige of the old Germanic system, preserved — ironically — in ceremonies celebrated in churches.

Kaufehe may not have been the earliest form of Germanic marriage. German historians have hypothesized that during an irretrievable past of the Germanic tribes, copulation that impregnated females was driven primarily by male sexual aggression and passion. The traditional marriage by purchase, therefore, may have been preceded by marriage by capture (*Raubehe*).[2] During periods of wandering and endemic warfare men undoubtedly committed rape and other physical violence to obtain women and establish exogamous unions. Some of these unions may have resulted in permanent marital relationships.

Lacking a term for marriage as an institution, Germanic languages were limited to the word that identified the institutionalizing ceremony. The origin and meaning of ON *brúð(h)laup* (wedding, with similar German cognates) remains under debate, but a likely interpretation conjures the image of a young woman in flight. The constitutive elements, *brúðr* (bride) and *(h)laup* (leap or run), suggest violence at the origin of matrimony.[3] During their expeditions abroad, viking men did, in fact, obtain women through force, keeping some as permanent companions whom they brought home as wives.[4] Some men continued this behavior after settling down in Iceland, and legal prohibitions against taking women in warfare were repeated through the centuries.[5]

Marriage by capture was dysfunctional in a settled society, however, and, most likely, it remained merely an occasional exception. By contrast, features of marriage by purchase were well established throughout the Germanic world. According to the earliest historical sources, couples lived in stable unions established by formal rules. Procreation was not limited to marriage, to be sure, but inheritance rules nonetheless privileged the offspring produced within this institution. Here, therefore, I examine marriage before reproduction.

Although the Germanic peoples had developed rules for formal marriage long before the advent of Christianity, the new religion greatly influenced marital customs of all tribes. Scarce Continental sources provide an incomplete picture of pagan marriage among the Germanic barbarians, but a comparison between the first marriage practices of Christians in Rome and the practices during the early Middle Ages on the Continent suggests that churchmen quickly accepted certain matrimonial features to which they had no objections. Blessed by the Church and certainly not in conflict with Christian principles, the celebration of the engagement and the wedding in two steps, for example, undoubtedly had Germanic roots. Amply demonstrated from the nordic sources, this model can also be found in the more meager Continental evidence.

Since Christian marriage was more complex than pagan union, one can arrive at an initial approximation of the pagan model by eliminating from the nordic literary and legal texts the features that bear a clear Christian imprint, such as consent and the extensive incest restrictions. Furthermore, because certain non-Christian features, in particular concubinage, persisted for centuries, the pagan image can be enhanced by a negative print, as it were, developed from the contemporary sagas and the meager charter material that, directly and indirectly, depict behavior churchmen strenuously attempted to eradicate. The sources from the north yield more details than those from the Continent, and one may speculate that the nordic regulations applied to the entire Germanic pagan world.

Originally formulated by pagans, the laws provide a definition of marriage that indicates pagan features left in place by churchmen and illustrated in specific cases from the sagas of Icelanders.[6] The laws, also record the first modifications necessitated by a Christian society; after codification, however, churchmen continued to introduce changes, which were subsequently stated in charters and separate ecclesiastical legislation. The contemporary sagas reveal the implementation of the new ideas. After a careful sifting of evidence, reasonably accurate pictures of pagan and Christian marriages emerge. Of course, the sketches are not perfect illustrations of the two ideologies, for the pagan model is blurred by the unavoidable mediation of the texts by Christian writers, and the ecclesiastical model represents a compromise between the new ideas of churchmen and native tradition.

An examination of marital problems offers a view of the problems inherent in the sources.[7] To what extent are the laws descriptive or prescriptive? Do they reflect a consensus of society as it existed, and if so, at what time? Do they provide a blueprint that lay and ecclesiastical leaders did not succeed in implementing as they sought to bring their society from its pagan past into a Christian future? Do the sagas of Icelanders draw on reliable oral information about paganism, or have the authors — despairing over the failures of their Christian goals — embossed their forebears with a patina of nostalgia? Is the timespan between events and authors of the contemporary sagas less important than the demands of ancient narrative technique and motifs, thus making these accounts less reliable as social resonances than a historian might expect? Though perhaps not fully answerable, these questions can at least be approached by comparing and evaluating three bodies of sources: the laws, flanked by the sagas of the Icelanders (*Íslendingasǫgur*) and the contemporary sagas (*samtíðarsǫgur*). The laws are grounded in the old world of paganism, but they openly incorporate new Christian rules; the sagas of the Icelanders pretend to provide an almost entirely pagan setting; and the contemporary narratives describe medieval Christian society. Since these genres were committed to writing at about the same time in a closely knit society that provided regular opportunities for social intercourse at festivities, þing meetings, and games, literary mimicry and societal forces naturally ensured mutual influence. The reader should be forewarned that to probe for pagan customs it is necessary to use circuitous routes. I shall often start with the authors' Christian foundation and work backward in time, occasionally shifting back and forth. Admittedly, this approach will create organizational problems and anomalies of interpretation.

PAGAN MARRIAGE

Marriage and Property

The German expression *Kaufehe,* captures the essential features of a woman's role and status in a pagan marriage, for it suggests the fundamental connection between marriage and property. When the Germanic tribes entered the Roman Empire in the late fourth century, they had begun to discourage unrestricted copulation and to develop a concept of legitimate marriage as a means to limit the number of children for whom one man was responsible economically. In the north the Old Norse term "lawfully wedded" (*skilfengin[n]*), which designates a legally acquired wife, and the corresponding "lawfully begotten" (*skilgetin[n]*), which refers to the legally conceived and born child, suggest the existence of other sexual partners and children, but the distinction (*skil*) implied in the process of sorting out the illegitimate candidates in both categories (*úskilfenginn* and *úskilgetinn*) carried no Christian connotations, merely identifying instead the rules already established by pagan society.[8]

Marriage was not necessarily monogamous, and in fact kings and powerful men were allowed several wives. Although polygamy is not mentioned in the nordic law codes, and even bigamy (*tvíkvenni*) was prohibited according to Icelandic law, narrative sources do refer to cases of polygamy.[9] As Tacitus suggests, it seems plausible that during ancient times chieftains and kings acquired multiple marriage partners legally if they were rich enough to pay the necessary bride price and support the numerous siblings born by multiple spouses. Such patterns continued among Norwegian royalty into the Middle Ages. As late as the mid–eleventh century, King Haraldr the Hard-Ruler (*harðráði*) was an open bigamist, and multiple sexual partners were common into the thirteenth century.[10]

Since no bride price was paid for concubines and slaves, they were less destructive of family property; in Iceland the resulting offspring did not inherit originally. In Norway unmarried parents may have been able to bequeath their property to children provided both parents were free and the man had admitted paternity.[11] Norwegian laws contain the same framework of engagement, bride price, and wedding as Icelandic laws, which suggests that the social goal toward which the former aspired included a clear distinction between marriage and other sexual relations and between legitimate and illegitimate heirs.[12] In contrast to Icelandic law, however, Norwegian (and Danish) laws allowed a man's children to inherit if they were produced in a public union with a free-born concubine with whom he had lived continuously without separation for twenty years or more and with whom he had gone to bed without concealment (*í ljósi;* NgL 1:54). In other words, Norwegians may have been more willing than Icelanders to accept established relationships, even when they were not legally sanctioned. Information is more limited for Norway than for Iceland, but this rule did not readily condone extramarital affairs, nor did it automatically recognize illegitimate children.

Pagan marriage was thus arranged to ensure the orderly passing of property from one generation to the next. In the north, and especially in Iceland, where people lived close to the margin of subsistence, property—including land, livestock, and valuable man-made possessions—was accumulated by, and belonged to, the individual only for his or her brief lifetime. Before and after, it formed part of the accumulated patrimony of the clan. Its orderly passage through the generations—a problem of utmost importance—was formally established by law. Although they emphasized the relationship between pro-creation and property, lawmakers were also conscious of the irrational power of sexuality and, accordingly, they severely curtailed the inheritance rights of children born to women who had not been acquired in legitimate marriage. The law also prohibited marriage for poor people, since their offspring would become a burden on the community. Once the connection between property and marriage has been grasped, even the seemingly bizarre aspects of pagan marriage fall into place. It is not surprising that marriage regulations were included in the secular laws dealing with commerce in the oldest preserved Norwegian laws.[13] In the more ample Icelandic law a special section was devoted to the engagement (*Festa þáttr*) which incorporated all aspects of marriage.[14]

The few restrictions on matrimony in pagan law involved property. The most stringent requirement was to stay within the social class into which one was born. The original distinction was between free and unfree, and the original marital requirement (*skil*) may simply have demanded that both partners belonged to the group of free people. Lack of freedom of one of the parents was as serious an impediment to the child as the lack of proper parental marriage. In Iceland a child born to a free woman and an unfree man could not inherit, even if the woman had freed the man in order to marry him; the same was true in reverse, although a man could free a slave woman for the purpose of marriage (*Gg* 1a:224, 192; 2:68, 190).[15] As the number of unfree people declined, this distinction lost importance, particularly in Iceland, but it was replaced by differences in wealth and prestige. Only individuals who were "an equal match" (*jafnræði*) could marry (*Gg* 1b:29, 241; 2:156, 162; 3:420). The term refers both to social prestige and to wealth, although the sagas suggest that an excess of the latter could compensate for deficiency in the former. In such cases, however, the girl most often married down, her family unable to resist the attraction of a wealthy suitor; the woman who was "married for money" (*gefin til fjár*) became a common topos in the sagas.[16] The fact that in the texts such marriages invariably developed problems later suggests that social class originally may have meant more than wealth.[17]

The proper progression of inheritance was apparently a concern, for a rule existed that limited the bride price allowable for an eighty-year old man — and further disinherited any subsequent children unless he received permission from his present heirs (*Gg* 1a:224; 2:68). A mixture of societal and private concerns lay behind the regulation that precluded inheritance for children born to a feeble-minded man who had married without permission (*Gg* 1a:222–23; 2:66–67).[18] Moreover, if a couple desired to marry, and the woman was still of childbearing age (*Gg* 1b:38; 2:167), fear of proliferating poor people mandated minimum property requirements beyond the everyday clothes (*hverdags klæðnað*). Similar concerns lay behind the permission to castrate beggars. People undertaking this task were not punished, even if they seriously wounded or even killed the victim in the process (*Gg* 1b:203, 2:151). Furthermore, if a foreigner fathered a child on an Icelandic woman and left the country, the baby was to be entrusted to a compatriot and taken to him (*Gg* 1b: 25, 2:149–50). In short, the rules restricting marriage and sexual activity were prompted more by a practical concern to safeguard property from reproductive despoliation than by social considerations.

Restrictions

Most of the personal and temporal restrictions on marriage included in the laws were of Christian origin. If pagan society had had similar limitations, they would have been replaced by these new rules, but both legal and literary sources suggest that pagans imposed few restrictions pertaining to persons within the framework of a contractual monogamous marriage. Marriage basically involved transfer of property, and the contracting parties could afford to wait for biological maturation, particularly in the case of girls. The law decreed no minimum age for either bride or groom. If a young girl with physical flaws became engaged, no final decision was made until she turned sixteen, giving her a chance to outgrow the impediments (*Gg* 2:162). The law also referred with equanimity to widows under the age of sixteen.[19] The sagas of Icelanders report very young brides in pagan setting, a pattern which continued into Christian times.[20]

Pagan interpersonal restrictions were likewise absent. Incest rules prohibiting sexual relations within the immediate nuclear family is a near universal human phenomenon, and it was presumably found among nordic people.[21] In the law codes, rules prohibiting a man from sleeping with his mother, sister, and daughter were grouped together with the broader incest restrictions including affinity and spiritual kinship that were developed by churchmen, a fact which adds to the difficulty of distinguishing between pagan and Christian components. Literary sources do, however, support the assertion that incest rules affecting the nearest family were of pagan origin. Intercourse between parents and children was frowned upon; if it did occur by mistake or deceit, such intergenerational unions were brought to an end.[22] Nor was incest between siblings tolerated. Snorri relates that the god Njǫrðr had been married to his sister while he was among his own group, the *vanir*, "because that was legal there," but in a comment that reflects an ancient aversion against the practice, he adds that among the *æsir* it was prohibited "to marry anyone that closely related" (*at byggva svá náit at frændsemi, Yn* 26.4:13). Even a royal baby, Knútr, was exposed in the forest because he was the product of a brother and sister (*Jms* 1:1–2). In *Vǫlsunga saga* Signý disguised herself in order to commit incest with her brother when she wanted to produce offspring capable of taking revenge against her husband. Although this case was reported without condemnation, the phenomenon was exceptional. In all probability pagan society had formulated rules against incest that were retained within the broader restrictions imported into the north by Christians. Even these simple and ancient rules apparently were not being followed without enforcement, however.[23] Not only in the north but throughout Christendom, churchmen felt compelled to repeat, century after century, both the recent ecclesiastical incest rules and the elemental restrictions shielding mother, sister, and daughter.[24]

The incest regulations that extended beyond the immediate family were patterned closely on canon law and followed its shifting evolution. It is therefore difficult to believe that they predated Christianity. In fact, it seems clear that pagan Icelanders did not avoid marriage alliances beyond the inner circle of the nuclear family. The sagas of Icelanders report at least one case of marriage between a woman and two brothers in sequence, in defiance of canon law operative during the time of writing the texts but probably also in accordance with social custom during the events (*Gí* 6.18:57 and *Erb* 4.12:20); the genders were reversed in the case of Hámundr the Darkskinned's (*heljarskinn*) successive marriages to two sisters (*Lnd* 1:266). A law speaker "lived with two women, mother and daughter" (*átti mæðgur tvær; Bs* 1:62). These examples, though few, do suggest that pagans were unaware of the elaborate restrictions based on kinship ties later imposed by churchmen.[25] If biological considerations were among the reasons for such rules, the problem may not have been acute in Iceland in the first years of settlement, because the colonists came from different areas of Norway and were not closely related. In addition, they brought numerous people from the islands in the west who were originally unrelated to the settlers. With all these different genetic strains, Iceland had become a veritable melting pot.[26] Unfortunately, much less is known about the marriage patterns of the Norwegians who stayed at home, but it is not implausible that long settlement in isolated communities had resulted in more inbreeding among the last generations of pagans, perhaps with negative biological consequences, a problem explored later.[27]

Marriage Regulations

What rules did the pagans obey? The first mention of marital matters appears in the Inheritance Section (*Arfa-þáttr*): "That man cannot inherit whose mother was not bought for a bride price of one mark or more, or with whom no wedding was held, or who was not engaged (*fostnoð* [from *fastna*])" (*Gg* 1a:222, 2:66). The full regulation was repeated later, and a few details were added in the Engagement Section (*Festa-þáttr*), but the basic framework was provided by the conditions necessary for inheritance. Logically they can be reduced to two, the engagement, in which the bride price was negotiated, and the marriage ceremony in which the spouses were joined. Whereas Roman and early Christian marriage had been contracted in a single act during the early Middle Ages, pagan marriage in the north required distinct steps.[28]

Engagement. The first condition for a successful marriage negotiation was that the two parties were "evenly matched" (*jafnræði*), a term that referred both to social standing and wealth. Property concerns would have rendered the matchmaking of interest to both sets of parents. The father of a girl might, in fact, have been interested more in acquiring the immediate help of a new son-in-law than in the distant prospect of grandchildren, especially if he had no sons of his own. The narrative literature nevertheless states unequivocally that the father of a girl could do nothing to initiate the marriage of his daughter but had to wait for a suitable candidate to appear. Repeated visits by an unwelcome male in search of sexual pleasure (the topos of "the illicit love visit") offered the only occasion for a father to intervene actively on behalf of his thus compromised daughter.[29]

Surviving into Christian times, this tradition of paternal passivity on the bride's side is most clearly exemplified in the short story (*þáttr*) about Eindriði and Sigríðr (*Eindriða þáttr ok Erlings*).[30] Early in the eleventh century the young Norwegian Eindriði agrees to bring Sigríðr on his ship to her father Erlingr. When they arrive, her family accuses Eindriði of having slept with her on the way, and he is forced to clear himself of the charge by the hot iron ordeal, a procedure introduced by churchmen for such cases. Perceiving Eindriði's anger, Erlingr's son (Sigríðr's brother) suggests that their father now offer Sigríðr in marriage to the young man, but Erlingr answers: "When has anybody ever heard that I should offer my daughter to any man. It would be more suitable if he asked me for her; then I would give her to him." Nevertheless, Erlingr is willing to let his son make the offer. Understanding that Erlingr stands behind it, Eindriði accepts, confessing that there was no woman in Norway he would rather marry, but he also admits that nobody can fully appreciate what it cost a father to propose his daughter to another man. When he meets Erlingr, he makes sure that he has understood correctly: "Is it your intention, Erlingr, to offer me your daughter?" Since Eindriði's own father feels that his son's ordeal has affronted the family honor, he is only slightly mollified by Eindriði's explanation that they cannot expect greater honor than Erlingr's own proposal. Admitting this, Eindriði's father adds: "If it is true," which only increases the reader's awareness of the unique situation.[31]

The normal procedure of engagement was for the father or other relative of the young man, often the suitor himself, to pay a visit to the father or guardian of the girl in the company of nine to eleven kinsmen and friends.[32] The spokesman for the visiting party was to broach the subject only after a few days. The desirable qualities of a potential son-in-law are listed by Ófeigr, when he answers the question why his daughters were not married: "Because no men have yet presented themselves who are both rich in goods and have sufficient estates and are also of good family and themselves accomplished men. Although I am not rich, I am demanding in my choice concerning family and honor" (*Bdm* [*Möðruvallabók*] 7.9:339–40).

Fathers were free to turn down the proposal and often did so when the suitor was a berserk (*berserkr*) or generally known as an uncontrolled or unpleasant man. This refusal was not tendered out of consideration for the daughter, however, but to prevent violence in the community.[33] A suitor could also be refused if the social distinction (*manna munr*) was too great, or if he was a foreigner.[34] Gunnlaugr was turned down because the girl's father thought he lacked stability, for he did not yet know whether he wished to get married or travel abroad. As a compromise the father offered the girl, not as an engaged woman (*festarkona*), but as the less binding "promised woman" (*heitkona*), who was obligated to wait for three years (*Gnl* 3.5:67).[35] Finally, the brittle notion of honor could cause even the most promising match to disintegrate.[36]

Assuming that a candidate looked auspicious, initial negotiations took place between the spokesman for the groom and the person who had the right to arrange the girl's marriage, her *marieur* or, in the Old Norse terminology, her "engager" (*fastnandi*) or "legal guardian" (*lǫgráðandi*). This person was either her legitimate son over sixteen, son-in-law, father, or brother. In a family that lacked these suitable men, a mother could arrange the marriage of her daughter, but the law specified this condition as the only one that allowed a woman to take charge of another woman's marriage (*Gg* 1b:29; 2:155).

It may initially appear strange that the list of guardians was headed by the prospective bride's son and son-in-law, thus singling out women who already were mothers. Since it was specified that the son acting as a guardian must be legitimate, the woman would have been either widowed or divorced, with either a grown son or a married daughter. As the sagas suggest, most marriages of Icelandic women were arranged by fathers. In conformity with the sequence of inheritance, however, the father's appearance was set back to the third place in the laws. The law allowed a father to inherit from his deceased offspring only when the latter had neither son nor daughter (*Gg* 1a:218–19; 2:63). The most surprising feature of the sequence of marital guardians is the presence of the woman's male in-laws, her son-in-law at the second place and her brother-in-law after her mother. As non-kin, they were not among her heirs, but as her husband's kinsmen they shared responsibility for her marital and sexual fate. With the addition of her husband, this group was also charged with prosecuting sexual crimes committed against her (*Gg* 1b:48; 2:177).[37]

The connection between marriage and property was further accentuated during the negotiations between the groom and the guardian. The former, now speaking for himself, would "recount the marriage deal" (*tína mundarmál; Gg* 2:162), that is, promise the bride price (*mundr*), the payment from the groom's family, stipulated by Icelandic law at a minimum of one mark. (In Norway the lower limit was set 50 percent higher, at twelve ounces (*aurar*), a sum designated as "poverty level" (*ǫreigð;* NgL 1:27, 54). In the sagas, however, bride prices are often much higher. Norwegian laws introduced an additional contribution from the groom, the so-called "supplementary gift" (*tilgjǫf*), which eventually was added in the later *Jónsbók*.[38] From the bride's family the guardian spelled out the exact proportion of the girl's dowry (*heimanfylgja*), the initial payment of her parental inheritance which was due to the couple at the wedding. Again the sagas reveal that considerable sums often were negotiated. When Hrútr arranges his marriage with Mǫrðr's daughter Unnr, for example, the father provides "sixty hundreds" as her dowry, the equivalent of eighty cows (*Nj* 12.2:9). In another case a much larger sum—two hundred ounces of silver—is offered by a third party to a father who is not able to come up with a dowry for his daughter (*Bdm* 7.9:343).[39]

The Icelandic mundr and the heimanfylgja, the contributions of the two parental families to the new conjugal unit, thus correspond to the initial capital with which young Germanic couples had begun life together a thousand years earlier, as reported by Tacitus (*Germania,* chap. 18). Using a general term, the Roman author referred to the *dos* brought by the husband for which the bride reciprocated with specific gifts of arms. By the time of the Lombard laws the two contributions were known as the *meta* and the *faderfio* respectively.[40]

When agreement had been reached, witnesses were called in and the two men repeated the conditions. The *Staðarhólsbók* version has preserved the formula used by the groom (*Gg* 2:162). Listing the terms of the engagement, he should make the guardian repeat the heimanfylgja, swear that he had the right to arrange the girl's marriage (*heimild*), and assure the groom that she was "without flaw" (*heilt ráð*). This last condition was defined to mean that she had no impediments that would have diminished her value in case she had been a slave. To seal the bargain, the two men shook hands (*tókusk í hendr*). The commercial character of the transaction is clear from the formula — the agreeing on a price, the witnesses, the handshake — the same formula used to negotiate three other important acquisitions, land, a chieftainship, and an ocean-going vessel.

Although the woman had the greatest interest in the arrangement, she was totally absent from the negotiations. Indeed, no meeting between the young couple was required. The law nowhere implies that a woman in pagan times was asked for her approval, but clearly states the father's right to force his daughter into a marriage he desired. According to an addition to the law made probably around 1200 and found only in one manuscript, a father was prohibited from forcing his daughter to marry if she wanted to become a nun (*Gg* 2:156).[41] With only two nunneries in Iceland, this possibility could not have accommodated many women, but the regulation is one of churchmen's first attempts to ameliorate the female premarital position. It implies, however, that paternal enforcement was normal and accepted in other situations. A few cases do appear to suggest a pagan notion of consent, but it is notable that the majority of the marriages in the sagas were arranged completely without the women's knowledge, let alone their approval. A passage treating the remarriage of widows offers further indication of paternal coercion. A widow was granted the right to agree to a proposed candidate, unless her father was in charge, in which case he had the final word (*Gg* 1b:29; 2:156). In other words, although a widow need not accept her son's or son-in-law's proposal, she still had to comply with her father's wish.[42] The law granted self-determination to a few other women as well. A divorced woman did not need her relatives' permission to remarry her former husband, provided the marriage had not been forbidden in the first place, a statement that invokes Christian regulation. If a guardian had refused two worthy parties (*jafnræði*) for his ward and a third suitor of similar caliber appeared, a girl could engage herself, provided she obtained the approval of another relative and was at least twenty years of age. A similar stipulation, but without the age limit, applied to widows and divorced women. If several brothers were in charge of a sister's marriage but could not agree, the advice of the one who concurred with her inclination was to be followed (*Gg* 1b:29; 2:156). These rules are rarely, if ever, illustrated in the narrative sources.

The narrative literature indicates that political as well as economic issues were at stake in marriage negotiations. Men used the marriages of their womenfolk to create alliances in anticipation of hostilities or to cement unions between formerly feuding parties. Exchanged like pawns, women had to start new lives among people they did not know or whom they hitherto had considered enemies. The marital fate of two sisters in *Hœnsa-Þóris saga* strikingly illustrates these problems. Most of the story narrates dealings of the unpleasant protagonist which culminated in the burning of the respected Blund-Ketill. Young and promising but lacking sufficient support, Blund-Ketill's son Hersteinn was responsible for avenging his father. He appealed to Þorkell Fringe (*trefill*), "a wise man, with many friends, and extremely rich" (*Hn* 3.1:6). Promising help but not revealing his plans, Þorkell immediately takes Hersteinn on an expedition before news about the burning has spread. Their goal is the farm of a certain Gunnarr Hlífarson, father of two daughters. Gunnarr has played no role in the story thus far, and he does not know the two men. Arriving late in the evening, the two men force Gunnarr from bed and outside the house despite extremely cold weather. Announcing that "we have a lot to talk about," they squeeze Gunnarr between them, Þorkell explaining that Hersteinn wants to marry his daughter Þuríðr and that they expect an immediate answer. Protesting the haste, Gunnarr asks to consult Þórðr the Yeller (*gellir*), his powerful brother-in-law, but Þorkell replies that they do not want to be the woman's "waiting suitors" (*vánbiðlar*) for long. Turning to Hersteinn, Þorkell promises whatever "help" (*lið;* a word most often used in contexts of feuds and war) necessary to bring about the desired arrangement, if Gunnarr does not understand what is honorable. Sensing the threat, Gunnarr stretches out his hand; Hersteinn immediately calls witnesses and engages himself to the daughter. Only then is Gunnarr informed of the murder of Hersteinn's father (*Hn* 3.10: 29–30).

If Gunnarr felt duped, he did not let on. The next morning he urges his two guests to go with him to his brother-in-law at Hvammur, where his daughter is staying. Gunnarr is more interested in the reaction of his brother-in-law than of his daughter. To persuade the former, he tells the white lie that Blund-Ketill is willing to give up his farm and let Hersteinn take over. He persuades Þórðr to arrange Þuríðr's engagement to Hersteinn and even talks him into celebrating their wedding at his farm in a week's time.[43] Only when they are mounted and ready to leave does Gunnarr inform Þórðr of Blund-Ketill's murder. An angry Þórðr retorts that had he known he would not have agreed so readily. Exploiting his success, Gunnarr identifies Hersteinn as Þórðr's relative (*mágr*) and expresses confidence that Þórðr will help them because "many have heard that you engaged the woman and this was done with your advice" (*Hn* 3.11: 31–33). At the wedding talk revolves around revenge for Blund-Ketill.

If Þuríðr's engagement answered her future husband's need for an alliance by strengthening his position in an upcoming feud, her sister Jófríðr's marriage illustrates how a marriage could end a feud. Helped by his father-in-law and Þórðr, Hersteinn fights against Oddr Ǫnundarson and his sons, the supporters of Hœnsa-Þórir in the burning of Blund-Ketill. After Hœnsa-Þórir himself has been killed, a friendship develops between a young couple from opposing sides, Jófríðr, Gunnarr's other daughter, and Oddr's son Þóroddr. The two fathers are not pleased and continue the fight, but Gunnarr eventually accepts the match. Oddr is reconciled to the idea only after his son threatens to fight him.[44]

Most narratives confirm the impression gained from the laws that women were not asked to approve their future husband. The sagas even report cases where the girl was told about her engagement after the fact.[45] At the conclusion of the contract the young man went home, and the couple did not meet again until the wedding. The date of the wedding was stipulated in the engagement contract and normally fixed within a year, but a waiting period of three years was not unusual, necessitated by Icelanders' frequent and prolonged journeys to Norway.[46] Whatever her feelings, however, a young girl was not likely to spend the waiting period trying to persuade her guardian to abandon his plans, for serious legal consequences made success unlikely. Although the groom could cancel the arrangement with impunity provided he paid the bride price, the situation differed for the guardian and his ward. If the bride was not delivered on the appointed day, the groom had the right to appear and demand admittance to the house. By a solemn oath (*lýritr*) he could forbid the bride to be locked up to prevent access to her; he could demand her dowry and the expenses the guardian had agreed to pay toward the festivities. The guardian and people who sheltered the girl were punished with outlawry. No punishment was decreed for the woman, but it is clear that she would have been captured by the groom in the end (*Gg* 1b:33; 2:160).[47] By designating as open robbery (*rán*) the guardian's crime of cheating the groom, Norwegian laws underscored the commercial character of the arrangement (NgL 1:27).

Wedding. In contrast to the engagement, in which property considerations were paramount, the wedding was dominated by the themes of sex and reproduction. Old Norse has no special word for the institution of marriage, but the term *hjón* or *hjún* indicates the married couple, with equal emphasis placed on the reproductive and sexual functions, on the one hand, and the socioeconomic issues, on the other. The latter meaning can be assumed when the word is used to indicate the entire household, including domestic servants. As noted previously, the specific marriage ceremony was designated as brúð(h)laup. The second syllable (h)laup (leap or run) may imply a preparatory or pre-procreative movement of or toward the bride. The entire word brúð(h)laup may suggest the completed motion that would make copulation possible, for in modern Icelandic it is connected with the expression *hleypa til*—normally used to describe the bringing together of male and female animals.[48] In a similar way, in a ritual that stressed the sexual and reproductive purposes of marriage, the groom was brought to the bride, who awaited him in bed. Although poorly illustrated in the narratives, this ceremony is undoubtedly behind the expression in the law that "six witnesses must see the groom go in the same bed as the woman without concealment" (*í ljósi; Gg* 1a:222, 2:66).[49] Another term in the Icelandic sources that designates the marriage ceremony is the word *eiginorð*, which may also imply the couple's mutual consent.[50]

Children were considered to belong to the male parent, as revealed by the nomenclature (which still prevails) that identified a person as the son or the daughter of a man by affixing *-son* and *-dóttir* to his name.[51] Thus, two of Guðný's children with Sturla were known as Snorri Sturluson and Vigdís Sturludóttir. Only if a father predeceased the mother during the child's infancy would he or she be identified by the maternal name. In the traditional genealogy, a wife was simply the instrument through which a man acquired a child. This fact is expressed in the verb *kvángask* (to marry), used only about a man and indicating that he took a wife (*kván*), thereby becoming a "wifed man." (The equivalent female term *giptask* implies that the woman had been given by one man to another.) The sagas often note that a man was married (*kvángaðr*) and had a son or daughter but offer no further information about the woman than her husband's reproductive use of her.[52]

According to the evidence from the sagas, the wedding usually took place at the bride's house. The general rule may have assigned the wedding festivities to the more prestigious family.[53] The legal definition of a wedding is found in the Inheritance Section and repeated in the Engagement Section (*Gg* 2:66, 204; see also 1a:222). Assuming that the guardian had concluded a proper engagement contract, the wedding was legal if six witnesses had been present to see "the husband openly go to bed with the wife" (*gangi brúðgumi í ljósi í sama sæng konu*). The bedding was preceded by a lavish banquet, described in unusual detail in *Njála* (12.34:87–90). The festivities lasted several days, and the guests were given important gifts when they departed.

The commercial character of marriage is further reinforced by the option that a man could turn over his wife and other property to another man when he suspected his impending death.[54] This ancient tradition was not always appreciated, as suggested by a certain Sigríðr who hanged herself in the temple when her husband swapped lands and wife with a friend (*Lnd* 1:78–79).

A pagan marriage, then, took the form of a commercial contract consisting of two steps and negotiated between two males of equal standing. The guardian handed over to the groom a third human, the bride. Both families re-linquished property, thus enabling the new couple to establish themselves and provide for the offspring they were expected to produce. Although this pagan model stipulated only one legal wife, it did not preclude other sexual contacts. Since it allowed for divorce, neither did it imply a lifelong union.

Multiple Sexual Partners and Extramarital Sex Life

This pagan ideal of marriage as a stable association providing a peaceful transfer of property from one generation to the next was often eroded by other realities. Many unions were of short duration, for divorce was easy to obtain. Moreover, the continual decimation of men in battle or foreign travel and women in childbirth set remaining partners free to remarry. Equally impor-tant, marriage did not preclude other sexual outlets for men.[55]

Contemporary sagas. Tacitus's suggestion of polygyny among Germanic chieftains (*Germania,* chap. 18) is amply confirmed for pagan nordic kings. Around 900 the Norwegian Haraldr Fairhair (*hárfagri*), for example, is said to have dismissed nine mistresses before marrying the Danish princess Ragn-hildr.[56] More common was "resource polygyny," to use a term favored by anthropologists to indicate a system in which powerful men dispose of sev-eral women. The kings' sagas make it clear that from the ninth century to the mid–thirteenth century all kings were adulterous and almost all contenders between Óláfr *helgi* (St. Óláfr) in the first half of the eleventh century and Magnús Hákonarson in the late thirteenth century were illegitimate. Marriage gradually assumed greater importance, as may perhaps be inferred from the bigamy of King Haraldr the Hard-Ruler (*harðráði*) in the mid–eleventh cen-tury: in addition to Ellisif, the wife he had acquired in Russia, he married the Norwegian Þóra after his return.[57]

Even the most casual reading of *Sturlunga saga* makes it clear that few prominent men lived in monogamous marriage; most added concubines (*fril-lur*) openly to their wives or established informal unions with official mistresses (*fylgikonur*).[58] As indicated by ecclesiastical court cases and preserved char-ters, concubinage for lay and ecclesiastical leaders and informal unions among ordinary people persisted as serious problems throughout the fourteenth and fifteenth centuries.[59] Jón Arason, the last Catholic bishop in Iceland, for ex-ample, had six known children with his acknowledged mistress (*fylgikona*).

Laws. Granted that Icelandic men had multiple sexual partners during the Christian era, what was the origin of this behavior? Does it represent a moral decline peculiar to Iceland which vitiated the earlier marital rules established under paganism? Were multiple sexual partners and extramarital activities a privilege only for kings in the pagan era, or did more ordinary men behave likewise? The legal evidence records both pagan and Christian features. *Grágás* rarely focuses directly on concubines but frequently addresses the concomitant problem of illegitimate intercourse. In fact, the extensive treatment in the law suggests that this problem was endemic, and, significantly, the legal classification and vocabulary make it clear that it was of pagan origin. Identifying a series of sexual crimes ranging from stealing kisses to sleeping with and impregnating women, the law graded penalties, from payment of fines, to lesser outlawry (*fjǫrbaugsgarðr*), to greater outlawry (*skóggangr*), and, finally, to granting the right for a man to kill on the spot any male caught in flagrante delicto with one of six women under the avenger's jurisdiction (wife, daughter, mother, sister, foster daughter, and foster mother; *Gg* 1b:47; 2:176). Identifying illegal intercourse as *legorð* (literally, a case of having lain), the law did not distinguish between married and unmarried women, a clear indication of pagan origin. The only indication that adultery was considered more serious than fornication comes from a paragraph that included the former among cases for which settlement could not be made without the permission of the alþingi (*Gg* 1b:49, 2:180). Since, however, the other cases involved not only kinship but also affinal ties and spiritual kinship, this passage clearly exhibits ecclesiastical influence.[60]

The law construed sexual crimes as being committed against the families who controlled women's sexual and reproductive capabilities, not against women as individuals. The purpose was to protect the sexual integrity of the woman in order to reserve it exclusively for the husband, or, before marriage, to keep the young girl intact to maintain her value on the marriage market. If the guardian discovered later that his ward was pregnant at the moment of engagement, he was obligated to inform the groom immediately. Only a statement from a jury upholding by oath his ignorance when the arrangement was made could exonerate him. If he tried to hide a pregnancy, the punishment was outlawry (*Gg* 1b:36, 2:163, 200). The subsuming of the woman to the family is also suggested by the regulation that fines paid by the guilty person accrued, not to the woman herself, but to her guardian. Sexual crimes thus attacked the honor of the woman's family, whether natal or marital.[61]

In cases of illegitimate intercourse (*legorð*), the role of prosecutor (*aðili*) fell to the woman's five nearest relatives in sequence, followed in the sixth place by her mother. Since women had few opportunities to initiate prosecution, a mother was not expected to prosecute (*sœkja*), but would have to turn the case over (*selja*) to other male relatives listed further down the list (*Gg* 1b:48, 2: 177).[62] Intercourse with beggar women, not surprisingly, was left unpunished. Indigent people had no family to take care of them, hence nobody could be offended by their sexual exploitation. Therefore, as *Grágás* tried to curb free men's sexual use of women from their own class, it also revealed the ubiquity of the problem by admitting that other women were accessible.

In *Jónsbók,* the later law, the crime of legorð was understood as occurring between a man and another man's wife (*Jn* 67). Secular law may have considered adultery more serious than fornication, but both phenomena persisted. Bishop Árni's so-called New Christian Law from 1275 distinguished between the two crimes by referring to fornication as "single whoredom" (*einfaldr hórdómr*) and adultery as "double whoredom" (*tvífaldr hórdómr*), defined for men and women according to their marital status (NgL 5:39). This law also distinguished between whether a man took a woman as his wife (*eiginkona*) or used her for "bodily lust" (*líkams losti;* NgL 5:40–41). The laws clearly provide ample evidence that extramarital intercourse and concubinage were endemic in pagan as well as Christian society.

Sagas of Icelanders. Given this background, it comes as a surprise that the sagas of Icelanders, which were explicitly set in pagan times, are not illustrated with specific examples of concubinage and extramarital intercourse. In fact, these narratives only occasionally mention mistresses and illegitimate children. The nearly two score extant narratives in this genre contain a mere handful of mistresses and informal marriages, a few casual sexual encounters, and perhaps a dozen illegitimate children among literally hundreds of seemingly faithful and stable couples and their legitimate offspring. This fidelity is even more remarkable considering that men often were away on extended trips within Iceland and abroad. In *Egils saga,* for example, despite the hero's numerous and yearlong travels to Norway and England, first as a viking and later on more peaceful missions, he sires no illegitimate children and has relations only with his wife Ásgerðr.[63] The contemporary sagas present a stark contrast to this pagan restraint, asserting that throughout the twelfth and thirteenth centuries it was unremarkable for laity and clergy alike to live openly with concubines, thus inflating the illegitimacy rates. Read as a continuous narrative of nordic sexuality from pagan through Christian times, the sagas of Icelanders and the contemporary sagas would seem to suggest that the ancient pagan Icelanders disciplined their sexuality more closely than their Christian descendants.

A more careful reading of the sagas of Icelanders will reveal, however, that the impression of marital bliss is deceptive and that, in fact, these texts do confirm the impression from the laws and the contemporary sagas of pervasive sexual aggression. Under the seemingly placid surface of sexual calm, strong undercurrents of violence and aggression can be detected. The most obvious sign is the frequent topos of "the illicit love visit." [64] Found in fifteen sagas, the theme appears more than twenty times. An unmarried male, having taken a fancy to a girl, visits her regularly without making a marriage proposal. Displeased and offended, her relatives tell him to cease his visits, and his refusal initiates a series of murderous actions which often dominates the rest of the narrative. The topos does not necessarily convey historical episodes in accurate details, but its popularity suggests that the thirteenth-century authors of the sagas of Icelanders were conscious of the ecclesiastical criticism of men's sexual behavior in their own time and acknowledged the potential of uncontrolled male sexuality. In recounting the illicit love visits of their pagan ancestors, they recognized the deep historical roots of extramarital sexual relations and of male sexual aggression.

The violent deaths that befell almost all visitors suggest that the authors may have disapproved of this behavior. One of the few men who avoided death was Bjǫrn (*Erb*), who had the only long-standing, nonmarital sexual relationship with a woman (Þuríðr) from his own social class, although it possibly had been initiated by her. At any rate, their child was accepted by Þuríðr's husband, but in the end Bjǫrn was forced to leave Iceland. Less overt references to extramarital sex occur: Hǫskuldr, Njáll's illegitimate son, was of the same age as his other children and thus must have been conceived during his father's marriage. No mention is made of the initial relationship between Njáll and his concubine, but Hǫskuldr's mother Hróðný was a respected and well-connected woman in the community who maintained friendly relations with Njáll and his family. When her son was killed, she brought his body to Njáll's house and addressed Njáll's wife with the rare word co-wife (*elja; Nj* 12.98:251). Similarly, Þorgrímr had both a wife and a concubine (*frilla; Vtn* 8.37:97). In a reversal of genders, Þóra settled down in a relationship with a man hired to help her run the farm after her husband's death. Their son Már played a prominent role in the next generation (*Erb* 4.11:19). Fornication is obvious in the case of Friðgerðr, a young girl friendly with several young men. Finding herself pregnant, she named one of them as the father, but her failure to prove his paternity by the ordeal performed under the auspices of a priest (the event occurred in the late eleventh century) produced a long-lasting feud between the families (*Ljs* 10.12(22)–13(23):63–73).

A few other cases merely hint at the phenomenon of extramarital sex between men and free women. Who can guess the activities of two brothers known as "restless and improvident in love affairs (*kvennafar*) and law suits" (*Ljs* 10.1:4)? And what about "the case concerning a woman" (*konumál*) that forced a certain Þórir to leave his region (*Vtn* 8.39:101)? In a curious twist of justice, Óspakr Ósvífrsson was not prosecuted for his participation in the killing of Kjartan because he was already being sued in none other than a paternity case (*Lx* 5.50:156).[65]

A few extramarital affairs between high-ranking men and lower-class women or slaves likewise come to light. The most famous one concerns the beautiful slave Melkorka, whom Hǫskuldr bought on a trip to Norway and who became the mother of his favorite son Óláfr Peacock (*pái*). The author prepares his readers by stating that Hǫskuldr and his wife got on well together "but were usually rather reserved with one another" (*Lx* 5.9:18). He goes out of his way, however, to explain that when Hǫskuldr had installed Melkorka in his household "he slept with his wife every night and had nothing to do with his concubine" (*Lx* 5.13:26–27). When he paid the slave merchant three marks for Melkorka, Hǫskuldr noted that this was three times the normal slave price. The law, in fact, did permit a price of twelve ounces (*aurir;* one and one-half marks) for a slave bought for carnal pleasure (*til karnaðar; Gg* 1a:192). Because of changing silver content, prices are always difficult to compare, but if these two statements are juxtaposed, they suggest that a man was allowed to pay more than the normal rate for a slave acquired for sexual purposes, a sign that youth and beauty had their price.[66]

Cross-cultural comparison would indicate that Icelandic slaves were, however, sexually available for their masters at all times, although cases do not surface in the sources.[67] A vignette describing an episode in Greenland suggests that slave women provided sexual services for visitors (*Ftb* 6.21:225). In this case the status of the woman herself (Sigríðr) is not indicated, but she "lived with" (*honum fylgði at lagi . . . Sigríðr*) a certain Loðinn, a man who was identified as a "work slave" (*verkþræll*).

Servant girls occupied a niche between slaves and freeborn women, and several stories indicate their sexual availability for employers and guests. Staying overnight in a farmer's house, Grettir had a sexual encounter with the servant girl (*griðkona*), whereas the daughter of the house escaped (*Gr* 7.76: 238–41).[68] Visiting his old love who was at the shieling in the summer pastures with female servants, Hallfreðr announced that he was going to sleep with her and added: "I have promised my friends that they can do as they like." The author continued: "There were several huts and it was said that each man got a woman for the night" (*Hlf* 8.9:181). Offering her body may also have been included among the duties expected of the woman, slave or free, who regularly was assigned to a visitor in order to "serve" (*þjóna*) him.[69] A consummated affair between a visitor and a free woman is evident in the touching story of Oddný. Mute since birth, she expresses her hesitation to wait on (*þjóna*) the visiting Ívarr by writing runes on a stick. When the visitor impregnates her, she informs her brother in the same manner (*Þux* 13.3:346–47).

These scattered examples collected in the interstices of the narratives make it hard to accept the Christian comportment in sexual matters with which the sagas of Icelanders normally credit Icelandic men. Like their Christian descendants depicted in the contemporary sagas, pagan men were not sexually deprived. Legal marriage, established concubinage, aggressive sexual behavior toward women from their own class, unlimited access to slaves, and availability of female workers and servants provided abundant outlets. To be sure, some of this behavior was frowned upon by the native tradition, and churchmen sharpened the restrictions. Although slaves disappeared, men were not inclined to change their habits, however, and, increasingly, they turned to free women, thus further provoking churchmen's fulminations. Painfully aware of their own and their contemporaries' shortcomings, these authors may be embellishing their stories of their forefathers to conceal this aspect of the pagan social world, thereby adjusting it to the Christian program of their own era. Such obfuscation may have seemed further justified because men's relations with marginal women were accepted as normal but not memorable. Since the mistress and her offspring were rarely important enough to enter the narrative of the sagas of Icelanders, the genre exhibits a relatively placid sexual surface, portraying most couples as enjoying calm, monogamous marriages that ensured the propertied character of the institution.[70] By passing over in silence the problem of multiple sexual partners in the pagan era, the authors of the sagas of Icelanders reveal simultaneously native and Christian concerns.

CHRISTIAN MARRIAGE

What changes did Christianity propose to this pagan model of marriage? The Church's marital and sexual program was, of course, basically the same in the north as in the rest of Europe, but local conditions and resistance caused churchmen to shift emphasis in the program from time to time. It is clear at the outset that the Christian program envisioned more regulation of marriage and restriction on sexuality than the nordic people were ready to accept. Evolving over centuries, the Christian program was not yet perfected when it was introduced into the north. Whereas in the south, Stoic and Epicurean philosophies and regimes prescribed by physicians had attempted to discipline human sexuality before the Christian hegemony, in the north, particularly in Iceland, where nature remained relatively untamed and unexploited, humans resisted external restraints on their sexual freedom.

The first Christian limitations were directed toward the clergy to encourage them to accept celibacy. In the north a few generations telescoped the long evolution on the Continent during which women lost their respected positions as bishops' and priests' wives and were relegated to the demeaning status of concubines, who, to cap their misfortune, were assigned full responsibility for the broken vows of their celibate lovers.[71]

Although the Christian marriage doctrine had been formulated by the

Church Father Augustine, its legislative implementation was not perfected until the eleventh and twelfth centuries, when it was codified in the *Decretum* of the canonist Gratian and in the *Sentences* of the theologian Peter the Lombard. The most striking contrast between native Germanic tradition and the Christian model implicated the nature of the agreement. Churchmen did not object to the financial arrangements in marriage, which, of course, families continued to negotiate, but they insisted that Christian marriage was not a contract but a sacrament, a bond comparable to the mystical union between Christ and his Church. Promising fidelity for life—indeed a faith corresponding to religious belief—the young couple voluntarily entered a monogamous, indissoluble union.

Once this concept had been agreed upon in principle, however, churchmen were willing to compromise with preexisting rules. Little is known about the earliest form of Christian marriage, but it seems originally to have followed the Roman custom and consisted of a single act. Influenced, however, by the system found among the Continental Germanic tribes whom they sought to convert, churchmen accepted a scheme of marriage that consisted of two separate steps. From the middle of the twelfth century canon lawyers distinguished between *verba de futuro* and *verba de presenti,* of which the former, the engagement, entailed a promise of future marriage and the latter an immediately binding commitment, the marriage itself. There is little evidence that engagement existed in Roman and early Christian marriages; it was most likely adopted from the Germanic tribes to become the first step in Christian marriage.[72] On the surface, therefore, the marital program imported into the north by churchmen conformed to the twofold Germanic process.

Churchmen applied their specific principles of monogamy, fidelity, consent, and indissolubility to this model, expanded incest limits, and added ceremonial instructions for weddings. A Christian marriage thus restricted sexual interaction to a monogamous couple who had entered the union voluntarily and expected it to last for life. Different aspects of this ambitious program were emphasized at different times. Although the indissolubility of the marriage vow was stressed in a letter from Alexander III to the Norwegian archbishop as early as the 1170s, churchmen did allow room for divorce. Pagan marriage, however, had not only allowed divorce, but had not precluded other simultaneous sexual relations, and the continued existence of concubinage was the most vexing of all marital problems facing churchmen. (In fact, forced to forsake marriage, they themselves used concubinage to answer their own sexual needs.) Churchmen not only condoned one ingrained practice, divorce, while combatting another, concubinage, but they also actively promoted a new idea, consent.

Fidelity

Beginning in the late twelfth century churchmen impugned lay leaders (and some from their own ranks) who engaged in sexual relations with women to whom they were not wedded.[73] Extramarital affairs that resulted in innumerable illegitimate children abound in the contemporary accounts, both in the Sturlung complex and the episcopal sagas. Here, two cases suffice to illuminate the lives of a man and a woman, respectively, and to show the clergy's involvement on both sides of the issue. The first story concerns Jón Loftsson, the most prominent chieftain of his generation until his death in 1197. He was married to a certain Halldóra, with whom he had two children. Although an ordained deacon, he kept with him at his house—during the lifetime of his wife—Ragnheiðr, the sister of Þorlákr, bishop of Skálholt and the first church leader who tried to enforce celibacy among clergy and monogamy among lay leaders. Jón and Ragnheiðr had loved each other since childhood. Although she also had children by other men, she lived with Jón and their two children. In addition, Jón—in accordance with his reputation as a womanizer—had three children with various other women. Bishop Þorlákr was understandably upset. He told Jón that it was "intolerable . . . that the bishops cannot take away from you the whores (*hórkonor*) whom you keep against all customs of the country" (*Bs* 1:283–84).

Þorlákr anathematized Jón and Ragnheiðr's relationship, but to no effect. On a later occasion the bishop wanted to excommunicate Jón not only for his marital behavior, but also for his control of church land and buildings. In a tense encounter between the two men at the entry to the churchyard, Jón defied the bishop's excommunication with the proud words cherished by all Icelanders: "I know that your excommunication is just and the charge sufficient, and I am willing to suffer your sentence in this way, that I will go into Þórsmǫrk or any other place where the common people cannot have conversations with me, and I will stay there with the woman you are so upset about as long as I want, and your excommunication shall not make me part from my troubles nor any other man's interference, until God breathes into my heart to part with them willingly" (*Bs* 1:290–91). The chaplain implored the bishop not to excommunicate Jón but to wait for him to part with Ragnheiðr on his own, as he had indicated he would. Þorlákr agreed and Jón later sent Ragnheiðr away. She married and had several more children, while Jón himself planned to build a monastery and retire as a monk. He died in 1197, his plans unrealized.

The second case involves Yngvildr, a woman who was married to a man named Halldórr.[74] Unhappy in her marriage, she left her husband when her father died. When, in turn, her husband died abroad, her brother served as her guardian, but they did not get along. In 1157 Yngvildr moved in with her brother-in-law and met a young man by the name of Þorvarðr. They evidently became fond of each other, because the next year Þorvarðr moved to Yngvildr's district, and she built a house near him and withdrew from her family. She gave birth to a girl but pretended that the child belonged to another woman who had come to the farm late in her term. When people became suspicious, her brother demanded that Þorvarðr undergo the hot iron ordeal; he did, was cleared by the bishop, and the brother was ordered to pay a fine. A short time later Þorvarðr, now eighteen years old, went abroad, and Yngvildr, hair cut and dressed as a man, fled to join him, thus revealing their relationship. She and Þorvarðr eventually returned to Iceland but did not resume their relationship. Indeed, Yngvildr gave birth to a girl named Jóra, the acknowledged daughter of Bishop Klængr. Jóra was married by 1180; assuming that she—like most women—was married when she was about twenty, her mother and the bishop must have had their affair after he became bishop in 1152. The tale is all the more remarkable because Klængr and Yngvildr were first cousins.[75]

A reading of *Sturlunga saga* leaves the impression that extramarital affairs were so common that if the sentence of lesser outlawry (*fjörbaugsgarðr*), which required all men who had fathered illegitimate children to be absent for three years, had been enforced, the island would have been cleared of grown males. In a country without an executive power, however, only powerful men could enforce the law, and even they seem to have accepted the current mores. In fact, promiscuity was so common that the right granted by law to kill on the spot any man caught in flagrante delicto with one of six women under the avenger's jurisdiction appears to have been disregarded, at least judged by one husband's comment to a visitor: "I even witnessed that you slept with my wife Guðrún three times" (*St* 1:198–99). It is not surprising that in *Jónsbók* the punishment was reduced to a simple fine (*Jn* 67).

Prominent married men took mistresses, but ordinary folk ignored marriage altogether and lived in informal unions. The expression "live together by mutual agreement" (*fylgja at lagi*) identified a woman who "followed" a man or couples who lived in established and public unions but had omitted the normal rituals.[76] Rarely found in the sagas of Icelanders, the expression is frequent in the contemporary sagas.[77] The phenomenon became almost institutionalized among the clergy in the pre-Reformation period, when the term fylgikona designated the acknowledged mistress of priests and bishops.

Clearly, high rates of illegitimacy necessitated accommodations in the inheritance patterns, and the practical politics of *Sturlunga saga* suggest that illegitimacy was often overlooked when legacies were distributed. Sæmundr Jónsson, for example, half-brother of Ormr, "behaved well in that he gave Ormr's whole inheritance to his children although they were illegitimate" (*St* 1:270; his own legitimate status would have placed him ahead of his nephews).

Likewise, legitimacy did not seriously restrict succession to the Norwegian throne until the mid-thirteenth century.[78]

It is likely that many women willingly joined men in these informal unions. Some may have exploited their youth and beauty to promote themselves and their offspring through association with important men. Descendants of vikings, nevertheless, did not easily forget the possibilities provided by warfare for procuring women by force. No longer feasible on foreign soil, this practice flourished in Norway during the civil wars from the mid-twelfth to the mid-thirteenth century. Preparing to issue a New Christian Law at the beginning of his reign (1177–1202), King Sverrir—still remembering the preceding wars—included excommunication against men who "capture and rape women" (*renna a hendr konom ok brjóta þær til svæfnis;* NgL 1:409). Reissuing the old Frostathing Law in the mid-thirteenth century, King Hákon Hákonarson—who also came to the throne after prolonged warfare—felt compelled to add an introduction dealing with manslaughter, including a paragraph that described women's fate during wartime:

> It has also frequently occurred, though it is neither good nor decent, that wicked men have run away with the wives of other men; and many have atoned very little for this and some not at all. Since we expect that wise men will consider these cases as more important both before God and men than certain other [crimes], it is our will that all men shall know that those convicted of such misdeeds shall be considered as being outside the law both in the sight of king and men; [they may] be stricken down and slain wherever they are found, and [they shall] not be buried at church.[79]

Although the country was at peace during the following generation, Hákon's son Magnús—nicknamed Law-Amender (*laga-bœtir*) for his extensive legislative work—found occasion to repeat the enactment in his reissue of the Christian Law. He further applied the sanctions to men who ran away with other men's wives even in peaceful times.[80] In 1176 the Norwegian archbishop Eysteinn included Iceland in a general prohibition against taking women as war booty (*herfang;* DI 1:234), but it does not seem to have been a problem there.

When Bishop Þorlákr sought to induce Jón Loftsson to change his marital behavior to fit church rules, he enlisted the support of the international hierarchy. In the 1170s and 1180s letters from the archbishops of Niðaróss (Trondheim) upbraided the Icelandic secular and religious leaders for their sexual misdemeanors. Archbishop Eysteinn had heard of men "who have left their wives and taken mistresses instead. Some keep both their wives and mistresses under their roof and live such unholy lives that it tempts all Christian men to sin" (DI 1:221). In another letter addressed to Þorlákr and five named chieftains headed by Jón, the archbishop blamed them for not living according to God's law, and he singled out their behavior toward women as most objectionable: "You, the most famous of men, disgracefully lead lives of cattle, paying no heed to matrimony, although you know that it is a holy bond that must not be broken" (DI 1:262–63).[81] Þorlákr was also able to stir the papacy with his concern. Innocent III opened his reign with letters to the Icelandic clergy in which he admonished them to live virtuous lives (DI 1:298–301).

More general measures were aimed at chieftains as well as ordinary people. Bishop Magnús took a first step in 1226. Formulating extensive regulations for the Icelandic church service, this married bishop wisely ignored matrimony. His sole liturgical concern regarding marriage focused on illegitimacy and concubinage. Women who had given birth to illegitimate children were not allowed the use of a lighted candle with which new mothers normally were received on the festive occasion of their readmission to church after their confinement.[82] In the next generation (1269) Bishop Árni reiterated the decree discriminating against unmarried women, but he now extended the distinction to corpses of women who died in childbirth. When a body of a married woman was carried into the church for funeral it was to be preceded by a woman carrying a candle, but corpses of unmarried mothers were not granted this privilege (DI 2:27, 31 note the rule and DI 2:37 the exception). Churchmen did not attempt to punish the man for his share in the unwanted child, perhaps because the woman was successful in keeping the father's name secret.[83] Men were, however, targeted by a rule stipulating that if they openly lived with concubines (*frillur*), they were refused the eucharist unless they promised the priest in front of witnesses to marry their companion or separate from her.[84] The effect of such a prohibition in the north is unknown; it is not inconceivable that men considered regular church attendance more a burden than a benefit. To be deprived of the last sacrament—churchmen's last consolation for sick and dying people—was doubtless a more serious sentence. In the early fourteenth century it was specifically imposed on sick and unmarried women, unless their lovers promised to marry them or they agreed to separate from the men if they got better (DI 2:549).[85] Disciplining men by withholding the eucharist but punishing women by denying them the more serious last rites exemplifies the misogyny of churchmen. Meanwhile, members of the clergy were as guilty as laymen, hence the rule that if a priest's unclean life (*saurlífi*) became public knowledge through procreation (*barngetnaðr*), he was not to celebrate mass until he had spoken to the bishop, thereby risking that his church would be deconsecrated (DI 2:30, 34).

To his liturgical rules Bishop Magnús added marital regulations from enactments promulgated at the Fourth Lateran Council in 1215 and known in

Iceland in 1217. "If" a priest was asked to "consecrate the couple" (*hjón saman vígia*), he must first read the banns in his church on three consecutive Sundays before the engagement could be negotiated (DI 2:26–27, 36). The novelty of involving a priest is clear from the formulation. As churchmen gained confidence in performing the ceremony, however, they adopted a new verb, "to celebrate marriage" (*púsa*), to denote their role, and they developed a special service known as the nuptial mass (*púsan* or *púsaðarmessa*).[86] Borrowed from their Continental colleagues, the vocabulary was coined directly from Latin *sponsare* and Old French *espuser* (to marry) and confirmed the full force of ecclesiastical influence. These features were not fully worked out until the fourteenth century, although churchmen became increasingly visible at weddings, first informally, as honored guests.[87] They also succeeded in incorporating into the Christian law section of *Grágás* regulations that limited the work allowed for people on their way to a Saturday wedding. The secular law encapsulated prohibitions against celebrating marriages on particular days, primarily Saturdays before an ecclesiastical feast day (*Gg* 1a:27, 1b:39, 241; 2:31, 35, 167–68; 3:29, 35). A comparison of wedding dates, however, shows remarkable continuity between the sagas of Icelanders and the contemporary sagas. It seems likely that throughout Europe churchmen coordinated the church calendar — with its implications for celebration of marriage — to seasonal food supplies.[88]

If churchmen initially attempted to impose gender equality among lay people in certain areas of human conduct, they quickly singled out women for harsher punishment in sexual crimes. Defining fornication (*einfaldr hórdómr*), for example, the New Christian Law for Norway and Iceland specified that a wife was to pay a fine of three marks to the bishop — out of her dowry if necessary — whereas the husband was exempt (NgL 2:371; 5:39). The secular law further placed the woman's entire inheritance in jeopardy by decreeing that "if a wife sleeps with a man while married to her husband" (*undir bónda sinn*), she will lose her "supplementary gift" (*tilgjǫf*; the new Norwegian word for dowry; *Jn* 75).

Incest

To the simple pagan ban on sexual relations within the immediate nuclear family, churchmen added prohibitions against marriage and procreation within a vast network of relatives and friends. Set down by the late ninth century and effective until the Fourth Lateran Council in 1215, the three principles of consanguinity (relationship by blood; ON *frændsemi*), affinity (relationship by marriage; ON *sifjar*), and spiritual kinship (relationship through sacraments; ON *guðsifjar*) prevented two individuals from marrying if they were related within the seventh *generatio*, or "as far as memory could go back."[89]

The addition of affinal kin may originally have been a Germanic idea, but it was accepted with enthusiasm by churchmen.[90] The underlying principle that a couple's sexual relations in marriage created a corporal unity not only between themselves but also between their relatives logically led to the inclusion of extramarital relations as well. In a society where fidelity had not yet been accepted, the lists of candidates not available for marriage would naturally swell.[91] Furthermore, churchmen perceived of spiritual kinship as existing between a person who had played a role in the sacraments of *prímsigning* (a ceremony preliminary to baptism), baptism, and confirmation.[92] These rules limited even more severely the number of marital candidates, as they excluded close friends and relatives who had previously been considered eligible. In Old Norse the crime of overstepping the three boundaries of consanguinity (*frændsemi*), affinity (*sifjar*), and spiritual kinship (*guðsifjar*) was indicated by the suffix -damage (-*spell*) and these terms signaled a lawsuit.

Judging by their sheer bulk in the law codes, the ecclesiastical rules on this issue were numerous.[93] The oldest Icelandic and Norwegian laws contain the traditional Christian prohibition against marriage within the seventh degree of kinship. Given churchmen's heavy involvement in creating and writing down the laws, these codifications may tell more about intent than implementation. Distinguishing between marriages clearly allowed, that is, beyond the seventh degree, and those clearly illegal—within the fifth degree—*Grágás* identifies a gray area where churchmen themselves took an ambivalent stance, permitting marriages against the payment of fines, an issue included in the engagement negotiations (*Gg* 1b:30; 2:156). Since churchmen were not able to enforce the full scope of the seventh degree anywhere in Christendom, they were willing to compromise on the fifth degree of kinship in the north, a limit acceptable to secular leaders. In other areas of life—inheritance, responsibility for the destitute, and revenge—this limit accorded with the native boundaries of kinship. When churchmen relaxed the universal rule from the seventh to the fourth degree in 1215 (at the Fourth Lateran Council), the change was immediately registered in Iceland as elsewhere in the north and applied to kinship by blood and affinity (*Gg* 1a:37; 2:157).[94]

Nevertheless, it was difficult even after 1215 to comply with the vast complex of rules. According to Icelandic law, the husband was expected to appear at the þing after his wedding and explain that no legal impediments existed between him and his wife; nonappearance incurred penalties (*Gg* 1a:37, 60; 2:164, 166). In addition to reducing the degrees of kinship, the Fourth Lateran Council instigated the reading of banns. The Old Norse term was to *lýsa* (literally, throw light on). Used in its native context in connection with crime, the word's sense of proclamation fits the ecclesiastical significance well. The underlying purpose of the banns was to make public the couple's intention, thereby offering others the opportunity to reveal any impediments to the marriage. The regulations about the banns are found only in ecclesiastical legislation. In contrast to pagan custom, insufficient property did not prevent a Christian marriage, and *Jónsbók* makes it clear that destitute people did marry, although in practice poverty undoubtedly often prevented it.[95]

Consent

   Churchmen privileged the idea of consent above all others in their program, because it exemplified the doctrine of the equality of the sexes. The promise of mutual fidelity and the Pauline notion of the mutual marital debt were manifested in the Christian doctrine of consent.[96] Its entry into the legislation of the north, about which the evidence is relatively abundant, provides an opportunity to determine whether laws were prescriptive or descriptive.[97] One would expect some correlation at least between legal texts and social practice.

   Contemporary sagas. The contemporary kings' sagas that portray the highest level of nordic society show little interest in women and marital problems. Authors seem to take for granted that marriages were arranged by the groom and the bride's parents, and they describe only a few cases in which high churchmen were involved that show any attention to female consent.[98] One exception is the story of the Norwegian Cecilía Sigurðardóttir, King Sverrir's sister, who in an argument with Archbishop Eysteinn in the 1180s used lack of consent in her first marriage as justification to obtain an annulment, thus leaving her free to marry a man of her own choice and of whom her brother approved (*Bg* 2:26–27).[99]
   Among *Sturlunga saga*'s reports of countless marriages of Icelandic chieftains not a single case can be found in which women's wishes were considered. Rather, men arranged the marriages of their womenfolk according to their own economic and political advantages. Even the limited rights granted by *Grágás* to widows and divorced women were ignored.[100]

   Law. Despite ancient Roman roots, consent in marriage—interpreted not as parental consent but as that of the young couple—was not fully formulated as Christian doctrine until Peter the Lombard defined it at the middle of the twelfth century.[101] Already by the 1180s churchmen propagated the doctrine in Norway and in Iceland. In 1189 Archbishop Eiríkr of Niðaróss (Trondheim) wrote to the two Icelandic bishops, declaring that full matrimony was established as soon as a man had betrothed a woman "with her own yes-word" (*með jákvæði hennar sjálfrar;* DI 1:287) in the presence of witnesses.
   Audible female consent became the hallmark of Christian marriage legisla-

tion in the north. Judged solely by the legal texts, the change from the older ceremony is striking. The pagan woman did not even witness the two men's solemn handshake that sealed her fate. Silently and passively, she was transferred between her father and her husband. The Christian formula, by contrast, did not mention relatives but placed the woman in the center of the stage where her performative "yes" became the speech-act that loudly and publicly instituted marriage.[102] The clergy's insistence on this feature grew from their concern to extend to women the freedom in matrimonial matters that Germanic law accorded to men and of which churchmen approved. Female consent accommodated and facilitated two ideals held by churchmen in principle if not always in practice: gender equality and the extension of the Christian family beyond inherited tribal and social restrictions.

Not content to articulate this rule within ecclesiastical writing merely, clergymen succeeded in incorporating consent into Christian legislation at the provincial and national level. In Norway it is already found in the oldest existing versions of these laws, for example, in the so-called Older Borgarthing Christian Law. According to this text, a man seeking to marry should first obtain the advice of the woman's relatives, but next he must ask her own opinion. In a stumbling and cumbersome way the text explains how witnesses representing the future groom and bride respectively were to listen whether "the woman says no to the request for marriage or yes. If she says yes or is silent, the marriage can be concluded according to both lay and ecclesiastical law . . . But if she says no, the marriage cannot be concluded legally" (NgL 1:382). Although historians have dated the law to the first half of the twelfth century, this advanced concept of consent suggests that the particular passage was included later.[103] Furthermore, it is clear that the passive role traditionally attributed to women in matrimonial arrangements convinced churchmen to accept a bride's silence as a positive answer. In the Older Frostathing Law, thought to be slightly later, the obligation to ascertain the woman's response was placed on her guardian (NgL 1:155). The passage interpreting the woman's silence positively is also found here, suggesting that it was not only an accommodation to shy women but an attempt as well to attenuate the radical idea of mutual consent; it seems plausible that it was accepted with greater reluctance by the woman's parents than by the groom and his parents.

Christian laws in Norway dating from the mid–thirteenth century were phrased more elegantly. In one case the law no longer retained the need to consult the woman's relatives but instructed the suitor to go directly to the woman he wished to marry. Assuming that ecclesiastical impediments did not prevent the union, he should take her hand in the presence of witnesses, mention her name, and declare that he betrothed her in accordance with the law of God. The witnesses were to hear the woman's "yes-word (*jáyrði*) because it was prohibited according to God's law that a man should marry a woman or a maiden against her will" (*kona eða mey nauðga;* NgL 2:299–300, 319, 333).[104] The total absence of the woman's relatives, however, was apparently not acceptable, because they were reinstated in the next version of the Norwegian Christian Law drafted by Archbishop Jón in 1277 (NgL 2:367–68). Although intended for all Norway, this law was probably never implemented but remained an influential model for later legislation.

Similar steps were taken in Iceland. In 1269 Bishop Árni Þorláksson (1269–1298) introduced new rules for the Church service that included brief references to female consent (DI 2:29). Further elaborated and incorporating consultation with the woman's kin, these rules also became part of the so-called New Christian Law accepted by the alþingi in 1275.[105] According to this law and Bishop Jón's Christian Law for Norway, the formal engagement where witnesses heard the woman give her assent could not take place until the banns had been read, but the man had also to consult the woman before arranging the reading with the priest. In other words, the law now specified two occasions on which the suitor should confer with his future wife.

Secular laws were also revised during this period. Ecclesiastical control over marriage was not exclusive, because secular legislation still regulated property. Like the older secular laws, the Inheritance Section consolidated varied versions issued by Norwegian kings for Norway and Iceland. Here the old rules of family control over a daughter's marriage remained intact. The Christian notion of gender equality was acknowledged, not for the bride, however, but for her mother. Whereas the older laws accorded men the right to arrange the marriages of their female relatives and included the mother only in the absence of male relatives, the new laws stated that both "father and mother shall decide on their daughters' marriage" (NgL 2:227; *Jn* 70). Not only was the bride's consent not mentioned, but the laws stated specifically that if a woman married without her kin's advice, she forfeited her inheritance to the next in line (NgL 2:75, 227–28; *Jn* 71). Surely this threat was a powerful deterrent for any woman inclined to follow her own wishes; it was doubtless considered necessary because of the new freedom offered by ecclesiastical legislation. The idea was evidently so drastic that lay society felt compelled to protect itself. Culminating in this radical conclusion, consent validated secret marriages of young people as well, which became an undesirable consequence for propertied parents anywhere.[106]

The inherent conflict between lay and ecclesiastical perceptions in Iceland came into the open in 1281 when *Jónsbók,* the new secular law, was presented at the alþingi by the representative of the Norwegian king. After the General Assembly's acceptance of the New Christian Law (including consent) only a few years earlier, Bishop Árni now claimed that only the bishop exercised jurisdiction over marital matters. In particular, he protested against *Jónsbók*'s regulations concerning "the giving away of women . . . in matrimony and the inheritance of those women who had been seduced at home as well as those who marry secretly."[107] Notwithstanding the bishop's objection, however, the alþingi accepted *Jónsbók*.

Sagas of Icelanders. Although Christian in origin, consent is occasionally found in the sagas of Icelanders, which has persuaded some scholars that pagan women also had the right to accept or refuse a suitor.[108] The alleged right often surfaced indirectly only after it had been ignored. When Guðrún, for example, was not consulted about her first marriage contracted at the age of fifteen, "she let it be known that she was displeased" (*Lx* 5.34:93). Informed of her father's plans for her marriage, Hallgerðr responded: "Now I am certain of what I have been suspecting for a long time, namely, that you do not love me as much as you always have said you did, since you did not think it necessary to discuss this proposal with me; besides, I do not find this marriage as prestigious as you had promised me" (*Nj* 12.10:31). When fathers or other male relatives consulted the young girls, they apparently took their opinions seriously. Egill thus assured his daughter that his answer to the spokesman for her suitor would depend on her reaction to the proposal. When he was not able to persuade her, he transmitted her negative answer (*Lx* 5.23:63–64).[109]

Most often, however, girls yielded to their father's wishes. Occasionally their consent was offered in positive terms, as when Oddný willingly agreed to her father's suggestion of a betrothal to Bjǫrn because "she knew him beforehand and they had loved each other dearly" (*BHd* 3.2:114), but in most cases the acceptance was tacit and passive: the girl "did not refuse" (*Þhv* 11.4:8), or "did not say no as far as she was concerned and asked her father to decide" (*Lx* 5.45: 137), or "it was not against her will" (*Krm* 8.17:264). Rarely did a woman object as strenuously, as Þorgerðr who stated when her father tried to convince her that Óláfr would be a good match: "I have heard you say that you love me most of your children, but now it seems to me that you are going against that if you plan to marry me to a concubine's son, although he is handsome and fond of fine clothing" (*Lx* 5.23:63). On a milder note, Þuríðr answered her father's proposal of marriage by saying that "she wasn't that eager for a husband that it did not seem just as good to stay home" (*Hn* 3.11:32). (In both instances the marriage nonetheless took place.) In still other cases the woman imposed conditions to be fulfilled before agreeing to the arrangement.[110]

What is the explanation for this presumably Christian privilege permeating a pagan world? Certainly, other aspects of the Christian marital program were not implemented without resistance. Despite churchmen's efforts, married and unmarried men carried on with their concubines, and fathers continued to decide on spouses for their daughters. Rather than concentrating on what churchmen wanted to abolish from the old society—extramarital activities and concubinage—their sexual program might be cast positively, in terms of what they wished to introduce into the new world—marital fidelity. This shift of emphasis allows a comparison of the treatment of marital fidelity with the other new proposal—consent—in the sagas of Icelanders, the laws, and the contemporary sagas. Put most simply, the authors of the sagas of Icelanders asserted that both ideas existed in the world of their pagan forefathers; both issues exist also in the laws, where, however, the Christian influence is obvious; and both notions were unmistakably absent from the contemporary sagas. One assumes, then, that the Christian authors and scribes of the three genres in principle opposed the un-Christian behavior of their contemporaries. They found it impossible to dissimulate the objectionable behavior of their own contemporaries, but they could eliminate most references to the peccadillos of their distant ancestors, thereby idealizing the past and accommodating the pagan world to their dreams for the future. The assertion that female consent already existed during paganism may have been the first result, albeit only literary, of local churchmen's attempts to curtail male control. The didactic intent is clarified by the fact that in these narratives all five of the marriages that were contracted against the expressed will of the women ended in disaster.[111] Arranged marriages for women, ubiquitous presence of concubines, and extramarital activities for men, not only dominated the discourse on sexual behavior in the thirteenth century but were also, in fact, constitutive of the very subject of pagan sexuality in the north.

Other Literary Genres. The majority of the marriages in the sagas of Icelanders were contracted without female consent, as allowed by secular law; the few (and notably spectacular) cases of female consent were, one concludes, the result of ecclesiastical propaganda. Evidence of consent, however, is also found in other genres of Icelandic literature, including the kings' sagas (*konungasǫgur*), the chivalric sagas (*riddarasǫgur*), and the heroic sagas (*fornaldarsǫgur*). To test the hypothesis of Christian origins one must look at the marriages in the kings' sagas, which were placed in the distant past, long before the authors' own time, and which included, therefore, pagan as well as Christian settings. These accounts are not, of course, reliable transcripts of historical fact, but, like the sagas of the Icelanders, they do illuminate their authors' mental outlook.

No case of consent can be found in those sagas that describe the pagan and mythical periods of Scandinavian history.[112] Marriages involving consent do appear, but they are limited to the period after the late tenth century, when Christianity first became known in the north. A closer analysis of these incidents uncovers two features. First, the idea is used anachronistically. The kings' sagas introduce consent into the north at a time when it had not yet been incorporated into Christian laws elsewhere. Although associated with Christianity, consent is thus alleged to have existed in the north at a time when it could not have been known there as a Christian principle. Second, when the same event is treated by several authors, the later versions are more likely to introduce consent than the earlier.[113] Writing at the time when church leaders were propounding consent, the authors of the kings' sagas clearly understood the connection between Christianity and female consent. Although they were mistaken as to when the ideal was first promulgated, their writings record the growing perception of its propriety for Christian women.

If the kings' sagas thus reveal the chronological and conceptual origins of consent, the two other genres, sometimes grouped together under the common label "the lying sagas," illuminate the nordic perception of the geographic spread of the notion.[114] Perhaps prompted by a Norwegian translation of the Tristan and Iseut story from 1226, a handful of poetic French texts — most important, the works of Chrétien de Troyes — were reworked into Old Norse prose. These works inspired in turn a body of native tales with settings and subject matters drawn from the past. The bulkiest and the most popular Old Norse literature, these narratives, inspired by French romances and composed during the fourteenth and fifteenth centuries, can be divided into two groups according to their geographic setting. The chivalric or romantic sagas treat the larger European world; the heroic sagas include stories where the action was limited to the north. The common term "lying sagas" evokes the atmosphere of fantasy which permeates both genres. Like the kings' sagas set in ancient times, they deserve little credence as historical sources, but they can still be used to gauge perception of the distant past at home and abroad.

We shall first examine the chivalric sagas to ascertain how these tales perceived consent outside Scandinavia. An analysis of the two dozen original Icelandic chivalric sagas reveals that, on the issue of consent at any rate, the authors pictured Europe as divided into two large sections, a northern area stretching roughly halfway down the European continent and including England and Ireland, and a southern area surrounding the Mediterranean's northern and southern coastlines and also encompassing distant places such as India, which likewise was considered to be Christian. In the north the marriage of a woman was most often decided by her male kin, whereas in the south women were almost always asked about and frequently given full choice of their marriage partners. In the north women demurely accepted their male relatives' decisions and only occasionally murmured about the suitor being too old or exhibited fear of their fathers.

Only one story with a northern setting appears to contradict this generalization. In *Bærings saga*, Vilfríðr, the daughter of a northerner, King Pippin of Paris, is asked in marriage by the emperor of Greece.[115] The archbishop advises the union, and her father is prepared to comply if she agrees. When she expresses willingness, the two are engaged, but at that moment the extremely handsome Bæringr, the hero of the story, enters the hall. Falling madly in love, Vilfríðr regrets her engagement and eludes the marriage in the sole way acceptable to churchmen—by pretending to seek entry into a nunnery (chaps. 14, 16). In this case, in which a northern woman was asked for her approval before a decision was made, both an archbishop and a groom from southern Europe were present, features that might have suggested to the author that female consent was appropriate.

One saga may illustrate the northern and the southern patterns simultaneously in order to reflect the travels of the heroes. In *Mágus saga*, for example, Matthildr from Saxland was married to the protagonist through negotiations held exclusively between her future husband, her father, and her brothers, whereas Erminga, daughter of King Húgon in Mikligarðr (the Old Norse term for Byzantium) discussed with her father the marriage proposal from Emperor Játmundr and eventually accepted it (RS 2.14:196–200; 2:141–46). When the entire action took place in the south, however, practically all women were given the opportunity to express an opinion, and many were free to choose. The farther the action was removed from the author's homeland, the more firmly established the doctrine of consent seemed to be. When accorded free choice by her father, for example, Princess Gratiana of Greece had already turned down several suitors.[116] It seems clear, then, that the idea of consent originated from and belonged to countries that had long been Christian, and that elsewhere its existence was closely associated with important clergymen.

The heroic sagas suggest how consent was perceived in Scandinavia's distant past. Almost one hundred marriage arrangements can be identified in the approximately two dozen stories. Two-thirds of those arrangements were negotiated by male relatives who paid no attention to the women's wishes. In the remaining cases some familiarity with consent emerges. Deeply rooted in pagan times, these tales cannot, of course, show the explicit influence of churchmen. A father's plausible reason for permitting a daughter to express preference may occasionally result from his own inability to choose between two equally qualified contenders or from fear of a suitor. Ingibjǫrg (who appeared in two sagas) was courted by two men.[117] Unable to choose between them, her father, the king of Sweden, asked her to make the decision. The Swedish princess Húnvǫr was requested by a man with the frightening name of Hárekr Iron Skull (*járnhauss;* the author was not sure whether he was a man or giant). When Hárekr demanded not only Húnvǫr, but also the kingdom, in return for which he promised only to refrain from killing the father, the king's considered reply was: "I think it would be a good idea to find out what she will answer." [118]

It is unclear whether pagan fathers in the distant past of Scandinavia or Europe were in the habit of letting daughters express opinions about prospective husbands, but Icelandic authors working between the twelfth and the fifteenth centuries certainly did not think so. These stories corroborate the conclusion drawn from the sagas of Icelanders that the consent situated in a pagan setting was, in fact, part of clerical propaganda at the time of the writing. According to the new evidence from the chivalric and the heroic sagas, in the distant past the choice of a husband did not rest with the woman directly but with her father or other male guardian. In the authors' minds, consent was limited to the ancient Christian countries of the south, and appeared in northern Europe only with the introduction of the new faith and, most specifically, by the mediation of high ecclesiastical officials.

It appears, therefore, that the evidence in the medieval north for social implementation of consent is far slimmer in the contemporary sagas than in the prescriptive and fictitious works. It is worth remembering, however, that the contemporary sagas described the highest levels of society, that is, the people with influence and wealth for whom the marriages of their children were of great import. As on the Continent, they conceded to their children free choice over family concerns only with the greatest of reluctance. Given the fact, however, that churchmen increasingly encouraged families to allow women to decide on their marriage partners, in the nordic world as elsewhere in western Christendom, one might reasonably presume that men less important than those in the pages of *Sturlunga saga* would continue to do their best to find suitable husbands for their daughters. Even if fathers were not legally obliged and only rarely did choose to discuss these matters formally, they may well have known their daughters' preferences and perhaps in many cases respected them. With churchmen insisting on consent, men may have been persuaded to turn the decision over to their daughters.

Linguistic evidence may help to corroborate this conclusion. Churchmen had developed new words (the verb "to marry" [*púsa*] and the noun "nuptial mass" [*púsan* or *púsaðarmessa*]) to identify their own role and the new clerical ceremony that came to precede the traditional wedding feast (*veizla*). Emphasizing the equality inherent in the doctrine of consent, the words designating the bride and the groom were *púsa* and *púsi*, respectively, identical terms differentiated only by grammatical gender. The similarly gendered ON *frilla* and *friðill* are occasionally used about a couple living together but not married. The new vocabulary was undoubtedly created by Continental churchmen, but a scrutiny of the Norse texts suggests that the words entered the north through the translated French literature and shortly thereafter appeared in the native chivalric sagas.[119] Only when the vocabulary was established in literature and, very likely, in common parlance, did churchmen incorporate it into their legislation. Indicative of a change in marriage customs, the new discourse also reinforced that change. A father who cared little whether or not his daughter was consulted in marriage may have been persuaded by his priest to accept the new words and the accompanying doctrine. Although the vocabulary eventually went out of fashion, the doctrine persisted. Sponsored by Christianity, consent became a fundamental right for women throughout the Western world.

TWO MARRIAGES

Despite its distinct ideals, Christianity succeeded in effecting only minor changes on ancient marriage in Iceland, which had been established by the colonists on the Norwegian pattern. Among leading families especially, Christian marriages continued to seal reconciliation between two families by transferring wealth and a woman, thus retaining the pagan character of a political and commercial contract. Churchmen tried to stress fidelity and to curb extramarital sexuality, but to little avail. They may have had more success with consent, but most evidence for contemporary practice must be teased from sources describing the earlier pagan society and is therefore inconclusive.

A comparative analysis of two marital arrangements and celebrations, one from the pagan world of the sagas of the Icelanders and the other from the Christian society of the thirteenth century, reveals the conservative continuity of nordic marriage throughout the Middle Ages. Judging by the internal chronology of *Njáls saga*, the wedding of Hallgerðr Hǫskuldsdóttir and Gunnarr Hámundarson, her third husband, must have been celebrated sometime during the fall of 974 or 975.[120] On 18 October 1253 the thirteen-year-old Ingibjǫrg Sturludóttir was married to Hallr Gizurarson at Flugumýrr, the farm that belonged to Hallr's father, Gizurr. Four days later the farm was attacked and burned down. Although the fire was widely noted, only *Íslendinga saga* (the most important part of *Sturlunga saga*) provides information about the wedding.[121]

Celebrated at the same time of the year, both marriages were arranged to seal reconciliations after long-standing feuds between two families. Gunnarr had been the opponent of Hallgerðr's uncle Hrútr since he retrieved the dowry of his relative Unnr, Hrútr's first wife (*Nj* 12.21:58–59). The long-lasting feud between the families of Sturla and Gizurr can be traced to Sturla's uncle Sighvatr's dislike of Gizurr as a young boy (*St* 1:299–300). Both weddings were preceded by careful financial arrangements. Few of these details are available in Hallgerðr's case because her relationship with Gunnarr began with mutual infatuation, a situation unique within the sagas of Icelanders. Although Hallgerðr's uncle disparagingly referred to the emotional involvement as a "match dictated by desire" (*girndarráð*), he and her father arranged with Gunnarr a formal engagement contract (*kaupmáli,* literally, purchase agreement) that detailed the financial exchange.[122] The arrangement was done in Hallgerðr's presence, and she announced her own engagement (12.33:87). Ingibjǫrg's marriage was preceded by complicated financial transactions that involved great outlays by her father and her maternal grandmother Jóreiðr (*St* 1:480).

The pagan Hallgerðr had accorded her consent, but no indication suggests that Ingibjǫrg had been asked to approve of Hallr. Almost thirty years earlier, Jóreiðr, Ingibjǫrg's maternal grandmother, had refused remarriage to an ally of Sturla Sighvatsson, her son-in-law's cousin, because she wanted to keep her property intact for her daughter. To persuade Jóreiðr, Sturla had resorted to force and removed her to his farm, and she had responded by a hunger strike. To be sure, Jóreiðr prevailed in the end, but the story suggests that although consent may have been understood by a few women, it had not yet gained respect from men in cases where property was involved.[123]

The two wedding ceremonies were also strikingly similar. The main celebration consisted of a large party where relatives and friends were separated by gender and seated at tables in carefully arranged order. At Hallgerðr's wedding Gunnarr, the groom, and Njáll occupied the place of honor at the middle of the table facing Hallgerðr's father and uncle on the other side, and the bride was placed at the middle of the women's table (*Nj* 12.34:88–89). At Ingibjǫrg's wedding the two fathers held the places of honor, but the women's seating was not mentioned (*St* 1:482–83). Food and, later, drink were served liberally; verbal games and speeches undoubtedly provided the entertainment.[124] At Ingibjǫrg's wedding the host, her father-in-law Gizurr, made a speech. Emphasizing the important reconciliation of the feuding parties obtained through marital affinity (*mágsemð*), Gizurr still felt it necessary to offer truce (*grið*) for everybody present (*St* 1:483). At the end of both celebrations the guests were offered gifts before they departed.

Indeed, the similarities between the two celebrations are so numerous that differences are difficult to identify. The most evident is the consent accorded to the pagan Hallgerðr, which is omitted for the Christian Ingibjǫrg. This anomaly may be accounted for by literary tradition. Consent was on the agenda of the authors of the sagas of Icelanders as they revised the image of pagan marriage and it may have become so common in the days of *Íslendinga saga* that it no longer called for comment. Fitting the pagan context, Hallgerðr's wedding also became the occasion for the divorce and immediate remarriage of Þráinn. Irked by his wife's sarcastic verse about his roaming eye, he angrily divorced her on the spot and asked to marry Þorgerðr, the fourteen-year-old daughter of the bride. With a slight change of the seating arrangement, the celebration was transformed into a double wedding. Perhaps another noticeable difference between the two parties, pagan and Christian, concerns the visibility of the women. In addition to twenty-four named male guests, the author of *Njála* included seven named women, and "many . . . other women" (*mart . . . annarra kvenna*) who came with Þorgerðr, Hallgerðr's daughter. Two of them were in charge of serving the food. When the question of Þorgerðr's marriage arose, both she and her mother were asked for their opinion, and Hallgerðr herself engaged her.[125] In contrast, Ingibjǫrg was not mentioned by name a single time at her own wedding, nor was any other woman. The only reference to female presence is the observation that "four men poured for the women." Apart from the factor of the double wedding, this difference may be accounted for by the greater visibility of women in the personal stories of the sagas of Icelanders than in the political preoccupations of contemporary sagas.[126]

One might explain the similarities between the two accounts by noting that the author of *Njála* described Hallgerðr's wedding in terms of contemporary celebrations with which both he and Sturla Þórðarson, the author of *Íslendinga saga,* were familiar. Nonetheless, the almost total lack of Christian ambience at Ingibjǫrg's wedding must still be addressed. During the thirteenth century churchmen attempted to gain influence over marriage policies, but Ingibjǫrg's wedding took place before these rules were established. Sturla Þórðarson died in 1284, before their full implementation. Even discounting this background, the traditional character of Ingibjǫrg's wedding is nonetheless remarkable. As late as the middle of the thirteenth century, two hundred and fifty years after the acceptance of Chrisianity, the most prominent Icelandic families still arranged and celebrated marriages with few traces of Christian influence. Only the mention that church pews (*kirkjustólar*) had been borrowed for the occasion and Gizurr's request for the Lord's blessing at the beginning of his speech indicate that Ingibjǫrg's wedding took place in a Christian society.

DIVORCE AND WIDOWHOOD

Marriage ended with death or divorce. Þráinn's divorce of his wife Þórhildr at Hallgerðr's wedding is unusual in the specific context of the sagas of the Icelanders because it was the husband and not the wife who took the initiative, but the incident does suggest the ease of divorce in ancient Iceland. Þráinn remarried immediately, but no further information survives about Þórhildr. Divorced women still in their childbearing years frequently remarried. Although the narratives have little to say about widowers, widows clearly attracted the attention of saga authors.

Divorce

Law. In *Grágás* Icelandic marital policy was largely limited to the ancient pagan tradition, but churchmen's efforts to promote Christian marriage were included only in the Christian Law added later and in separate ecclesiastical legislation. A quick, superficial look at *Grágás* might suggest, however, that on the specific issue of divorce—a cardinal point in the ecclesiastical program on the Continent—churchmen were already in control. The law states boldly and unequivocally that "divorce shall not exist in this country" (*Gg* 1b, 39; 2: 168). This proclamation must be merely a rhetorical flourish, however, to appease ecclesiastical leaders, because in both major manuscripts it is followed by nearly a dozen closely argued pages that first deal with automatic exceptions equivocating the rule and then assign determining roles to the two bishops who can grant divorce in specific circumstances. Moreover, in the sagas of Icelanders—the genre that, together with the law, purports to offer the most authentic pagan context—divorces are relatively frequent.

On two other cardinal points in churchmen's new marital program—fidelity and consent—the authors of the sagas of Icelanders asserted that they were found already in the pagan world of their forefathers, despite the law's statement to the contrary. Working at the same time, other authors amply demonstrated that in the contemporary world of the thirteenth century ancient sexual and marital customs continued unabated despite churchmen's efforts to eradicate them. For these reasons I am not inclined to accept the testimony of the sagas of Icelanders on these two issues. On this new issue, however, the detailed regulations from the law allowing divorce (despite its initial proclamation to the contrary) can be illustrated by specific cases from the sagas of Icelanders. Thus I am willing to accept the evidence from the narratives in this case. Divorce was easy to obtain, and in fact may have been a common phenomenon in the pagan society described in the sagas of Icelanders. Realizing the futility of promoting the specific doctrine of indissolubility, ecclesiastical leaders therefore compromised with native tradition by allowing exceptions, provided, however, that they were left to the bishop's supervision and discretion.[127]

Property, the foundational premise of a couple's entering marriage, loomed equally large when divorce (*skilnaðr*) was considered. The law enumerated four conditions that granted divorce automatically, two of which concerned property. The first dealt with the couple's financial responsibilities for children and kin. If a couple was so poor that they could not maintain their children, or if one of the spouses had needy relatives for whom the other was not willing to spend his or her assets as demanded by Iceland's system of poor laws, a divorce could be obtained automatically.[128] In the first case the prosecutor was the nearest relative responsible for the needy children; in the second case, the wealthier of the spouses assumed the prosecuting role. In both cases the law gave specific instructions on the verbal procedure (*Gg* 1b:39, 40; 2:168–69; 3:35, 420–21).[129] As a justification for divorce, however, poverty was abolished in a later paragraph, identified as "new law" (*nýmæli*) in one text and grouped together with rules for incest and extramarital procreation, which thereby revealed Christian influence (*Gg* 1b:236; 2:203; 3:457).

The other situation was presented by the husband who wanted to take his wife's property out of the country against her will. She simply had to call in witnesses and declare herself divorced (*Gg* 1b:44; 2:172; 3:421). The chief concern was less the woman's well-being than the family's fear that the husband might leave with the property (in which her relatives had a stake), as stated in the preceding paragraph: "If the husband wants to leave the country (*hlaupa af landi á brott*) with his wife's property, she has the right to turn the case over to whomever she wishes, in order to prohibit his journey, and, if necessary, to prosecute him as well as the men who will take him abroad."

The third justification in the law for immediate divorce was violence committed by one spouse against the other. The sagas also recognized such violence as reason for divorce but do not report the serious bodily damage required by law before an automatic divorce could be granted. According to the law, one partner had to inflict on the other injuries (*áverki*) that could be considered "greater wounds" (*hin meiri sár; Gg* 1b:40; 2:168; 3:35). Elsewhere these were defined as lesions penetrating the brain, the body cavity, and the marrow (*Gg*, 1a: 145, 147–48; 2:299, 352; 3:429). Easily aroused to violence, Icelandic husbands may well have transgressed these limits. Without ready access to weapons, however, women did not have the same opportunities, but churchmen's insistence on gender equality perhaps induced lawmakers to use the neutral pronoun (*þau*), thus suggesting that either spouse could be guilty.[130]

The fourth condition for automatic divorce was, not surprisingly, marriage within the prohibited degrees of kinship (*Gg* 1b:40–41, 235; 2:168–69, 204–5). In Iceland, as throughout Europe, the simultaneous promotion of ecclesiastical incest regulations and the indissolubility of marriage brought the two principles into conflict. Privileging the former, churchmen were increasingly forced to accommodate the latter by allowing annulment. A practical form of divorce also occurred when a husband failed to sleep with his wife for three years because of negligence (*úrækt* or *úrækð*). Her family was permitted to regain the property and, as a sign of her juridical return, fines for her eventual seduction accrued to her family, although, as a special privilege, the woman was allowed to administer this property herself (*Gg* 1b:55; 2:170–71; 3:420–21).

In addition to these conditions, special permission for divorce could be obtained from the bishop in unusual circumstances (*Gg* 1b:39, 41–43; 2:168, 170,

204; 3:420). The chief excuse offered was incompatibility (*verða eigi samhuga*). The husband was to guarantee his wife's transportation back and forth, and the couple was required to meet with the bishop, preferably at the alþingi. The bishop was to make a decision by the following Saturday. If he did not grant a divorce, he could allow a separate domicile for the wife and a division of the property (*Gg* 1b:55; 2:206; 3:456). If the request was granted, the bishop would order the two partners to live singly (*einlát*) for a while. He could grant permission for remarriage, but if either party married without his license, new children were barred from inheritance (*Gg* 1a:224; 2:68–69, 173).

These rules suggest a society in which divorce was obtainable and of long-standing tradition. Seriously troubled by extramarital sexual activities and not yet ready to face the issue of indissolubility, church leaders made the best of an equivocal situation by accepting the prevailing practice on divorce, but they insisted on introducing the bishop's authority in certain cases. Churchmen were forced to come to terms with entire categories of people who previously had been free to marry. They continued to do so, but now, as wedded couples, they were forced to divorce or at least to pay fines because of the new regime. Until the new incest restrictions had been assimilated in practice, it would have appeared futile, if not hypocritical, to insist on indissolubility.

This legislation reflects a slight undercurrent of concern for women as the weaker partner in marriage. As noted previously, the bishop could grant a wife permission to live apart from her husband, and the husband was required to provide his wife transportation to the meeting with the bishop. In the first case the husband's normal right to demand her return no longer obtained (*Gg* 1b: 55; 2:206–7; 3:457). The law further granted that if a wife wanted a divorce after it was discovered that she and her husband were related within the semi-forbidden degrees (fifth to seventh), friends and neighbors were no longer prevented from providing hospitality (*innihǫfn*) after her departure, even if the husband had taken the solemn *lýritr* oath to prevent it (*Gg* 1b:40; 2:169).

Sagas of Icelanders. This underlying concern for wives may have been fostered by churchmen's habitual view that women belonged to the weaker and unprotected classes. It may also have been caused by a lingering perception that women had been largely responsible for divorces in pagan society, an observation with which the modern reader of the sagas of Icelanders might concur.[131]

The narrative sources corroborate the law's stipulation that violence was sufficient cause for divorce, but they rarely substantiate the suggestion of gender symmetry: husbands in the sagas more often committed violence against their wives than they received it. Prudently refraining from retaliation, a wife instead would leave her husband, thus skewing the divorce rate in the favor of women. Male violence was the most frequent reason for divorce in the sagas. Þorvaldr's slap of Guðrún (*Lx*) and Bǫrkr's of Þórdís (*Erb* and *Gí*) provoked the two women to divorce. Guðrún reinforced her case by tricking Þorvaldr to wear feminine clothing; Þórdis's action was fueled indirectly by her husband's support of her brother's killer, but prompted directly by the slap.[132] Violence leading to divorce could also be committed by women. When a wife tried to awaken her husband by throwing pillows at him in jest, he retaliated in kind. When she progressed to stones, he declared himself divorced and added that he could not tolerate her tyranny (*ofríki; Hǫv* 3.43:327–28).[133] A more serious case is reported in the kings' sagas where the pagan Guðrún tried to stab her husband, the Christian king Óláfr Tryggvason, on their wedding night. Snorri assures his readers that "Guðrún did not return to the same bed as the king" (*ÓT* 26.71:318–19).[134]

It comes as no surprise that divorce formed an integral part of female discourse; as part of the image of the female inciter, women used the threat of divorce to incite men.[135] Half a dozen women egged their husbands into action using this incentive. Conscious of her marital assets, a wife could issue sexual or financial ultimatums ("you shall never come in my bed again," or "I shall let my father repossess my property"), often delivered in bed.[136] Since most of these couples had not been getting along, the threats may say more about the acceleration of the incitement process than about divorce, as the wife quickly resorted to the ultimate weapon. In one unique bed scene, however, a woman calmly asks her husband to support her brother, urging "and you must do it for my sake." The husband agrees immediately because "they had a good marriage" and she does not need to egg him (*Flm* 13.19:271, 18:268). Unsurprisingly, none of the threatened divorces in the sagas of Icelanders occur because the women get their way.[137]

To be an effective weapon, divorce initiated by wives must be shown to be possible. In a score of completed divorces in the narratives wives take the initiative twice as often as men. Unsuccessful goading also results in divorce on occasion, as suggested by the couple Vigdís and Þórðr who appear in several sagas. Although Vigdís dominates the marriage, she can not prevent her husband from making plans to kill her uncle. As a consequence, "she displayed hostility (*fjándskapr*) and declared herself divorced" (*Lx* 5:16.37). Her animosity likely included verbal egging.

The most unexpected aspect of divorce in the sagas is the latitude given to personal incompatibility, a justification that accorded with the bishop's permission to grant divorces in similar cases in the law. The discord can be described in vague terms ("they were not alike in temperament;" *Rkd* 10.11:176), or caused by specific problems ("because of their disagreement"; *VGl* 9.16:50; "their relationship was not good; *Lx* 5.30:80). The blame is occasionally placed on both partners, but more often the husband is at fault. The wife leaves on her own, or is sent back to her father.[138] Sometimes a wife has a sexual complaint, such as Unnr's famous case of lack of consummation. In other cases no reasons are offered: the reader remains in the dark, for instance, as to why Rannveig left her husband. She adds insult to injury, throwing his clothes into the cesspool, forcing him, girded only in bedclothes, to seek help from a neighbor (*Dpl* 11.8:158). One Halla encourages her husband to find a new wife for an altruistic reason—her poor health—but she and her family become upset when he complies.[139]

The woman's personal honor is involved in some cases. When her husband kills her friend Steinólfr in a jealous rage, Þórdís immediately declares that she will no longer be his wife from that day. The author adds that she "never came into the same bed" (*VGl* 9.21:68). When Steingerðr's husband Bersi is wounded in a humiliating way (his buttocks are sliced), she "took an intense dislike to him and wanted to divorce him;" *Krm* 8.13:254). In both cases the women are not hurt or directly involved, but their personal honor has been infringed by their husbands' emotional or physical flaws.[140] Male honor tinged with monetary concerns is Barði's reason for divorcing Guðrún; he declares that he can no longer stand her father's stinginess (*Hðv* 3.32:311).

In a pagan marriage the injured party could initiate a divorce without recourse to authority beyond the couple. It was not even necessary to tell the spouse immediately, but the validity of the divorce required the presence of witnesses at the initial declaration. Therefore the party desiring the divorce would call in witnesses (*váttar*), state the reason (*sǫk*), and declare him- or herself divorced (*skiliðr*) from the other. Unnr's divorce of Hrútr, caused by his inability to consummate the marriage, provides the fullest illustration. Instructing his daughter in the proper procedure, Mǫrðr told Unnr to choose a time for leaving when her husband was not at home. Before her departure she was to take witnesses to their bed, declare herself legally divorced according to the rules of the alþingi and the common law of the land and repeat them by the main door in front of witnesses (*Nj* 12.7:24). Later the announcement had to be reiterated at a þing. Since a woman was not empowered to undertake this last step herself, Mǫrðr acted for his daughter. A man could reduce the whole procedure by going directly to the alþingi.[141] These details, particularly those concerning witnesses, are confirmed by the laws.

The female initiative in divorce may seem unusual, but financial arrangements, such as characterize Guðrún's first marriage to Þorvaldr, may suggest an explanation. After "they have come into the same bed," she is to be in charge of all their property and be entitled to one half of the estate "no matter how long or how short their marriage lasted" (*Lx* 5.34:93). In other words, women retained their economic independence both in marriage and after. Although the husband was in charge of his wife's property (consisting of the mundr from his family and the heimanfylgja from her parents), she received both portions in an eventual divorce if the husband was at fault. If she was the cause, she nonetheless received her dowry (*Gg* 1b 42–43; 2:171). Ásgerðr, therefore, offers no idle threat when she warns her husband (in a bed scene elaborated later) that her father will retrieve both her bride price and dowry if he does not do as she requests (*Gí* 6.9:33). Normally a wife took her personal belongings (*gripir*) when she left her husband's house;[142] but she expected her kin family to take care of the division of the couple's property (*féskipti*). With its assets restored, the family was usually happy to have the woman back and sheltered her until a new marriage candidate appeared, which occurred not infrequently.[143] As depicted in the narratives and confirmed by law, therefore, unsatisfied wives who were well-to-do and still young could afford to regard divorce as an attractive option, because they were financially secure and confident in their continued reproductive capability.

Contemporary Sagas. Since churchmen were not entirely adverse to the traditional nordic divorce, one might expect frequent divorces in the contemporary world of *Sturlunga saga* and the other contemporary sagas. However, no more than a handful of examples can be discerned. The most common cause in these is personal incompatibility experienced in particular by the woman. For example, the unhappy marriage begun in 1172 between the priest Ingimundr, the uncle of Bishop Guðmundr, and Sigríðr Tumadóttir ended a year later. Ingimundr left, but no formal divorce (*skilnaðr*) was announced, although Sigríðr later remarries (*St* 1:53, 54, 124). Snorri Sturluson's daughter Hallbera was divorced from her first husband in 1224 (*St* 1:304); her relationship with the second was so bad that divorce was preempted only by her death in 1231 (*St* 1:319, 333, 335, 345). That same year Snorri's other daughter, Ingibjǫrg, was also divorced from her husband Gizurr Þorvaldsson after an unhappy seven-year marriage (*St* 1:346).[144] The property division was arranged by the men in these cases. Since personal matters did not surface easily in the crowded narrative of *Sturlunga saga,* except for the most prominent families, the problem may have been more common than the sources reveal. The Sturlung divorces were likely reported because the individuals involved had close kinship to the author of the saga, but, as a rule, others may have been omitted. Although the divorces were excused by incompatibility, the bishop does not seem to have been consulted. Churchmen's rules on incest could also be manipulated. A father occasionally used these rules to refuse a suitor whose marriage proposal he opposed.[145] In other cases churchmen were unable to force a couple to separate after their kinship was revealed but were content to arrange a compromise that allowed the couple to stay together for a limited time.[146]

Anthropologists argue that marital stability is closely related to economic development; the pivotal point is the introduction of agriculture. During the viking age, when Iceland was being settled, the economy may have more closely resembled a hunting and gathering stage than the settled agricultural and pastoral regime that prevailed during the twelfth and thirteenth centuries. It is plausible that divorce was more accepted in the earlier pagan than in the later Christian stage when immovable property and its inheritance dominated the economy.[147] The easy divorce in the sagas of Icelanders may reflect earlier practices that were modified first by underlying economic development and only later by an active Christian policy. It is equally possible that divorce was as common in the contemporary world as in the saga age. Since *Sturlunga saga* was largely devoted to political issues, the authors might have chosen to discuss divorce only when important people were involved.

Widowhood

If well-to-do and still in their reproductive years, women often remarried after divorce or the decease of their husbands. After menopause, bereft of reproductive capabilities and perhaps losing sexual attractiveness, older women did not remarry—and often enjoyed their greatest independence as widows. Saga women were frequently admired for qualities normally associated with men. This "gender blurring" was most often expressed by the author, but women themselves also articulated such ideals.[148] Words with a masculine semantic range—"valiant" (*drengr*) and "forceful" (*skǫrungr*), for example— characterized numerous men and a few admired women, mostly middle-aged or beyond. Older women no longer inspired fear and jealousy in men, but even the most impressive among these manly and forceful women exercised their authority best in the absence of their husbands. Thus, Þorbjǫrg, described as "very forceful" (*skǫrungr mikill*), "was in charge of the district and made all the decisions when Vermundr [her husband] was not at home" (*Gr* 7.52:169).[149]

Women themselves were aware of the restrictions imposed by a husband. A particularly illuminating case is Guðrún Ósvífrsdóttir's fourth wedding, a story preserved in two versions.[150] When the wedding festivities had begun and the widow Guðrún was already seated on the bridal bench clad in her finest, Þorkell, her new husband, became aware that she was sheltering a fugitive, Gunnarr Þiðrandabani. In one version Þorkell orders Gunnarr to be seized in fulfillment of an earlier promise to a friend to have him killed. Guðrún, however, rises from the bench and orders her own men to protect Gunnarr. Since she "had a much larger force," Þorkell settles for sending Gunnarr away that evening. In the other version he is forced to be content with even less. When he demands Gunnarr's departure, Guðrún replies that her groom-to-be could leave as he had come because she did not care to have him as her husband, adding "I am not willing to turn over to your weapons those men I want to keep." Guðrún realized that as a mature but married woman she did not have the same independence that she had enjoyed in her previous state of widowhood. The fact that she was still fertile—she bore a son for Þorkell—may have induced her to remarry.[151]

From these cases it appears that a widow was best able to embody masculine ideals. She was not under the guardianship of father or husband; her sons were usually grown and gone, or they were so young that they did not yet exercise authority over her; her own dowry and the bride price paid by her husband, as well as other inheritances assembled over time, secured sufficient wealth to hire male help who, among other services, protected her against sexual advances of strange men. Even when she was no longer sexually attractive her advanced years need not be a burden. The narrative corpus contains several examples of independent, older widows who confirm that a woman at this stage of life enjoyed her greatest power.[152]

Best known is Auðr/Unnr Ketilsdóttir, the daughter of a Norwegian chieftain and wife of a Norse king in Dublin. Little is known about her until both her husband and son were killed and she became responsible for a large household, including several granddaughters and a grandson. At that moment "she had a ship built secretly in a forest, and when it was completed she loaded it with valuables and prepared for a voyage. She took all her surviving kinsfolk with her. It is generally agreed that it would be hard to find another example of a woman (*kvennmaðr*) escaping from such hazards with so much wealth and such a large retinue. From this it can be seen what a paragon amongst women she was (*hon var mikit afbragð annarra kvenna*)."[153]

Auðr was clearly an exceptional woman. Aware of the authority that male kinsmen could exercise—especially younger male in-laws—she wisely scattered her granddaughters on islands in the Atlantic and married them to local men whose authority she avoided by proceeding to Iceland with her young grandson. Ignoring the restrictions on land claim (*landnám*) that applied to women, she claimed as much land as any man.[154] She lived until she had arranged her grandson's marriage and died with dignity during the wedding festivities. Even if no longer physically attractive to men, Auðr/Unnr, rich, powerful, and independent, passed the last phase of her life in conformity with the masculine model available to mature men.

This type found particular favor with the author of *Fóstbrœðra saga*, who included no less than eight such powerful women, three of whom dwelt in Greenland.[155] The most impressive is Sigrfljóð, who arranged the killing of two obstreperous neighbors and later convinced their kinsman to accept compensation, which she paid personally from her own purse (*fésjóð*; *Ftb* 6.5:

138–42).[156] Equally masculine in her behavior is the widow Katla, who, in the manner of princes and kings, accepted a praise poem (*lof*) on behalf of her daughter, rewarded the poet with the gift of a ring, and bestowed a name on him (*Ftb* 6.11:171–72).[157]

In many traditional cultures a woman gained wealth, influence, and prestige as she moved through the biological stages of life, often reaching her apogee as a widow. Powerful widows are not as numerous in the contemporary sagas as in the sagas of Icelanders, a discrepancy caused, perhaps, by changing economic and political situations. The presence, however, of Guðný Bǫðvarsdóttir, one of the two pivotal women evoked in the first chapter of this book, and, from the following cohort, Jóreiðr Hallsdóttir, great-grandmother and grandmother respectively of Ingibjǫrg (Jóreiðr resisted remarriage by going on a hunger strike), is enough to suggest that the powerful widow continued as a social phenomenon into Christian times.[158]

It is difficult to establish definitive conclusions about pagan and Christian marriage and divorce. Obstacles are presented by the differing historical contexts of the three major groups of sources, the pagan setting of the sagas of Icelanders, the mixed pagan and Christian content of the laws, and the Christian world of thirteenth-century Iceland and Norway in the contemporary sagas. Style also creates difficulties. The dry, dense, detailed prose of the laws differs markedly from the narrative flow of the sagas. Meanwhile, the slow, deliberate style of the sagas of Icelanders, in which every detail is pregnant with meaning, contrasts with the rapid pace of the contemporary sagas, in which the reader is overwhelmed by political detail but often deprived of the social information I am seeking here.

The chief obstacle, however, is the turbulent cross-current stirred up by the white stream of Christian mediation emanating from all sources and by the clear flow of continuity from ancient pagan practices, to evoke again the image of the two streams of water in the Blanda. Despite the chronological anchoring of all sources in the present, authors were receptive to the current from the past and reported in a reasonably faithful manner what had been passed down to them about their history. They occasionally succumbed to urgent concerns in their own day which they tried to contextualize within the past. These anachronisms are easily identified, however, and rather than muddying the pagan and Christian sketches they can help fill in the details. Thus, I do not trust the authors of the sagas of Icelanders when they intimate that the Christian notions of marital fidelity and female consent existed in the pagan past, when the negative print of these ideals—concubinage and extramarital affairs—can be read out of both laws and the contemporary sagas. When, however, the authors more soberly accept another Christian defeat, that of indissolubility, by admitting that divorce was relatively frequent in the ancient setting, I am willing to believe them because the phenomenon existed both in laws and the contemporary narratives. The native institution of marriage as a twofold arrangement of engagement and wedding negotiated by men for women under their control and accompanied by financial arrangements persists throughout all the evidence. Hindsight suggests that the most successful aspect of the Christian program was female consent, but since it may have been accepted more easily by people with little means than among the propertied classes who appear in the sources, the process by which it was accomplished is not entirely clear.

CHAPTER THREE

Reproduction

CONCEPTION:
THEORY AND KNOWLEDGE

Although most peoples have believed that human conception requires both a woman and man, the specific roles
assigned to the two partners have varied historically.
The ancient Hebrews and the Greek Aristotle, for example, attributed conception solely to the man's seed
and limited the woman's task to providing nurture for
the fetus.[1] The Greek physicians Hippocratus and Galen,
however, assumed that the woman contributed her seed as
well to the reproductive process.[2] It is difficult to discern the
thoughts of nordic people on these issues since theoretical
discourse on human physiology is virtually lacking.[3] Like
most humans, they doubtless concluded that both women
and men participated in some manner. The Norwegian Gulathing Law, for example, enjoined an engaged couple to appear at their wedding and designated
a delinquent man as "he who flees the female sex organ" (*fuðflogi*) and an
absent woman as "she who flees the male sex organ" (*flannfluga;* NgL, 1:28,
4:6). Since the law assumed the reproductive purpose of marriage, the terms
thereby attributed roles to both sexes to some degree.[4]

Poor soil, however, magnified the dependence of nordic people on animal
husbandry, particularly in Iceland. Able to control and manipulate the reproductive life of their beasts, farmers throughout the northern world—like
people from other pastoral societies—compared animal and human physiology and benefited from their experience with the former. In one case, a father
wished to alleviate his daughter's intense pain. Known as a "good doctor," he
placed her on his lap and examined her body. Discovering a large malodorous

boil above her navel, he declared: "If any of my cattle suffered from such a disease I would cut it out, but here I do not dare for the sake of God" (*Bs* 1:252).[5] This man hesitated, but in other instances human surgery was performed. In a well-known case, the famous physician Hrafn Sveinbjarnarson operated on a man who suffered so badly from a gallstone that he swelled to the size of an ox. Pushing the stone down into the penis and tying the ends with threads, Hrafn "made an incision lengthwise, removed two stones, anointed the wound and cured him" (*Bs* 1:644).[6]

Most male animals were castrated (the technical term was "to cut out the testicles" [*gelda* or *afeista*]), which left only a few for breeding.[7] On a more ominous note, human males were also subject to the gelder's knife; as noted earlier, beggars were castrated in Iceland in order to limit their offspring. In Norway a person who committed bestiality risked both gelding and outlawry (*NgL* 1:18, 2:496). The fact that castration was explicitly prohibited in all but the aforenamed cases (*Gg* 1a:148) suggests that it was occasionally used in hostile encounters, as the narrative sources confirm. In the turmoil that habitually followed Bishop Guðmundr, a priest was killed and two others were gelded (*afeista; Bs* 2:118). In one notorious case Sturla Sighvatsson ordered the blinding and emasculation of his cousin Órækja, son of Snorri Sturluson. Sturla performed the castration himself, urging Órækja to think of his wife Arnbjǫrg. Only one eye and one testicle were removed, however, and Arnbjǫrg was assured that her husband "retained his sight and was sound" (*hefði sýn sína ok var heill; St* 1:395–96); the second term implied hope for Órækja's future sexual performance.[8]

Familiarity with the human reproductive process is also suggested by a humorous treatment of the subject in a later heroic saga. Before committing suicide, a father suggested that his six children live as three couples but without "increasing their number" (*eigi fjǫlgi þér lið yðvart*). To comply, the young people "studded themselves with wooden pegs and wrapped woolen cloth around their bodies so they could not touch each other's bare skin." Aware that she had been impregnated by a visitor, one of the daughters—she was named Snotra (wise) as the most clever in the family—loosened the cloth around her face while pretending to be asleep. Because he had accidentally touched her cheek, her brother assumed he was responsible for her condition (*Gtr, FSN* 4.1:4–6).

Conception was conveyed by the verbs *ala* and *geta,* referring in the plural to the couple's activity or in the singular to either partner, although the former was preferred for the woman and the latter for the man.[9] Emphasis on the man's role is suggested by the terms "conceiving limb" (*getnaðarlimr* or *getnaðarliðr*) in contexts where medical problems of the penis, not procreation, are treated (*Bs* 1:614, 644; 2:25).

An emphasis on the male role is further confirmed by two terms of genealogical descent, *langfeðgar* and *kvennkné*. That Icelanders named their children after paternal or maternal relatives and identified themselves through
both male and female ancestors indicate that they used the bilateral descent
system. A woman was included in a genealogical chain, however, only if she
provided a more prestigious family than her husband. The privileging of the
male is clear from the proud use of the first of the two terms. Langfeðgar
literally means a long list of agnatic ancestors and indicates a lineage of forefathers extending over an unspecified sequence (*Eg* 2.1:4), but it is also employed when only two generations are involved (*Eg* 2:50:128). The extended
term langfeðgatal indicates long dynasties stretching back through fathers into
mythical times.[10]

The second term, kvennkné, which literally means female knee or link, was
devalued when it was associated with royal succession. Attempting to establish a marital program consisting of monogamy, indissolubility, and legitimacy
for the nordic population in general, churchmen concluded that if they could
impose this policy on royalty, the devastating wars of succession that plagued
Norway during the twelfth- and the first half of the thirteenth century would
cease.[11] In 1165 the archbishop of Trondheim (Niðaróss) was willing to support the young boy Magnús Erlingsson as king because his mother was a royal
princess and both she and her son were born in legitimate unions (*ME* 28.21:
396). Upon Magnús's coronation, a law of succession was drawn up, stipulating
that the oldest legitimate son (*skilgetinn*) should inherit the throne, but it was
disregarded in the struggles between pretenders during the next half-century
because it allowed maternal descent. Against this argument new pretenders —
Sverrir and Hákon — contended that only a man who was himself the son of a
king and who could trace his ancestry back to other kings without any female
intermediary (*kvennkné*) should be considered a royal candidate. The idea was
discussed extensively in the early part of the thirteenth century during the
minority of King Hákon, himself an illegitimate son of King Sverrir. It was
defended by leading chieftains, who argued that the custom was as old as heathen times and had been legally sanctioned by saintly King Óláfr (*helgi*).[12] This
principle is the Norwegian equivalent of the patrilineality of the Salic law in
France, also not identifiable in ancient legal texts but invoked in the early fourteenth century to prevent the claim of the English king to the French throne
through a female link when the male line of the Capetian dynasty came to
an end.

The foregoing theoretical discussion of procreation suggests that, although
cognizant of the participation of the two sexes, the nordic peoples nonetheless
privileged the male role.

HETEROSEXUAL LOVEMAKING

Unfortunately, Old Norse sources are not explicit on the subject of love-making, preferring euphemisms and opaque physical descriptions. Neverthe-less, by sequencing scenes from the sagas in which men and women become erotically excited and make bodily contact, one can construct a prosopogra-phy, as it were, of lovemaking.

First, arousal is obviously necessary. From at least Roman times western European tradition has been dominated by a particular "male gaze" that identifies women as erotic objects through descriptions of female beauty.[13] Although Germanic Europe eventually adopted this stance, it had previously experimented with a less gender-specific focus on perceptions of beauty. The sagas of Icelanders demonstrate that scopophilia, the pleasure of beholding, was derived from handsome men as well as from beautiful women. An almost identical vocabulary was deployed for both sexes, but male beauty was de-scribed in greater corporal and sartorial detail than female.[14] Sober and ob-jective, these descriptions articulate an appreciation of human—particularly male—beauty, but without erotic connotations and without resulting sexual encounters. Of particular interest, therefore, are the few occurrences in which a man's sexual arousal is provoked by female beauty and, even more rarely, those in which couples are mutually excited.[15] Among the first group is the aging Þráinn, who during a family celebration becomes so inflamed by the young Þorgerðr that he "could not keep his eyes" from her (*var starsýnn; Nj* 12.34:89). When his wife makes a snide remark, he divorces her and marries the young woman on the spot.[16] The case of Þorbjǫrg and Þormóðr offers an example of mutual excitation. In the author's opinion, the woman (Þorbjǫrg) "was not particularly beautiful," but Þormóðr considers her attractive (*lízk honum vel á hana*), and she reciprocates by finding him handsome (*verðr henni hann vel at skapi; Ftb* 6.11:170) as they engage in amorous conversation.[17] Only rarely did saga authors provide a romantic atmosphere for couples' brief meetings.[18]

An analysis of sexual relations is further impeded by the habitual use of euphemisms, as illustrated in the frequent topos of the illicit love visit.[19] Although not all these visits result in pregnancy, they leave no doubt about the man's intentions as he repeatedly calls on a woman against her family's wishes. Nevertheless, almost without exception, saga authors claim that the man comes "in order to talk with" the girl (*til tals við*). That gestures and ca-resses are more important than words is obvious from a scene in which the lover "placed her [his mistress] on his lap . . . and *talked* with her so all could *see* it" (*Hlf* 8.4:145). The gestures visible at a distance are clearly not the talking lips but the caressing arms and hands.

A related obstacle is the use of certain words that denote pleasure in general but at times imply sexual intercourse. One such term is "to amuse oneself" (*at skemmta sér*). It most often refers to a couple's pleasurable activities, denoting a card game (*Gnl* 3.4:60) or innocent conversation (*Lx* 5.42:127) as well as illicit intercourse (*Nj* 12.87:211). Frequently used in connection with "talk" (*tala*), the two expressions—mingled and redolent with double entendres—are employed to good effect in a scene of *Laxdœla saga*. As Bolli is talking with Ingibjǫrg in Norway (*sitr á tali*), Bolli blames him for forgetting the pleasures (*til skemmtanar*) in Iceland where Guðrún is waiting for him (*Lx* 5.41: 126).[20] A similar term is "to enjoy" or "to derive benefit from" (*njóta*), used in a general way in single- and double-sex relations, but frequently referring to sexual intercourse. The magician Þórveig thus places a curse on Kormakr that he never "enjoy" his beloved Steingerðr (*Krm* 8.5:222; 6:223).[21] Thus these words can imply the entire process of lovemaking.

More specific are the terms *faðmr* and *faðmlag*. Associated with measurements that refer to the length of an arm, the words suggest sexual embrace. When Hrafn betrays and kills Gunnlaugr, the man whom his wife Helga loves, he offers as his excuse: "I could not bear the thought that you should enjoy Helga's embrace" (*faðmlagsins Helgu; Gnl* 3.12:102).[22] A glimpse of marital lovemaking is conveyed in a story concerning a shipbuilder. Described as "fond of women" (*kvennsamr*), he thinks he sees his beautiful wife board the ship on which he is working. Approaching her, "he puts her down gently (*hann bregðr á bliðlæti við hana*), because they were used to this kind of game. Now he lies with this woman (*legst hann með þessari konu*), . . . but as they separated, he seemed to understand that she was not his wife but an unclean spirit" (*Bs* 1:605).

Foreplay

Beyond the general terms covering the entire cycle of lovemaking, the sources occasionally permit glimpses of couples caught in intimate situations. When a man is depicted as taking a woman by the hand and leading her off (*Nj* 12.87:211), one may assume a relationship already existed.[23] First acquaintance may have occurred at drinking feasts, where women—always in the minority—were assigned by lot to men. Each couple shared a horn in *tvímenningr*, leaving some men to drink alone.[24] A young Swedish girl was not too pleased with the assignment of the inexperienced Egill, but she eventually warmed up when he "picked her up and placed her next to himself." Hints of sexuality are conveyed in the description of this woman's looks and behavior. Not surprisingly, "they drank all evening and became very happy" (*allkát; Eg* 2.48:120–21).[25]

Egill's gesture, "placing her next to himself," is a saga formula denoting intimacy and a first contact between bodies.²⁶ As a next step, the man would place the woman on his lap (*setja í kné sér*). Hallfreðr exhibits his intimacy with his mistress Kolfinna in this way, as does Þórðr with his wife Oddný (*Hlf* 8.4:145; *BHd* 3.12:142). This action was normal in lovemaking, but the two men also wanted to annoy the woman's future husband and former lover, respectively, who were watching. It is rare to find a woman in this posture; one saga attributes it twice to a certain Yngvildr, but she uses it to betray the man whom she pretends to seduce (*Svf* 9.18:172–73).²⁷

Having placed the woman on his lap, the man proceeds to kiss her (*kyssir hana*), as do both Hallfreðr and Þórðr in the episodes just mentioned.²⁸ Although in this case Þórðr is tender (*blíðr*) with his wife, kisses could entail a brusque treatment, as suggested by the verbs *kippir* and *sveigir*, used when a man violently pulls a woman toward him.²⁹ Men seemed to take the initiative, but women naturally reciprocated, as implied by the comment from a man who has smashed his opponent's jaw; he is glad that the widow with whom the victim lives would now find her lover less pleasant to kiss (*Hör* 3.31:306). It was to be expected, of course, that the Norwegian Queen Gunnhildr—having herself initiated an affair with the visiting Hrútr—should kiss him at his departure (*Nj* 12.6:21).³⁰

The degree of intimacy between Kjartan and the Norwegian princess Ingibjǫrg, is left vague. Before departing, Kjartan "embraced Ingibjǫrg" (*hvarf til Ingibjargar; Lx* 5.43:131). With a general meaning of "turning toward," *hverfa til* suggests bodily or facial contact. It does not denote an erotic kiss, however, but one exchanged on solemn occasions either between a man and a woman or between men, thus making "to embrace" a better rendition. Since Kjartan never saw Ingibjǫrg again, its use here is fitting. When Ásdís likewise sent her son Grettir away for the last time, she "embraced him" (*hvarf til hans; Gr* 7.47: 153). Anticipating the serious events that would befall his son Þórolfr, the old Kveld-Úlfr walked him to his ship with foreboding and "embraced him." In the next generation Þórolfr's brother Skalla-Grímr took final leave of his son Egill with the same gesture (*Eg* 2.6:15; 58:173).³¹ Used under similar circumstances, the word *minnask*, perhaps etymologically related to "mouth," more clearly implied kissing, but it was used primarily about men, as they greeted or took leave of one another.³² No evidence has surfaced in the narratives of women kissing and embracing each other, but the penitential of Bishop Þorlákr from 1178 punished lovemaking between women as harshly as adultery and bestiality (*DI* 1:243).³³

Intimacy is signaled when a man places his head in a woman's lap and her hands frame his face. Ormr assumed this position with Sigríðr, although she warned him that she was engaged to his brother (*Þhr* 14.5:187–88). Occasionally, the purpose was to delouse, a service a slave mistress performed for Stígandi.³⁴ Although the man was betrayed in this case, by allowing himself to fall asleep with his head in her lap, he demonstrated his confidence that a woman's attention to a man's hair was a token of love. The mistress who washes her lover's hair is a frequent topos, and wives continued to provide this grooming for husbands.[35]

A woman could also show her love by making clothes, rendering the shirt a sure love token before marriage. Whereas Steingerðr refused Kormákr's request, Valgerðr made "all the clothes that demanded the most elaborate work" for Ingólfr (*Krm* 8.17:264; *Vtn* 8.38:101). Wives continued to assume responsibility for their husbands' clothes after marriage, of course, but the pleasure turned to drudgery, as suggested by a conversation between two women, Ásgerðr and Auðr, married to two brothers. While both were busy sewing, Ásgerðr asked Auðr to cut a shirt for her husband Þorkell. Apparently tired of the work herself, she assumed that Auðr's previous relationship with him would make it an attractive task for her sister-in-law (*Gí* 6.9:30).[36] Although Auðr refused, her rejoinder—that Ásgerðr would not have asked her if the task had involved a shirt for Vésteinn, Auðr's brother and Ásgerðr's current lover—confirms that the shirt was a token of pre- or extramarital love. Thus, too, a woman on shipboard is pictured in the daily task of tightening the wide sleeves for a man, in this case her lover Grettir (*Gr* 7.17:53).[37]

So far in this analysis, women's active role in lovemaking has been confined to men's hair and clothing, with no skin contact. Women are, however, seen putting their arms around men's necks. Although this embrace mainly signifies marital affection, it is to be expected that the sexually charged Queen Gunnhildr behaves toward her lover Hrútr in this way (*Nj* 12.6:20).[38] The gesture undoubtedly denoted genuine affection, but it was frequently used by wives to obtain favors from their husbands. To persuade her husband to let her foster father stay with them, Hallgerðr "put her arms around his [her husband's] neck" (*lagði hendr upp um háls honum; Nj* 12.15:47). Ásgerðr bragged to Auðr that she planned to use the same gesture in bed to obtain her husband's forgiveness after he had overheard the two women admit to earlier affairs in the sewing episode just mentioned (*Gí* 6.9:31).[39]

Intercourse

Ásgerðr's plan for the night provides a good approach to the final act of lovemaking, because the author permits the reader to watch Ásgerðr and her husband in bed together.[40] Despite her earlier boasting to Auðr, Ásgerðr's plan does not work out at first, because Þorkell is so upset by her revelation that he refuses to allow her to join him under the covers. Offering him the choice between pretending that nothing has happened and an immediate divorce, Ásgerðr makes sure that he understands that divorce means financial loss as well as the end of their marital relations (*hvílaþrǫng*, literally, crowding together in bed). In resignation, Þorkell tells her to do what she wants, and Ásgerðr climbs in next to him. The author comments that "they had not been lying together long before they settled their problem as if nothing had happened" (*Gí* 6.9:32–33). Obvious intimacy notwithstanding, the vague expressions — crowded bed, lying together, settled their problem — provide little specific information about past and present lovemaking.

The same saga, fortunately, contains another episode that suggests the act of marital intercourse (although it ends in murder). Having decided that he must kill his brother-in-law Þorgrímr — his sister Þórdís's husband — Gísli goes to the couple's farm at night. Approaching their bed, Gísli sets in motion a remarkable scene that deserves to be quoted in full:

> He goes up and feels about and touches her breast; she lay nearest the outside. Then Þórdís said: "Why is your hand so cold, Þorgrímr?" and wakes him. Þorgrímr said: "Do you want me to turn toward you?" She thought he had laid his arm over her. Then Gísli waits a while and warms his hand in his shirt, and they both fall asleep. Now he touches Þorgrímr softly, so that he wakes him up. He thought that Þórdís had woken him and then turns toward her. Then Gísli pulls the covers off them with one hand and with the other he spears Þorgrímr through with Grásíða [his sword], so that it sticks in the bed.[41]

Scholars have long pondered why Gísli created an erotic situation at this moment, but the point is that such a situation is indeed established. By touching her breast Gísli makes Þórdís think that her husband "had laid his arm over her," signaling his desire. In Eddic poetry this expression (*leggja hǫnd* [or *arm* (arm) or *lær* (thigh)] *yfir*) is a frequent euphemism for lovemaking.[42] Only half-awake, Þorgrímr undoubtedly does not notice her question about the cold hand, but perceives only that she has awakened him. He wants to make sure of her intentions and asks whether she wishes him to "turn toward" her. Having warmed his hand, Gísli makes a new move, this time awakening Þorgrímr. Assuming that Þórdís has again announced her desire, her husband does not ask about her intentions but simply "turned toward her," ready for action. Instead, he is himself gored by Gísli's sword.[43] The expression (*snúask at*) is elsewhere used as preliminary to, or as a metaphor for, sexual intercourse. When the Norwegian king Magnús, for example, joins the reluctant Margrét in bed, "he turned toward her (*snýsk hann til hennar*), spoke tenderly to her, and explained that he was going to do her a great favor if she would only cooperate" (*Msk* 122).[44] More explicit is an episode involving King Helgi, who allows a female in tattered clothes to spend the night next to him in bed but "turned away from her" (*snýr sér frá henni*). When she is transformed into a beautiful woman, the king "quickly turned toward her (*snýr sér þá skjótt at henni*) with tenderness." Having obtained the miraculous transformation she had hoped for by sleeping next to a king, the woman wants to leave. Without getting out of bed, Helgi declares he will arrange a "hasty wedding" (*skyndi-brullaup*), and "they spent the night together."[45] The next morning the woman declares that the king had behaved "with desire" (*með lostum*) and that she is pregnant (*Hrkr, FSN* 1.15:28). Another author leaves no doubt about the activity when he describes a groom who on his wedding night "turned toward the bride intending to destroy her maidenhood" (*SN, LMIR* 2.21:52–53).[46]

If these scenes suggest only the emotional aspects of love and use metaphorical terms for the act itself, a small drama in *Njála*, played out in several episodes, approaches an almost clinical description of intercourse. I have already touched upon the love affair between Queen Gunnhildr and Hrútr several times. Engaged to Unnr, Hrútr is forced to postpone their marriage because of pressing business in Norway. Here he encounters the aging Queen Gunnhildr, whose sexual appetite is illustrated in several sagas. Providing him with beautiful clothes, Gunnhildr tells him: "You shall lie with me in the upper chamber (*liggja í lopti hjá mér*) tonight; we two alone.'" The saga author continues: "Afterwards they went to bed upstairs, and she locked the door from the inside" (*Nj* 12.3:11–15).

After a year in Norway, Hrútr becomes homesick. Taking notice, the queen asks whether he has a woman in Iceland. He denies it, but she does not believe him. When he leaves, Gunnhildr gives him a bracelet, but she places a curse on him: "You shall not be able to satisfy your desire with the woman you intend in Iceland, but you may have your will with others" (*þú megir engri munúð fram koma við konu þá, er þú ætlar þér á Íslandi, en fremja skalt þú mega vilja þinn við aðrar konur; Nj* 12.6:21). The crucial expression is *munúð* (desire), from *munhugð* (*mun* [love] and *hugr* [mind]), a word that stresses the cerebral aspect of desire.[47] Returning home, Hrútr marries Unnr, but the queen's curse takes effect, as indicated by the statement that "little was happening in their relationship" (*fátt var um með þeim Hrúti um samfarar*), where the last word, *samfǫr* (literally, traveling together) is a euphemism for intercourse (*Nj* 12.6:22). After several years Unnr finally tells her father that she wants a divorce because, as she explains, her husband "is not able to consummate our marriage (*hann má ekki hjúskaparfar eiga við mik*) so I may enjoy him (*njóta hans*), although he is as virile as the best of men in every other respect" (*Nj* 12.7:24).[48] Asked by her father to be more specific, Unnr provides details: "As soon as he touches me, his skin (*hǫrund,* here a euphemism for penis) is so enlarged that he cannot have pleasure (*eptirlæti;* literally, lasting sensory impressions) from me, although we both wish sincerely that we might reach fulfillment (*hǫfum vit bæði breytni til þess á alla vega at vit mættim njótask*), but it is impossible. And yet, before we draw apart (*vit skilim*), he proves that he is by nature (*i œði sínu*) as normal as other men (*Nj* 12.7:24)."

Provided with this information, her father gives her detailed instructions on how to divorce Hrútr.[49] Meanwhile, the other part of the queen's prediction also comes true. Another narrative reports that Hrútr married two other women, with whom he had sixteen sons and ten daughters (*Lx* 5.19:48–49). His mishap with Unnr, however, left a final trace in *Njála* which is of interest here because it provides the most explicit term for the male role in sexual intercourse.

After Unnr leaves, Hrútr refuses to return her dowry to her father and instead challenges him to single combat at the alþingi. Since the father has pressed the claim with "greed and aggression," sympathy is on Hrútr's side. The case catches the imagination of everyone, including children. On the way back from the meeting, Hrútr and his brother stop overnight with friends. Two boys and a girl are playing on the floor; the boys reenact the drama several times: "One of the boys said: 'I'll be Mǫrðr [Unnr's father] and divorce you from your wife on the grounds that you couldn't have intercourse with her (*þú hafir ekki sorðit hana*).' The other boy replied: 'Then I'll be Hrútr and invalidate your dowry claim if you don't dare fight with me' " (*Nj* 12.8:29).[50]

The crucial term is *sorðit*, from *serða*, a verb indicating the male role in intercourse. Its precise translation would be to penetrate, to screw, or to fuck.[51] This appearance is a unique use of the word in the active sense, however. More common is its passive form, *sorðinn* (to be used sexually by a man, to be penetrated, or to be screwed), which describes the passive male in homosexual relations.[52] In its active form *serða* therefore indicates the male role in sexual intercourse toward the same or opposite sex. Another word with the same meaning, *streða*, was created by metathesis. In *Grágás* and in the Norwegian laws the past participles of these words, *sorðinn* and *stroðinn*, were joined by the adjective *ragr* in a paragraph listing the accusations (*ýki*) that men might direct against each other. Whether carved in wood—visible but silent—or spoken aloud, such insults resulted in outlawry for the offender.[53] The specifically sexual meaning of *ragr* implied the general condition of being effeminate, while the two other words referred explicitly to the sex act in which one man, designated as having been *stroðinn* or *sorðinn*, played the passive role, while the other performed the action of *streða* or *serða*.[54] The passage from *Njála* indicates that the word originally could be used about heterosexual relations as well, a conclusion confirmed by the poem *Grettisfœrsla*. Alluded to in the saga named after the protagonist (*Gr* 7.52:168), this poem was erased from a single fifteenth-century manuscript, but it has been partially restored through the use of ultraviolet light.[55] Describing Grettir's irrepressible sexuality, it employs the active voice of *streða* and *serða* about his relations with both sexes as well as with animals. The use of these words in homosexual situations eventually endowed them with obscene connotations.

The voices of the lovemakers themselves can be amplified by echoes from third parties as they provide suggestive comments on what couples might be doing privately. Although such remarks are often colored by jealousy or hostility, the details are nonetheless useful because the observers draw on personal experience. Threatening her men with death, the aging Queen Gunnhildr had prohibited them from telling others about her tryst with the handsome Hrútr. The men undoubtedly gossiped among themselves but rumors about this or her other affairs with even younger men have not survived.[56] *Eyrbyggja saga,* however, contains vignettes of two other women, Katla and Þórgunna, who were less successful but no less interested in young men than the powerful queen.[57]

The arresting story of the magician Katla, who was desperately in love with the young Gunnlaugr, is of special interest for the purpose of providing details concerning intercourse. With a son the same age as Gunnlaugr, Katla is no longer young but still "beautiful to behold" (*fríð kona sýnum*).[58] Gunnlaugr makes frequent visits to the neighboring farm to learn magic from Geirríðr, a woman of Katla's age. Oddr, Katla's son, often accompanies him. When they return to Katla's farm, she invariably invites Gunnlaugr to spend the night, but he always refuses and returns home. One night Geirríðr warns the young men about the return trip, but since they will be traveling together for most of the journey, they are not afraid. When they come to Katla's farm it is so late that "Katla was already in bed; she asked Oddr to invite Gunnlaugr to stay. Oddr replies that he has already asked him, 'but he [Gunnlaugr] insists on going home.'" Her response, "Let him go, then, and meet what he has caused," prepares the reader for the subsequent disaster. Gunnlaugr does not return home but is found the next morning outside his father's house, unconscious and badly wounded.[59] Oddr spreads the rumor that Geirríðr "had ridden him," but Katla eventually confesses to the crime herself (*Erb* 4.15–16, 20:26–30, 54). The account is permeated by Katla's jealousy and sexual frustration, which become palpable in a conversation with Gunnlaugr when she bluntly accuses him of going to Geirríðr in order to "caress the old woman's crotch" (*klappa um kerlingar nárann; Erb* 4.15:28).

A similar obscenity is applied to the young woman who attends to Grettir's sleeves on board ship. The couple inspires sexual fantasies among the shipmates, who vent their irritation by declaring that Grettir "liked better to stroke the belly of Bárðr's wife" (*klappa um kviðinn á konu Bárðar; Gr* 7.17:51–52]) than to work.[60] The suggestion of the missionary position is even more explicit in the case of Þjóstólfr, who reveals his jealousy by accusing Hallgerðr's husband of having strength only for "romping on Hallgerðr's belly" (*brǫlta á maga Hallgerði; Nj* 12.17:49).

Although references to sexuality are most often couched in modest and clinical terms, the preceding episodes suggest that in the Old Norse world, as in most societies, sex was rarely far from people's minds. These scenes involve jealousy or other frustration, but occasionally sexual imagery appears in more normal situations. *Stúfs þáttr*, an epilogue to *Laxdœla saga*, preserves a dialogue between the Norwegian king Haraldr *harðráði* (Hard-Ruler) and Stúfr, the son of Þórðr, nicknamed *kǫttr* (cat). Puzzled by Þórðr's unusual name, the king asks Stúfr whether his father was "the hard or the soft cat" (*kǫttrinn . . . inn hvati eða inn blauði;* 5:283). When the young man "clasped his hands together and laughed but did not answer," the king admits that he had asked a foolish question, since "the person who is soft (*blauðr*) could not be a father." Used to designate male animals, *hvatr* (roused, sharp, eager, vigorous) evokes the image of an erect penis, and *blauðr* suggests female suppleness.[61]

The sources are reticent about female penetration.[62] In a rare exception, however, a late saga graphically describes an attempted rape in Norway. Refr, the irate husband, kills the culprit Grani, one of the king's favorites, although his wife assures him that Grani "had in no way damaged his property" (her). Wishing to leave the country, Refr is required to inform the king of his deed. To gain time he employs such elaborate circumlocutions that his message is understood only after he makes his escape. Pondering Refr's statement that Grani had wanted to "mountain-gorge my wife" (*fjallskerða konu mina*), the king finally interprets it to mean that Grani had wanted to "sleep with her (*hvíla með henni;* literally, rest with her), because that is what it is called when women are penetrated (*giljaðar*), but the chasms are mountain gorges" (*en gilin eru fjallskǫrð; KrR* 14.16–17:152–55). Penetration is here evoked by images of canyons.[63]

Akin to sexuality is nakedness. Given the reticence of the sources, it is not surprising that the entire literary corpus yields only two cases of female nakedness, both of which inspire horror. The first instance involves a corpse, and the second describes a woman who uses her semi-nakedness as defense against her enemies. The Christian Þórgunna had made arrangements for her own burial at Skálaholt because she foresaw its future prominence as the episcopal see.[64] When the men who transported her body, "wrapped in an un-stitched linen shroud," are refused hospitality at a farm, they are forced to spend the night "without food" (*matlausir*), but Þórgunna herself appears in the kitchen, "stark-naked, not a stitch of clothing on her," and starts preparing a meal. Her apparition frightens the inhospitable hosts into offering the men everything they need (*Erb* 4.51:141–44).[65] Saga people were accustomed to revenants; thus it was Þórgunna's nakedness, not her ghostly presence, that was fearsome. This conclusion is confirmed by the other episode, which involves the pregnant Freydís in Vínland. Under attack by Indians, Freydís grabs a sword from one of her fallen compatriots and pursues the invaders. When they turn to confront her, "she pulled out her breast from her clothing and slapped it with the sword" (*Erð* 4.11:229, 430). The natives (*skrælingar*) flee, displaying the same reaction to nakedness as nordic people.

SEXUAL INITIATIVE

An analysis of lovemaking as it occurs in the pagan setting of the sagas of Icelanders suggests a pattern of male initiative and female passivity. Describing a society permeated with Christian consciousness, the contemporary sagas, however, reveal shifts in perceptions, promoted by churchmen. They transferred responsibility for sexual activity, in particular for breaking the sexual code, from men to women. Since priests and even bishops were regularly married, the clergy were exposed to the same sexual tensions over wives and daughters as the laity. Not only did churchmen punish women earlier and more severely than men for concubinage and illegitimacy,[66] but when they themselves are depicted in sexual encounters, they invariably assign responsibility to the female partner.[67]

An episode occurring around 1100, elaborated both in a saga of Icelanders (*Ljs*) and in a contemporary saga (*ÞH* in *St*), highlights the different treatment in the two genres and the growing tendency of churchmen to blame women. The story describes a scuffle between the priest Ketill Þorsteinsson and a certain Guðmundr in which each loses an eye. Ketill attacks Guðmundr, blinding him in one eye, because he has heard that the latter seduced (*fíflði*) his wife Gróa (in fact, the daughter of a bishop). Guðmundr responds with the biblical injunction of an eye for an eye (*Ljs* 10.21(31):105). The use of "seduce" (*fífla*) suggests that the saga author blames Guðmundr for the affair.[68] In the later version Ketill himself told the story in 1122 a short time before he became bishop (*St* 1:46–48). According to native tradition, Ketill could have charged his opponent with his humiliation, but he was conditioned by his clerical training. Although the case involved his own wife, he chose to place the fault on the woman: "She was not faithful to me," (*hon gerði mik eigi einhlítan;* literally, she did not rely on me alone).

The ecclesiastical requirement of celibacy for the clergy was instituted only with difficulty. The process of accepting this rule demonstrates most clearly the shift from male to female responsibility for sexual transgression. Those clergymen whose sexual fantasies appeared in female form found it natural to blame women for their own shortcomings in the perpetual battle to maintain chastity. This attitude is occasionally illustrated in the episcopal sagas, a subgenre of the contemporary sagas. Guðmundr Arason the Good (*góði*), a native bishop of the northern see of Hólar, took the demands of chastity seriously for himself as well as for the Icelandic church.[69] His *Life* includes a series of miracles, one of which is an Old Norse adaptation of the well-known vision of Tundalus.[70] Known as "Rannveig's vision," (*Rannveigar leizla*), one episode narrows the original focus on general sinfulness to sexual transgression, and changes the protagonist from male to female. The author was thereby enabled to blame breaches of clerical celibacy on women, where he felt it belonged.[71] Rannveig, the mistress of one priest, "had previously lived with another. Although she had few scruples about this, she was a pious woman in other ways." Leaving a bathhouse one day, she falls into a trance and lies as if dead for several hours. After awakening, she reports her vision to Guðmundr:

> She had been seized by demons, bruised and scratched as they dragged her across a lava field where she saw many people in suffering and torment. The demons did not let go of her until they came to a place where she saw in front of her a huge cauldron or a deep, wide pit; it was filled with boiling pitch and around it were blazing fires. Inside she saw many men, both those living at that time and those who were deceased, and she recognized some of them. There she saw nearly all the chieftains who had misused their authority. Then the demons addressed her saying: 'Down into this pit you shall be cast, for such are your deserts. You have shared in the same sin as those who are down there, namely loathsome lechery, which you committed when you lay with two priests and so defiled their office. To this you have added vanity and avarice. Now here you shall remain, since you would never abandon our services, and in many ways we shall torment you.'

Although she is burned in the boiling pit, she is rescued when, in her distress, she calls on Mary and the saints, and she is finally shown the abode where all the Icelandic bishops dwell in bliss.[72] Despite the happy ending for Rannveig, this brief glimpse into future judgment makes it clear that women were assigned sole responsibility for the sexual transgression of the clergy.

In conclusion, then: although fundamentally modest and reticent, the Old Norse sources offer occasional glimpses of heterosexual activity. Homosexual relations between men were not only recognized as a social phenomenon but were also implicated in the verbal accusations punishable by law. Same-sex and even bestial activities were therefore treated more openly in both legal and narrative sources, but these subjects lie outside my focus on women and gender, and I omit them here.[73]

PREGNANCY AND BIRTH

However a society might theorize conception, it is obvious that women bear the greatest burden in reproduction. Immediately after the sexual act neither partner knows the result. If insemination has occurred, the woman will eventually become aware of her pregnancy, but the man may never know. If the woman chooses to inform him and he accepts paternity, his obligations most often take effect only after birth and are mainly of a financial nature. Meanwhile the woman has had to cope with the effects of pregnancy, her reduced capability for physical work, her greater need for food, the responsibility for carrying the fetus to term—problems that culminate in the pain, danger, and uncertainty of the birth itself and are followed by a period of recovery and lactation during which the task of nurturing the child remains entirely hers. In a stable marriage, the husband can and will support his wife in this period, but in societies where extramarital affairs are common—as in ancient and medieval Iceland and Scandinavia—a different situation predominates. If the woman is not married or if her husband questions his liability, her position is far more complicated.

The sagas of Icelanders show no interest in conception, but the later imaginary narratives do occasionally address the subject.[74] One assumes that impregnation usually took place in bed and at night. The secretive circumstances under which irregular sexuality occurred is signaled by the terms identifying the results. A "bush child" (*hrísungr*) was the offspring of a free man and an unfree woman, and a "corner child" (*hornungr*) was the product of a free woman and an unfree man. These terms suggest that the man had to indulge his secret pleasures outside, but that the woman was in control of the house and could find a private space with her lover. In a similar way, "wolf drop" (*vargdropi*) and "child of the stall" (*bæsingr*) designated the progeny of an outlawed man and an outlawed woman, respectively. The first term suggests a meeting in the wilderness, whereas the second indicates a meeting within the confines of the farm. All four expressions thus convey the important gender distinction of the man's greater distance from the foyer (*Gg* 1a:224; 2:68).[75]

The condition of being pregnant is most often signaled by the euphemism "The woman was not well" (*kona var eigi heil*) or "She was not alone" (*fara eigi einsaman* or *einsǫmul*).[76] It is rare to find as detailed a description as the one the unmarried Friðgerðr gave of herself to her employer: "As you know I have demonstrated here that I can work hard, but now it has become more difficult for me because I am growing larger and I have trouble walking. I have not needed help from others before, but now I seem to be needing assistance the way things are going, because I am pregnant" (*Ljs* 10.12(22):65).

Despite Friðgerðr's protestations, women appear to have worked up until the last minute before giving birth; nor did their condition prevent travel. One woman produced twin boys unattended while she was shepherding sheep in the pastures, and she brought the babies home the same night (*Svf* 9.12:153). When Ingimundr traveled about Iceland looking for a place to settle, his wife was pregnant. Feeling birth pangs, she asked for a little rest and gave birth to a daughter (*Vtn* 8.15:41). Under the more settled conditions of Norway, a husband tried to dissuade his pregnant wife from accompanying him on a sea journey, but she insisted. When the birth was imminent, she wanted to go ashore. The party obtained local hospitality; the wife was taken to the woman's quarters (*kvenna hús*) while her husband waited in the main house (*skáli*). After three days' rest, she was ready to continue (*QO*, FSN 2.1:202–3).[77]

The birth itself was expressed in the image of the woman "becoming lighter" (*verða léttari*). What little is revealed about the birth process suggests that delivery techniques were universal and changed little over time.[78] Only women were present. The normal birth position was for the woman to kneel on the floor, with helpers ready at her knees or supporting her arms.[79] As the birth progressed, she would shift to a knee-elbow position, and the child would be received from behind. Runes and songs were offered as age-old remedies for difficult births, probably performed by a helping woman (*bjargrýgr*) trained through experience and apprenticeship. Although the sagas of Icelanders report surprisingly few cases of death in childbirth and no difficult births, the miracles performed by Icelandic saints narrate many realistic stories of prolonged and difficult births, dismemberment of infants, and problems with lactation.[80] In Iceland, manuscripts containing the story of the early Christian martyr Margaret of Antioch (*Margrétar saga*) were secured for women experiencing difficult births. The Icelandic versions contained a prayer spoken by the saint herself that "no dead or lame child" be born in a house where her vita was found.[81]

During Christian times a new mother was considered unclean for a period after the birth. Although this notion cannot be documented from the sources set in the pagan era, it is common in other non-Christian cultures. Churchmen had adopted the idea from Jewish sources, and since they apparently faced few objections instituting the ceremony of receiving a woman back into the church after her confinement, the belief in the new mother's impurity probably had native roots (NgL 1:16, 384).[82] To curb illegitimacy, the Norwegian church prohibited this ceremony entirely for unmarried women, but the Icelandic clergy, as previously noted, banned only the lighted candle with which new mothers were normally greeted (NgL 3:261; DI 1:437).

Like women in all traditional societies, medieval nordic mothers nursed their children and returned to work almost immediately. A touching scene shows a poor farmer and his wife busy at harvest, he cutting the hay and she raking it while she "carried a swaddled baby on her back which she nursed at

her breast" (*St* 1:221). Churchmen appear to have understood women's special dietary needs when they exempted pregnant women and nursing mothers
from fasting during the first Lent after delivery; if they nursed for two more
Lenten periods, they were expected to fast.[83] These rules suggest a nursing
period of two to two and a half years (*Gg* 1a:35; 2:44). A late text reports that
one mother weaned her daughter from the breast at the age of two, thereby
enabling her to leave the child with her husband before going to visit her father
(*Fld* 11.10:238–39).

Tacitus praised Germanic mothers for nursing their babies (*Germania*, chap.
20), and until the advent of modern technology, it was the norm in all traditional societies for children to receive their first nourishment from lactating women. At some point during the late Middle Ages, however, Icelandic
mothers came to regard their own milk as inferior. Rather than nursing their
children, they gave them cows' milk and even cream. Even more destructive
of their health, children were fed meat and fish, prechewed and thinned with
melted butter, from their third or fourth month. The results were disastrous,
and Iceland suffered from unusually high infant mortality even by the standards of the seventeenth century, when foreign travelers first brought attention
to the problem and identified malnutrition as the cause.[84]

Children appear to have been spaced at regular intervals, perhaps following
the rhythm dictated by nursing.[85] The reproductive potential of many women
was exploited to capacity, resulting in scores of children. Hallfríðr Einarsdóttir,
the third wife of Snorri the Chieftain (*goði*), for example, gave birth to six sons
and seven daughters. Men, of course, were potentially even more fertile. In
fact, Snorri provides an extreme illustration of the masculine reproductive capacity. In addition to the thirteen children produced with Hallfríðr, he fathered
another six legitimate and three illegitimate children. His last child was born
afer he died at the age of seventy-seven after a long illness (*ÆSn* 4:185–86).[86]
Hrútr Herjólfsson had sixteen sons and ten daughters with two wives; one
son (Kári) was twelve when his father was eighty. When Hrútr appears at the
þing with fourteen sons, the saga author comments: "This is mentioned because it seemed to be a sign of great splendor and power; all his sons were
accomplished men" (*Lx* 5.19:48–49; 37:105–6). As this comment implies, paternal pride was rarely inhibited. Comparable expressions of maternal pride are
nonexistent because authors rarely noticed women, but mothers likely took
similar pleasure in their children.[87]

PATERNITY

After the woman had carried the pregnancy to successful term, the child's
future remained uncertain. The Norwegian Frostathing Law stated categori-
cally that "every child must have a father" (NgL 1:130).[88] After birth the baby

was brought to the man in a ritual equal in importance to the birth itself.[89] Ingimundr's son, for example, "was carried (or born; *borinn*) to him and he was to decide on the name" (*Vtn* 8.13:37).[90] The naming was often accompanied by sprinkling of water, a ceremony more common among pagan royalty than among Icelandic farmers.[91] Its importance is suggested by the declaration that "it was called murder when children were killed after water had been poured over them" (*Hrð* 13.8:22). A child not accepted by the father was "un-carried" (*úborinn*), a condition with serious legal consequences.[92]

Assuming that the father accepted the child, it was brought back to the mother and fed. Scholars have seen a conflict between the father's right to name and sprinkle the child in the acceptance ceremony found in the narrative sources, and the statement in the law that "the child whose mother is bought with a bride price can inherit if it is born alive and has received food" (*Gg* 1a: 222; 2:98; 3:413). It would be a mistake, however, to interpret the law as a remnant of an older practice by which mothers decided their children's right to live by feeding them immediately after birth.[93] The Christian section of the Older Borgarthing Law stipulated that women who helped the birthing mother must stay "until the child is born and they must not leave until they have placed it at her breast" (NgL 1:340). This suggests that the interval between the birth and the coming-in of the mother's milk was used to present the child to the father.[94] When the man was the mother's husband, the task of bringing the baby to him was uncomplicated. Most husbands accepted all children produced by their wives, although gossip might indicate otherwise.[95]

An unmarried woman who gave birth to a child faced further obstacles. She was obliged to journey to the father, even if he was on the move, and give birth nearby to make him accept the child. In the early tenth century, Þóra, impregnated by King Haraldr Fairhair, traveled to the king when her term neared. Taken on board ship by Earl Sigurðr, she did not reach the king in time but gave birth to a boy, the future King Hákon *Aðalsteinsfóstri,* on a stone near the shore. The earl fortunately "sprinkled the boy with water and called him Hákon after his own father" (*Hhf* 26.37:143). Three centuries later, in 1223, Þórdís Snorradóttir managed better timing. Late in her pregnancy, she followed her lover, the married Oddr Álason, on his erratic journey throughout the country. A widow with an involved love life of her own and children by several men, this prominent daugher of Snorri Sturluson felt obliged to stay close to Oddr until she had given birth to his baby girl. After resting three days, she returned home. Although not explicitly stated in the text, Þórdís's purpose was to present the infant to Oddr in order to secure his acceptance and support.[96] By this date Christianity had guaranteed the child's right to live, but Þórdis was sorely in need of the father's material assistance.

The underlying concern to identify the father was surely economic. The

climatic and economic conditions of the north were unfavorable to unre-
strained human sexuality, and its reproductive results could not be tolerated
even within marriage in the case of poor people. Couples who met the property
qualifications necessary for marriage shared the expense of raising children:
the husband paid two-thirds and the wife one-third; dowries for daughters
were provided in the same proportions (*Gg* 1b:46; 2:106, 108, 175–76). When
Geirmundr abandoned his wife and infant daughter in Iceland without leaving
money for the upkeep of the child, his wife retaliated by secretly placing the
child next to him on his ship and stealing his sword (*Lx* 5.30:80–83). The father
(or his relatives) of an illegitimate child was responsible for its maintenance
until age sixteen (*Gg,* 1b:23; 2:135), although the law sought to protect paternal
and maternal relatives against the reproductive excesses of a sexually active
young man by making them responsible for supporting only the first two of
his illegitimate offspring (*Gg* 1b:28; 2:150). These rules, which ignore Christian
monogamy and charity, likely reflect ancient pagan practice.

Already during the pagan period general poverty and the man's economic
responsibility for the child (regardless of the marital relationship between the
parents) made the identification of the father an utmost concern. Ancient
society allowed infanticide, however, and many children lacking fathers were
exposed. The prohibition against this ancient custom came with Christianity.
The identification of the man who had impregnated an unmarried woman
now became even more important to her relatives, lest they become liable
for the child's upkeep. Rules designed to elicit paternal information from unmarried women antedated Christianity, but the prohibition against infanticide
combined with high illegitimacy rates assured their continued enforcement in
law. In Iceland a woman was obliged to identify the father of her unborn child
if asked by her guardian to do so. If she refused, the guardian was entitled
to return with five neighbors and together they were to "torture her" (*pína
hana*), but without leaving wounds or blue marks, until she revealed the name.
If her lover conspired to hide his identity, no settlement could be reached on
paternity without special permission from the law court. The woman was also
obliged to reveal the place where she and her lover had met and where the
child was conceived (*Gg* 1b:58–59; 2:182–83; 3:422–23). Once identified, the
man was prosecuted by the woman's family and made to pay for the child's
upkeep.

Rather than prescribing torture, Norwegian lawmakers took advantage of
the woman's vulnerability during labor. According to the Older Borgarthing
Law, for example, her guardian was to stand in the door leading into her room
at the commencement of labor and ask for the name of the child's father. If she
pronounced a name that was audible to the people at the door, her word was to
be attested to by female or male witnesses. The man so designated was known

as the child's "half-father," with corresponding economic responsibilites. Her statement was accepted until a month after delivery, but if she kept silent the child was considered a slave after this time and the mother was held responsible for its support as well as for a fine payable to the king (NgL 1: 358, 367, 419). Permission to torture a pregnant unmarried woman was found in the secular section of Icelandic law, whereas Norwegian lawmakers placed their corresponding regulation in the Christian Law Sections; they were among the oldest of this genre and some probably written before 1150.[97] The new religion may have attenuated the harshness of an older procedure on how to ferret paternal information from a pregnant woman, but the Icelandic and the Norwegian laws make clear the urgent need to designate the father for both pagans and Christians.

Whereas pagan society thus placed the entire burden for identifying paternity on the woman, churchmen eventually provided in the ordeal (*skírsla*) a procedure to balance the sexes. Although it never became a regularized method of proof, it allowed a man to prove his innocence in paternity cases by carrying hot iron (*járnburðr*) and permitted the woman to support her claim against her impregnator by retrieving stones from the bottom of a kettle of boiling water (*ketiltak*).[98] Replacing the old jury (*kviðr*), the ordeal (*skírsla;* it was sometimes classified as a *nýmæli*) was cited more frequently in the more recent *Staðarhólsbók* than in the older *Konungsbók*. This distribution and the slight interval between the two manuscripts suggest a gradual acceptance of the new rule, which attenuated the older regime and conferred equal responsibility on the two partners for identifying extramarital pregnancies. Since, however, the purpose of the man's ordeal was to prove his innocence and that of the woman's to demonstrate his guilt, the system could work at cross-purposes if applied to the same case. Whatever the outcome in individual cases, distrust of the procedure is suggested by the practice of allowing bishops to readminster an ordeal in paternity cases "if they thought it necessary, and then the last one shall be valid" (*Gg* 1b:216; 2:58; 3:20, 146, 456).[99]

Once a man knew that a woman under his guardianship had been with a lover or impregnated, he assumed the principal legal responsibility in the case, becoming the *aðili* who prosecuted at the alþingi. The list of prosecutors (*aðiljar*) was similar to the sequence of guardians in inheritance and engagement, with the exception that the husband and the father preceded the son and son-in-law. This change may reflect the fact that younger women whose children were not yet grown and therefore unable to act as guardians were more frequently involved in illegal intercourse (*legorð*) than were older women. This crime was separate from paternity, and whereas several men could be prosecuted simultaneously for illegal intercourse, only one man could be sued at a time for paternity. Intercourse without consequence could be forgotten if the activity ceased, but a paternity case never became moot and could be prosecuted whenever the guardian became aware of the existence of an illegitimate child.

The prosecutor had the right to demand lesser or greater outlawry for the man, who was also obligated to pay the personal fine (*réttr*) to the guardian. In Iceland (but not in Norway) this fine was identical for all classes: at six marks, or forty-eight ounces (*aurar*) —, or six times the minimum bride price, the same amount as for killings. Lesser settlements arranged through private agreement were apparently not uncommon, but permission from the alþingi was needed. A fine of six marks was imposed if permission had not been obtained. The original and the new case could be prosecuted by anybody who was inclined to take the trouble. A woman's refusal to name the father precluded settlement for a smaller fine (*Gg* 1b:48–56; 2:176–203).

INFANTICIDE

The laws' preoccupation with identifying paternity suggests persistent but changing societal attitudes toward the problem of unwanted children. In pagan society all fathers had the right to refuse the infants presented to them by their wives or mistresses.[100] Although a wife might stand a better chance of having her child approved than would a mistress, considerations of the child's sex, health, looks, the number and composition of the father's present offspring, and even his feelings toward the mother could influence his decision. If rejected, the child was exposed out of doors, a fate calculated to be fatal given the climate of the north, although in the eight individual cases of "carrying out of children" (*barna útburðr*) in the narratives, the child was saved (no doubt the reason for recording the story).[101] In the case of an unmarried mother unwilling or unable to reveal her child's father, the decision rested with her male relatives. Special conditions might occasionally allow such a woman to keep her child, but the chance for life was definitely slimmer for children in this category than for those of married women or established mistresses. The fate of exposure also threatened children of slaves.

No matter how self-evident it may seem, it should be noted that the problem of infanticide is of particular concern to women.[102] Nine months' pregnancy — involving, under the best of circumstances, discomfort, nausea, and restricted movement, and culminating in a painful, prolonged, sometimes dangerous delivery — heightened the mother's interest in the baby over that of the father. To have the child summarily removed, not knowing whether it would be returned, was traumatic. If the child was exposed, the mother was denied the intermittent respite provided by nursing, forced instead into immediate unrelenting work performed with an aching, bleeding, and lactating body. Infanticide was most often inflicted on baby girls, which may have exacerbated the mother's grief.

Iceland

I deal briefly with the problem of female demography in ancient Iceland before following the process by which infanticide was abolished there and in Norway. Among the names of four hundred original settlers on the island, *Landnámabók* identifies thirteen women who claimed land on their own. In addition, ninety wives who accompanied their husband are included among the original female settlers.[103] Other wives remained nameless and unmentioned, and many more women came as sisters and daughters of the first settlers. Celtic slaves — both men and women — were imported from Ireland and the other Norse outposts in the North Atlantic where the colonists often stopped over, sometimes for generations. The statistics suggest that the sex ratio — defined by modern demographers as the number of men available per one hundred women [104] — must have been extremely high among the first few generations of Icelanders. In other words, in ancient Iceland as in all colonial societies, women were scarce and, as a consequence, highly valued for their sexual and reproductive services as well as for their physical labor.[105] The problem of too few women is evoked succinctly by the author of *Eiríks saga rauða* in a vignette from the New World, where the problem was even more severe: "There was a profound division between the men on account of the women, for the unmarried men fell foul of the married which led to serious disturbances" (*Erð* 4.12:233, 432).[106]

Although traditional societies habitually dispose of more female infants than male, there are indications that baby girls were welcomed in pagan Iceland. In fact, one of the very first births recorded on the island was that of the girl Þórdís, daughter of Vigdís and Ingimundr Þorsteinsson, a founding father. The couple had immigrated to Iceland with their three sons, and Vigdís, who was pregnant during her husband's prolonged search for a suitable place to settle, gave birth to Þórdís at the place that became the family's permanent home (*Lnd* 1:217–20; *Vtn* 8.13:36–37; 15:41).[107] Equally poignant is an episode in which a baby girl survives a shipwreck in northern Iceland with her parents. On shore a man, known as "a viking and a bad man," killed the couple but "took the girl and raised her" (*Lnd* 1:200).[108]

Regardless of their social and economic status, this girl and other women in their reproductive years easily found husbands among the first generations of settlers. According to *Landnámabók*, the first generation of named settlers contained nearly six times as many men as women.[109] Given this imbalance, it is remarkable that almost three-quarters of the men in this first cohort managed to establish families. Nearly two-thirds of these, however, were identified only by the name of the father and his children with no indication of whether he was a widower or of the children's legal status. Who were these unknown women who produced the first generation of native Icelanders? One intriguing proposition is that they were Irish slaves whose names were suppressed because their ancestry was not worthy of comment and added little luster to the family. These Celtic women may have contributed their distinct genes to the Icelandic melting pot, with important biological consequences.

Demography, therefore, suggests that conditions in Iceland's initial period of colonization favored the survival of baby girls and allowed reproduction for all adult women. The situation most likely reverted to a traditional pattern later, as women became more numerous through local growth and continued immigration. For a while, female infants may have been exposed more frequently than male, and poor women's fertility was restricted. Eventually, however, churchmen succeeded in abolishing the exposure of both baby girls and boys. Fortunately, the sources fill in this hypothetical sketch.[110]

The surest evidence of infanticide in pagan Iceland comes from Ari Þorgilsson's sober description of the voluntary acceptance of Christianity in the year 1000: "It became established by law that everybody should be Christian and undergo baptism, those in the country who were still unbaptized; but concerning child exposure (*barnaútburðr*) and the eating of horse meat (*hrossakjǫtsát*) the old law should remain valid. People could sacrifice (*blóta*) in secret if they wished, but they would incur the lesser outlawry if witnesses were present. But after a few years this heathenism was abolished like the rest (*Ísl* 1.7:17)."[111]

By the year 1000 itinerant Icelanders had encountered Christianity abroad; some returned with full baptism or the "first blessing" (*prima signatio;* the Latin term was taken over in Old Norse). Others had met the new religion via the missionary efforts of compatriots and foreigners sent to Iceland by Óláfr Tryggvason, the first Norwegian king to proselytize.[112] At the alþingi in 1000 one of the most influential leaders was Gizurr Teitsson, who had accepted baptism from Þangbrandr, Óláfr's missionary, a short time earlier and who had just returned from Norway with a message from King Óláfr, his second cousin. The rule against infanticide was well established in England, where Archbishop Theodore of Tarsus's penitential imposed a penance of fifteen years for the crime.[113] The connection between the English church and the two Norwegian missionary-minded kings, both named Óláfr, is clear.[114] It seems obvious that when an adult was baptized, in this case Gizurr, he would have been told about infant baptism, and the Christian corollary against infanticide would have been explained. Óláfr and Gizurr must have discussed the social consequences of accepting the new religion, and it is likely that Icelanders were aware of the Christian stance on this issue before the general conversion in 1000.[115]

Ari's summary details ("after a few years this heathenism [infanticide and the eating of horse meat] was abolished like the rest") are augmented by Snorri's *Heimskringla*. His account is more recent, but it adds important nuances he might have learned during his stay in Norway. In the second decade of the eleventh century the new Norwegian king Óláfr *helgi,* whose sainthood—identified by his nickname—suggests that he was as devout a Christian as his namesake, attempted to modify the existing laws throughout his lands. He made "every effort to reduce paganism and the old customs he thought went against Christianity." [116] Inquiring about conditions in Iceland, Óláfr was told that "there it was allowed according to law to eat horse meat and to expose children like pagan people and still other things that were against Christianity." [117] When his informants identified Skapti Þóroddsson as the man who, as law speaker, had the most influence on the laws, the king sent him a message, ordering the removal of features he deemed most offensive to Christianity (*mest í móti kristnum dómi;* (*Óh* 27.58:73–74, 60:77). Later, Óláfr shipped timber and a bell to be used for a church at Þingvellir, because, in Snorri's words, "the Icelanders had changed their law and established the Christian law according to the word they had received from King Óláfr" (*Óh* 27.124:214). The Icelanders had apparently agreed not to expose children and not to eat horse meat. [118]

The king's pressure on Icelandic leaders can be detected in local law as well. The Christian Law was presumably recited at the alþingi like the secular laws. By the early decades of the eleventh century the recitation would thus have included Óláfr's demands concerning children and horse meat. A century later the secular laws were committed to writing (1117), but, although formulated, the Christian Law was not yet inserted. Its inclusion was sponsored by the two bishops, and it was appended to *Grágás* in the period 1122–1133 (*Gg* 1a:36; 2: 45–46; 3:291–92). [119] As a preamble to the secular laws, the Christian Law opens both existing versions of *Grágás* with a proud declaration: "This is the beginning of our law that all people in this country must be Christian and believe in one God, Father, Son and Holy Ghost. Every child that is born shall be brought to baptism as soon as possible, regardless of how deformed it may be" (*Gg* 1a:3). [120]

In a country where Christianity was still young, the second statement about infant baptism was naturally the tool to achieve the goal of total conversion announced in the first. Despite lingering resistance from adult political leaders, the entire population would be Christian in the course of one generation if every newborn was baptized. [121] The statement is followed by five closely argued pages that provide details for baptism. Although in the pagan context birth was not a sufficient entry to life unless the father accepted and named the child, in the new Christian world, unconditional baptism replaced paternal acceptance and identification; baptism and naming occurred simultaneously.

The phrase "regardless of how deformed it may be" echoes negotiations between the Norwegian king and Icelandic men, who may have been reasserting their ancient right to deny life to a child. One version of the Christian Law stipulates that the child should be baptized regardless of its shape, provided it had a human voice (*Gg* 3:137); this provision suggests that exposure might still occur in extreme cases. Perhaps the king had insisted on the right to life for all children but had been willing to accommodate the ancient right of exposure provided it was limited to grossly deformed children. The kings had conceded this amendment in Norway, but in Iceland the Christian program was accepted, resulting in the triumphant words of the law.

Norway

Óláfr *helgi* (St. Óláfr) may have won the battle easily in Iceland, but he met serious opposition in Norway. According to Snorri, Óláfr was aided by priests and, in particular, by Grímkell, his "court bishop," *hirðbyskup*, as he sought to formulate Christian law for Norway (*Óh* 27.57:72, 58:73). Equipped with this new law, Óláfr traveled around the country:

> At every þing he allowed the Christian law to be read out aloud and the commandments that followed from it. In that way he abolished many wrong customs and pagan ideas, because while the earls had kept well the old law and the law of the country, concerning Christianity they had let people do as they wanted. The result was that people were mostly baptized in the towns along the coast, but the Christian law was unknown to most; in the valleys and the mountain villages paganism still prevailed widely, because when people can decide on their own, they remember best the faith they have learned as children (*Óh* 27.60:77).

Unfortunately, scant information has survived about Óláfr's Christian Law. It was formulated in the first decades of the eleventh century, but its only extant parts are embedded in the Gulathing Law, where they were combined with Magnús Erlingsson's legislation drawn up in the 1160s.[122] The laws of the two kings were merged, but on a number of issues dealing with sexual, marital, and reproductive questions where Óláfr and Magnús did not agree their decisions were kept separate. Magnús's rules are most often listed first, or the differences are summarized in a chapter heading giving Magnús's new rule. This distribution suggests that Magnús's rules were meant to take effect, whereas the earlier ones were included for the sake of completeness or historical interest (NgL 1:8, 11, 13). In these double paragraphs, as it were, an increased emphasis on Christian norms and behavior can be discerned.[123] On infanticide, chapter twenty-one, entitled "Magnús revoked this in part" (NgL 1:12), states that "every child born in our country is to be nourished," but, introduced by an "O" (for Óláfr), the following exception is added: "unless it is born with such deformity that the face is turned where the back of the neck should be or the toes where the heels should be. Such a child must be taken into the church and be converted from paganism and laid down in the church and left to die."[124]

It is impossible to be sure that the inscription against infanticide in the existing versions of *Grágás* had been accepted already in the early eleventh century in Iceland, although Óláfr's appreciation suggests that the population there had complied early. The Gulathing Law indicates, however, that the king did not have similar success in Norway, but was forced to accommodate the tradition of infanticide by allowing the exposure of deformed children. A century later, nonetheless, Magnús—who owed his position to the church's collaboration—felt strong enough to legislate as Óláfr had wanted. But before examining Magnús's success, I shall probe more deeply the issue of infant deformity.

Because of the size and diversity of Norway, other provincial laws were codified that also include sections of the Christian Law. The laws for the Borgarthing and Eidsivathing, for example, are as old as the existing version of Óláfr's Christian Law and represent a similar tradition. Claiming that there were many deformed children, the Borgarthing Law distinguished between two groups of infants. The first included children born with the same inversion or transposition (the medical term is *situs retroversus*) described in the Gulathing Law, but they also displayed animal features such as seal fins and dog heads. They were to be buried alive in a place where "neither humans nor cattle walk." Infants in the second group simply had facial hair, and they were to be taken to church and blessed (*láta prímsigna*). Retaining these categories but reversing the fates, the Eidsivathing Law allowed the first group to be fed, taken to church, and baptized, but authorized the bishop to decide the child's ultimate fate, whereas the second group was to be baptized and buried alive within the churchyard in a grave covered by a stone, to prevent dogs and ravens from exhuming the corpse. No dirt was to be shoveled in until the infant was dead. The text added, either piously or cynically: "Let it live as long as it may" (NgL 1:339, 363, 376, 395).[125] In the case of slave children, the master or even the slave father himself was expected to perform the act (NgL 1:131).

It seems, therefore, that pagan society had exposed both deformed and healthy babies, among the latter females in greater numbers than males.[126] When the Norwegian authorities, both political and ecclesiastical, encountered native resistance to the Christian principle that every human being had a right to be nourished, they were first forced to compromise on the issue of badly deformed children. Emboldened by their success with healthy children, churchmen became more aggressive in the next legislative campaign. By the late thirteenth century Magnús Hákonarson initiated extensive legislation that resulted in a comprehensive Land Law and the so-called Newer Christian Law, of which two distinct local versions are preserved. Although not as bold as his namesake Magnús Óláfsson, who a century earlier had declared bluntly that every child born should be raised, this Magnús stated that "every child born shall be raised even if it is slightly deformed, as long as it has a human head" (*ala skall barn huært er borit værdr oc manz hafud er a þo at nockor orkymli se;* NgL 2:293).[127] Now parents were expected to nourish infants with slight deformities.[128]

The popular support for infanticide which persisted in Norway hindered legislators from obtaining the sweeping Christian victory that Óláfr had won in Iceland in the early eleventh century. Instead of obligating parents to raise all children regardless of physical shape, Norwegian leaders started slowly, and they never dared to include all newborn children in their sweeping obligation to parents to take care of all their offspring.

The difference in the treatment of infanticide in Iceland and Norway can also be gauged by the punishments inflicted for transgressions. Unmentioned in Icelandic laws, punishment for infanticide underwent an evolution in Norway which demonstrates an increasingly aggressive Christian policy in the period between Óláfr and Magnús.[129] Chapter twenty-two of the Christian Law of the Older Gulathing Law states that Magnús demanded outlawry for the crimes for which Óláfr had imposed a fine of three marks, and the following paragraph provides details: "If a man exposes his child, whether it has been baptized or is pagan, and it perishes and he is accused and convicted of this, he has forfeited peace and property, for we call that the greatest murder" (*morð et mikla;*" NgL 1:13). Óláfr may have judged that victory for his views was imminent and monetary fines sufficient to discourage infraction, or he may have been realistic, knowing that people would be willing to pay for the privilege of continuing the practice. Magnús's strong language and stiff penalties a century later suggest that infanticide continued but was increasingly frowned upon. The Gulathing Law placed this problem under the king's jurisdiction, but the growing involvement of churchmen can be seen in the contemporary Frostathing Law wherein the crime was assigned to churchmen's jurisdiction. Under the heading "Child Exposure," the law states: "If a man exposes (*slær utt*) his child, he must go to confession and pay a fine of three marks in God's name to the bishop" (NgL 1:131).[130]

Why were infants accepted more readily in Iceland than in Norway? Scholars have traced textual influence from Continental sources on the regulations concerning impairment, but the similarities are not striking.[131] The deformities mentioned can scarcely be identified medically and biologically in modern times, and it is worth considering whether the laws envisaged problems raised by constant inbreeding.[132] The narrow confines of the deep Norwegian valleys had compelled local communities to live together and to intermarry for centuries. With insufficient differentiation in their genetic makeup, closely related couples may have produced biological enormities that were routinely exterminated. Even churchmen were forced to admit that such beings could not achieve a viable existence, although priests and bishops were ready to bless and even baptize them. Eventually, the expanded ecclesiastical rules against incest sought to mitigate against inbreeding and resultant deformities. The genetic profile of Icelanders, meanwhile, was different. Arriving from diverse areas of Norway, the immigrants possessed greatly expanded gene pools from which the new Icelanders were generated. In addition, by sojourning among the Celts of the North Atlantic islands, at times intermarrying and staying for generations, and by bringing Celtic slaves to Iceland, the colonists further enlarged their genetic resources.[133] Deformed babies were probably far less numerous in the colony than in the mother country. When the Norwegian king outlawed infanticide, the Icelanders could readily comply because they were rarely faced with the serious problems encountered in Norway. The Icelandic texts retain only slight traces of formulations used in previous negotiations between the Norwegian king and his subjects.

Like extramarital sexuality, infanticide did not disappear overnight, at least not in Norway, and, as in the case of adultery, churchmen shifted the responsibility from men to women. In pagan society the decision to expose a newborn was the father's prerogative, and the mother was left with no say in the fate of her child. Following ecclesiastical efforts to abolish exposure, the practice was changed from being considered a male right to becoming a female crime, a shift that was further exacerbated by the concern of political and ecclesiastical leaders over extramarital pregnancies. Churchmen were among the first to accuse women of killing infants. The late twelfth-century Bjarkö Law contains a paragraph instructing the bishop's official what to do if he learned that a woman had exposed (*sleget utt*) her child. Only an oath from the parturient woman's helper that the child was stillborn would save the mother from a fine (NgL 1:303). After stipulating that women who assisted the birth must remain until the child had been placed at the mother's breast, the Borgarthing Law continued:

> If the child has died when people return to her [the mother] and they can determine by marks, by hands or by bands, that the child has been strangled

or suffocated, and if she is conscious, then she is the murderer of her child. She is to forfeit her property and peace in the country as well as her chattel. She must go to a pagan country and never live where Christian people are. The murder of a pagan is worse than the murder of a Christian because the soul of the person who dies a pagan is lost (NgL 1:340).

Even more explicit, the Eidsivathing Law admonished men called in as witnesses to examine the dead child to ascertain that "it is neither blue nor bloodied and does not have a string (*dregill*) around its neck" (NgL 1:376). A mistress (*ambátt*) who had given birth to a stillborn child was, not surprisingly, treated with particular suspicion (NgL 1:377). The antipathy of churchmen to extramarital affairs may have encouraged mothers to do away with illegitimate children. Fear of childbirth itself, mounting attacks from the pulpit against illegitimacy, and perhaps even wishful thinking find touching expression in stories of miracles in which the Virgin Mary or one of the Icelandic saints offers help in difficult births; at times they remove the child or even dispose of the mother's soiled clothing (*Bs* 2:167, 169; *Mr* 157).[134]

BAPTISM

Whereas a pagan father both accepted his child and named it at the same time, among Christians naming took place at baptism. Fathers (or parents) still chose the name, of course, but under normal conditions its bestowal was assigned to the clergy when they administered baptism. The Icelandic and Norwegian laws agree, however, that lay people could perform the ceremony in an emergency—when the child was ill and might die unbaptized, thereby jeopardizing salvation and forfeiting a Christian burial. In these circumstances men were preferred to women as officiants, but *Grágás* notes that "if a man does not know the words or the gestures, it is proper that a woman teach him" (*Gg* 1a:6; 2:5). According to ancient Church doctrine, however, the person who baptizes a child contracts a spiritual kinship (*compaternitas*) with its family and becomes its godparent, a bond which precludes marriage with the child's relations.[135] For this reason celibate clergymen were preferred baptizers. Because spiritual kinship was incurred when the father performed emergency baptism, the couple was required to separate to avoid future incest. Since this expedient may have been a frequent necessity on the isolated farmsteads in Iceland, other male relatives or neighbors were usually chosen as baptizers until this extreme consequence was eventually abandoned (*Gg* 1a:4–6, b:215; 2: 4–6; NgL 2:293–94).

Only in the utmost emergencies, when the child was at the brink of death and no man was available, was a woman permitted to baptize (*Gg* 2:5; 3:6, 58,

150). The privileging of males prompted some texts to add that if a young boy was present, the woman was to place his hands on the infant she was about to baptize (*Gg* 2:5; 3:297). This limited right, as well as the repeated injunction for women to teach the ritual to men, resulted in the requirement that every adult know the *credo* and *pater noster* from the age of twelve so as to be able to administer the sacrament.[136] Women incurred the same punishment as men if they were deficient (*Gg* 1a:7; 2:6).

As an accommodation to emergency baptisms of sick infants, churchmen allowed any liquid to be used, including fresh water, dew, ocean water, snow or ice if melted and softened, and even spittle (*Gg* 1a:6, 2:4; NgL 1:132). Judging by a papal ordinance from the early thirteenth century prohibiting beer, this beverage was also apparently employed.[137] As the use of fresh water was increasingly encouraged, churchmen assigned further responsibilities to women for baptism. By the end of the century the new Norwegian Christian Laws enjoined all pregnant women to assure the supply of water while they were still capable before the commencement of birth pangs (NgL 2:311, 327). Archbishop Árni's statute from the middle of the fourteenth century specified that a birthing woman keep next to her bed "a suitable container with water" (*viðirkuemelikit kerald með vatne;* NgL 3:297). Thus, churchmen assigned women greater responsibility for both body and soul of their infants.

REPRODUCTION AND ROYAL SUCCESSION

The objectives of an ordinary woman and her family in pursuing her seducer were to make the biological father pay for maintenance and to provide a legacy for the child. The stakes were much higher, however, for women who consorted with men of royal stock.[138] Among all Germanic tribes the leaders' sexual behavior shaped the primitive stage of monarchy. Distributing their genes through polygyny, polycoity, or serial monogamy, early Germanic rulers produced innumerable offspring, each with competing claims to the throne. This system resulted in serious problems over royal succession, as multiple candidates fought for the office, and as others were accommodated through joint rule of the entire kingdom or after fissiparism through individual rule of minor territories. In this process a mother's support of her son in his quest for power could be of crucial importance. As the tribes became increasingly settled, geographic expansion was curtailed and the landed domain of a single ruling family became too small to tolerate further subdivision. As a result, competition intensified, creating greater scope for ambitious mothers to work for their sons, regardless of their own marital relationship with the father. Eventually, the monarchs worked out a system of orderly transfer of power. On the Continent the German Saxons and French Capetians secured control for their dynasties by devising the twin tools of legitimacy and primogeniture, thus assigning to only one woman—the legally married wife—the monopoly of producing the next king. Since these ideas correspond closely to the new ecclesiastical marriage policy for the entire population, churchmen worked hand in hand with political leaders to create social and political stability through these principles.[139]

The transitional step—in which many contenders vied for the single prize of the kingship but were willing to settle for fissiparism or joint rule—is particularly well illustrated in Norway, where these options persisted into the thirteenth century.[140] In the north, ancient sexual mores involving several partners were more common and lasted longer among royalty than in the population at large. These ingrained habits were reinforced by the viking expeditions. Rarely accompanied by their wives and female friends, viking men established sexual contacts with foreign women, some of whom they brought back to Scandinavia or to the new world in Iceland. Around the millennium, when the viking voyages declined, these opportunities ceased for most men. The Norwegian kings, however, were slow to realize that their political role in the Western waters had been played out, and they continued to lead expeditions to Ireland, the Isle of Man, the Orkneys, and the Shetlands into the eleventh, twelfth, and even thirteenth centuries in hopes of reinforcing their traditional presence. On the eve of the north's eclipse in international politics, Haraldr Sigurðarson the Hard-Ruler, for example, was defeated and died at Stamford Bridge in 1066 as he competed for the English throne. Magnús *berfœttr* (Bare-Legs) lost his life in a local battle in Ireland in 1104. As late as 1263 the aging Hákon Hákonarson succumbed to illness on the Orkneys, where he spent the winter after a successful military expedition. Beyond their liaisons with native mistresses at home, these kings—with the exception of Hákon Hákonarson—procreated with foreign women with whom they formed casual relationships.

For a long time, therefore, Norway suffered the consequences of the interaction between politics and sexuality in its leading families. Although common to the entire Germanic world, the issues were magnified in Norway by the legacy of the roaming viking male. These linked problems resulted in more than a century of continuous civil war (1130–1240), threatening the country's very existence. No fewer than forty-six candidates of royal descent emerged, all seeking acceptance as kings. In addition to a royal father, a contestant also needed a local þing willing to certify him (a process known as the *konungstekja*). Only then could he hope that other assemblies would join his struggle against rivals. Among these candidates, about half (twenty-four) became kings for a short time; only two sustained their authority over the country as a whole. Among the total number twelve or thirteen were born in legitimate marriages; among the successful contenders only five could claim this distinction. Three rivals stressed their legitimacy to reinforce a more questionable claim through the female line (the concept of *kvennkné* examined earlier), and a fourth was a half-brother of a king. In other words, only one king in this period, Ingi Haraldsson, could boast of being the legitimate son of a king. The deciding factor remained paternity, not legitimacy.[141]

In most cases, the names of the royal bedmates and their progeny were public knowledge. As long as a young man of royal paternity stayed in court circles, his claim was not disputed. Before death, a king might admit that he had also fathered a son abroad, in which case the young man would be accepted on his arrival in Norway, as happened with Eysteinn Haraldsson who traveled from Scotland in the 1140s. Problems did occur, however, when unknown young men appeared from abroad supported only by their mothers' claim of royal conception. Arriving from the Faroe Islands early in the thirteenth century, a man named Erlingr, for example, claimed to be the son of King Sverrir. His candidacy was supported by his half-sister Kristín, although Sverrir himself had declared on his deathbed that he had no other heir but (the illegitimate) Hákon, regardless of how many might come from the West pretending to be his sons. In this instance, a striking family resemblance may have caused Kristín to vouch for Erlingr, for his mother was either Sverrir's first cousin or, possibly, his half-sister.[142] Other cases were resolved by the hot iron ordeal.[143]

Women who consorted with prominent men often endured hardship as they tried to protect and promote their offspring. The saga dealing with Hákon Hákonarson (1217–1263) contains a rare glimpse into the brief but decisive relationship between his parents. During the fall of 1203, the young Inga from the Varteig family stayed with the unmarried king Hákon Sverrisson in Bergen. Only a few of the king's men were aware that she shared his bed, and even she may not have known that she was pregnant when the king died on 1 January 1204, for Hákon Hákonarson was not born until the next summer. It is unclear whether Inga was a willing or a reluctant partner, but, once pregnant, she came to share the fate of other young women who carried to term the offspring of married monarchs, or kings now dead or absent. Rejected by her family, Inga sought refuge with friends and gave birth to her son secretly at a priest's house.

Foreign women impregnated by Norwegian kings confronted serious problems. Most often the children's sole providers, they saw their first responsibility to name the offspring after his royal father, thus publicizing his paternal origin. When the son came of age, his mother accompanied him to Norway and helped him to assert his royal claim. One saga reports a meeting in England between two boys in their teens, a Norwegian named Kali and an Irishman called Gillikristr who informed Kali that he was the son of Magnús *berfœttr* (Bare-Legs), that he carried the royal name Haraldr, and that his mother's family came from the Hebrides and Ireland (*Ork* 34.59:130–31; *Mgs* 28.26: 265).[144] Although the young men often were required to undergo ordeals, in the final analysis it was the woman who could best vouch for paternity. Her testimony carried weight, not only with her son, as might be expected, but also with those deciding whether he should be accepted.

The most remarkable example of a woman who promoted her illegitimate offspring is found in *Sverris saga*. The section under consideration here was actually written under the king's own auspices. Born in 1151 in Norway, Sverrir was assumed to be the son of Gunnhildr and her husband Únáss *kambari* (comb-maker). At age five he was sent to the Faeroes to be fostered by Únáss's brother, Bishop Hrói. Twenty years later, on a pilgrimage to Rome, Gunnhildr confessed that Sverrir's father was not her husband but King Sigurðr Haraldsson, nicknamed *munnr* (mouth). The case was presented to the pope, who instructed Gunnhildr to go to the Faeroes and inform her son. A year later Sverrir made his way to Norway, where he eventually became king and the progenitor of an illustrious lineage. Historians have since debated the truth of the mother's story and considered whether Sverrir was simply a more talented impostor than his competitors. The question is unimportant in this context. If Sverrir was indeed of royal stock, he nonetheless depended — like other contenders — on his mother; if an impostor, his story still shows that a woman's claim was accepted, even outside royal circles.[145]

By promoting her royal offspring, a woman gained advantages for herself. The birth of a boy recognized as royal guaranteed her a place at her lover's court; if her son became king, she was taken care of for life. Álfhildr, the mistress of Óláfr *helgi* and mother of his only son, Magnús, passed her life with the married king. When Magnús succeeded his father, he kept his mother at court with great honor, although her presence caused friction with his stepmother, Ástríðr, Óláfr *helgi*'s widow. A royal mistress was likewise able to introduce into the royal entourage children fathered by other men before or after her cohabitation with the king. More distant kin, such as brothers or uncles, were also favored. The term "king's brother" became in fact a quasi-title for the reigning king's maternal half-brother, who possessed no royal blood but had shared the same womb. By the second half of the thirteenth century, however, Norwegian monarchs finally accepted the program of monogamy, primogeniture, and legitimacy. In this way they not only promoted political stability, but they also brought to a close opportunities for female self-promotion through reproduction, a chapter that had already ended on the Continent among the Merovingians and the Carolingians.

CHAPTER FOUR

Leisure

WORK BEFORE LEISURE

The few women among the first settlers accepted the urgent task of procreating a new cohort of native Icelanders, thereby rectifying the imbalance in the sex ratio.[1] But this function did not excuse them from the equally onerous burden of production. The natural conditions in Iceland required early settlers to work hard the year round. The empty island encouraged an equal start for all settlers. Abandoning Norwegian class differences, the original colonists retained only the basic social distinction between landowners and slaves. As the population grew, usable land became scarce. The cessation of the viking expeditions precluded fresh supplies of slaves from abroad. Already *Landnámabók* noticed that numerous slaves who had arrived with the original settlers were freed and became established as tenant farmers on their former masters' land, a form of exploitation that was often more convenient and cheaper to maintain than large households of slaves. As a result, slavery disappeared, and the free class divided into groups. The rich and powerful exploited the work capacity of people with fewer resources, and an upper class was created whose male members devoted less time to work and more to politics and leisure. Fully evident in the contemporary sagas, this aristocratic class also appears in the ancient context of the sagas of Icelanders.[2] During the entire period covered by the sources, however, lower-class people were reduced to such hard labor that any respite was considered a reward. Free time was often used simply to sleep. When Gunnarr, for example, was informed by his shepherd about a planned attempt on his life and henceforth allowed the young man to choose his own work, further rewarding him with the day off, "the boy lay down and immediately fell asleep" (*Nj* 12.54:136).

In the accepted ethos, however, unrelenting work continued to be perceived as the natural and normal human condition. The description of a certain Þorbjǫrn as "a great worker who was never idle" would fit most Icelanders (*Gr* 7.48:153).[3] Defining a beggar as a poor person who went from farm to farm "aimlessly" (*nenningarlaust*), *Grágás* further characterizes such behavior as "not normal for human beings" (*úmennzka*). The compiler of *Staðarhólsbók* logically places permission to geld poor men at this point in the text (*Gg* 2: 151; 1b:28, 203). Another passage defines a vagrant as "a man so strong and able-bodied that he could earn his keep if he would do the work of which he is capable" (*Gg* 1a:140). Here the lawmakers' outrage jumps from the page, finding relief only by imposing the law's severest penalty, outlawry.

The margin of survival in Iceland was so slim that humans were expected not only to work hard but also to use all natural resources and to allow nothing to go to waste. The law, for example, prohibited the abandoning of farms. If the owner could not use the land himself, he was to rent it to the nearest neighbor at the beginning of the summer to let the hay be consumed by another family's animals (*Gg* 1b:92, 2: 461–62).

Like settlers elsewhere, the first colonists brought their own seed and animals to Iceland. They expected to continue the mixture of agriculture and husbandry that had sustained them in Norway. By 1100, however, they realized that except in the south, the climate would not support cultivation even of barley, the hardiest of grains.[4] The most important yield of the land therefore became the indigenous grasses, dried and stored as hay and used as animal fodder during the winter, and the economy became dependent on sheep and cattle.[5] Although agriculture and animal husbandry are both seasonally determined, the physical work of the former is more demanding at certain seasons, providing lulls at other times, whereas the latter requires more regular, though less strenuous, work throughout the year. These factors influence the gender division of labor and leisure.

GENDER

Like people everywhere, couples in the saga world occasionally discussed which of the two worked harder. Urging everybody on his farm to keep busy, Þórðr asserted to his wife that "I am doing more work on our farm than you" (*BHd* 3.12:139–40). According to law, work was gender specific, with men in charge of outside work and women responsible for inside work. Þórðr's statement may have described his own situation correctly, but in fact most women participated in practically all varieties of outside labor in addition to their housework. Before I analyze the work normally performed by the two genders, however, I examine the way men and women spent their nonworking hours, an inquiry that also illuminates the gender distribution of work.

Although the "frontier era" in which the sagas of Icelanders is set demanded constant work from everybody—at least during the first generations—the narratives themselves were written at a time of less toil and of greater social differentiation. They therefore depict men who spend considerable time not working. Men used their leisure time—grouped according to an ascending scale of social importance—to be bored or lazy, to sleep while others worked, to engage in sports and games, to tell stories, to drink and jest, to indulge their grief by composing poetry or luxuriating in bed, and to participate in the politics of the island. Women shared only few of these activities and are often depicted as working while men played. Women are rarely seen socializing among themselves without working at the same time, and Þórðr's statement likely did not hold true for society as a whole. Women, in fact, worked longer and harder than men, although because women were not central to the sagas' focus on feuding and politics, the authors regularly diminished the role and status of females.[6] It is safe to assume that women in Iceland, as in most societies, socialized and played among themselves unobserved by male authors.

To examine men's leisure activities, I draw again on the combined fund of evidence provided by the laws, the sagas of Icelanders, and the contemporary sagas. Despite Christian mediation in all sources, the analysis of marriage and reproduction indicates an ideological break between the demise of paganism and the acceptance of the new religion on issues where churchmen attempted to make nordic people modify their moral behavior. Leisure, by contrast, exhibits general continuity. Since the law has little to say about these matters (with the exception of politics), I draw my information here primarily from the combined narratives of the sagas of Icelanders and the contemporary sagas.

IDLENESS AND SLEEP

Women were nearly always seen working, but a few men were caught in boredom or idleness despite the general work ethos. Þormóðr (in *Fóstbrœðra saga*) complains constantly that life is boring (*daufligt*). Although this feeling was undoubtedly justified when he was an outlaw living alone in a cave in Greenland during his early twenties, it is not clear why he was idle enough to be regularly bored, regardless of the season, while he was staying on his father's new farm in Iceland a few years earlier (*Ftb* 6.23:238; 9:161, 162; 11:169).[7]

In a similar vein, Þorkell (in *Gísla saga*) is consistently depicted as being showy and lazy. Sharing a domicile with his brother, he "was very vain and did not work on the farm, whereas Gísli worked night and day" (*Gí* 6.9:29). Even during the harvest, when the brother takes advantage of a perfect day and orders every man to be busy with the hay, Þorkell remains in the heated house and sleeps after breakfast. Self-conscious about his bizarre behavior, he usually thanks Gísli for working when the brother returns each evening (9:32). After overhearing his wife admit her lasting passion for Vésteinn, Gísli's brother-in-law (in a scene examined earlier), Þorkell finally decides to divide the property with Gísli and leave the farm. His justification is not emotional tension, however, but the damage caused by his slothful behavior.[8] The reader is not surprised to learn that after Þorkell chooses the movables, leaving his brother the land, the farm is no worse off than before (10:34–35).

Normally a farm was run by a nuclear family, but Þorkell is one of the few married men who shared a house with another couple, first with his brother and later his brother-in-law and their respective wives. His laziness provides a plausible explanation for this unusual arrangement, but his behavior does not change when he and his wife finally established their own farm. At this stage Gísli, now an outlaw, comes seeking help, but, knowing his brother, he instinctively heads for the "sleeping quarters" (*svefnhús*) where, in fact, "Þorkell was lying" (23:74).[9] It seems entirely emblematic that at the moment when Þorkell is killed, he is seated, watching his goods being unloaded from a ship, while his companion is busy making their tent ready (28:89–90).[10]

Þorkell is not the only male character who sleeps while others work. Þórðr (in *Laxdœla saga*), Guðrún's second husband, is rumored to be hard at work, improving their house while she stays in the mountains with the sheep. He and his father-in-law are nevertheless still asleep at daybreak when his former wife arrives to seek revenge. Bolli, Guðrún's third husband, behaves no better. After giving the workers instructions for the day, he returns to bed (*Lx* 5.35:97–98; 55:166).[11] In the contemporary sagas a certain Sigmundr Hook (*snagi*), having spent the morning transporting hay, returns to bed "while it was still light." He rises again only when his mistress informs him that the children need water (*St* 1:308). Since it is the first Friday of the new year (1225), when daylight is shortest, Sigmundr can not have been out of bed for many hours, but it may be his way of enduring the hunger imposed by the Friday fast.[12]

Numerous examples show that women regularly went to bed later than men and arose earlier.[13] Ljótr is asleep when Hávarðr arrives, but his wife and other women are still up (*Hsí* 6.12:329). Likewise, Þórðr is already in bed when his wife Oddný tries to find space next to him (*BHd* 3.14:149). Returning home late at night, Ingimundr's sons automatically call for the housekeeper (*húsfreyja*) to explain why the floor is wet (*Vtn* 8.22:62).[14] In the morning, meanwhile, two women, a maid and the farmer's daughter, are the first to enter the room where a visitor had sought refuge for the night (*Gr* 7.75:239). Going out to the stable in the morning after a turbulent night, a woman discovers that nine cows had been killed (*Bdm* 7.12:362 [text in Möðruvallabók]).[15]

Congruent with these situations is the frequent topos of a woman waking a sleeping man in the morning. Evidently, these preludes to important occurrences are included in order to convey the impression of normal practice. Whereas the men are remembered from the subsequent unusual happenings, the saga authors capture women, often unimportant servants, in these fleeting glimpses of quotidian life.[16]

Although women spent less time in bed, they also slept more lightly and fretfully, awakening at the slightest provocation and frequently becoming aware of troubles before men.[17] When a man comes secretly to a farm late at night and steals embers from the fire, only a woman is alert. When a hostile party quietly arrives during the night, a woman is the first to notice (*St* 1:322; 513). As a wealthy widow, it is not proper for Þórelfr to go to the door herself when someone knocks late at night, but she is the first to hear. Asking a male servant to respond, she, characteristically, has trouble rousing him (*Ftb* 6.3:131). Suspicious of the visitor Rindill, Þorgerðr does not go to bed at all, but her husband Þorkell falls asleep several times, oblivious to the locking and unlocking of doors (*Ljs* 10.8(18):50–51).[18] Briefly stated, in work and sleep medieval Icelanders displayed gender differences that can be observed in other cultures, ancient and modern.

SPORT AND GAMES

The daily monotony of life was broken by sports and games. The most physically taxing games were reserved for men, but women were sometimes included in more cerebral amusements.

Despite its rigor, the nordic climate did not discourage swimming, and both men and women occasionally used this exercise not only as transportation or escape but also as a sport.[19] Competitive swimming did not aim for speed but for underwater endurance. As demonstrated by Kjartan and an unknown man who turns out to be King Óláfr Tryggvason, two men generally sought to keep each other under water as long as possible (*Lx* 5.40:117). Three men competed in a more spectacular case in which "nobody thought they would come up alive." When they finally emerged, two of them bled profusely from their noses and had to be helped to shore (*QO*, FSN 2.26:309).[20] Wrestling, which seems to have occupied young boys much of the time, also pitted two men against each other.[21]

Most common was the ball game *knattleikr*, a kind of hockey played by teams of men with a ball and sticks on a flat surface, preferably ice, after the

Yule celebrations, when seasonal work was lowest. As demonstrated by Kjartan, the game demanded both strength (*afl*) and skill (*fimleikr; Lx* 5.45:136). Matched according to competence, only men at their physical peak were allowed to participate. At the two extremes, an overly aggressive person and a man past his prime were relegated to spectator status (Þórðr in *Erb* 4.43:115 and Skeggi in *Þhr* 14.3:177).[22] Women were occasionally among the onlookers during small and local contests. At games held in the fall, they would sit on a nearby slope when "the weather was good" (*Hlf* 8.2:142; *Vtn* 8.37:98). Even when "snow was on the ground" (*Gí* 6.18:58), they remained outside until the cold forced them indoors.

In suitable areas, ball games were arranged on a large scale, drawing people from an entire district. Shelters were built, and men came from afar, staying as long as two weeks. The cooking was done by men, indicating that women were present neither as spectators nor as helpers.[23] An integral part of Norse social life, these games were introduced in the New World by the few settlers (*Gn* 4.8:265). They often became outlets for pent-up male energy during winter months and could result in quarrels and even killings.[24]

Whereas ball games enlivened the winter season, group amusements during the summer took place at horse fairs (*hestaþing* or *hestavíg*), where male aggression was channeled into horse fights. As two men pitted and goaded their horses against each other, they took more than vicarious pleasure in the animals' combat. Urging his own horse with a stick, a man often used it against his human opponent as well. Although male spectators were numerous, the only female present was a mare tied nearby to further excite the stallions.[25] *Sturlunga saga* does contain a single vignette of a man who met his girlfriend at a horse fair (*hestaþing;* 1:102).[26] Since horse fights were dangerous, however, it is likely that women preferred to stay clear. Their absence is further indicated by the practice of reciting scurrilous poems about women at these meetings, an amusement that female presence would have inhibited.[27] That women were aware of the potential violence is suggested by Hildigunnr's egging of her brothers and cousins to match their horse against Gunnarr's (*Nj* 12.58–59:147–51).

From the age of five or six boys engaged in their own team sport (*sveinaleikr;* literally, boys' game). The sport was likely quite violent; one group of boys, for example, admitted only those who had killed something living. In, one hopes, an exceptional case, the five-year-old Þorgils slew his father's favorite horse to qualify (*Flm* 13.10:250–51).[28]

Board games constituted a physically less taxing leisure activity. In the Eddic poem *Vǫluspá* chess games are reserved for the male gods, but this ancient war game of foreign origin was a male amusement also in the human world.[29] The "golden pieces" (*gullnar tǫflor;* str. 61) found in the grass when the gods return must refer to individual chess pieces.[30] Used in the singular, *tafla* more likely denotes the board on which the pieces were moved. A scene set in 1237 and describing the end of a game between two men provides details. A large contraption installed on the floor, the board impedes one of the players when he stands up; it needed dismantling and storage after each use (*St* 1:398). Like other forms of competition, these games could lead to violence. On a tense evening at Guðmundr *dýri*'s farm many men "fought over games and women and stole from each other" (*St* 1:202).[31] Accusing her husband of being lazy because he is always "at the game" (*at tafli*), a wife strikes him with one of the pieces (*Gr* 7.70:226).

Requiring cerebral, not physical, agility, board games could readily be played by women. By the twelfth century it was the most popular game in Europe among upper classes of both genders. In the saga world, a man and a woman were occasionally seen playing together as, for example, Gunnlaugr and Helga (*Gnl* 3.4:60), Leiknir and Ásdís (*Hǫv* 3.4:221), and Víglundr and Ketilríðr (*Vgl* 14.14:90). Ordinary women apparently did not play together, but two supernatural women play a special kind of chess known as *hnettafl* or *hnefatafl* (*Þskf* 13.14:205).

STORYTELLING

In contrast to board games, which involved only two people, storytelling gave pleasure to groups and was entirely cerebral, since the teller relied on memory or reading. Women were reputed for their knowledge of past events. Ari Þorgilsson, author of the venerable "Book of Icelanders" (*Íslendingabók*), for example, praises one of his informers, a woman, Þuríðr Snorradóttir, for being "wise and truthful" (*Ísl* 1.1:4).[32] Snorri repeats Ari's words in the prologue to his *Heimskringla* (27:7), and presumably the two men credit her with more than recalling small details. Women undoubtedly told stories privately to their children, but public performance was limited to men and prophetesses.[33] Þuríðr and other females divulged information about the past, and the prophetess or sibyl (*vǫlva*) predicted the future. Þuríðr offers her revelations to Ari privately, the vǫlva performed in public to those assembled around her. Undoubtedly, prophetesses had been common in the distant past among both the Continental tribes and the nordic peoples, but in Norse sources these sibyls or sorceresses (*vǫlur*) appear only outside Iceland, although this anomaly may be due to accidental loss of evidence.[34]

In contrast to women, men created entire stories about living kings, distant ancestors, or mythical beings and performed them publicly. The narratives contain a few passages that describe the subject matter, creation, and performance of storytelling, including precious information about saga creation.

"Great entertainment" occurred at a þing meeting in Greenland, as people formed a circle on the ground listening to Þorgrímr. Seated on a chair, he "excellently and amusingly" told a story that involved his own deeds (*Ftb* 6.23:231).[35] Known for their storytelling, Icelanders were often asked to entertain abroad. A certain Þorsteinn stayed with King Haraldr Sigurðarson, nicknamed the Hard-Ruler (*harðráði*) (1046–1066), and his skill made him popular (*þokkasæll*) with the king and his men, who rewarded him with clothing and weapons. By Christmas he had exhausted his repertoire, but he reserved for the holiday entertainment the story about the king's own trip to Byzantium (his *útfararsaga*), which he claimed to have heard in yearly installments at the alþingi from Halldórr Snorrason, one of the king's companions (*Þsf* 11: 335–36).[36]

The passage that has attracted the most scholarly comment is found in a description of Helga Yngvildardóttir's and Ólafr's wedding in 1119 in Reykjahólar.[37] According to this account, written long after the event, the seven days of festivities included "great merriment and cheer, good amusement (*skemmtan*), and many kinds of games (*leikar*), including dances, wrestling, and storytelling" (*sagnaskemmtan; St* 1:27). One saga was recited by the host Ingimundr, a priest (with whom the mother of the bride was living), who had a reputation as a skald and a storyteller, and three were told by Hrólfr, one of the guests. These tales belonged to the genre characterized by King Sverrir as "lying sagas" (*lygisǫgur*). The term, as well as the subject matter and the stanzas included, place these tales among the heroic sagas (*fornaldarsǫgur*).[38]

Most trustworthy from a historical standpoint is a vignette concerning Sturla Þórðarson. He was exiled from Iceland in 1263 and forced to seek refuge in Norway despite King Hákon's hostility, and he gained the confidence of the king's son Magnús because of his skill at reciting.[39] The crucial event took place on board ship, where sailors were accustomed to hear stories before going to sleep. Telling the sailors the lost *Huldar saga* about a troll-woman "better and more cleverly than any had ever heard before," Sturla was invited to repeat it to the king and queen. After he also had declaimed two poems about Magnús and Hákon, the king declared that Sturla recited (*kveðr*) better than the pope.

DRINKING AND WORD GAMES

The prophetess and the male storyteller were individuals who gave virtuoso performances. In contrast, groups of men engaged in word games to entertain themselves during drinking fests, the most important social diversion of the nordic world.[40] Originally tied to pagan sacrifices, these celebrations included both seasonal feasts that punctuated the year, and others that commemorated personal events.[41] Although Christian leaders attempted to purge these rituals of pagan features, they were careful to retain the timing of the old celebrations, which they associated with important Christian events. In the north, for example, the birth of Christ was so successfully conjoined with the pagan midwinter *jól* that the Latin Christmas has never displaced the native term and its synonyms.

All private events were toasted with drink. The Danish word *barsel* (childbirth) apparently derives from Old Norse *barnsǫl* (child-beer). It is tempting to assume that from earliest times nordic people honored the mother and greeted the newborn by drinking, and indeed such a custom did actually appear in the Early Modern Period. Barsel is extremely rare in Old Norse sources, however, and not more frequent in later medieval Danish texts, indicating that it lacked medieval roots.[42] At the end of life the deceased was honored by an inheritance beer (*erfiǫl*) provided by the heir, who came rightfully into his legacy through this rite. Only one woman was reported to be honored in this way, and, characteristically, she was an older widow no longer under male guardianship.[43] Weddings naturally celebrated both the bride and the groom, but men were the normal focus of individual celebrations.[44] Because men did most of the traveling, they alone were the recipients of going-away (*brotferðarǫl*) and the opposite, welcome-home (*fagnaðarǫl*) parties. Often including games and entertainments, these feasts also entailed meat and vast quantities of beer and ale. Since imbibing was rarer and more memorable than eating, drinking was privileged in the stories and collective memory. *Drykkja* (the noun) and *drekka* (the verb) became the shorthand for feasts. A wedding was often identified by the term to "drink the wedding" (*drekka brullaup*).

An elaborate drinking culture was therefore well developed by the time the Norwegian vikings started traveling abroad. When they settled in new colonies in the West, they naturally continued their drinking culture. Climate hampered the growing of grain and the production of malt in Iceland. Limited local supplies were supplemented with imported raw and finished materials, but alcoholic beverages never became as readily available in Iceland as in Norway. Consequently, drinking patterns developed somewhat differently in the two countries. The vocabulary employed for the feasts is identical in Norway and Iceland, but given the short supplies on the island, it is natural that the specifics of beverages and drinking are often omitted in the Icelandic setting. Descriptions of Norwegian feasts (*veizlur*) almost always include the words beer (*ǫl*) or drink (*drykkja*), while in Iceland the term *veizla* and its synonyms *boð* and *heimaboð* are most often used alone, and references to drinking are rare. Not that people abstained; the "happiness and amusement" (*gleði ok skemmtan*) that characterized the autumn feast (*haustboð*) at Hjarðarholt were not fueled by conversation and sociability alone (*Lx* 5.46:140). Undoubtedly, a ceremonial toast was always offered at weddings and funerals, but supplies rarely allowed the extensive drinking common in Norway.

It is likely no coincidence that the sagas report more details of games and entertainment in Iceland but reveal more drunkenness in Norway. The broad range of amusements enjoyed during feasts — celebration, talking, joking, playing games, and telling stories — was no doubt more fully developed when and where drinking was curtailed. The full spectrum of conviviality was surely present in Norway from the beginning, but as supplies of drink became abundant, imbibing was privileged, and — as a physiological consequence — other activities declined.

More striking than differences imposed by climate and geography, however, were distinctions in men's and women's drinking behavior. Celebrations clearly provided respite from toil and opportunities for bodily relaxation. The author of *Hungrvaka*, a short history of the Icelandic bishops, notes alcohol's soothing effect on grief (*Bs* 1:78). To what extent did these pleasures include men and women equally? Although men dominated drinking festivities as they did other social activities, women were nonetheless involved in specific aspects of the drinking culture. Best known is the traditional female role of serving, practiced by all Germanic tribes and shared with the Huns. Wealhtheow hands the cup to the men in Heorot; Guðrún greets Atli with the same gesture. From the beginning, nordic mythology had encapsulated the serving woman in the figure of the valkyrie who pours drinks for the fallen heroes in groups in Valhǫll; Eddic poetry contains other mythical women cast in the same role. In nordic human settings, the daughter of the house serves beer for the occasional viking who arrived for a friendly visit.[45] In the traditional Icelandic society, serving was likewise normally done by women. A man was cast in the role only to make him appear ridiculous.[46] Foreign influence, however, eventually reassigned the traditional female role to male cupbearers in royal and aristocratic circles.[47]

Although serving required work, it still provided women with a measure of pleasurable sociability. How fully they participated in the drinking culture by imbibing is, however, less clear. Indications from mythology and myth suggest that females drank in mixed company. In the Eddic poem *Lokasenna* gods and goddesses drink together at Ægir's banquet, while "the beer served itself" — the dream of any host (prose before str. 1). When Brynhildr is awakened by Sigurðr on the mountain top, she likewise suggests that they drink together, and she miraculously produces a container and beer (*Vls* 21:49).

In human society the custom of "drinking in pairs" (*tvímenningr*) offered women an occasion to drink. Snorri Sturluson informs us that drinking patterns varied according to the king's law and viking custom. According to the king's law, men and women drank together at feasts, each couple sharing a horn (*tvímenningr*), but among vikings, all men drank together from a common horn in party drinking (*sveitardrykkja*). If women were present, they drank singly from individual horns (*einmenningr; Yn* 26.37:67–68). Offering the visiting King Hjǫrvarðr a horn from which she had drunk, the Swedish princess Hildiguðr introduced "couple drinking" (*tvímenningr*) to these vikings, and the custom eventually came to dominate all mixed drinking. Drinking by couples sought to prevent trouble over women: they were assigned by lot, leaving the remaining men to drink by themselves. Each important man enjoyed the exclusive company of a girl, an arrangement intended to prevent her from flirting with other men and thus provoke jealousy. Viking practice, however, did not obtain in Iceland. When the custom of couple drinking was evoked under circumstances less awesome than a viking visit, it was always set in contexts abroad.[48] Instances of this new custom in the sagas, therefore, do not permit the conclusion that Icelandic women participated in drinking festivities. By the time of the later kings' sagas, the older custom of "party drinking" had gone out of fashion, but general drinking, especially at night, remained common. A few upper-class women are specifically mentioned as drinking in male company.[49]

Evidence of female drinking in Iceland is, in fact, less clear. As depicted in the sagas of Icelanders, relatively little drinking took place on the island in pagan times.[50] The most graphic scenes of Norse drunken behavior are found in the sagas of Icelanders, but they occur in Norway, when Icelandic men, perhaps unaccustomed to Norwegian abundance, have difficulty holding their liquor.[51] In contrast, *Sturlunga saga* provides evidence of heavier drinking in contemporary Icelandic society. Greatly dependent on imports, it was largely limited to upper-class men who had become sufficiently rich to indulge a habit often acquired abroad.[52] Since women rarely traveled outside Iceland, they did not acquire the taste. Limited supplies may have also increased men's reluctance to share alcoholic beverages, thus reducing the proportion available for female consumption compared to that in Norway. Men frequently controlled the supplies of grain and malt, and husbands and wives may have argued over whether such supplies should be used for gruel or beer in times of need.[53]

When marriages were celebrated, supplies were sufficient for everybody, including women, to "drink the wedding," at least in a single toast (*Nj* 12.6:22).[54] One must also assume that women drank at regular feasts, as, for example, at the winter celebrations honoring the god Freyr which occurred simultaneously at two neighboring farms, Gísli's at Hóll and Þorgrímr's at Sæból. At Sæból "men began to drink at night and went to bed afterwards to sleep." (Nobody even notices that Gísli entered the room quietly and murdered Þorgrímr in bed.) Meanwhile, at Hóll, all men (*menn allir;* plural masculine) are drunk (*olœrir*) when they go to bed. Auðr remains awake and lets her husband in after the deed (*Gí* 6.15–16:49–54). Assuming that she too has been drinking, she is sober enough to stay awake and wait for Gísli's return. Although the corpus does not contain a single reference to female drinking in Iceland, women undoubtedly imbibed when the texts imply group drinking, but they consumed far less than men. At Ingibjǫrg's famous wedding in 1253 an unspecified number of men and women were seated in six rows. Probably more men than women were present, for eight men served "each of the rows of men," whereas four sufficed to serve the women present (*St* 1:483). It seems safe to conclude that Norse women did drink with men, but neither mythic nor human women drank in their own company.[55] On rare occasions when ordinary women were seen alone, they were likely to be working or gossiping, but not drinking.[56]

Men did their most serious drinking when no women were present. Furthermore, only men showed the psychological and physiological effects of alcohol also in mixed company. The proper way to drink was "without restraint" (*ú-sleituliga*). When the horn was passed, a man could not refuse. A reluctant drinker who tried to drink "with restraint" (*við sleitur*) was penalized by being forced to drain an extra cup, a "sconce drink" (*vítishorn*); only old age and sickness excused a man from less than his share.[57] The term *kappdrykkja* (from *kapp*, contest) suggests that drinking involved competition.

As a first sign of the influence of alcohol a man became "cheerful or happy," a mood conveyed by the word *kátr*. In drinking episodes the word can also suggest sexual arousal (as in *kåt*, the modern equivalent in Swedish and Norwegian), but more often it is employed in opposition to taciturn (*hljóðr*); it thus indicates a loosening of the tongue. As men became talkative, the lack of restraint did not result in mere loquaciousness but was directed into organized word games. Generally known as "beer cheerfulness" (*olteiti*) and specifically designated as "sarcastic drink words" (*hnœfilyrði* or *hnýfilyrði*), toasts (*minni*), solemn vows (*heitstrenging*), or comparison of men (*mannjafnaðr*), these amusements could be innocent self-praises, such as the three-year old Egill performed as part of the amusement (*olteiti*) at his grandfather's party (*Eg* 2.31:81).[58] At other times men indulged in increasingly coarse ridicule of the physical weaknesses of other male guests. At Helga's wedding in Reykjahólar in 1119, "there was no shortage of good drink."[59] Before the storytelling begins, Ingimundr, the host, suggests that toasts (*minni*) be offered. After a while, as "they all drank heavily and became rather intoxicated," they proceed to hurl gibes and jokes (*kerskiyrði*) at the old, foul-breathed Þórðr Þorvaldsson. Ingimundr starts, and others chime in. Þórðr, also known as a skald, at first responds in kind, but eventually he asks that the most vociferous guest be told to leave; when his request is refused, he becomes so upset that he departs himself (*St* 1:23–26). Promises of extravagant actions in the future were involved in heitstrenging, and verbal duels comparing leaders in mannjafnaðr. An inebriated man was tempted to make statements he normally would have kept hidden. Thus he bragged about himself and his leader and teased and insulted others. This provocation required new, perhaps coarser replies, which were facilitated by the loss of inhibition exacerbated by more drink. Although the contest opened verbally, the enhancement of verbal skills through drinking increased competition, resulting in both competitive dispute (*kappmæli*) and competitive drinking (*kappdrykkja*). The goal was to improve oral performance without showing the effects of alcohol. Among the criteria listed to determine whether a man was competent to keep his property, the Norwegian Gulathing Law stated that he had to be "able to manage his horse and his beer" (*hestfœrr ok ǫlfœrr;* NgL 1:54).

Episodes of competitive disputes and competitive drinking are found in all genres and periods of Norse literature.[60] Women, however, did not participate in these orgies of drunken boasting. Since wives of kings and rulers were frequently not present when visiting dignitaries were convivially received, it is not surprising that they were able to help their husbands negotiate the extravagant promises made under the influence of drink.[61] Although widowed or single female rulers received visiting male colleagues, they generally appear to have emulated the topos of "the sober queen." The single Ólof of Saxland (*Hrkr*) and the widowed Sigríðr of Sweden (*ÓT*) both drank heavily with a visiting, amorous king. Feigning willingness to join him in bed, each waited until the man fell asleep, then they escaped and proceeded to scheme against him (FSN 1.7:14-15; 26.43:287-89). In Sigríðr's case the text states that "the king was dead drunk and so were they both." Sigríðr thus qualifies as the only woman in the narrative corpus to be charged with drunkenness. Like "the woman serving drinks," "the sober queen" possesses a venerable pedigree in Germanic poetry. *Atlakviða,* perhaps the oldest of the Eddic poems, preserves the unforgettable image of Guðrún who "was far from drunk with ale" as she received her brothers at Atli's court and prepared her revenge (str. 15).[62]

The topos of "the sober queen" eliminates the argument that women drank less than men because their bodies tolerated less. The absence of women from these verbal and imbibing competitions opens up the largely uncharted territory of the relationship between language and the acquisition of power. The purveyor of the instinctive noises of screams, cries, and laughter and of the structured sounds of language, the voice bridges the body and the symbolic, materiality and meaning, nature and culture, and, possibly, male and female domains.[63] It is no coincidence that the traditional role of expressing grief through inarticulate wailing has been assumed by women, but — although women taught their children to speak — in practically all cultures men have appropriated formal and public speaking, leaving women to make silences expressive.[64]

Alcohol will, of course, loosen the tongue of man and woman alike, but, already in control of language, Norse men's linguistic leadership was increased by the first drink, resulting in competitive speaking and drinking. Lagging behind men in verbal power, women were not sufficiently emboldened by the first drink to engage in verbal competition. With no incentive to drink further, they imbibed less than men, distanced from both forms of competition. Old Norse women were not at loss for words, however, as demonstrated by their roles as inciters, but their whetting was done in private and never under the influence of drink.[65]

On occasion the saga authors imply that their ancestors were prone to drink regularly at night (*Erb* 4.31:83–84; 37:98). As argued already, the scarcity of alcoholic beverages even on solemn occasions suggests that nightly drinking probably happened rarely, but when it did, such sessions are depicted as being entirely dominated by men. On one memorable occasion an enterprising young man by the name of Brandr invents a new game — a mock court that uses an imaginary law known as the "law from Syrpa's þing" (*Syrpuþingslǫg*). Containing "all sorts of teasing and verbal insults," the game eventually became standard entertainment in the whole country. The first occasion, which takes place while Brandr is staying with Þorkell, is described in the following terms: "Men came from far and wide from other farms, making a lot of noise. Þorkell sat at drink with only one other man. Eventually it was reported to Þorkell that the women found the verdicts of the mock court rather strong. They could not defend themselves and were not at liberty to come and go as they pleased (*Vbr* 10.2(9):129–30)."[66] The association between *Syrpuþingslǫg* and one of the possible meanings of *syrpa* (dirty woman) makes it easy to imagine that these games involved sexual harassment in words, gestures, and body contact, as the men played and prevented the women from doing their work.[67]

EMOTIONAL DISTRESS

Gender influences the way men and women cope with grief and emotional distress. No evidence has surfaced among the Germanic people of ululation, the ritual female mourning of gestures and inarticulate noises which is well known from the Mediterranean region. Eventually, however, men and women alike learned to articulate grief over personal loss in songs of lament.[68] The first recorded instance appears to be Procopius's story of the Vandal king Gelimer, who after a defeat in 533 composed and performed a song describing his life and sorrow.[69] Gelimer's grief may have derived more from public misfortune in warfare than from private devastation over the loss of a human being. Later, however, the loss of friends and family became the preferred object of lament songs. Given the persistent male bonding in the *Männerbund* of the Germanic *comitatus* and of the viking band, it is unsurprising that men were the first to articulate their loss, in this case, of comrades fallen in battle.[70] Eventually, they learned to express heterosexual longings and grief as well. Women were late-comers to the genre, but later Eddic poetry includes beautiful articulations of female grief and mourning. Despite the overt female voice, the themes of loss of lover or husband suggest that these lays were composed by male poets.

In the saga world women did not yet articulate mourning but coped with grief by keeping busy with everyday tasks. In contrast, men allowed themselves time and leisure to indulge their heterosexual longings and grief for fallen kin and comrades.[71] The classic example is Egill's *Sonatorrek,* the beautiful poem inserted in *Egils saga* in which he laments the loss of his sons.[72] Before Egill plays out this theme in full, preparatory chords are struck by his grandfather in a prelude within the saga. When old Kveld-Úlfr receives the news that his son Þórólfr has been killed by the Norwegian king, he becomes so distressed (*hryggr*) that his grief (*harmr*) brings him to bed. Skalla-Grímr, his other son, encourages him to cheer up (*hressa sik*) and argues that revenge or any other solution is better than losing one's dignity in bed. Complaining that he is too old for action, Kveld-Úlfr finds release in composing a single stanza (*Eg* 2.24:60).

Two generations later, Egill loses his own favorite son, Bǫðvarr, by drowning. In this case violence is not an option, because revenge against the gods was not possible. The father retrieves his son's body from the ocean, buries it in the mound next to his own father, goes home to bed, locks the door to the alcove, and refuses to eat, apparently with the intention of starving himself to death. After several days his wife sends for Þorgerðr, their oldest daughter, who, having traveled all night, likewise refuses the food her mother has pre-pared, and joins her father in bed. Praising her desire to die with him, Egill declares: "How can anyone expect that I should want to live with a grief such as this?" (*Hver ván er, at ek muna lifa vilja við harm þenna*). Þorgerðr tricks her father into drinking milk and subsequently encourages him to compose an eulogy (*erfikvæði*) for Bǫðvarr rather than to die. The result is the magnificent poem *Sonatorrek.* As Þorgerðr undoubtedly anticipated, Egill cheers up (*tók at hressask*) as the poem progresses (2.78:242–57).[73]

Lesser men also took to their bed under similar circumstances; some died of grief.[74] The old Hávarðr spends three years in bed, grieving the death of his son Óláfr, leaving all the daily tasks to his wife (*HsÍ* 6.5:308; 6:309; 7:315). Informed at the alþingi of his son Hallr's death, Guðmundr goes to bed in his booth and dies of grief a month after his return home (*Hðv* 3.14:254). In these two cases the wives arrange the revenge. The theme is richly illustrated in the sagas of Icelanders and is also found in the contemporary accounts. After Brandr Kolbeinsson's death in 1246, his father is so distressed that he "enjoyed neither sleep nor food." Traveling to his daughter, he becomes ill and dies a week later. Those who knew him realize that his death was caused by his loss (*mannamissir; St* 2:82–83). As men indulged their grief, women assured that life continued.

POLITICS

The political life must also be included among nonproductive male activities. Men ran the meetings at the alþingi and the local assemblies as active executors of justice and as receivers and supplicants.[75] They also found time for visiting, socializing, and drinking. A group of four men were accused of spending so much time drinking that they neglected their political obligations.[76] Women were expressly excluded from prosecuting manslaughter (*Gg* 2:335), and they were allowed to arrange a daughter's engagement only when no close male relative was alive (*Gg* 1b:29; 2:155). When they were granted to act as principals (*aðiljar*), in the few cases that involved their personal and economic safety and integrity, they were not expected to prosecute (*sœkja*) on their own but to delegate (*selja*) the task to male relatives. If they agreed to let these surrogates reach a compromise with the defendant (the term was *setja*), the men were not allowed to settle for less than the fines imposed by law.[77]

Certain of the positions created to make the law function specifically called for men. In order to be appointed to the court (*dómr*), for example, one had to be "a male (*karlmaðr*), sixteen or older, capable of taking responsibility for his word and oath, and a free man with a fixed domicile" (*Gg* 1a:38).[78] Even minor positions, such as witnesses (*váttar*), called for "men (*karlar*) capable of understanding an oath, twelve years or older, and free with fixed domicile" (*Gg* 1a: 153; 2:312). Without including the word *karl* to specify a male, the law achieved the same stipulation with the term "assembly-fit" (*þingfœrr;* literally, able to travel to the þing). To be assembly-fit was defined as a person (*maðr*) "able to ride full-day journeys, bring his own hobbled horse to resting places, and find his way alone where the route is known to him" (*Gg* 1a:160; 2:321). Although the term maðr could apply to both genders, its restriction to males in this case is clear from the subsequent paragraph where a woman and an unfit man are grouped together as ineligible for jury duty (*kviðr*). The law identified four males (son, stepson, son-in-law, or foster son) who were allowed to appear in place of the unfit man and added the woman's husband as a fifth possibility, in case she owned the farm and her husband resided with her (*Gg* 1a:160–61; 2: 322). In other words, although a female proprietor of farm in most cases would be as "assembly-fit" as any man, she was not considered capable of jury duty.

This definition of assembly-fit obviously excluded women not only from jury duty but also from participation at the local þing and the alþingi. Horses were the chief means of transport, and women were of course capable of riding. The sagas often report their presence at the alþingi, but they apparently came for social purposes exclusively. Marriageable women were often present at assembly meetings, doubtless to be seen by prospective suitors. Once married, however, women were too busy.[79] Þing meetings took place during the spring and summer when weather was less likely to hinder travel. In other words, neither the women's physical fitness nor geography and climate would furnish compelling reasons for their exclusion. Lawmakers may have argued that pregnancy and lactation hindered frequent and regular attendance and therefore justified the exclusion of all females. In the category of unfit men, however, it is worth noticing that the law granted specific allowance for occasional male illness, excusing men from jury duty if it seemed unlikely that they would regain health in time and even permitting sworn testimony at sickbed to be conveyed by others to the meeting (*Gg* 1a:58, 202; 2:330–33; 3:432). Whereas young boys, according to the law, were expected to outgrow physical weakness and mental immaturity at the age of twelve or sixteen, young girls—doubtless as capable riders and as mature as boys—were never considered assembly-fit and were therefore effectively barred from participating in the political and juridical functions of their society.

This analysis of gender roles and leisure time suggests that medieval Icelanders established daily routines that provided considerably more leisure—structured as well as unstructured—for men than for women. Women may not have worked all the time that men played, but they obviously spent more hours at work than men did.

CHAPTER FIVE

Work

My chief concern in this chapter is women's labor within the total work force of ancient and medieval Iceland, but I include men's work to provide a gendered context. The female deployment of distaff and loom bore far-flung consequences for exchange and export which in turn implicated the island's economic life in general.

¶As outlined in previous chapters, the sources reveal a perceptual divide between paganism and Christianity on social problems concerning marriage and sexuality. A somewhat parallel shift in technology occurred as settlers increased their mastery over the difficult, unusual, and hitherto untamed terrain. By exploiting the hot springs, by producing a surplus of wool, by perfecting weaving techniques, and by introducing the homespun as a means of exchange, Icelandic men and women of the twelfth and thirteenth centuries not only sustained the colony initiated by their ancestors but created a more comfortable and pleasant life on a formerly inhospitable and barren island. Although the sources are relatively plentiful, the subject has not been treated in this way before.[1] More than usual, however, in this case information must be ferreted from inadvertent details in the sagas, dense legal paragraphs, and the interstices of the narrative genres. In contrast to the break in marital and sexual patterns, which, we recall, originated in ecclesiastical ideology, the technological divide was the result of the growing expertise of ordinary Icelanders in handling everyday problems. Promoted with fanfare, the ecclesiastical program could not be missed, and it may have made saga writers self-conscious regardless of their response. Authors were much less aware of the precise development of technological shifts, and they may in fact have portrayed the material transformations with greater historical accuracy than the foreign religious and moral impositions.

GENDER DIVISION OF LABOR

Although men and women were assigned different tasks, they needed to work together to enable society as well as the individual farm to function successfully. This fundamental condition is expressed directly in the vocabulary in the broad term *hjón,* which not only designated the marital couple but embraced the entire household, including servants. As wives, mothers, daughters, sisters, and housekeepers, women fulfilled sexual, reproductive, and labor needs. Only the last function is explicitly mentioned or implied in the sources with any regularity. A man possessing a farm but lacking a wife, or whose wife was unwilling to manage the household, had to find another woman for the task. Conversely, a woman could not manage without male help. A widow, for example, whose sons were too young to help, would hire a male manager, even a priest.[2] In one case a husband whose wife had left him went to his father-in-law and asked his help in retrieving her because, as he argued, he could not manage the farm without her (*Rkd* 10.16:197–98).[3] Lacking this option, an unmarried man would hire a housekeeper (*matselja*).[4] When an unmarried man was too busy to undertake the farm duties himself, he hired both a male and female manager, frequently a married couple, referred to as the *ráðamaðr* and *ráðakona* (literally, the man or woman in charge). In 1197, at age twenty-seven, Sighvatr Sturluson established his own estate at Hjarðarholt and hired his sister and her husband as managers. The next year he married, and after a few months he and his wife "took over the estate and managed it alone" (*taka . . . við búi sínu ok réðu ein fyrir; St* 1:234–35). He doubtless soon dismissed his sister.

The housekeeper was the single prestigious female position on a farm. When advising his son Sturla (albeit sarcastically) about the chief positions the young man needed to fill on his growing estates, Sighvatr Sturluson assigned seven positions from eleven candidates, among them only one female, the housekeeper (*St* 1:407–8). On large estates the male title eventually was transformed into the more prestigious bailiff (*bryti*), while the female title disappeared, although the wife of a married bailiff continued to work.[5]

Wives of bishops received special recognition for managing their families as well as the large episcopal estates. Of particular fame was Herdis, wife of Bishop Páll in Skálholt (1195–1211), who raised nine children and also "looked after all the things the estate needed with great skill in management and wisdom." In 1207 she and two of the children traveled to Skarð to inspect a farm owned by her and her husband. Although the weather turned bad, she insisted on returning, because "many things needed to be taken care of at home." She and most of her party were drowned as they tried to cross a river by boat. The bishop was inconsolable, but their fourteen-year-old daughter Þóra "took over the management" (*tók til forráða fyrir innan stokk; Bs* 1:137–40).[6]

The size of the household in which a person lived depended on biological and social status. Remaining with parents or foster parents during their youth, young men and women were required to find work at different domiciles from the age of sixteen and twenty respectively (*Gg* 1a:129; 2:265). Since housework was the only option for the landless, they might never leave the profession of service. If their financial circumstances allowed them to marry, their goal was to establish independent households. Joint households were temporary. A daughter-in-law, for example, rarely moved into the house of her husband's family unless her mother-in-law was no longer alive. Despite this nuclear aspect, many households were nonetheless large. Other arrangements, such as unmarried brothers living together, are also found in both the law and the narratives.[7]

The smaller the farm and, consequently, the fewer the hjón, the greater the involvement of husband and wife in all aspects of work. In larger, wealthier households, however, certain jobs were considered below the dignity of the owners. Angry at his wife, Þórðr proposes that she milk the sheep, although he admits that she is unaccustomed to this chore. In retaliation she urges him to clean out the pens (*BHd* 3.12:139–40). Unsurprisingly, neither performs the assigned tasks.[8]

A division of work was generally established between women and men. Most clearly articulated in law, the rule specified — without making it an obligation — that a wife was to manage the couple's affairs that pertained within the house (*fyrir innan stokk*; literally, "within the threshold"), and it was understood that the husband was in charge of everything outside (*fyrir útan stokk*; literally, "outside the threshold"; *Gg* 1b:44; 2:173).[9] Several saga passages confirm that after the wedding the husband turned the household over to his wife (*Nj* 12.6:22, 65:162; *Kjn* 14.2:6) or designated another woman to be responsible (*Vtn* 8.44:116).[10] Recently arrived from Norway with her husband and mother, Droplaug does not wish to be in charge of "the inside work on the farm" (*búi fyrir innan stokk*) at first and turns it over to her mother. Four years later, when the older woman dies, Droplaug is better prepared. After her husband's death she is courted by another man, a widower with two sons who earlier had handled his own situation by "letting various women manage the household."[11] Moving to his farm, Droplaug benefits from her previous experience, as she "took over the entire management, both inside and outside" (*fyrir útan stokk ok innan; Fld* 11.7:233–34, 23–24:289–91). At Helgafell, the mother of the unmarried Snorri is in charge of the inside work (*fyrir innan stokk*). Since

Snorri is busy with politics, his farm work is handled by his uncle who, with a comparable expression, "took over the management of the farm" (*tók forráð fyrir búi; Erb* 4.15:26).[12]

OUTDOOR WORK

The word *stokkr* (nominative case) in these two expressions designates the threshold into which the outer door locked. Although the term should not be taken in a literal or architectural sense, it does seem clear that the masculine domain of work was entirely outside. More interested in feuds and interpersonal relations, the authors of the sagas of Icelanders refer to men's work only as backdrop to these more dramatic events. On two occasions in *Njála,* for example, when Gunnarr and Hǫskuldr are engaged in the seemingly peaceful occupation of sowing, the author is less concerned with their work—despite the valuable detail that they kept the seed in a sieve (*kornkippa*)—and more attentive to the arrival of their killers. Impending violence is suggested by the added particular that both men are armed, Gunnarr with an axe and Hǫskuldr with a sword, and both wear expensive capes, each emblematic in the lives of the wearers but totally unsuited for field work (*Nj* 12.53:134, 111:280).[13]

Narrative demands naturally compelled authors to focus on the high drama of feuds and politics. And indeed these activities so consumed their time that saga heroes were limited to the overall management and organization of their farms, relegating the actual work to others. As Flosi and his hundred men are planning the final attack on Njáll and his sons, they return home to "manage their farms during the summer while the hay harvest was on." On two other occasions an additional incentive is to allow the sex-starved men to "find their wives" (*finna konur sínar;* 131:341–42, 134:353). Taking leave of his own farm later, Flosi "gave orders to all his workers (*heimamenn*) as to what work they were to do during his absence" (124:316–17, 126:322). Even during periods of relative peace, well-to-do men performed less physical work than poor people. When the rich Bjarni is engaged in a duel with his poor neighbor Þorsteinn, he asks for a drink of water, because "I am less used to working than you are" (*Þst* 11:75).

Because of their preoccupation with feuds and politics, the contemporary sagas pay even less attention than the sagas of Icelanders to men's physical work. One must therefore turn to the law for information on how Þorsteinn— he was known for doing the work of three—and countless others unrecorded in the sagas extracted a living from the harsh Icelandic soil. The management and exploitation of land and its transfer from one generation to the next occasioned innumerable disputes. The ensuing violence was brought under control by applying specific rules that were "laid down," thus becoming "law" over time as implied in the etymology of *lǫg* (law).[14] The result was a long chapter, "Land Claims" (*Landabrigðis þáttr*), running to sixty pages in the *Konungsbók* manuscript and twice as long in *Staðarhólsbók*. Dealing primarily with social issues, such as transfer of landed property, these texts also offer vivid glimpses into the challenges posed by nature.

The law contains little evidence of agricultural farming. An ancient precept for guaranteeing peace, the so-called truce formula (*trygðamál*) refers to sowing seed as being done by men (*karlar; Gg* 1a:206).[15] Most often a male occupation, sowing had undoubtedly been more widespread in Norway than in Iceland. More congruent with Icelandic nature are references to digging and fertilizing the home field. The connection between manure (*tað*) and hay (*taða*) suggests that even grass had to be coaxed into existence by human efforts (*Gg* 1b:89).[16] Manure was so important that it was included in property divisions (*Gg* 1b:106). Produced both by humans and animals, it was collected and stored on farms during the winter. Men spread cow dung on the home field as fertilizer for the rich grasses that, dried as hay, fed the animals during winter. Scattered randomly by sheep and cows in the pastures, manure also increased summer grazing. As trees disappeared, sheep dung was used for fuel. These details point to the overwhelming importance of animal husbandry for the Icelandic economy.

Left on their own, animals will wander wherever they find food. To preserve property rights to animals and land, men branded beasts and built fences. Numerous chapters in the law dealt with these activities, which are largely ignored by saga authors. Cattle, sheep, pigs, and even birds were to be clearly identified with the owner's mark (*einkunn; Gg* 1b: 154–55, 159). To be legally accepted, a fence had to be built of stone and turf; it should taper from five feet at the ground to three feet at the top, reaching the shoulder of a full-grown man, and it should be furnished with gates at the crossing of roads. Fence building was so important and time-consuming that the law specified three months of the summer as fence season (*garðǫnn; Gg* 1b:90–91, 2:450–51). Fences also enclosed haystacks to protect against men, animals, and weather (*Gg* 1b:97–98).[17]

Despite these efforts, animals still strayed and hay was scattered by wind and water. The law allowed farmers to build a "starvation pen" (*sveltikví*) for animals belonging to others, thus separating them until fetched by their owners (*Gg* 1b:118–19). Left on their own most of the year, sheep were rounded up from the mountains in the fall and brought down to a common pen. Owners sorted them, the new lambs accompanying their mothers (*Gg* 1b:155–56). In case "the ocean, water or bad weather" caused hay harvested by one farmer to be mixed with that of others, the law offered elaborate provisions for retrieval (*Gg* 1b:106–7).

The mountains, islands, and coastlines provided other resources for work and income, and the law specified tasks that involved cutting brush and wood, producing charcoal, fishing and collecting eggs, as well as reaping the bounty of winds and waves. Taking the worker far away from home and demanding physical energy beyond the capacity of most women, these tasks were—and still are—most often performed by men.[18]

Masculine activities can be sorted out by examining the Christian Law section of *Grágás*. Imposing a period of rest from Saturday afternoon through Sunday, churchmen specified the tasks which were permitted during this time and the longer holy seasons of Christmas and Easter. Among chores specifically or most likely reserved for men but dependent on the season, were the driving of the animals to and from pastures and grazing areas and the cleaning of the stalls during the long Christmas holiday. Permission to fish and hunt after mass, provided that one fifth of the catch was given to the church within a week, was also accorded to men, although the sagas occasionally refer to women fishing.[19] Emergency measures to restore damages by fire, floods, and shipwreck were also, not surprisingly, granted.[20] Men's work out of doors (*fyrir útan stokk*) therefore involved the fundamental tasks of subduing, taming, and exploiting the harsh Icelandic nature.

Women Sharing the Male Domain

The observation that men's work involved outdoor tasks should not lead one to conclude that women's domain was confined entirely to the indoors. The basic distinction between male and female work was that men exploited nature directly, bringing back grain and hay, slaughtered animals, fish and eggs, whereas women's work primarily consisted of processing and converting the results of male work for short-term consumption and long-term preservation. Some of these tasks were performed outdoors, others inside the house.

In addition to the obvious indoor tasks, the secular law added that the wife also was in charge of dairy operations (*smala nyt; Gg* 1b:44, 2:173). During winter, when animals were kept on the farm, milking took place in the barn. During summer they were sent to pastures in the mountains and uplands, tended by a shepherd and women, sometimes including the housewife herself. Living in cottages or shielings, the women milked the animals and preserved the surplus in various dairy foods.

Specifying tasks allowed during holy days, the Christian Law likewise drew attention to everyday functions performed in and around the house. It confirmed the secular law designation of milking as female work by allowing women (*konur*) to transport milk and to prepare dairy products (*Gg* 1a:23, 2:28).[21] Itemizing other chores permitted on Saturday afternoon, Sunday, and holy days, the law either employed the passive mode or referred in the active voice to "person" in the singular or plural (*maðr* or *menn*), terms that did not exclusively imply the male sex but were used for women as well (including pregnant women). Only the terms *karl* and *kona* ensure unambiguous gender specificity. Cross-cultural comparisons suggest, however, that in addition to milking, Icelandic women were also allowed on holidays to make fire, butcher slaughtered animals, cook, brew beer, dry and mend clothes, and pick small amounts of berries for immediate consumption (*Gg* 1a:23–24, 2:28, 32).[22]

Work was conditioned by the social status of both genders. The lower a woman's position, the harder her work, which doubtless included male tasks. It is perhaps no accident that the only recorded case of odor from perspiration due to physical work came from a female slave (*Gí* 6.27:85). In the everyday world of the sagas women were, in fact, involved in practically all outdoor tasks, including animal husbandry. Except for milking, animals were normally tended by men; cattle and sheep may have been relatively small in Iceland, but they could be strong and dangerous.[23] Male shepherds were therefore normally in charge of the pastures, but an occasional shepherdess can be found.[24] A very young girl (*meystelpa*) in charge of cattle belonging to two brothers, for example, was bullied by their neighbor (*St* 1:182).[25] Women and young girls also helped men drive animals and herd them into pens.[26] A woman supervised the task of channeling a stream under the house (*Hrð* 13.31:77). The law specified as male tasks the pulling ashore (*skipsdráttr*) and launching (*framdráttr*) of a boat. All farmers from the neighborhood were to appear with their workmen (*húskarlar*), but one saga episode shows women from the shipowner's farm pulling with the men.[27]

In poor families women also participated in field work during harvest. As men cut, women raked and turned the grass to dry it before the hay was tied, stacked, and stored by men. Recall, too, the mother who nursed a swaddled child as she raked behind her scything husband (*St* 1:221).[28] In wealthier families women were not expected to help with the harvest; they remained at home doing other work (*Gí* 6.9:30). During his final night, Gunnarr was alone with his wife and mother while the rest of the household was away for the hay harvest (*heyverk*; *Nj* 12.76–77:185–91; see also 68:169). As a result of continued viking activities, women became familiar with men's work; when husbands went away, they placed their wives in charge with confidence. Authors employ the formulaic refrain: the wives "managed farm and children" (*varðveita bú ok børn*).[29]

The Female Domain

Gathering. Included in the exploitation of nature were not only agriculture and animal husbandry but also gathering. These three stages—gathering and hunting, animal husbandry, and agriculture—illustrate the chronological development of the economic life of a culture accompanied by decreasing female involvement. Anthropologists have shown that in gathering and hunting societies the activity of gathering is nutritionally more important than that of hunting; furthermore, it is clear from cross-cultural comparisons that gathering has been dominated by women. Particularly important in Iceland during the period of settlement, gathering continued to provide calories and vitamins to the daily diet. Churchmen were aware of its importance, considered it work, and included it among the chores prohibited on Sunday.[30] The law does not allow a clear gender distinction between these tasks, but scattered references in the sagas confirm the suggestion from cross-cultural comparisons that women were in charge of collecting berries, mosses, angelica, seaweed, and eggs from birds nesting in meadows, whereas male physical strength was required to handle the occasional stranded whale and to fetch bird and eggs from the cliffs.[31] Narratives and legal texts pay scant attention to collecting berries, but the carving up of stranded whales and the distribution of other (heavy) beachfalls provided opportunities for disputes among men, which in due course generated legal provisions and left traces in the narratives.[32] Since the results of women's gathering were less spectacular or exceptional, disputes (if any) did not result in feuds and law cases, and their activities merited neither recording in narratives nor legal enactment.

Dairy Work. The primary responsibility of women in animal husbandry was milking, an activity that brought them out of doors much of the year. Pastured in the uplands and on islands during the summer, sheep and cattle required continual attention.[33] Often the whole family moved to the pasture (*í sel*) with the animals, necessitating a trek from the regular farm (*vetrhús*) to primitive shielings in the mountains for a period of three to four months.[34] In more important families the housewife accompanied a shepherd (*smalamaðr*) in the uplands while her husband was away at the alþingi.[35] One woman thus produced twins and "returned home with the boys at night" (*Svf* 9.12:153). In another case a twelve-year old girl gave birth to an illegitimate son in the pastures.[36] Children were apparently socialized to their adult roles early; a wife could be found in the pastures with two young daughters while her husband stayed at home with two sons, of whom the youngest was nine (*Hǫv* 3.12: 248–49).[37]

Milking was done at least once every twenty-four hours. The women went to the cows in the pastures, but the ewes were herded inside movable pens by the shepherd (*smalamaðr*).[38] By the mid–fifteenth century milking had become professionalized, and three women would be expected to milk eighty ewes and twelve cows a day.[39] The law that allowed women to transport milk and dairy products on Sundays was a necessity resulting from the shieling's size. Consisting of sleeping quarters (*svefnsel*) and a small shed (*búr; Lx* 5.55:166), the shieling provided facilities only for separating the milk into curds (*skyr*) and whey (*sýra*); hard cheese and butter were produced on the farm.[40]

Laundry and Bathing. Washing clothes also brought women outside. As in all preindustrial societies, laundry was done in streams, which were often distant from the house.[41] The hot springs and warm streams found frequently in the country made laundry less of a chore than elsewhere, and it was inevitably combined with baths. Saturday was variously referred to as "bath day" (*laugardagr*) or "laundry day" (*þváttdagr*). Hot water made it possible to wash clothes year round, thus facilitating the apparent custom of a wife presenting her husband and sons with clean shirts on Sunday morning (*Hǫv* 3.12:249). As suggested by this detail and confirmed by episodes depicting women washing linen out of doors, washing was a female task.[42] A brief mention of a lost shirt furnishes the incidental information that "the women had forgotten it in the wash" (*St* 1:381). The sagas offer occasional glimpses of the laundry implements, such as the bat (*vífl*). Normally it was used to beat the clothes, but it caught the saga author's attention only when it was picked up by a man to defend himself against an attacker (*Rkd* 10.22:220). At times washing could also be dangerous for women. When a wife broke her foot washing her linen in a brook, her husband commemorated the place by building a church (*Flm* 13.35: 325–26). Later accounts report women losing their lives while washing.[43]

Wet clothes needed to be dried, of course, a process that depended on good weather and contraptions — poles and lines — for hanging. The latter were especially necessary during the process of fulling and drying the woven cloth before it was cut for clothing. Sunshine was always useful, but clothes were hung outside all year round on poles or beams erected near the washing places. It is symptomatic of the male focus of the narratives that drying scenes concerning the nature-given conditions of weather are rare and include references to women (or miracles), while scenes involving men and poles are more frequent, not merely because the men erected or repaired the contraptions but because they at times found them useful for more violent purposes.[44]

Hot springs and streams invited bathing while washing clothes. Often designating both functions, the word bath (*laug*) is found in numerous place-names. The Icelanders were proud of their bathing culture. Describing a bath arranged for the Norwegian king, one author commented condescendingly that a bathtub (*kerlaug*) was necessary "because no other facilities for bathing (*annarra lauga kostr*) existed in Norway" (*BHd* 3.9:133).[45] The baths provided plentiful opportunities for socializing, as women came to wash clothes and men to bathe.[46] Bringing her wash, the beautiful Sigríðr met her two suitors at the bath (*Þhr* 14.3:176, 5:185).[47]

The bathing and washing culture is far more developed and more frequently mentioned in the contemporary sagas than in the sagas of Icelanders. From the beginning the settlers had utilized the hot streams and springs, but their thirteenth-century descendants had learned to exploit this unusual natural resource far more efficiently. Given the nature of the sources, they do not necessarily reflect a precise historical development of this technological improvement, but they do demonstrate that the authors of the sagas of Icelanders were aware of recent progress. They themselves enjoyed the relatively sophisticated bathing facilities described in the contemporary sagas, and they do not credit their ancestors with an equally advanced technique.[48] This observation is all the more pertinent because comments about bathing would seem to belong to the casual and inadvertent details normal in the detailed narratives of the sagas of Icelanders but easily obscured in the rapid pace of *Sturlunga saga*. The frequency of such comments in the contemporary sagas compared to their relative scarcity in the sagas of Icelanders suggests, in fact, that the authors of the latter genre are reporting an actual historical change.

In the contemporary narratives a broad distinction can be made between two words for bath, *laug* and *bað*. People generally rode on horseback to the "bath" (*laug*), thus giving rise to the term "bath travel" (*laugarfǫr*), whereas the local "bath" (*bað*) was on the premises of the farm.[49] Shelters were built near the distant bath (*laug*) and served not only visiting bathers and washing women but also transients.[50] The numerous hot springs allowed many farms to have a bath nearby, around which a shelter was built either as a separate building or an addition to the back of the main house (*St* 1:366). The terms "bath" (*bað*) and "bath room" (*baðstofa*) seem to have been used interchangeably; the latter only rarely implied the steam of the sauna.[51] Requiring a fire, the normal sauna may have created difficulties in Iceland as wood became scarce, but steam could be generated by throwing the natural boiling water from the springs directly on stones.[52] Although steam baths were eventually abandoned, the term baðstofa continued for the bath and later the living room, as people retreated to this heated area of the house.[53]

Known by any of the variants for bath, the facilities not only promoted hygiene and contributed a sense of well-being in a cold climate, but, like swimming pools in modern Iceland, they also served as sites for political deals and gossip. Unarmed only in the bath, men were occasionally wounded or even dragged out and killed.[54] Given the preoccupations of *Sturlunga saga*, it is not surprising that the bath scenes included mainly men, although a few passages suggest that men and women bathed together.[55] Specifying penalties for adultery, Bishop Árni Þorláksson's penitential of 1269 warned against bað and laug (DI 2:40), but certainly working women combined washing clothes and bathing.[56] Bathing occurred usually after the evening meal; it had become so routinized that the time after dinner was referred to simply as bathtime (*baðferð; Bs* 1:849).[57]

INDOOR WORK

The main preparation and preservation of the farm's resources was done inside the house (*fyrir innan stokk*). Aimed at providing bodily comfort, these endeavors also included grooming, as well as the preparation of food and clothing for immediate consumption as well as later export, and long-term cooking and preservation of edibles. Given the male perspective that dominates all genres, it is not surprising that the sources provide little information about these activities. Close attention to inadvertent details nevertheless reveals at least an outline of women's domestic work and sheds light on gender differences. In three areas women contributed direct service to others: grooming, preservation and cooking of food, and production of cloth and clothing. The last activity also had far-flung consequences for the Icelandic economy.

Body Service

Washing of hair was located at the interstices between laundering and bathing, work and pleasure, indoors and outdoors. In the saga world it was performed only by women for men, children, and themselves individually, but not for other women, if we trust the silence of the narratives on this point. Noted relatively frequently in the sagas of Icelanders, hair washing took place mainly out of doors, whereas — reflective of recent comfort — the single occurrence mentioned in *Sturlunga saga* located it in the heated house (*eldahús;* 2: 101). The most famous hair-washing scene was a love token (*Vgl* 14.18:98), but normally the task was simply a domestic chore performed by wives for their husbands (*Ljs* 10.14[24]:77), housewives for their male assistants (*Hðv* 3.21: 273), or mothers for their children (*BHd* 3.33:205; *Svf* 9.2:131–32). When women were alone, they washed their own hair (*Dpl* 11.1:138; *Brð* 13.12:141). Women also attended men in the baths in the contemporary world, as suggested by an episode from one of the bath scenes in *Sturlunga saga* where a man asked the woman who was drying him also to rub his itching neck (2:97).[58]

Female help in washing and bathing, however, represents only the most visible evidence of a large number of personal services which women rendered to others. Men were the primary beneficiaries, but well-to-do housewives also enjoyed the privilege. Covered by the verb "to serve" (*þjóna*), the work included every imaginable body service a woman could provide, including sexual availability. A wife was supposed to care for her husband as well as visiting guests.[59] At the simplest level women waited on men at table (*HrF* 11.3:

104). As wives and mothers, women served meals to their families, and, as in many traditional societies, they did not take seats themselves except on special occasions such as weddings.[60]

An important service consisted of helping people in and out of clothes. Particularly appreciated in a wet and cold climate, this was performed for women as well as for men. Undressing her mistress Jórunn, the slave Melkorka gets into a fight with her (*Lx* 5.13:27–28).[61] The woman was to be available at all hours. A father promised his daughter that she could stay close to him day and night and thereby avoid Hákon, a visiting suitor whom she had been assigned to attend (*þjóna; Vgl* 14.13:87). The sexual service implied in this story is revealed openly by the jealousy that provokes Loðinn to attack the visitor whom his bedmate Sigríðr had attended in this way (*Ftb* 6.21–2:225–28). Recall also the consummated affair between the mute Oddný and the visiting Ívarr whom she had been assigned to serve against her will (*Þux* 13.3:346–47). Not all men demanded sexual service, of course, but even a bishop appreciated a massage on sore spots (*Bs* 1:462). A direct body service was rendered by the woman Hallfríðr who warmed Gizurr between her thighs after he had spent several hours shivering in a tub of cold whey (*St* 1:493).[62]

The sewing up of men's sleeves was a little observed chore that medieval Icelandic women shared with their Continental sisters. Until the middle of the fourteenth century, when a new fashion, perhaps inspired from men's plate armor, created the inserted sleeve and replaced the older T-shaped style, sleeves were wide, and since they were rarely buttoned, they needed to be sewn close to the wrists to provide maximum warmth and freedom to work. This task was performed by women morning and night. Thus the young and beautiful wife of the captain sews Grettir's sleeves. Showing his gratitude in two stanzas, he thanks her for helping him overcome his laziness and enabling him to work (*Gr* 7.17:53–54; str. 15, 16). After a bath on New Year's Eve in 1241 Gizurr got dressed and "let himself be sewn by the wrists" (*lét sauma at hǫndum sér; St* 1:458).[63]

Always rendered but rarely mentioned, these services may explain the large number of nameless women whose presence is assumed in the saga pages. Their work was taken so much for granted that it is often expressed anonymously and indirectly: "clothes were taken off" or "food was carried in."[64] Doing their menial jobs and causing trouble neither among themselves nor for the men, these women are nearly invisible among the male actors of the sagas.

Food Preparation and Storage

Relatively little is known about food.[65] Describing the native Iceland of Bishop Guðmundr, his biographer Abbot Arngrímr mentions that "grain grows a few places in the south, but only barley. The normal food consists of fish caught in the ocean and animal products" (*Bs* 2:5). I follow this tripartite division in an examination of the production of grain, the catch of fish, and the yield from animals in the form of dairy products and meat.

Grain. Scarcity of grain meant that in Iceland, unlike in continental Europe, bread never became a staple. It was in fact so rare that people dreamt about it (*ÞSH* 11.5:314–15), and one man received the nickname "Butter-Ring" (*smjǫr-hringr*) from his favorite food of bread and butter (*Rkd* 10.12:181).[66] Scarcity of grain and ovens made flat bread the preferred form in most of the north, but even in this form it never became important in the Icelandic diet.[67] Grain was instead diluted in gruel and porridge, probably the most important food on ocean travel and a preferred dish for elderly (toothless) people.[68] The requisite grinding is never mentioned in the narratives and can be inferred only from the millstones specified in charters and found on archaeological sites. Poetic sources suggest that grinding was a task performed by lower-class women.[69]

Grain was also used for brewing. Requiring fire and the warmth of the kitchen, brewing was allowed even during the Christmas holiday. Traditionally, women have been associated with this work and it remained a female task throughout the medieval period. In one of the heroic sagas a king resolved the jealousy between his two wives by deciding to keep the one who presented him with the better beer on his return from war (*HáH*, FSN 2.1:95). As late as the end of the fourteenth century a laysister was superintendent of brewing in Vadstena, a Swedish monastery that accommodated men and women.[70] Describing a brewing in honor of Bishop Páll, a vignette states specifically that the housewife was in charge.[71] On important farms the physical work needed for large quantities may have demanded male help, as suggested from a brief glimpse at the farm at Stafaholt where the female housekeeper (*húsfreyja*), assisted by the male manager (*ræðismaðr*), replenished the stores of beer depleted by the visit of fourteen unexpected guests (*St* 2:129).[72] Consumed at the alþingi, beer was commonly brewed on the spot, but there the quantities demanded and the scarcity of women made it a male task.[73] Mentioned rarely in the sagas, brewing was a difficult process and occasionally required divine assistance mediated through miracles credited to Icelandic bishops.

Fish. Fish was extremely important in the daily diet. Abundantly available in streams, lakes, and the ocean, fish had attracted the first settlers (*Lx* 5.2:5). Preserved by drying and known as *skreið*, it was used year round, and its consumption increased when Christian fasting rules were accepted.[74] Dried fish was stored inside the house, and extra supplies kept on islands.[75] Despite its dietary importance, fish rarely is mentioned in the narratives, perhaps because fishing and hunting took place in the wild rather than in the controlled environment of the farm.[76] Until the early twentieth century farming remained the preferred and idealized way of life, and fishing was merely tolerated in silence.[77] Although held in contempt, men's fishing was as economically indispensable as women's work, but, like the latter, it was not considered memorable.[78] Perhaps reflecting everyday life more accurately, the miracles attributed to Icelandic bishops include frequent references both to fishing and female chores.[79]

It is more surprising that the sources rarely reveal disputes generated on fishing expeditions. Performed from small boats by the same men who became irate on land when their neighbor's animals strayed onto their property, fishing would surely be expected to engender disputes. On the larger viking boats occasional tension did occur.[80] The intensity of the work, however, the small size of the boats and crew, and the vast expanse as well as the unpredictability of the ocean may have tempered conflict. A further reason for the relative calm is suggested by the author of *Laxdœla saga* who, in a rare reference to a populous and rewarding fishing station, commented that "wise men thought it very important that people got along well in fishing stations, because it was believed that men would lose their fishing luck if they quarreled" (*Lx* 5.14:29).[81] It is hard to believe that men never fought while fishing, but disputes were not remembered after landing and thus did not become the stuff of stories. Disputes did not enter the law, which further suggests that they were minor. Once off the boat, however, men fought over the division of the catch (as detailed immediately after the comment in *Lx*), the division of stranded whales, and the burden of launching or pulling up the boats.[82]

Dairy Products and Meat. Hard as a board, dried fish was softened by being beaten and was served with butter.[83] The results of long processes of preserving milk, butter and cheese were accepted by lay and ecclesiastical authorities as payment of rent.[84] Heavily salted, butter could be kept for decades; large stores were accumulated, like gold, by wealthy landowners. By the time of the Reformation the bishopric in Hólar possessed a mountain of butter calculated to weigh twenty-five tons.[85] Further down the preservation process were various soft cheeses and the ubiquitous curds. The remaining whey was not discarded but used either as a beverage or a preservative.[86] Although scarcely mentioned, the fabrication of these dairy products was clearly women's work.

In Iceland, dairy food nevertheless enjoyed higher prestige than meat, as suggested by a scene in *Njála*. During "a great famine" people lacked both "hay and food [*hey ok mat*]."[87] Having shared his stores with others, Gunnarr has difficulty in obtaining new supplies either by purchase or gift when his own supply runs out. The next summer—before the harvest was in—Gunnarr's wife Hallgerðr sends a servant to steal food, specifying that she wants butter and cheese.[88] Suspicious of the provenance of these products on his table, Gunnarr orders them removed and replaced with meat (*slátr; Nj* 12.47–48:121–28). In times of need, therefore, grain and its products—gruel, bread, and beer—vanished from the menu. The necessities of life were reduced to "food" (*matr,* a general term) for humans and hay and grass for animals. When animals were fed, butter and cheese were available. With insufficient fodder, however, the only matr was meat, for it became necessary to slaughter (*slátra*) the animals and consume the meat (*slátr*) directly. For people on the move, however, meat was more usual and valued than dairy products. Providing prolonged sustenance and always fresh and available on the hoof, it was consumed in large quantities by the bands of men who devastated the countryside during the political turmoil of the Sturlung age.[89]

Cooking. Once processed, dairy foods, the indirect benefit of animals, needed little preparation and cooking, in contrast to direct products such as meat from cows, sheep, and—until prohibited by churchmen—horses. Men slaughtered the animals (*Krm* 8.4:216), but women cut up the meat, at times spending most of the night at the task (*Hǫv* 3.19:272, 23:281). Cooking followed techniques and employed utensils that changed little over time. A comparison between the kitchen equipment buried with the woman entombed in the Oseberg burial in Norway in August or September 834 and the household recommendations of 1585 by the Swedish Count Per Brahe for his wife shows remarkable little change over a span of seven centuries.[90] As suggested by these two sources, cooking remained women's business. When Gunnarr—in the scene just examined—asks his wife where she obtained the butter and cheese, she tells him not to worry because "it is not for men to get mixed up in the preparation of food" (*Nj* 12.48:124). Scenes showing women preparing food are nevertheless rare. Only a few cooking episodes involving females surface in the sagas and the use of fire is not certain.[91] Men, assigned by lot, did their own cooking when women were absent, as for example on board ship and abroad, at the alþingi, or at games. The overwhelming male perspective of the narratives accounts for the anomalous fact that more scenes show men cooking than women.[92] As was the case with fishing, scenes evoked in the miracles attributed to Icelandic bishops were most likely closer to everyday life than the sagas, and the former invariably depict women in charge of preparing food.[93]

A unique passage in the *Staðarhólsbók* version of *Grágás* states that three buildings on a farm were protected against fire through insurance paid by the community, the hall (*stofa*), the heated room (*eldhús*), and "the room in which women prepare food" (*búr þat er konor hafa matreiðo í; Gg* 2:260).[94] It is not entirely clear what room is meant by the last statement. It would seem fitting to prepare food in the room where the fire was kept (*eldhús*), but the room (*búr*) most often referred to in connection with food is the outside storage room (*útibúr*). Cooking and storing food require hot and cold temperatures, respectively. It is likely that food already prepared, such as cheese, curds, and cooked or cured meat and fish, was served directly from the pantry. Perhaps in connection with the slaughtering season, dishes in need of cooking were occasionally prepared in a special house referred to in some texts as a cooking house (*soðhús*), where meat was cooked in a pot (*soðketill*).[95] A more general use of fire is suggested by the term "house with a fire" (*eldhús*), also a separate building.[96] A scene in a contemporary saga shows a couple busy "doing the cooking outside at night in the house equipped with fire" (*úti í eldahúsi um nótt at soðningu; St* 2:91).[97] Other texts mention a pantry (*matbúr*) connected to the main house. It seems probable that the fire needed for preparing food was found in or near this room.[98]

Fire was required not only for cooking but also for warmth and for drying clothes and people. Under normal circumstances embers were kept over night, but in times of turmoil the fire was extinguished to prevent, or at least discourage, arsonists, who—prepared for this eventuality—often brought their own torches or added tar from containers to set fire to buildings more readily.[99] Since ignition was not easy, embers from existing fires were likewise welcomed.

These and other references to fire clarify the problem of where the cooking took place. The texts distinguish between the plural long fires (*langeldar*) and the singular meal fire (*máleldr*). The former consisted of large fires built in the middle of the room. Soaked by rain as they traveled home from the alþingi, Hǫskuldr and Hrútr were grateful for Þjóstólfr's langeldar at Lundr where they stopped for the night (*Nj* 12.8:28).[100] The difference between the long fire and the meal fire is particularly well illustrated in several scenes of *Eyrbyggja saga*. The smaller meal fire was built in the evening near suppertime, often in a different room from the one that (on other occasions) held the long fire. People sat by the fire a long time before eating, since the hearth served not only to warm people and to prepare food, but also to provide light. Stones heated in the flames were used to warm milk and other liquids.[101] In a scene describing Snorri and his men "sitting by the meal fire" (*máleldr*) at his farm, one manuscript substitutes "by the dining table" (*yfir matborði; Erb* 4.26:66). The large fire and the small meal fire, as well as references to heating stones and "other benefits of the fire," occur in the text during the ghost episode at Snorri's sister's farm at Fróðá (*Erb* 52:145; 54:148–49).[102] The food was most likely taken from the adjacent pantry (*matbúr*), cooked on the meal fire in the presence of the entire household, and perhaps brought back to the pantry for final serving.[103]

The use of stones for heating milk calls attention to the scarcity of vessels suitable for heating over fire. It is all the more surprising, therefore, that meat was not roasted but boiled. When reporting that a group of brigands roasted a cow directly on the fire, the author (Sturla Þórðarson) explained this unusual procedure by the absence of a kettle (*St* 1:211). Boiling required large containers. The kettle from which the hapless Sǫlvi had just lifted boiled meat was so large that when he was thrown head first into the still boiling soup, he died instantly (*Nj* 12.145:407).[104] Kettles obviously were precious. Forming part of a wife's dowry, a particularly fine specimen caused trouble for the husband who parted with it.[105]

The Storage Room (Útibúr). Quotidian, regular, and usually performed by women, cooking rarely attracted the attention of saga writers. They refer much more frequently to the útibúr, not because of its accustomed purpose of storing food and raw materials for cooking—the domain of the women—but because as the only locked room on the farm it also contained other valuables entirely under male jurisdiction and served the political function of sheltering people on the run.

In addition to the general word "storage room" more specialized uses were implied by *gervibúr, sǫðlabúr, matbúr,* and *skyrbúr.* Originally the "war room" (*gervibúr*) stored gear and clothing associated with warfare (*gervi* or *gǫrvi*). Securing war equipment may have been the original motive for locking a room, but this purpose was served only in times of relative peace; when trouble was expected, weapons had to be ready at hand. Through Gróa's foresight all shields were taken from the storage area (*útibúr*) and brought inside the house the evening before the unexpected attack and arson on Flugumýrr in 1253 (*St* 1:487). As indicated by the first half of the word, the "saddle room" (*sǫðlabúr*) stored saddles, but eventually both gervibúr and sǫðlabúr, as well as the more general útibúr, came to designate places where foreign merchants kept their merchandise both for display and for safety.[106] Icelanders themselves also stored valuables other than food in this area. Illugi was surprised to see his storeroom opened and a number of rolls of cloth and pack cushions taken out (*Gnl* 3.4:59). Ropes and sharpening stones were stored in there, and, in one case, corpses.[107] Merchandise and food could be stolen from a storehouse even when guarded by a slave (*Hrð* 13.27:68). Occasionally equipped with a window, the "pantry" (*matbúr*) and "curd room" (*skyrbúr*) referred to storage rooms for food in general (matr) and curds (skyr) in particular.[108] On large farms the production of curds was sufficiently specialized to require its own locale. Such a skyrbúr might have a southern exposure, as indicated by the term "southern room" (*suðrbúr*), suggesting that the sun's heat was used to further fermentation. Different containers (*skyrker* and *sýruker*) stored the curds and whey and were large enough to hide a man.[109]

On smaller farms the pantry stored all kinds of food, as demonstrated by

Otkell's storage house from which Hallgerðr orders her slave to steal butter and cheese (*Nj* 12.48:123). This room was probably a wing of the farmhouse, since the owner attributes the fire—started by the thief to hide his crime—to the fact that the area is attached to the heated part of the house (*eldhús*).[110] In most cases the pantry was a separate house standing at some distance from the main buildings and guarded in times of trouble.[111] Built on high, dry sites as befitted the preservation of food, the storage houses in the Norse colonies in Greenland still survive as visible ruins.[112] In the Icelandic narratives the best-equipped storage house belonged to Atli in Otradalr who "owned a large pantry stocked with all kinds of good things. In it were large piles and all kinds of meat, dried fish, and cheeses and everything that anyone could wish" (*Hsí* 6.15:342).[113] Atli was so fond of this place that he and his wife slept there every night.[114]

To be safe for valuables, the storage room was locked. The person possessing the know-how could lock (*læsa*) and unlock (*upp lúka*) the room; other people used force to break it open (*brjóta upp*).[115] Traditional notions of housewives in charge of food supplies may conjure up images of women with rings of keys at their belt, but few passages confirm such impressions. A single reference to storage-room keys (*búrluklar*) seems more rhetorical than real: in 1242 a woman attempted to goad her reluctant husband to join her brother in an action of revenge by threatening to take up arms herself and offering him the keys instead (*St* 2:6).[116] References to keys involve only the locking of trunks of foreign origin.[117] Storage rooms seem rather to have been secured with a latch (*láss*) that only authorized people knew how to open; having learned it, they did not forget. Otherwise it is difficult to explain the scene in which Hallgerðr's slave, who earlier had been in Otkell's service, opened (*lauk upp*) the pantry of his former master (*Nj* 12.48:123). It is unlikely that he would have been allowed to keep a key.

In this case a slave had access to the storage room; in another instance the prestigious housekeeper (*matselja*) was asked to carry a light and open up the pantry (*búr*), "the only locked room (*hús*) on the farm," for those who came to make a legal search (*rannsaka*; *Erb* 4.20:51). The husband and wife also had access to the storage area, but since narrators were more interested in the fugitives occasionally kept safe inside than in the food, men more often than women are seen locking and unlocking the door. This detail may imply more than narrative focus, however, because it is a mistake to assume that women were in sole charge of the distribution of food. Men seem to have had at least as much to say about supplies; they kept extra stores of dried fish and flour on islands and brought them to the farm only as needed (*Nj* 12.11:34). Husbands, not wives, were likewise in charge of inviting guests to banquets and feasts.[118]

As the sole part of the farm that could be secured, the storage room provided safety for fugitives, a privilege granted by both male and female owners to favorites. The sheep barn (*sauðahús*) occasionally served the same purpose, but since it could not be locked, it was not as effective.[119] The most notorious fugitive in the narrative corpus is the Norwegian merchant Gunnarr found in several sagas.[120] In his first appearance, he is sitting in a storage room (*útibúr*) in which his merchandise is kept (264). Earning his nickname Þiðrandabani from the name of a man (Þiðrandi) he killed, he spends the next years as a fugitive. During the first winter he is hidden by two brothers in their goat shed (*geitahús*) in the mountains (202, 267-70). Forced to leave, he is then sheltered by Sveinungr and barely escapes after close encounters with his pursuers (203–7, 273-81). The following winter Helgi Ásbjarnarson gives him refuge in his storage room, in charge of which he places his wife during his absence. She not only feeds Gunnarr in his confinement but also manages to foil her brother's threat to "break open the pantry if you will not unlock it" (207-9, 282-85). Only Helgi's friend Guðrún Ósvífrsdóttir dares to give Gunnarr access to the house (209-10, 286-88).[121]

Wives also used the storage rooms to shelter relatives, and a few women in flight themselves benefited from the facility. Having placed her distant relative Þórólfr inside her pantry, the forceful Vigdís locks it and keeps him there for the winter despite her husband's disapproval (*Lx* 5.14:31).[122] On a lighter note, Steingerðr's father locks her inside the pantry to protect her from Kormákr's advances (*Krm* 8.5:218). Architectural details suggest that refuge was as important as food storage. The útibúr that a mother used as a place of safe-keeping for her son is described as an earth-house (*jarðhús*), standing in the middle of the homefield (*tún*) and half buried in the ground (*HrG* 8.2:322). An occasional log cabin (*stokkabúr*) built of horizontal logs undoubtedly afforded more protection than the ordinary turf building.[123]

A spectacular game of hide-and-seek staged in a storage room saved Gizurr Þorvaldsson from certain death. Gizurr celebrated the marriage between his son Hallr and the young Ingibjǫrg at his farm Flugumýrr in October 1253. Four days later his enemies attacked. The men inside the farm defended themselves so valiantly that the attackers—fearing being trapped between the defenders and the men from the neighborhood coming to Gizurr's aid—resorted to fire. Although he suffered badly from smoke inhalation, Gizurr was determined not to leave the house and sought refuge in the curd room. He shed his armor and helmet but kept his sword and climbed into a tub full of whey. Dressed in underwear and immersed to his chest in the ice-cold liquid, he was hidden by the darkness and a sheltering curd vat (*skyrker*) on a rack above him. When a party of men with torches entered, looking for him and discussing the torture that awaited him, Gizurr deflected the pursuers' probes and suffered numerous but minor wounds. He later reported that before the search party had arrived, his shivers caused ripples in the whey, but at the height of danger he was calm

(*St* 1:492–93).[124] This episode appears in *Sturlunga saga,* but its arresting drama should not obscure the fact that the contemporary sagas offer few such cases in comparison to the sagas of Icelanders.[125] During the tumultuous events of the Sturlung age, when the country suffered near-civil war, the fragile storage room seldom provided sufficient protection. In another sign of improved technology noticeable in many areas, people learned to bolt the doors to their houses or in desperation chose churches as refuge, but both places could be breached by persistent pursuers.[126]

Wool

By preparing and preserving food, women served immediate short-term needs. Whatever time remained after these chores was spent on the preparation of thread, cloth, and clothes, endeavors with long-lasting effects not only for the immediate families but also for the economy of the entire society.[127]

The female role in Icelandic material culture is highlighted by the importance and ubiquitous presence of homespun (*vaðmál*) produced from sheep's fleece. Clothing the entire population from cradle to grave and even occasionally protecting sick animals, homespun was also used for bedding, sails, wall-hangings, packs, and sacks of all kinds.[128] Most impressive, it replaced silver as the standard commodity against which other products were evaluated within Iceland. As the country's exclusive export, it procured necessities and luxuries only available abroad. The result, the unique system of "the homespun standard," governed Icelandic economic life for centuries.[129] I deal with the latter issue in the subsequent chapter; here, I am concerned with the production of homespun.

It is characteristic of the male perspective of the sources that although references to homespun as units of value are ubiquitous and information about the quality and measurement of the export cloth are full and detailed — all areas under male jurisdiction — the narratives are all but silent on the essential preliminaries of spinning the thread and weaving the cloth. As in most comparable societies, these tasks were almost surely performed by women, but it is difficult to substantiate this premise in detail. The solitary tasks of spinning and weaving rarely led to conflicts, did not demand legal attention, and did not reach the ears of storytellers, and thus bequeathed nothing but silence to law and literature. Other steps in the wool production required cooperation mainly among female workers, but these tasks do not surface in the sources, either, again implying that women's disputes were considered unworthy of notice or perhaps even that women were less prone to quarrel over their work than men.[130]

Production of Cloth: Preliminary Steps. When settlers first arrived in Iceland they brought a few animals and limited supplies of food, clothing, weapons, and silver. With the food depleted before the clothes wore out, the two necessities of eating and keeping warm were accomplished sequentially but with an intervening delay, as men and women immediately set to fishing and gathering food, waiting for the domestic animals to proliferate sufficiently to contribute clothing as well as food. Skalla-Grímr, one of the first settlers, depended heavily on fishing and gathering because "in the beginning they had few animals compared to how many were needed, considering the number of humans" (*Eg* 2.29:75). Additional ships "laden with cattle" apparently arrived regularly (*Lnd* 1:235), and sheep and cattle reproduced quickly to provide dairy products, meat, skin, and raw wool in abundance.

Norwegian women brought to Iceland the age-old skills of spinning and weaving, which they had learned as children at home. Confident both of her own expertise and the availability of raw materials, one of the first female settlers refused to accept land as an uncompensated gift from a relative, but insisted on giving him "a spotted cloak and wanted to call it a purchase, thinking that it would strengthen the deal."[131] She and other women applied their craft to the first harvest of raw wool in Iceland and in the process taught their daughters the requisite steps to transform the fleece that had warmed the sheep to a form that could be shared by humans.[132]

The first task, to remove the wool from the backs of the sheep, was originally accomplished by plucking (*reyfa* or *rýja*) the fleece at the time of shedding, thus producing a "handful" (*reyfi*) of wool. The sheep were eventually sheared, and—if the animal was slaughtered immediately thereafter—a new product resulted, a shorn sheepskin (*klippingr*).[133] Rarely mentioned in the sources, this first task was undoubtedly performed—then as now—primarily by women, although men may have helped after they had driven the animals into the shearing pens.[134] The next step was to clean and wash the wool, a job never mentioned in medieval sources. In the twentieth century it was performed by women and children, using a mixture of water and urine.[135] This process produced the cleaned and dried but unspun wool (*tó*). To prepare this raw wool for spinning, it was worked or carded with fingers or a special comb (*ullkambr*), in order to straighten it and arrange the fibers in parallel strands.[136] If the spinning did not commence immediately, the prepared wool was kept in a wool basket (*ulllaupr*), such as the one in which Earl Sigurðr's mother sarcastically chided him that she would have kept him had she thought he would live forever (*Ork* 34.11:24).

The spinning required a simple tool, the distaff, consisting of two parts known as a *rokkr* and a *snælda,* terms also used interchangeably for the whole instrument. Rokkr does not refer to a spinning wheel, as implied by the equivalent terms in modern Scandinavian languages, but to a simple distaff or stick on which a bundle of wool was fastened. With this rokkr secured under her belt or arm, the woman had both hands free to pull out a thread and fasten it to the spindle (snælda). Twisting and turning the spindle as she threw it to the ground, she manipulated the thread as it came off the distaff and picked up the spindle on which she wound the length of thread, repeating these steps over again. Since the mechanism was easy to carry, women undoubtedly spun whenever their hands were free from other chores.[137]

Weaving. When enough thread had been spun, the weaving could commence. Again, the mechanism was simple.[138] The loom (*vefr* or *vefstaðr*) was the standing loom, the so-called warp-weighted loom, known throughout the world.[139] Leaning against the wall when in use and taken down afterwards, it consisted of two posts or uprights (*hleinar*), on top of which rested a crossbeam (*rifr*). On this was attached the warp (*varp* or *garn*), long threads weighted down with stones (*kljár*).[140] Secured through a hole in the weight and wound around it, each thread was kept straight, lengthening as the cloth grew. Toward the bottom of the posts (*hleinar*) a crossbar (*yllir*) separated the front and the back warp, each half consisting of every other thread. Halfway down the posts was a movable rod (*skapt*) connected with loops to the back threads. The crossbar thus created a space between the two layers through which the woman quickly passed the woof (*vipta*) attached to the shuttle (*hræll*), as she walked from one side of the loom to the other and alternated the position of the layers by moving the rod. The rod thus eliminated the painstaking task of plaiting the woof between the individual varp threads.[141] As the cloth was slowly woven from the top down, the space between the two layers of the warp also allowed for the insertion of a large beater (*skeið*), with which the woof was pushed in place. As it increased in length, cloth was rolled up on the crossbeam equipped with a handle for this purpose. The space between the beam and the roof rafters of the house would determine the possible length of the finished cloth.[142]

No medieval looms have survived intact, but reconstructions are possible from archaeological fragments and later drawings. The most detailed written information resides in literary descriptions of two imaginary looms, one allegedly worked by supernatural valkyries, as reconstructed in prose from a man's vision as well as narrated by the valkyries themselves in the famous poem *Darraðarljóð*, and another that a woman perceived in a dream.[143]

The scarcity of information about the loom and the weaving process is indicated by the fact that *Darraðarljóð* and the valkyrie vision not only contain the fullest account of the loom but also provide the most detailed evidence that weaving was women's work.[144] The poem recounts a battle in Ireland involving a young king and an earl. It is preserved in *Njáls saga* where the contextual prose connects it to the battle at Clontarf in 1014 (12.157:454–60).[145]

Valkyries traditionally were depicted as martial figures on horseback, hovering over men in battle as they determined winners and losers. This portrayal is seen, for example, in *Hákonarmál*, Eyvindr Finnsson's poem from the second half of the tenth century (see especially str. 10–11).[146] In a radical shift from this imagery, the poet of *Darraðarljóð* chose the metaphor of weaving as the vehicle for representing the valkyries' task of deciding warriors' fates in battle, a change that significantly domesticated and feminized the earlier masculine image.[147] Although no longer present at the scene, the valkyries were still in charge, as they wove men's destinies while the battle raged at a distance.

The crucial concept is the difficult expression "web of war" (*vefr darraðar*), which is repeated in the refrain "let us wind, let us wind / the web of war" (*vindum, vindum / vef darraðar;* str. 4, 5, 6). Outside the poem this kenning is found solely in Egill's poem "Head-Ransom" (*Hǫfuðlausn*), where it is used as a metaphor for the turmoil and confusion of battle (str. 5; 2.60:187). Although feminist scholars have preferred to interpret *Darraðarljóð* as evidence for the importance of weaving — perhaps even as a "work song," Klaus von See is undoubtedly correct in insisting that war and not weaving was the poem's salient concern.[148] It better fits the category of praise poems honoring rulers, in this case "the young king" (str. 4, 5, 10) present at the battle, than the virtually nonexistent genre of work songs. Von See's argument can be further corroborated by the number of valkyries present. Six are mentioned by name in the poem (str. 3, 5), but the man watching outside observed twelve.[149] Weaving is a solitary occupation. Although two women might alleviate the tedium of walking the shuttle back and forth, it is hard to see how six or, worse, twelve women could operate a single loom efficiently. But if several women attenuate the weaving metaphor, they enhance the battle's turmoil conjured by the kenning "web of war" (*vefr darraðar*). The use of the singular genitive (*darraðar*), which troubles von See, actually accentuates the image of confusion, as six or twelve weavers compete for just one *darraðr* (sword), here serving as the beater.[150]

It should also be noted that weaving on these looms was not a rhythmic activity that lent itself to a work song. Turning the beam as the cloth grew — the only heavy work for which the song could be used — surely did not occur often enough to insert the refrain three times within the poem. Von See points to incitement songs for men connected with battles and burnings. The apparently rhythmic encouragement and urging that a gang of men employed as they pulled a ship ashore further suggest that work songs also accommodate men's work.[151] Although the valkyries' role of deciding men's fate in war is feminized by the metaphor of the loom, the expression "web of war" (*vefr darraðar*) retains the ambience of battle. The rhythm inherent in the poem's meter and made audible through the valkyries' recitation further associate weaving not with solitary female work but with masculine cooperative work facilitated by song.[152]

Known in Iceland at least since 1200, *Darraðarljóð* was inscribed in *Njála*. In his narrative frame, the saga author indicates what he understands and tries to make the best of what he does not comprehend. He clearly grasps the function and operation of a loom but is puzzled by the expression "web of war" (*vefr darraðar*). Having described the battle of Clontarf in Ireland in detail and carefully dated it to Good Friday 1014, he adapts the enigmatic kenning and creates the otherwise unknown character, Dǫrruðr, a man allegedly living in Katanes (Caithnes) in Scotland at the time. Exiting his house early in the morning of the battle, Dǫrruðr notices twelve persons—their gender is not revealed—arriving on horseback and entering a *dyngja*, the term for women's quarters of a house and associated with weaving. As Dǫrruðr peered through the window, he ascertains that the riders are women now setting up a loom. Understanding its construction perhaps better than a modern reader, the prose author extracts the necessary information from the poem, as he describes the loom in the preceding prose. Woof and warp consist of men's entrails; the weighing stones are fashioned from men's heads; the shuttle is an arrow, and the beater a sword.[153] Having set up the loom, the women start to work, reciting the poem's eleven stanzas while Dǫrruðr listens and watches. Providing closure after the last stanza, the prose author describes how the valkyries—having finished their song presumably at the end of battle—pull the cloth from the loom and tear it to pieces, each carrying off her shred. They remount their horses and depart, six to the south and six north.[154]

The poem retains the horses, the valkyries' old accouterments from Eddic and skaldic poetry. Novel, but still befitting their traditional warlike role, are the loom's implements—arrow and spears—as well as the grisly products of war, male heads and entrails, from which the cloth is created. Consonant with the valkyries' ancient role is also the final act of shredding the cloth. Although retaining and enhancing the war attributes of the poem, the prose author accentuates the feminization of the valkyries suggested by their weaving. Removed from the battle and safely installed within the female quarters of the house, they first "set up their loom." Having finished, they take off the cloth and dismantle the implement. Although war still permeates the atmosphere, the radical shift from a masculine martial stance on horseback to a feminine posture at the loom is remarkable within the history of valkyrie representation. In effect *Darraðarljóð* pursues to a logical conclusion the image of the norns, who were female figures in control of the thread of fate. Attributed to the norns in Eddic poetry, the theme was also known from classical literature. If the norns decided on the length of a person's life by cutting thread at a pre-determined length, other similarly empowered women surely wove an equally fateful cloth.[155]

It is difficult to imagine a more powerful metaphor of complex gender relations than that created by the *Darraðarljóð* poet. Struck by its power but unable to understand it fully, the prose author of *Njála* further elaborated the image as he inscribed the poem into his narrative. The underlying concept is *de*struction in war both of and by men. War is not condemned, however, and the content of the woven cloth as well as its tearing at the end retain the notion of wartime devastation. The contrasting image of women's *con*struction through weaving is scarcely articulated. These valkyrie images were the last in a succession of representations of women as ancient supernatural powers. At first they were personified as goddesses and wise women, later as prominent women in male roles — the traditional valkyries on horseback and maiden warriors, for example — and now finally domesticated as weaving women.[156] The constructive activity of female weaving is undercut by the gruesome products of masculine destruction and amplified by the violent gesture of destroying the cloth at the end. The poem, particularly in its use in *Njála,* articulates a transition in the male imagination from the predominantly warlike conditions of the early viking age to a more settled life in the new colony where men habitually observed women at the loom.

Compared to these powerful mythical females involved in gruesome weaving, the few references to human women at the same task in ordinary settings are disappointing. Most important — because of its matter-of-fact nature — is a statement by Refr, a man of flowery and circumlocutionary language. Seeking to gain time to escape, Refr confesses to the king that he has killed a man and declares that he "cloth-worked (*váðvirkta*) him [the victim] at the end." Reflecting on the meaning of this and other bizarre expressions, the king recalls that this term was a "set phrase (*málsháttr*) in Iceland when women finish their web" (*KrR* 14.16:153, 17:155). The brevity of this remark reveals that weaving was so obviously female work that it needed no comment.[157]

Spinning and weaving had become professionalized as female occupations by the late Middle Ages. According to the fifteenth-century *Búalög* (household laws), a spinning woman was expected to process a pound (5.2 kg) of wool in a week and in the same period a weaver (*vefkona*) was to weave twenty-two ells of cloth. The women were not to be disturbed (*frátafin*) and could have a light if they desired.[158] As long as the vertical loom prevailed, women were undoubtedly in charge of weaving throughout Europe. When it was replaced with the horizontal loom, which was first introduced in Flanders during the twelfth century, men took over the profession. As the only kind available in Iceland until the late eighteenth century, the vertical loom assured female employment there, but when the new loom was introduced, its operation was taught and assigned chiefly to men.[159]

Fulling (þæfa). Much of the homespun was put to immediate use, but often the next step of fulling (*þæfa*) was needed. When the cloth was soaked and pressed in a mixture of fermented urine and hot water, the lanolin interacted with the ammonia, causing the fat to coagulate into a solid layer. The process shrank and tightened the cloth, making it stronger and warmer.[160] The result was the feltlike woolen cloth (*þófi*) particularly suited for coats (*þófastakkir*) and hoods (*þófahettir*). A common topos in the narratives is the magical coats and shirts provided by female magicians to protect their male favorites. The term *þófi* is not mentioned in connection with these garments, since it would have detracted from the sorceress' supernatural powers, but the belief in protective clothing may have its origins in this fabric.[161] By contrast, in the contemporary sagas where magic played a minor role, impregnability was directly attributed to the fulled cloth. The coat worn by Þorbjǫrn in a battle in 1234, for example, was specifically described as impenetrable and impossible to cut with a sword even when spread on a board (*St* 1:366).[162]

No reference to fulling exists in literature, beyond the mention of the need to wash and dry large pieces of cloth (*stórfǫt*), presumably after the fulling but before they had been cut for clothes or other purposes (*VGl* 9.26:88). According to the *Búalög*, fulling cloth was male work, and a man was expected to full twenty units (*voð*) a day.[163] During the final rinse of the fulling dye could be added. The cloth naturally reproduced the many shades of the sheep, ranging from white to black and including browns and grays. *Mórendr* (russet) was a technical term for the more expensive reddish homespun. Additional colors and shades could be added from the extracts of plants and roots.[164] Cloth of bright colors (*litklæði*), used primarily by men on special occasions, was of foreign origin.

With the sheep sheared, the wool washed and dried, the thread spun, and the cloth woven, fulled, and dyed, it is time now to look at the practical use — direct as well as indirect — of the homespun.

CHAPTER SIX

The Economics of Homespun

Although direct proof is scarce, few scholars doubt that women bore the chief responsibility for spinning and weaving in primitive societies, a conclusion supported by cross-cultural comparisons. Beginning in the late eleventh century, however, the upright loom, a fairly simple tool, was replaced in western Europe with the horizontal loom, a far more complicated instrument both to set up and to operate. This technological shift was accompanied by a change in gender, as women's domestic weaving on the old loom was replaced by professional weaving performed by men in urbanized capitalistic settings. In Iceland the horizontal loom was not introduced until the late eighteenth century. Until then, women were chiefly responsible for spinning and weaving. Naturally they continued to clothe their families and provide bedding and wall hangings for their houses throughout the entire period of domestic weaving, but for several centuries during the Middle Ages they also managed to produce large surpluses of the ubiquitous homespun, which was adopted as a standard measure of value. It was used as currency in Iceland and accepted abroad, where it was exchanged for supplies not available on the island. This sequence suggests the three phases in the consumption of cloth which I examine in turn: its primary use as protection against cold, its secondary function as a medium of exchange, and its ultimate role in export with the corollary requirement for standard measurements. Women's work naturally was the precondition for all three phases, and their contribution was most visible in the first. As in other traditional societies, however, economic policy and foreign trade in Iceland were controlled by men, and therefore once again I must treat both women's and men's work.

GENERAL USE

Once produced, the homespun and other types of cloth fashioned by women were consumed for a myriad of purposes by the entire population.[1] One of the less apparent but important products was sails. Women's role in supplying this fundamental prerequisite for the viking expeditions is vouchsafed by Óttarr the Black (*svarti*), an eleventh-century Icelandic skald who refers to "sails . . . spun by women."[2] A more tangible illustration is the "good long-ship sail" (*langskipssegl gott*) that Þórólfr brings the Norwegian king as a present from his father Skalla-Grímr (*Eg* 2.41:104).[3] The Norwegian *Speculum Regale* recommends, as a matter of course, that large amounts of homespun (*vaðmál*) be stored on ships together with needles and thread for the reparation of sails (Brenner 11). The spectacular Norwegian ship burials confirm these literary references to woolen sails.[4]

In addition, cargo was packed in sacks of homespun and further protected with skins (*Gg* 1b:71–72). Similar woolen sacks were used for inland transport (*Gnl* 3.4:59). Sick animals were wrapped in homespun (*Bs* 1:615). Private houses and churches were made warm and comfortable with wall hangings (*tjald*, plural *tjǫld*) on festive occasions and further adorned with narrow tapestries, often woven with patterns and pictures (*refill*; plural *reflar*) running the length of the walls.[5] Tents were made of homespun, and large pieces covered the booths at the yearly meetings of the alþingi.[6] Table cloths and towels for washing hands in connection with meals may have been made of linen, but bedclothes were of wool, at times stuffed with down.[7]

The most immediate and obvious application of women's work at the loom was, of course, clothing; indeed, homespun and linen protected people from the cradle to the grave. One text notes as unusual that a certain Þorkell, born in the northernmost part of Norway "where homespun was very scarce" was wrapped in sealskin "for protection," thereby earning the nickname "the Hide-Wrapped" (*skinnvefja; Brð* 13.3:108). A newborn baby, set out to be exposed, was "wrapped in a cloth" (*dúkr; Þux* 13.4:348). Likewise, Hǫrðr threw a blanket (*feldr*) over the body of the dead Sigurðr (*Hrð* 13.21:55), and Þórgunna's corpse was wrapped in "an unstitched linen cloth" before being carried to burial (*Erb* 4.51:143). The law prohibited the burial of naked corpses, specifying that they should be wrapped in linen or homespun and brought to church for interment (*Gg* 1a:8; 2:7–8).

COATS

The most specific information about homespun for clothing involves coats and cloaks worn by men outdoors.[8] The richness of the vocabulary—which cannot be matched in English—suggests the variety. Occasionally the coat was of unremarkable homespun, like the *vǫruváðarkufl* worn by the slave Bolli (*Hrð* 13.27:69).[9] More common was the gray coat (*gráfeldr*) or raincoat (*váskufl*) of the same color, often worn over fancier and more colorful dress clothes (*Lx* 5.29:79; 62:185). Homespun was available in the colors of the sheep. The wool was whiter when sheared in the spring than in the fall, thus explaining Grímr's appearance in a white homespun coat (*vararváðarstakki*) and white pants (*Þsk* 13.9:197).[10] At the other end of the spectrum, Snorri wears a black cape (*kápa*) when he goes abroad (*Erb* 4.13:23). A particular fancy two-colored coat (*tvílóðinn feldr*) is put to good use by Þormóðr when he—like members of modern street gangs—first wears it with its black side visible and, after a killing, disguises himself with the white (*Ftb* 6.23:231). A love of a two-colored (*hálflitr*) coat gave Gunnarr his nickname *helmingr* (half; *Qdm* 9:109).[11] Hrafn's cape (*kyrtill* or *slopr*) must have been of a particularly deep brown shade because the cloth used for its fabrication—a present from Bishop Guðmundr—had been dyed brown (*brunat*).[12] Among the natural sheep colors was russet, found in the reddish homespun cloak (*sǫluváðarkyrtill mórendr*) that Gunnarr wears on his trip to Hǫskuldr (*Nj* 12.22:59). Often fashioned with stripes, russet cloth (*mórendr*) was normally priced higher than ordinary homespun, but Þórhallr's reddish cape (*kast mórendt*) excites only scorn among Njáll's sons, even when, predicting Njáll's death, the young man declares that he will wear it until he had revenged his beloved foster father (*Nj* 12.118:295).

The dense fulled cloth (*þófi*) acted as a near substitute for armor, protecting the body against assaults. Most cloth was probably treated with a certain degree of fulling without becoming the feltlike *þófi*, but the natural lanolin rendered clothes not only warm but also water repellent, like Icelandic sweaters today.[13] All terms for garments that include the prefix *vás* (wet) clearly indicate their role as rain gear.[14] To increase its usefulness, a raincoat (*váskufl*) was often equipped with a hood. Stranded on an island close to the Norwegian coast, Grettir dons a tunic (*kufl*) and a pair of pants of ordinary homespun (*sǫluváðarbrœkr*) before he swims across to the mainland to fetch fire. At his arrival at a farmhouse his frozen clothes give him the appearance of a troll (*Gr* 7.38:130). A particularly apt illustration of the use of homespun as rain gear is found in the case of two brothers, Sæmundr and Guðmundr, who rode out on a rainy and foggy April morning in 1252. Sæmundr had thrown a large piece of ordinary homespun (*sǫluváð*) sewn together at the edges over his fancy clothing, perhaps to protect both him and his horse, and Guðmundr wore a striped overcoat (*yfirhǫfn*); the prefix *yfir* (over) suggests the coat's protective nature (*St* 2:98).

SHAGGY COATS (*VARARFELDIR*)

In addition to fulled or ordinary cloth coats made from smooth material, Icelandic women produced a more elaborate tufted cloth fashioned into shaggy coats, the so-called vararfeldir. Apparently greatly appreciated at home, these coats were marketed by Icelandic merchants abroad and became a significant item of export. It was also known as a tufted coat (*rǫggvarfeldr*) or a pile coat (*loðkápa*). It is likely that this item was implied in many cases when only the term *feldr* was used, and one may assume that when Þorsteinn wraps himself in a "thick coat" before going to the privy in the middle of the night, he is protected by a shaggy coat.[15]

The distinctive feature of this coat was the tufts or shag (*rǫggvar*) that created a furlike appearance. Scholars have often assumed that the vararfeldr was a single lambskin or a fur coat fashioned by sewing skins together, but the legal definition clearly precludes this assumption.[16] While *vara* (plural *vǫrur*) in the Norwegian context most often denoted fur, in Iceland it came to mean homespun.[17] Feldr, on the other hand, most often denoted a coat made of cloth, but it could also be used about a fur coat, as in modern Icelandic and Norwegian. The vararfeldr suggests both aspects, as it refers to a cloth coat made to look like fur. The variety of wildlife in Norway had undoubtedly accustomed the immigrants to a wide choice of fur coats, but lack of indigenous animals in Iceland required the settlers to replace fur with lambskin when flocks became sufficiently large for this purpose.[18] Meanwhile, Icelandic women may have attempted to substitute woven cloth for scarce fur and thereby invented the tufted fabric used for the shaggy coats.[19]

Practically all the vararfeldir, loðkápur, and rǫggvarfeldir mentioned in the texts specifically protect Icelandic men, often against especially bad weather or on board ship, a fact that supports the case for Icelandic origin. At first the garment identified the wearer as an Icelander, but travelers quickly began to use the coats as gifts or sold them for direct profit abroad. Lost in a bad winter storm at night in Iceland, Helgi and Grímr wear pants and shaggy coats, (vararfeldir), fastened at the wrists for extra protection (*Fld* 11.26:294). Braving bad weather to go to a wedding, Finnbogi and Bergr wear foot-long shaggy coats (loðkápur; *Fnb* 14.34:310). Grettir prepares for an encounter with a ghost by wrapping himself in his tufted coat (rǫggvarfeldr) and fastening one end under his feet and the other over his head, thus keeping watch through the neck opening (*Gr* 7.35:119).[20] In Norway the Icelanders Gestr and Eyjólfr wear pile coats (loðkápur).[21] Even more telling, when Egill takes leave of his host Álfr in Sweden, he gives him a pile cloak (*loðólpa*) that Álfr accepts with gratitude, and declaring that he plans to fashion it into a pile coat (loðkápa; *Eg* 2.74:232).[22]

A careful reading of a passage from *Fljótsdœla saga* provides the best evidence of the Icelandic origin of these coats. Shipwrecked on the Norwegian coast, Þorvaldr loses all his property but comes ashore "in his Icelandic clothes." He is received in the household of Earl Bjǫrgólfr, but because of his poor condition he is placed "on the lower bench where slaves and freedmen ate." A mood of gloom permeates the hall, but nobody explains its source to the visitor. Recounting to the earl a strange dream that uncannily matches previous events at court, Þorvaldr induces his host to reveal that his daughter Droplaug has been abducted. Þorvaldr specifies that in his dream he had been "at the shore wearing the same outfit I am used to wear everyday," in other words, the "Icelandic clothes" that he wore at his arrival but which had not yet been identified. Following his dream, however, Þorvaldr sets out alone the next night to rescue Droplaug. While battling a giant, he takes off his loðkápa and puts it around the young woman, thus revealing the unique character of his "Icelandic clothes" (*Rkd* 11.5:223-28).[23]

It seems clear that when faced with the men's demand for fur coats, further heightened by Icelandic weather, the women developed a fur substitute for the first settlers by experimenting with a novel weaving technique. Once a certain length of homespun had been completed, and the cloth was still on the loom, the weaver inserted a pile thread—the washed but untwisted tuft taken directly from the fleece of the sheep—under several warp threads, brought it up on the front of the fabric, carried it over two threads, and passed it under to the back side again. More wiry than spun thread, the pile was not pulled tight; thus, a loop was left on the front. The circumference of the pile could be varied according to the natural length of the fleece locks (6-11 inches). Each lock constituted a tuft or *rǫgg*, and the final product resembled a patchy lamb fleece.[24] An eleventh-century remnant of such a cloth was found at an archaeological site at Heynes in Akranes in 1959.[25] To provide additional warmth, the coats may have been lined with smooth cloth, resulting in the compound word *vararfeldr* and the two-colored coats occasionally encountered in the narratives. The coats were apparently not only warm but strong. It took a bear's mauling to turn Grettir's pile coat into tatters (*feldarslitr; Gr* 7.19:75-77).[26]

If the hypothesis of an Icelandic origin of the tufted coat is correct, one might expect to hear of specimens as soon as wool was available in sufficient amounts. According to a skaldic stanza attributed to Bjǫrn, this poet had received "a coat with beautiful tufts" (*feld . . . fagrrǫggvaðan*) from his rival Þórðr (*BHd* 3.14:148-49; str. 15).[27] Some scholars have charged that Bjǫrn's poems date from the time of the prose author and not of the more ancient hero.[28] Although it would be helpful to be able to date these coats from a stanza of the early eleventh century, Bjǫrn's mature years, it is not necessary, because other evidence is available. By 1200 the shaggy coats had gone out of fashion and had lost their economic importance. They do not appear in the contemporary narratives, nor is it likely that the authors of the sagas of Icelanders wore such garments themselves. Documented in charters and laws dating from the end of the eleventh century, however, the coats, whether mentioned in poetry or prose of the sagas of Icelanders, must represent a genuine item of material culture undoubtedly originating generations before they appeared in texts of literary interest. The shaggy coats thus represent one small detail in which the accuracy and historicity of the sagas is secure.

One final look at the tufts, the coats' distinctive feature: The law specified that a standard coat must have thirteen tufts across the width. Apparently, the coats could also be prepared with tufts of various length, as an episode in version C of *Ljósvetninga saga* illustrates. Having obtained merchandise from Helgi, a certain Þórir is to pay later in shaggy coats. Before the two men part, they agree on how thick-tufted (*þykkrǫggvaðir*) the coats are to be (*Ljs* 10.5[13]:22). Little is known about Þórir, but one surmises that he conveyed the specifics of the coats to his wife, mother, or other women.[29] The same saga contains an episode that further illustrates the length and the nature of the tufts. Forced by political circumstances to dissimulate depression, Guðmundr sits silent in church with his head buried in his tufted coat. When a small child's flatulence causes people to laugh, Guðmundr can not contain himself and chuckles inwardly, enough to make his tufts (*feldarrǫggvar*) tremble, as his brother astutely observes (10.6[17]:41–42). These tufts were clearly not the sturdy lamb fleece itself, the only fur available in Iceland, but the individual piles inserted by hand into the cloth and now vibrating in rhythm with Guðmundr's silent amusement.[30]

The coat also doubled as a blanket.[31] The most famous case involved the coat worn and used by the law speaker Þorgeirr in 1000 (or 999), when the alþingi asked him to resolve the crisis created by the new Christian religion which threatened to tear the country apart. Lying down on the ground at the law mountain, Þorgeirr spread his cloak over himself and remained silent the whole day and the following night, pondering his answer for the next morning.[32] Whatever the nature of Þorgeirr's cogitations, his cloak provided him shelter.[33]

Clothes Making

The fashioning of cloth into clothes was also performed by women, although again, few details survive. In the process referred to as *skera* (tailor), the emphasis is more on cutting than sewing. The few references to sewing (*sauma*) involve fine linen work or embroidery (*Ork* 34.55:118). The most famous sewing episode is the scene where Auðr and Ásgerðr discuss who is to make (*skera*) shirts for their husbands (*Gí* 6.9:30). Their conversation reveals, as noted earlier, that marriage turns the activity into a domestic chore, whereas it is a love token in the early phase of courtship.[34] Of course, women were expected to make clothes for the entire household. Having received a young child for fostering—a cousin of her deceased husband—Dalla immediately shows her affection by "cutting" clothes for him (*Fnb* 14.35:315).[35] Clothes were naturally passed down to younger children when the original owners outgrew them (*St* 2:106).

No special credit was assigned to women for making clothes, but some individuals, men and women, were noted for being skillful with their hands (*hagr*). When applied to women this notice seems to have referred to needlework, although the narratives do not provide specific examples.[36] In a unique case, Margrét, nicknamed the Skillful (*hin haga*), was celebrated as the most accomplished bone carver in Iceland during the time of Bishop Páll. Having fashioned an episcopal staff, she was asked to do an altar table (*Bs* 1:143–44).[37]

CLOTH AS MEDIUM OF EXCHANGE

Although the first settlers procured their basic needs of food and clothing by exploiting the resources of the island and their accompanying flocks, luxuries and even a few essentials had to be imported from abroad. These needs were prompted by new liturgical requirements of churchmen as well. Establishing fixed prices on imports, the law identified the items of flour, linen, timber, wax, and tar (*Gg* 1b:72).

In the beginning these commodities were purchased with silver. Brought by the settlers in large quantities to the island and replenished through looting as long as the colonists took part in viking expeditions, silver was available in bulk, as hack silver, or in foreign coins.[38] The metal was not counted, but weighed according to a system of ounces (*eyrir;* plural *aurar*) and marks (*mǫrk;* plural *merkr*), in which eight ounces, each weighing about twenty-seven grams, equalled one mark. Domestic trade was usually conducted by barter, but most commodities as well as legal fines and compensations were evaluated in silver money. In addition to foreign purchases, silver supplemented local transactions otherwise negotiated in kind.[39] Domestic silver supplies most likely became depleted when the cessation of the viking expeditions closed their source. As a consequence, the remaining silver, circulating in the relatively pure form of "burned silver" (*brannt silfr*), was mixed with alloy and became "pale silver" (*bleikt silfr*).[40]

As supplies of silver ran out, other media of exchange were substituted, but homespun eventually won out. A nonmetallic monetary standard deployed at a regional or national level and accepted abroad over a span of centuries is rare in Western economy, but the process by which this remarkable phenomenon developed can be reconstructed only with difficulty.[41] Because of the increase in sheep, Icelandic women evidently produced homespun in such abundance that it became the common denominator of local exchanges and the medium in which fines, compensations, and land were expressed.[42] Most significant, it was the currency in which taxes and tithes were measured and was used to obtain foreign goods.[43]

Lacking a centralized government, Iceland was ruled through traditional kinship structures that had prevailed in Norway before the creation of monarchial rule.[44] With the establishment of the alþingi, the activity of making laws started. Iceland possessed only one paid official, the law speaker, whose job was to recite the laws during the course of three annual sessions. In return for performing this important function, he was rewarded with two hundred ells of homespun in addition to half of the fines paid for designated crimes (*Gg* 1a:209). This tax did not impose a great burden. Increase in social stratification, however, resulted in the exploitation of the lower classes, whose productive efforts the chieftains expropriated. The original obligation for every free farmer to appear at þing meetings, provided he owned at least one cow for every member of his household, was replaced by the so-called "assembly attendance dues" (*þingfararkaup*), a tax payable to the chieftain, who in turn used part of it to reimburse the travel expenses of those farmers who did attend the meeting.[45] The amount of the tax is not revealed, but it is significant that the original property qualification was expressed in cows, suggesting that transition to the homespun standard had not yet occurred.

During the eleventh century, however, the needs of Christian churchmen added to the economic burden of the productive classes. Men and women were called upon to sustain the clergy whose chief function was emphatically not to produce material goods.[46] By the end of the century Bishop Gizurr persuaded Icelanders to accept tithing for the purpose of supporting the Icelandic church and improving society's ancient poor laws.[47] According to the historian Ari Þorgilsson (who died in 1148), people were to evaluate their property whether in land or movables, swear to the correctness of the assessment, and pay one-tenth of the amount. This arrangement was to last as long as the country was inhabited (*Ísl* 1.10:22).[48] For the purposes of this book, the most interesting feature is that the assessments were expressed in homespun, and ells of this cloth became the currency specified for most payments.[49] This first property assessment — an impressive achievement in any society and comparable to the contemporary Doomsday Book in England — became the pattern for all later assessments, which continued to be expressed in lengths of woolen cloth. Homespun was also produced by women in the other nordic countries, and the Norwegian laws indicate that certain payments could be rendered in lengths of woolen cloth in that country as well.[50] Because of the ubiquity of homespun in Iceland, however, documentation about different types of cloth and about rates of payment is far more abundant in that country.[51]

Icelandic homespun was admirably suited for these comprehensive purposes, although it did not manifest all the characteristics normally assigned to money. The only product in abundance on the island, it possessed intrinsic value, was transportable, did not spoil (it could be recovered and dried after shipwreck), and it commanded a market at home and abroad. Like other domestic products, homespun was originally evaluated in silver. One ounce (*eyrir*) of homespun was, appropriately, the amount of cloth that could be acquired for one ounce of silver. Neither counted nor weighed, the cloth was measured, and the unit was an ell (*alin* or *ǫln;* plural *alnir*), roughly the length of a grown man's forearm from elbow to fingertips. Eventually this measurement was introduced into the monetary system. Since small pieces of cloth were less useful than larger ones, the standard measure came to be the law ounce (*lǫgeyrir*) consisting of a piece of cloth six ells in length. Economic historians have come to the consensus that originally, when silver was plentiful and items for physical comfort scarce, one ounce of cloth (six ells) was worth one ounce of silver, but eventually a ratio of 4:1 was established.[52]

Around 1100 the transition from metal to woolen cloth became so well established that the alþingi inscribed a law that fixed prices for all imaginable items—including gold and silver—in lǫgeyrir or eyrir, reiterating the previous ratio of "six ells new and unused homespun per ounce."[53] Likewise, numerous charters endowing churches and monasteries expressed donations in hundreds of homespun.[54] The system was applied overseas as well. In 1083, exempting Icelanders from excise duties (*tollr*) in Norway, King Óláfr *helgi* (St. Óláfr) charged merchants harbor fees payable in homespun—cloaks and cloth—or silver.[55] During a famine in 1056 the Norwegian king Haraldr the Hard-Ruler (*harðráði*), sent four ships with flour to Iceland, setting maximum prices in homespun.[56]

This is not the place to follow the vagaries of the relative values of silver and homespun, but suffice it to say that increased cloth production and the relative scarcity of silver brought about a devaluation of homespun. The Germanic world originally operated on a duodecimal hundred system of one hundred and twenty units, which governed all economic and monetary transactions in Iceland.[57] In this system the silver standard had also operated with hundreds, but as cloth increasingly replaced silver, the multiplier of six (ells per ounce) easily brought payments, fines, and prices into the realm of large numbers, and this terminology became standard in expressing monetary values.

This arithmetic explains a striking difference between the sagas of Icelanders and the contemporary narratives. In the former, monetary transactions were most often expressed in terms of silver, and the term "hundred" is rare.[58] Even rarer and more recent are references to the devalued "three ells ounce."[59] In the contemporary sagas, however, the terminology of a hundred predominates, sometimes used alone, at other times with ells (*alnir*) or homespun added.[60] This difference not only confirms the archaic cast of the sagas of Icelanders, but it also demonstrates in economic terms that as silver became rare, it was replaced by homespun as the standard against which other goods were evaluated. Produced locally and of great bulk, homespun was doubtless more visible than silver ever had been, but one should not imagine bails of homespun rolling across the country and monopolizing all commercial negotiations. Many local transactions still took the form of barter, but the value of the goods was no longer expressed in silver but in hundreds of woolen cloth. Alternate values behind these figures (land, cattle, silver in coins or ornaments, scraps of metal, as well as rolls of homespun and piles of coats) appear in the sources and make it possible to follow the transition from silver to cloth in greater detail. Foreign trade, however, was measured entirely in homespun and coats. In the final analysis, homespun became both a tangible commodity and a universal standard of value.

In short, by the end of the eleventh century the previous silver standard, founded on men's violent and sporadic activities as vikings, had been replaced by the homespun standard, based on women's peaceful and steady work as weavers. This situation prevailed until around 1300 when dried fish (*skreið*) replaced homespun as the leading export. By this time expression of values in hundreds of cloth was so well established that homespun continued as a standard of value, although in actual exchange it had been replaced by dried fish. Women were involved in the preparation and preservation of the fish, but men were the primary procurers of the new commodity.[61]

By collecting references to payments of fines, arrangements of dowries, and other monetary transactions found in the two genres of sagas, one can follow the transition from silver to homespun and thereby assess the increasing importance of women's work for the general economy. The sagas of Icelanders reveal an older system of financial transactions in which silver currency changed hands immediately, whereas the later sagas of Icelanders and the contemporary narratives depict values and payments expressed in the Icelandic hundreds that stood for homespun.

Silver in the Sagas of Icelanders

The authors' ignorance about the method of payment in ancient times is suggested by their numerous references to nonspecific "wealth" (*fé*). Originally designating animals, this word eventually became a generic term for valuables. When a woman was married "with a great dowry" (*með miklu fé*), one must conclude that the author knew neither the amount nor its specific nature (*Lx* 5.9:17). Likewise, when it is merely stated that men paid "fines" (*fébœtr*) as compensation for crimes, neither the precise amount nor the currency is revealed.[62] Since the value of both land and animals was expressed in silver ounces (*aurar*), the term "loose ounces" (*lausa eyrir;* cf. Danish *løsøre*) was devised to indicate movable property. The two terms were occasionally combined in the redundant *lausafé.*[63] Thus, Kolskeggr and Gunnarr pay lausafé as fines to be able to hold on to landed property (*Nj* 12.67:167).

The authors of the sagas of Icelanders, however, frequently wish to convey the impression that transactions were negotiated in silver, but even expressions specifically mentioning the precious metal are at times so vague that neither the amount nor the metal itself is evident. When the texts refer to payments of fines in "one hundred silver" or "three marks silver" it is not clear what kind of silver is meant — pure or mixed — nor even whether ounces of silver or legal ounces in homespun are implied.[64] A good illustration of the confusion generated among even contemporary participants in the story is found in the misunderstanding that occurred when Gellir and Egill pronounced their verdict against Oddr which obligated him to pay the derisory sum of "thirteen ounces." One of the chieftains thought the two men meant "thirteen hundred ounces," presumably in homespun, another "one hundred and thirty ounces in silver" (*Bdm* 7.10:352).[65]

Of greater interest here are the cases in which the references are unmistakably to tangible and visible silver, as when the silver was stored in trunks, like the two chests "full of silver" which the English king asks Egill to give to his father as "son payment" (*sonargjǫld*) to compensate for the loss of Egill's brother (*Eg* 2.55:145). Egill never hands this wealth over to his father, but his friend Arinbjǫrn is more generous with the contents of his chest. He opens it and "weighed out forty marks of silver" to Egill as recompense for the payment (*fé*) Egill had earned elsewhere but was unable to collect (*Eg* 2.68:216). The silver may have been large items such as bracelets or bars, but which could be broken down into hack silver, portable in a purse. To serve as currency, however, silver had to be weighed. When Hǫskuldr negotiates the purchase of the slave Melkorka, he asks the merchant to fetch the scales (*vág*) and weigh the silver in the purse (*sjóðr*) he is carrying at his belt. The weighing (*reizla*) reveals that the purse contains exactly the "three marks silver" demanded by the merchant, a price Hǫskuldr finds exorbitant but nonetheless pays (*Lx* 5.12:23–24). Hack silver was occasionally of such poor quality that "nobody wanted it and it was scattered on the field."[66]

Because of the absence of kings or other seigneurial authorities, coins were never minted in Iceland. Foreign silver coins, such as the English penny, which were known for their purity, may have been accepted on the island.[67] They eliminated weighing, since they could be simply counted instead. Scenes involving pieces of silver kept in purses and of visibly good and regular quality are numerous in the narratives. As an intermediary stage such pieces may have been weighed once and kept in a purse for future use. This expedient may have been used by Njáll and Gunnarr in their escalating payments for the three sets of killings provoked by their wives, which are transacted in tangible and visible silver pieces.[68] In the first case the "twelve ounces silver" Njáll asks for the killing of his slave Svartr is paid immediately by Gunnarr, who must have carried it on his person. Kept in a purse (*sjóðr*) and brought by Njáll when he and his sons leave for the alþingi, it is used again when, in turn, news of Kolr's killing reaches the meeting. Njáll returns it to Gunnarr who "recognized the money (*fé*) as being the same he had paid Njáll" (*Nj* 12.36–37:94–99). The second set of killings involves free men and calls for settlements of a "hundred silver" (*Nj* 12.38:102, 40:105). In both cases the fine is paid immediately. Since the negotiations again take place at the alþingi, the transaction must have been done in portable currency. In the third case even the large sum of "two hundred silver" demanded for the killing of two men close to Njáll and Gunnarr, respectively, is also paid immediately when requested at the assembly (*Nj* 12.43:110, 45:118).[69] Silver in small uniform pieces, perhaps coins, may also be assumed from scenes in which payments are counted (*telja*) or poured (*steypa* or *hella*).[70] Occasionally silver accumulated in such quantities that it formed a pile.[71]

The money purse appears in several texts. The twelve ounces of silver needed to pay for the killing of a slave was delivered in a purse and placed on the owner's door (*Erb* 4.44:121).[72] Seemingly betraying her husband by accepting "three hundred silver" from Eyjólfr, Auðr places it in "a large purse" which she swings at the giver, giving him a bloody nose (*Gí* 6.32:100–1).[73] Settling with Vermundr, the widow Sigrfljóðr dips into her money purse (*fésjóðr*) tied to her belt and pays him "three hundred silver" (*Ftb* 6.5:141).[74] The most amusing case is found in *Bandamanna saga*. The old Ófeigr receives money from his son in "a large purse" which he intends to use as bribes to advance his son's cause. Hiding the purse under his cape, he lets it occasionally slip below the edge between his legs. Unable to resist this kind of monetary "flashing," his interlocutors can not avert their eyes and succumb to the bribes.[75] When a person gave only part of the purse's content and therefore was unwilling to part with it, he poured the money into the recipient's lap (*kné*) or the fold of his coat (*skikkjuskaut* or *kápuskaut*).[76] The general use of the money purse is also implied in the expression that to accept payment was not as satisfying as to take revenge: a man did not like "to carry his kin in his purse."[77]

An intermediary stage suggesting the transition from silver to homespun

can be detected in a few passages from the sagas of Icelanders and is most striking in an episode in *Gísla saga*. Wishing to warn his brother Gísli secretly about
a plot on his—Gísli's—life, Þorkell rides ahead of his companions, announcing that he has to collect a debt on the next farm. He borrows the housewife's
horse and rides away to find Gísli, instructing the woman to put a piece of
homespun on the saddle of his horse and tell his companions that he is inside
the house "counting silver" (*Gí* 6.19:63). In other words, the payment of her
alleged debt was conflated in homespun and in silver.[78]

Homespun in the Contemporary Sagas

The *Sturlunga saga* complex contains nearly a hundred cases of financial
transaction in which a second stage can be uncovered. With the disappearance
of silver as the standard of measurement, values were invariably fixed in multiples of the Icelandic hundreds (120 units). Payments, fines, and dowries were
also most often indicated in multiples of hundreds without revealing the fungible behind the figures. Although homespun thus was the common denominator, it was not practical as actual currency in many domestic transactions.
Since women on Icelandic farms produced homespun sufficient for their own
needs, the local demand might not be high. Supplies were accumulated, however, for travel and for foreign export. In about a dozen arrangements, extending from 1121 to 1262 and involving payments from twenty to two hundred
hundreds, the Sturlung compiler specifies the acceptable values in which these
payments could be rendered. I examine here a sample of these cases.
   In 1121, arranging a settlement of eighty hundred ounces calculated in
the three ells standard, Hafliði carefully specified the acceptable legal tender (*vǫruvirt fé*): designated real estate, gold, silver, Norwegian imports, iron
work, fine treasures, and gelded horses (*St* 1:49–50).[79] The most interesting
feature in this case is the expression vǫruvirt fé. Although merchandise (*vǫrur*)
other than homespun (*vara*) could be used as payments, their value (*virði*)
was measured against the cloth even in the case of silver, the ancient standard.
In 1181 Sturla Þórðarson awarded himself the enormous sum of two hundred
hundreds as compensation for a knife attack by the wife of one of his opponents. The sum was payable in "cloth and cattle, gold and pure silver or other
precious items" (*St* 1:111). An almost identical list headed by cloth is found in a
settlement from 1214 for one hundred hundreds (*St* 1:228). Around the middle
of the century, however, homespun disappeared from the list of fungibles,
which now, in addition to the usual items, included ships, animals, islands and
other forms of real estate, and driftwood.[80] The cloth's double role as a current
commodity and a fungible item of exchange continued to make it a valuable
gift at home and abroad.[81]

EXPORT OF CLOTH AND COATS

High among the available media for domestic exchange, homespun, the most abundant chief commodity, dominated the export trade. It was only natural for the colonists to retain connections with friends and relatives in Norway, and Icelandic men frequently went abroad. The expense of costly travel included not only food for the trip and compensation for the passage (if the traveler was not the owner of the boat), but also sustenance while abroad. In the sagas of Icelanders these needs were covered by the general term "means for travel" (*fararefni*).[82] From the end of the eleventh century Icelanders were charged harbor tolls in Norway payable in cloth, coats, or silver. It is possible, although not indicated in the narratives, that the original silver supplies were sufficient to permit re-exportation of the precious metal to Norway for a while. During this period enterprising Icelanders could also replenish their resources by joining the viking ventures of pirating ships and attacking coastal settlements, thus reducing the need to bring large supplies of silver from home. Concomitant with the decline in viking activities was a noticeable increase in homespun as part of the fararefni. Planning to go abroad without the leave of his father, Gunnlaugr takes from the storehouse a number of "cloth sacks . . . and . . . saddle pads," informing his surprised father that they were his travel money (*Gnl* 3.4:59). Using the same term, Grettir asks his father for supplies and is given "provisions (*hafnest*) and a little homespun" (*Gr* 7.17:49). When he arrives late to a ship, Arnbjǫrn assures the captain that it will not be necessary to open the cargo for his fararefni, which easily could be placed on top. In his baggage (*baggi*) are three hundred ells of homespun and twelve shaggy coats (*Erb* 4.39:105).[83] When Melkorka wants her son Óláfr to visit her family in Ireland, he explains that Hǫskuldr, his father, keeps his property "in land and cattle and has no Icelandic homespun lying around." Melkorka guesses that her suitor Þorbjǫrn would produce the cloth if she agreed to marry him (*Lx* 5.20:50).[84]

If the travel supplies were only occasionally identified and itemized in the sagas of Icelanders, the contemporary accounts make no secret of the means needed to sustain Icelandic men abroad. The old term fararefni is rare and, when used, is immediately identified as homespun (*vaðmál*).[85] The methods by which it was obtained is occasionally revealed. Homespun fell completely under male control after women had produced it. It is no wonder, then, that Guðrún "spoke blusteringly" when in 1198 — during her husband's absence — a party of fifteen men took "ten hundreds of russet homespun . . . which he had intended for his trip abroad."[86] Planning their journeys, men collected and invested in cloth ahead of time. Whenever a trip came up unexpectedly, they immediately solicited the wooly valuta from friends and relatives. The priest Ingimundr bought cloth "for sale and investment because he frequently went abroad" (*St* 1:130–31).[87] Absolving Órækja, Bishop Guðmundr gave him "ten hundred ells of homespun" and told him to go abroad (*St* 1:396). Not obtaining from his father Snorri Sturluson the property he needed in order to marry, Jón decided to go to Norway instead and solicited funds (*vara*) from his friends (*St* 1:335), as did his cousin Sturla prior to a journey (*St* 1:361). Members of the most prominent Icelandic families, these men were not necessary merchants.[88] The most important aspect of the homespun abroad, however, was its fungibility. Even men like Jón and Sturla doubtlessly invested cloth not needed for living expenses in commodities unobtainable in Iceland. Men of lesser importance did likewise, for profit, and soon a thriving trade developed.

This trade is best illustrated in the narrative sources, but it also emerges from an analysis of inscriptions and documentary evidence. Among the so-called owners' markers written in runes and recently found in Trondheim and Bergen are a number of names of Icelandic men and women. Since these markers, most likely, were attached to merchandise coming from Iceland, they indicate an important Icelandic share in the North Atlantic trade—in which, intriguingly, women were involved.[89] Conversely, aware of the large profits to be gained from transporting scarce items to the island, Norwegian merchants steered their ships there, laden with cargo for which they were paid in cloth. From Icelandic and Norwegian charters and documents, Hjalmar Falk has identified two types of Icelandic export cloth. The most common was the ordinary homespun (*søluváð* or *vøruváð,* also called *varningr* or simply *vara*), otherwise encountered as part of compound words designating specific pieces of clothing worn for everyday use or by poor people.[90] Of better quality was the so-called *hafnar vaðmál.* The association with *høfn* (gen. *hafnar*), cape or coat, suggests its use for outer clothing. Ordinary homespun was packed in bundles (*pakkar;* hence the occasional term *pakkavaðmál*), whereas the better cloth was shipped in rolls containing sixty ells, the so-called *spýtingar.*

The pricing and export of the special shaggy coats, the product of female ingenuity as weavers experimented with substitutes for fur, deserves special notice. These coats were so valuable at home that they also became legal forms of currency. Setting the value of one shaggy coat at two legal ounces, the alþingi in 1100 defined a standard coat as being "four thumb ells long and two wide with thirteen tufts across" (*Gg* 1b:192; DI 1:164). Boosted by this domestic success, traveling Icelanders anticipated ready markets in Norway. Treating the reign of King Haraldr Eiríksson, Snorri Sturluson includes an illuminating episode explaining how the king obtained his nickname Gray-cloak (*gráfeldr*). Landing in Norway with a cargo of vararfeldir, the captain of a ship discovers to his dismay that nobody is interested in buying them. He complains to King Haraldr, who promises to look at them. Requesting one as a present, the king puts it on, and, as to be expected, "before they rowed away every one of his men had bought a coat. A few days later so many men came to buy the coats that not even half of them could be accommodated." Capitalizing on the new fashion, Icelanders started a regular export (*Hgr* 26.7:211–12), as illustrated by the following comment. Setting out for Norway, Þorsteinn and Grímr brought with them "some pile coats (*vararfeldir*) as merchandise . . . as was the custom" and sold them for flour (*Bkr* 11.2:187–88). To satisfy this fashion craze, other Norwegians were less scrupulous, as in the example of the young men who pulled the shaggy coat off Geirr when he refused to sell it (*Hrð* 13.13:35–36).

The export and perhaps also the production of the shaggy coats came to a halt about 1200. The export of homespun continued, although it met increasing competition from dried fish, as mentioned previously and detailed in the following episodes. The shipwreck in 1323 off the coast of Norway of a boat that carried the bishop-elect Laurentius to his consecration became a memorable event. Initially the entire cargo was lost, but whereas the dried fish was consumed by the ocean, oil casks and homespun packed in bundles (*spýtingar* and *pakkar*) were eventually salvaged (*Bs* 1:842). About the same time (1340) an enactment demanding the payment of tithes by Norwegian merchants traveling to Iceland mentioned in passing that "a short time ago only small quantities of dried fish (*skreið*) was sent from Iceland . . . but then the most important export was homespun" (*vaðmál*; DI 2:729). Both the ordinary vaðmál and the better hafnarvaðmál continued to be produced and exported, however, although in 1329 the Norwegian king felt it necessary to remind the Icelanders to keep the quality of the cloth at the high level for which the products were renowned (DI 2:645–46).

MEASUREMENTS

The success of the homespun not only for local consumption but especially for export abroad raised the issue of the cloth's quality and standards. For homespun to work as a measure of value, fixed standards had to be devised. Variations in the length and breadth of the cloth could not be tolerated any more than tampering with the content of precious metal in coins. Once measurements had been established at visible and verifiable standards, however, the homespun was more resistant to manipulation than coins, even though, unlike coins, which were produced under the supervision of a single seigneurial authority, it was fabricated by a large number of unassociated individuals.

Since the ell was based on the length of the human arm, it suffered individual and gender variations. To complicate the issue further, the north operated with two ells of different lengths, a longer and a shorter, of which the latter, adopting the distance from the elbow to the thumb, seems to be older.[91] No wonder, then, that confusion arose from both genuine mistakes and calculated fraud. The vita of Bishop Páll (1195–1211) records that intolerable disorder existed over the length of the ell brought about by the injustice (*ranglæti*) of both Icelanders and foreigners. To remedy the situation the bishop recommended that "people should have sticks (*stikur*) that measured two ells in length." With the help of several named chieftains, this "law was laid down and has been held ever since" (*Bs* 1:135). This enactment was copied into certain manuscripts of *Grágás* with the addition that "people shall measure homespun and linen and all kinds of cloth according to a stick equal in length to ten yardsticks (*kvarði*) measuring twenty [ells] that is marked on the church wall at Þingvellir (the site of the alþingi), and [the person measuring] shall place his thumb after each stick" (DI 1:309–10). Another version contains the further suggestion that "all burial churches shall be marked with the length of the correct stick, so people can go there and measure in case discussion arose concerning the ell" (DI 1: 309; *Gg* 1b:250).[92]

Although the traditional ell and its doubling into the yard was well known by this time, the decimal — rather than the duodecimal — context on the church wall suggests that the double ell was a fairly recent innovation as a standard measurement. Economic historians have seen inspiration in the English yard introduced by King Henry I in 1101.[93] Although evidence for trade between England and Iceland is scarce, the conformity between the two measurements may be understood as attempts by Icelandic merchants to render their spouses' homespun marketable in England and enable them to bring back flour, malt, linen, wax and other necessities. Variants of the Old Norse word for homespun, vaðmál, in Low German (*wadmal, watmal*) confirm the cloth's role in the export trade.[94]

Since men sold the cloth, they were ultimately responsible for establishing correct length. To enable smooth transactions it was equally important to fix the width of the cloth. This task entailed not only establishing a standard but also concerned the quality of the weaving. If the selvages were made too tight and the woof not pushed up, the cloth bulged in the middle.[95] These problems concerned women directly because they set up the loom to the correct width and made sure that the woof was horizontal and the weave tight. The measurement law of 1200 which had regulated the ell's length also addressed the cloth's width. Correct homespun should measure one stick (*stika*), or two ells, in width. Wider fabric was undoubtedly more difficult to produce than more narrow. Good quality was rewarded by the stipulation that the buyer was allowed to choose whether he wanted the measuring for length done in the middle (*hryggr*) (where the bulge would make it longer), at the selvage (*jaðarr*) (where puckering made it shorter), or in between (DI 1:310).[96] Mistakes up to 5 percent were tolerated, but wrong and false measures resulted in the lesser outlawry for three years.[97]

I devote so much attention to the production, use, and export of homespun to uncover the extraordinary role that Icelandic women played in their country's economy for more than two hundred years. Saga authors virtually ignore the female activity at the loom and take little note of male export of cloth. Most readers hardly notice the occasional references to wool clothing because the demand for warm garments is assumed for a cold climate. Meanwhile, editors and translators of the sagas have done their best to clarify the frequent references to the strange "hundreds." The editors of the Íslenzk fornrit series, for example, consistently "translate" the hundreds in homespun into equivalent values in cows. It is true that medieval Icelanders also employed a "cow value" (*kúgildi*), the price of a cow within a certain age and related to fertility and milk production (DI 1:165), but regional differences and transportation obstacles rendered this term inappropriate as a national standard; nor were cows an item of export. Modern readers, more susceptible to clothes than to cows, may be well attuned to the original values expressed in garments. They can allow the thousands of hundreds of homespun to emerge from the texts and roll off the pages as the emblem, par excellence, of women's work.

FOREIGN CLOTH

Despite the importance of homespun to all aspects of domestic well-being and as a vehicle to obtain foreign goods, saga heroes — when given a choice — preferred to dress in clothes made from imported cloth. Not only were Icelandic men vain, but they were not unusual in preferring exotic imported clothes over the garments provided at home. The description, "the most clothes-conscious man (*inn mesti skartsmaðr í búningi*), doubtlessly characterized many more than the half-dozen men to whom it was directly affixed.[98] A "well-dressed man" (*skartsmaðr*) wore fancy clothes (*skrúðklæði*) made of colored cloth (*litklæði*) in far greater variety and brilliance than the natural colors of homespun that reflected the shades of sheep and the added hues of plants and roots.[99] Men showed off these fancy clothes, tailored abroad or cut and sewn by Icelandic women, as soon as they arrived home from their ships and on special occasions.[100] Hallfreðr and his men, for example, wore litklæði as they proceeded directly from the ship to Kolfinna's mountain hut (*Hlf* 8.9: 180). So did Sámr and his men returning from a long trading trip abroad (*HrF* 11.8:126). Back from England, Arinbjǫrn brought Egill a complete outfit of "English cloth in many colors" made to fit his friend's ample girth (*Eg* 2.67: 213). At Guðrún's fourth wedding the groom arrived with a party of sixty, "and that was a very select company because most of the men were in dress clothes" (*í litklæðum; Lx* 5.68:201). An amusing episode in *Grettis saga* demonstrates that even an outlaw could be susceptible to foreign finery.[101]

Vanity is also involved in a touching episode concerning two brothers, Sæmundr and Guðmundr, who wished to display their beautiful clothing at the moment of death. We left them riding on a rainy morning in April 1252. Under their rain gear of homespun each wore a cloak (*kyrtill*), Sæmundr's two-colored, red and green, and Guðmundr's blue. Unbeknownst to them, their uncle Ǫgmundr was lying in ambush, planning to kill them. When captured, the brothers asked for a priest, confessed, and received the sacrament. Thus prepared for the axe, the eighteen-year-old Sæmundr took off his raincoat, knelt, and buried his face in his hands, his beautiful clothes displayed to his uncle, whose face turned blood red as he ordered the beheading (*St* 2: 98–100).[102]

Found in both the sagas of Icelanders and the contemporary sagas, men's preference for colored clothing is beyond doubt.[103] The previous story suggests that colored clothing can also imply danger. The authors of the sagas of Icelanders, in fact, employed this motif with great skill. Most common is the use of blue (or black), which in the semiotics of the sagas invariably signified immediate violence or danger. Headed for revenge, a man would dress in blue.[104] The few women involved in aggressive acts did likewise: the magician Geirríðr — the only person in colored clothing — headed out in her blue cloak (*skikkja*) with thirteen men in hopes of exposing the tricks of her colleague Katla (*Erb* 4.20:53).[105] Although blue is a sign of impending trouble, a few scenes suggest that any colored clothing can signal danger or aggression. The author of *Laxdæla saga* paints a remarkable scene in which Helgi, watching an approaching party headed toward his shieling with the purpose of gaining revenge for his share in the killing of Bolli, identifies ten men from the shepherd's description of their clothes, weapons, and facial features observed at distance. Five are identified by garments made of cloth in brilliant colors, including blue, crimson, and yellow-green. Only one, Lambi Þorbjarnarson, wears an ordinary gray coat (*Lx* 5.63:187–88). Helgi knows the reason why each man joined the party, but he is puzzled by Lambi's presence. Helgi's surprise and the anger of Lambi's half-brother after Helgi's death are justified. The attentive reader will remember that Lambi had urged the killing of Bolli in revenge for Bolli's slaying of Lambi's half-brother Kjartan. Having personally participated in the attack on Bolli, Lambi is as guilty as Helgi himself. Lambi's gray coat of homespun therefore signals that his presence is not justified and that his heart is not committed to the cause.[106]

In another passage in *Laxdæla* which has puzzled scholars, Bolli, egged on by Guðrún, slays Kjartan, whom both he and Guðrún love. Receiving the news from Bolli, Guðrún comments: "Morning tasks are often uneven; I have spun yarn for twelve ells of cloth and you have killed Kjartan" ("*Misjǫfn verða morginverkin; ek hefi spunnit tólf álna garn, en þú hefir vegit Kjartan;*" Lx 5.49: 154). The crucial term "morning work" (*morginverkin*) is interpolated from a paper manuscript copied from a lost original that may rival the Möðruvallabók chosen by Einar Ól. Sveinsson for his edition in the Íslenzk Fornrit series. According to this version, Guðrún states: "Great are deeds of renown" (*mikil verða hermðarverk*).[107] The term *hermðarverk* is unusual, and it implies famous deeds, such as warfare or revenge. Basing his conclusions on paleographic evidence, Ólafur Halldórsson suggests that these readings are faulty, and he substitutes: "Great are the works of damage" (*Mikil verða hér váðaverkin*), where *váðaverk* implies accidental harm (cf. Danish *våde*). He suggests that Guðrún may be playing with words, identifying her own work as constructive spinning (*váðverk*) but Bolli's as destructive "damage work" (*váðaverk*).[108] Philological details aside, saga authors spend much time describing men killing each other, whereas they totally ignore weaving, the most important activity of women. This brief passage in *Laxdæla saga* offers a fleeting recognition by one author and several copyists, perhaps even shared by Guðrún herself, of a significant difference between constructive weaving and destructive killing.

Conclusion

This book argues that an underlying continuum characterizes issues of women and gender in the Germanic-
nordic world, a continuum modified by Christianity
and technological advances. I return now to the exchange between Guðrún Gjúkadóttir and Jóreiðr Hermundardóttir cited in the first chapter. Guðrún, the
sixth-century Germanic woman, answers the question of
the dreaming Jóreiðr, her thirteenth-century Icelandic sister, as to what she, a pagan, was doing in Christian Iceland:
"It should not be of any concern to you whether I am
Christian or heathen, because I am a friend to my friend"
(*Engu skal þik þat skipta hvárt ek em kristin eða heiðin, en
vinr em ek vinar míns; St* 1:521).[1]

I wish to consider the continuity implied in Guðrún's remark. Her protest
notwithstanding Guðrún's paganism is not negligible, for it reveals the primordial tradition from which Jóreiðr's world developed. My approach in this book
has been to analyze female and gender roles in Norse society from sources in
which Christian authors attempt to describe both the ancient/pagan and their
own medieval/Christian society. By subtracting from this evidence those features that carry an identifiable Christian imprint — the marital and family life
over which churchmen claimed jurisdiction — and by isolating the technological skills that the descendants of the original settlers developed over time —
weaving homespun and the utilization of hot springs — one perceives an approximation of the pagan and ancient society. When one turns to the medieval
and Christian world, however, it is not sufficient merely to restore the subtrac-
tions and eliminations, for certain facets of ancient life persisted with little or
no change into medieval times, among them the enduring commercial foun-

dations of marriage, most features of manual work, many aspects of law, and leisure activities.

Unfortunately, it is not a simple matter to separate old, new, and continuing aspects of the Old Norse world with a view to ascertaining the position of women. Some ideas, although new and Christian, reinforced elements already present in the old system. Moreover, as one classifies these aspects, one is tempted to assess them as advantages or liabilities to the quality of feminine life. Such evaluations contain serious risks—because no one can ever be sure how ancient and medieval Icelandic women themselves evaluated those factors, and, one is prone to be influenced by personal evaluations. I therefore limit the classification to similarities and differences, with the realization that it is difficult to eradicate totally my own values in the sorting process.

First, a brief sketch of women's lives in the ancient pagan world based on what I have explored in this book. Whatever aura of respect Icelandic women derived from pagan religion, their private life was a mixture of rights and limitations. Although they did not have the prerogative to refuse a suitor, which certain sagas of Icelanders had postulated, they could initiate divorce. They received property in marriage and could obtain more through inheritance; as widows they retained their assets, which they could then pass on to their heirs. They probably enjoyed less leisure than men, but when they went to bed at night they may have slept with the satisfaction of knowing that their work had kept their families fed and clothed.

Although some of these features are unusual in a general medieval context, the Norse world was profoundly patriarchal. As my analysis of widows indicated, the human ideal that was most admired and to which both men and women aspired was more masculine than feminine.[2] Carol Clover has suggested that the social binary of nordic society was not male/female, but a different sort of polarity: on one hand, a group of people consisting of most able-bodied men and a few outstanding women known for their exceptional mental strength and overpowering personalities, and, on the other, a kind of "rainbow coalition" of the rest of humanity, including most of the women, children, slaves, the old and disabled, and disenfranchised men.[3] The few women found in the first group were identified in terms normally associated with men.[4] Most of them were older women who had gained in material and social assets what they had lost in sexual attractiveness. Whereas the debility of old age might disqualify a man from the admired category, women were never expected to fight and age did not therefore affect their worth. Moreover, since exceptionality was measured in male terms, a capable woman was obviously most advantageously placed to demonstrate her worth in the absence of a husband. It is therefore not surprising that the narratives reveal a number of imposing women in the permanent stage of widowhood, between marriages, or in control of authority while their husbands were away.

Even the most powerful widow, however, was disenfranchised politically. Women were not allowed to participate in the political and juridical functions of society either as active participants or as legal supplicants. They could not act as chieftains (*goðar*), judges, or even witnesses; they were not allowed to prosecute, except in minor personal matters concerning themselves and their daughters, and even here they could not act directly but had to seek the mediation of male relatives. Although women owned property, it was under male administration. A wife was allowed to purchase at most one-half ounce (*eyrir*), or three ells worth of woolen cloth a year, and her handshake (*handsal*) was legally binding only if authorized by her husband.

A few young women, safely ensconced within powerful families, did succeed in joining the group of exceptional women.[5] Young women, however, were inevitably vulnerable to predatory males, as the topos of "the illicit love visit" reveals. In the final analysis, male sexual aggression may be in fact the most profound cause for gender inequality anywhere. In the Norse world, however, sexual crimes were not considered damaging to the female victim but to her male relatives. Their honor, sullied through her pain, could be restored either through immediate revenge against the aggressor or by fines — paid to the men, of course, not to the female victim.

This melange of rights and limitations describes female conditions in the north before the arrival of Christianity. To assess the transformation that occurred during the next three centuries, I divide prevailing conditions into three sets. In the first set belong tendencies already present in the ancient world which Christianity simply reinforced; the second set reflects aspects of female life which continued without submitting to reform; and the third set contains practices in which Christianity and advanced technology introduced measurable change.

In the first group belongs a decline of female participation in religion. My forthcoming book on female images shows that this decline had already begun in the pagan era. Here I briefly trace the continued decline both on the divine and the human level and the steady rise of misogyny. Perpetuating the patriarchal father-god Yahweh of the Jews, the Christian triune deity was dominated by a father and a son, which left little room for a goddess. The Virgin Mary was never fully attached to the godhead, but as elsewhere in Europe, she became increasingly venerated in Iceland. The best testimony of this local devotion is found in the highly original and widely circulated *Maríu saga*, probably written by Kygri-Bjǫrn Hjaltason, later bishop of Hólar, shortly after his return from the Fourth Lateran council in 1215. The printed version fills more than a thousand pages and the text includes not only a biography of Mary but a detailed account of Herod's reign, theological commentaries, and numerous miracles ascribed to Mary. She was also featured in skaldic poetry.[6] Mary's cult has often been interpreted as reviving notions of the ancient mother goddess in the Mediterranean area. Echoes of ancient supernatural females could still be heard in the north in the twelfth century when Mary's cult was first introduced, but the Virgin never enjoyed the official divinity of her early nordic forbearers. The Protestant Reformation, imported from Denmark to Iceland, exterminated her cult in the sixteenth century. Fifteen hundred years after Tacitus's description of the worship of the goddess Nerthus among the Germanic tribes on the Continent, this female element was eliminated from northern religion, and its decline was paralleled by a similar but delayed deterioration of women's religious and ritual functions.

The new religion did not open opportunities for women. When Christianity reached the north in the late tenth- and early eleventh centuries, its male hierarchy was well established, and local women were not recruited for the initial tasks of missions and the preparation of adults for baptism that their Mediterranean and Anglo-Saxon sisters had been allowed to perform. Nuns and abbesses were also less numerous than elsewhere in Europe. Iceland, for example, numbering no more than seventy thousand inhabitants during the medieval period, contained only two nunneries.[7] A few cases of Icelandic hermitesses, either attached to a nunnery or living as anchorites in the wilderness, appear in the sources.[8]

Powerful strains of misogyny, doubtless of native origin, underlay the pagan tradition.[9] The advent of Christianity exacerbated the nordic contempt for women in important ways. The new religion emphasized the pervasive image of Eve, first mother and ur-woman. Not only was she accused of introducing the vice gluttony when she offered Adam the fruit of the tree, but also that of primordial seduction for enticing her husband to disobey God. Although theologians debated her responsibility for the cosmic Fall into sin, she was nonetheless deeply implicated in the transmission of concupiscence through the sexual act. In stark contrast to Mary who conceived God without sex and sin, Eve's responsibility for the original transmission of evil was as undoubted as it was undefined. As descendants of the first mother, women were most feared for their sexuality. Although Icelandic clergy were unfamiliar with the restraints on the sexual drive proposed by reforming churchmen and were at first unwilling to accept the requirement of celibacy, when they did try to comply they were even more prone than their Continental colleagues to blame their mistresses and concubines for their failures.

At first, churchmen attempted to impose gender equality among lay people in certain areas of human conduct, but they quickly singled out women for harsher punishment in sexual crimes.[10] The discrimination, moreover, increased over the years. Espousing gender equality, the Christian definition of fornication and adultery held women as well as men responsible for breaking the marital vow of fidelity. Nonetheless, the new Christian law for Norway and Iceland imposed harsher fines on women than men. The rise of misogyny is particularly noticeable in liturgical matters where churchmen's authority was unopposed: thus unmarried mothers were not preceded by lighted candles on the festive occasion when a woman was received back in church after her confinement. Later the rule was extended to the mother's corpse if she died during childbirth and was brought in for burial. In the fourteenth century sick and dying concubines were denied the last sacrament unless their lovers promised to marry them or they agreed to separate from the men if they got better. Meanwhile, men were simply refused the eucharist if they lived with concubines unless they promised the priest to marry their companion or separate from her. As I suggested previously, the population may have considered less serious the withholding of the eucharist than the denial of the last rites.

So many features of women's lives continued unchanged after the acceptance of Christianity that it is impossible to enumerate them all, but several conditions deserve iteration here: in addition to manifold disenfranchisement, the traditional activities of agricultural work, and the enduring pleasures of amusements and games, women experienced the perpetuation of the twofold structure of marriage combined with property arrangements, and the persistence of extramarital sexuality, illegitimacy, and divorce.

Centuries before the appearance of the northern sources, Tacitus was impressed by the dignity and equality ordinary women derived from Germanic marriage (*Germania,* chap. 18–19). His brief description of the sharing of property, brought as gifts by the bride and the groom from their respective families, provides the first glimpse into the commercial foundations of the Germanic marriage. His version corresponds well with the reports of Continental laws in the second half of the first millennium and with the numerous details culled from Icelandic and Norwegian laws dating from the beginning of the next. The propertied nature of pagan marriage was embodied in the fundamental division between the betrothal, in which the terms of the commercial contract were negotiated, and the marriage proper, in which the agreement was concluded and the property transmitted. Although churchmen transformed matrimony from a commercial contract over property to a Christian sacrament between individuals, Christian marriage nonetheless retained the twofold structure. Families continued to make financial arrangements, and the traditional Germanic/nordic procedure of betrothal and marriage was accommodated by the churchmen's division into the engagement, the *verba de futuro,* and the wedding, the *verba de presenti.*

Pagan marriage was intended to control the flow of property, not to inhibit sexual energy—in the pagan north sexuality was by no means limited to the institution of matrimony. The goals of Christian marriage, in contrast, were to restrict sexuality to the married couple and to direct it to the sole purpose of procreation. With virtually no information on contraception, abortion, or other means of birth control, I cannot judge the effect of the latter goal, but certainly the requirement of fidelity was infringed quite matter-of-factly throughout thirteenth-century Iceland, according to the contemporary sagas. Despite the disintegration of the political order of the Sturlung age, these sexual transgressions should not be interpreted as a decline from a previously higher morality that the sagas of Icelanders ascribe to the ancient pagans. On the contrary, a close scrutiny of the narratives set in pre-Christian times and a comparison with the legal regulations then in effect, suggest that the behavior unconcealed in the contemporary accounts dates back to the pagan setting of the sagas of Icelanders. Pagan men most certainly did not allow marriage to inhibit their sexuality. Open concubinage, aggressive sexual behavior toward women from their own class (although frowned upon, to be sure), unlimited access to slaves, frequent use of female workers and servants, and sexual adventures during foreign travel provided them with abundant extramarital outlets.

Legislation, too, reveals the continued persistence of pagan sexual mores, as I described in the cases that demonstrate Christian misogyny. When Bishop Árni's Christian law distinguished between whether a man took a woman as his wife (*eiginkona*), or he used her for sex (*líkamslosti;* literally, bodily lust; NgL 5:40–41), the paragraphs not only convey a completely masculine perspective but likewise accept men's extramarital relations as normal.

The prevalence of extramarital affairs kept illegitimacy rates high. In the pagan period the problem had been controlled through infanticide, but the churchmen's success in prohibiting this custom, coupled with a continued definition of legitimate marriage, resulted in the survival of large numbers of illegitimate offspring whose claims on parental property was accommodated in both law and practice, at least outside royal circles.[11] In the legal terminology the expressions "conceived to inherit" (*til arfs alinn*) and "going to inherit" (*arfgengr;* Gg 1a:249, 1b:24, 2:99; 1a:224, 2:68) became shorthand for the male child born in marriage. In the sequence of fourteen categories of heirs in *Grágás*, the first eight list legitimate relatives in descending, ascending, and lateral groups, and the last six include illegitimate children and siblings (*laungetin(n)*; Gg 1a:218–19, 2:63–64). In other words, in the absence of legitimate heirs, illegitimate children and siblings could take their place. From the world of the contemporary sagas Sæmundr Jónsson's generosity stands out, when, in 1218, he let his brother Ormr's seven children inherit from their father "although they were illegitimate" (*St* 1:242–43, 270); thus he relinquished his own position as a legitimate uncle. Although these rules and episodes illustrate the declining accommodation of infanticide, they simultaneously demonstrate the persistence of ancient sexual mores.

Divorce is another feature that passed from pagan into Christian society. In contrast to extramarital sexuality, the prevalence of divorce in the sagas of Icelanders suggests that it was also a dominant feature of pre-Christian Iceland. Although divorce was excluded in principle from the Christian matrimonial program, it was treated extensively in *Grágás*, the law that was fully in effect during this period. This fact, combined with the inclusion of divorce in the subsequent laws, *Jónsbók* and Bishop Árni's New Christian Law, suggests its enduring existence. Although not as frequent in the society of the contemporary sagas as in the sagas of Icelanders, it continues to appear.

If salient features of the pagan legacy persisted throughout the millennium of the Germanic-nordic continuum, it is nonetheless true that Christianity introduced radical changes into women's lives. The new religion's most original contribution to the feminine condition was the insertion of gender equality into marriage and sexual relations. This program would obviously benefit most the gender that had suffered discrimination. Churchmen were unable — and indeed did not wish — to interfere in all areas where women were treated unequally, but in matrimonial matters they sought to establish gender symmetry. Most successful was their program concerning consent. In Roman law the father had exercised decisive authority over the marriages of both his sons and daughters; according to Germanic custom the men themselves chose their wives. Familiar with both systems, churchmen preferred the Germanic approach but sought to extend the marital choice to women as well. Consent in marriage meant little to Germanic and nordic men who already enjoyed this privilege, but, if and when implemented, it was an extraordinary change for women. The silent pagan bride, transferred like property from father to husband, was replaced by the articulate Christian woman who by her own "yes-word" (*jáyrði*) was allowed to affirm her willingness to share her life with a man who already had consulted her, not just her father. Fathers of daughters may have appreciated this new female freedom, but it was not necessarily received with favor by the groom or his kinsmen, who were more preoccupied with the economic and political advantages offered by the bride and her family than with personal relations. One may further speculate that affective marriages — that is, marriages containing mutual marital affection — were encouraged when a woman had given her consent.[12]

The doctrine of consent was introduced to the north through ecclesiastical correspondence between Norwegian and Icelandic prelates beginning in the late twelfth century, in which the Archbishop of Niðaróss (Trondheim) brought the new legislation to the attention of his suffragans. In Norway it was inserted into the oldest Christian laws, but no trace is evident in the manuscripts of the corresponding parts of *Grágás*. In Iceland the first legislative mention of consent occurs in new liturgical regulations from the middle of the thirteenth century, and it was incorporated into Bishop Árni's so-called New Christian Law accepted by the alþingi in 1275. Churchmen were less successful about including it in the secular laws. The new *Jónsbók*, adopted in 1281, included gender equality—not for the marital couple, but for the bride's parents. The law stated that both "father and mother shall decide on their daughters' marriage" (*Jn* 70). Another rule effectively curbed consent for wealthy females when it warned women that if they married without their kin's consent, they would forfeit their inheritance to the next in line (*Jn* 71). The fullest evidence for the acceptance of the ecclesiastical principle of consent into the north, therefore, comes from the sagas of Icelanders, whose authors attempted to anachronistically incorporate this Christian principle into the mores of their pagan forebears.

Gender equality is also evident in the stipulation that men and women were to be punished equally for sexual crimes other than illegitimacy. *Grágás* had defined unlawful intercourse (*legorð*) as the crime committed by a man when he slept with a woman over whom he had no sexual rights. In contrast, Bishop Árni's law distinguished fornication (*einfaldr hórdómr;* literally, single adultery) from adultery (*tvífaldr hórdómr;* literally, double adultery), and applied them to both men and women according to their marital status (NgL 5:39). Without using the term, the so-called Older Christian Borgarthing Law had already conceived of single adultery and had ordered both a married man and a married woman to pay a fine of three marks if they slept with an unmarried partner (NgL 1:351).

The principle of gender equality may derive from churchmen's underlying concern for humans as individuals. In the pagan culture only the man was accounted an individual who took responsibility not merely for his own actions but also for those of his wife and daughters. When a pagan woman committed a crime, her husband had to answer in court, as Gunnarr did for Hallgerðr after she ordered her slave to steal food. A pagan woman was not considered capable of committing sexual crimes but was regarded as damaged property. Churchmen, however, considered women as responsible as men and distributed punishment equally.

With a written ideology of universal application, the Christian marital and sexual program can be readily identified. The technological advances in the transition from ancient to medieval Iceland are far more difficult to detect. Providing an incalculable boon to a cold climate, hot springs were, naturally, used for washing and bathing from the beginning of settlement. It seems, however, that later generations exploited this resource with greater expertise, creating a more sophisticated bathing culture that provided not only personal hygiene and well-being but offered opportunities for social intercourse and entertainment.

Small but significant climatic differences between Norway and the new colony made Icelandic settlers realize quickly that the agriculture they had known in the old country was not feasible except perhaps in the south. Instead, they relied almost entirely on animals. Sheep became particularly important, not only because they could manage on their own in mountains and meadows for a good part of the year when not in need of milking but because of their multiple bounty of milk, meat, wool, skin, and manure. Of utmost importance, of course, was the wool. Icelandic women perfected the ancient spinning and weaving technique they had brought with them from Norway, and the abundance of raw wool enabled their medieval daughters to provide their family needs in clothing, bedding, wall hangings, and sails in the manner of their foremothers, as well as to produce a large surplus of homespun, which served as export to supply demands not met on the island. The significance of the cloth is demonstrated beyond doubt by its adaptation as currency and a standard of measure that persisted for centuries after its export had diminished.

With a weekly day of rest and numerous feast days, the Christian calendar clearly afforded more respite from work than the few seasonal celebrations of the pagan year. The medieval woman, nevertheless, worked as hard as her ancient sister, and she, too, went to bed exhausted by her labors. Her satisfaction, however, may have been less. Whereas the housewife in the ancient setting worked with the resources available on her farm to feed and clothe her family, the economic success of the new system of wool export entailed increased management, which most certainly fell under male control. The first task was to ensure flocks of sheep large enough to produce surpluses of raw wool. The mass production of raw wool into homespun may have been accomplished by women working in teams. Since large quantities of the finished product were sent to harbors to be shipped to foreign countries, its distribution, perhaps along with the management of spinning and weaving, was supervised by males. The medieval woman was as tired at bedtime as her ancient mother, but she may well have felt more exploited.

This change did not occur because of male conspiracy, of course; it was the unavoidable result of structural changes common to many societies. When human activities expand from small, familial, unstructured units to communal, regional, structured enterprises, the women who were directly involved and responsible in the first stage often slip to the background in the second and fall prey to exploitation. The change can also be observed in the social, political, and religious spheres.

The likelihood that numerous women were involved in spinning and weaving on the farms suggests a point at which the new Christian ideology may have intersected with technological progress. When churchmen applied gender equality to the prohibition against infanticide—forbidding the killing not only of boy babies, but also of girls—it had a double effect on women. As infants, they had somehow avoided the exposure to which their feminine sex was so often subjected in pagan times. As Christian mothers, they were permitted to keep the babies they bore. The extension to women of the right to survive and to be nourished after birth was behind the Icelandic economic miracle, for it enabled the female half of the Icelandic population to sustain itself despite biological dangers and the hardships of work and thereby increased the numbers of women available to produce the homespun that fueled the Icelandic economy.

Keeping in mind this Christian prerogative for mothers to keep their babies after birth and for all children to be cared for, I turn for the last time to Jóreiðr's dream in 1255, in which the burning of Gizurr's estate at Flugumýrr almost two years earlier figures prominently. In the dream-conversation between Guðrún and Jóreiðr, the issue of heathenism is raised several times. To the young girl's question as to the arsonists' goals, Guðrún responds that "in their wickedness they wanted to return heathenism to the entire country." After her initial fright ("I am afraid of you;" *Mér er ótti at þér; St* 1:520), Jóreiðr insists on knowing the dream-woman's name. When she understands that the apparition is none other than Guðrún Gjúkadóttir, her immediate reaction is, "What are pagan people doing here?" In 1255 a young woman like Jóreiðr may not have been fully aware of the perils that female infants confronted in pagan times, but she may have nonetheless harbored an instinctive fear of a distant, threatening past. With the soothing response "I am a friend to my friend," the pagan Guðrún was able to calm the young Christian's apprehensions and to assure her of the abiding continuity between their two worlds.

APPENDIX

Sources

Three genres of prose narratives and the compilations of law provide the textual basis of this study. The narratives consist of the sagas of Icelanders (*Íslendingasǫgur*), the kings' sagas (*konungasǫgur*), and the contemporary sagas (*samtíðarsǫgur*). At different times scholars have oscillated between faith and doubt and back to faith again over the issue of historicity concerning the four groups of evidence. This issue is of utmost importance here. Although the kings' sagas were written before the sagas of Icelanders, I nonetheless turn to the latter first, because the hermeneutic process is clearer and more fully completed there and because these narratives are particularly relevant to this book.[1]

SAGAS OF ICELANDERS

The pride of Icelandic literature, the sagas of Icelanders (*Íslendingasǫgur,* also known as the family sagas), provide rich opportunities for examining the lives of ordinary women, but they also are burdened with serious problems, among which the most important pertain to their historicity.[2] Written mainly during the thirteenth century and surviving in later manuscripts, the most complete of which belong to the fourteenth century, the fifty some extant sagas and short stories (*þættir*) vary in length from a dozen to several hundred pages. Among the most memorable are *Eyrbyggja saga* and *Kormáks saga,* not to mention the indisputable masterpieces, *Laxdœla saga* and *Njáls saga.* In long generational surges they describe the origins of the immigrants in Norway and their travels abroad during the ninth century until their final settlement in Iceland. They concentrate on the century following the establishment of the General Assembly (alþingi) in 930, which constitutes the so-called saga age. The tantalizing feature of these accounts is their apparent realism and verisimilitude. Unparallelled in European literature until the nineteenth century, the narratives brim with minute details of everyday life and purport to reveal the inner workings of this northern society with an intimacy unmatched in other medieval sources.[3] They are particularly remarkable for the dialogues that vivify innumerable saga characters—virtually introducing them to the reader's personal acquaintance.[4]

It would, for example, be difficult to find a more realistic and detailed picture of a farm woman and her work than that of the Icelander Katla spinning wool, arranging her living room, giving orders to have a locked storeroom opened, and playing with her favorite goat (*Erb* 4.20:50–54). The problem consists in determining which society is covered in this vignette. Does it accurately portray the tenth century of Katla's allegedly historical lifespan, the thirteenth century of the medieval author, the author's perception of Katla's age, or a conflation of all three? Since the acceptance of Christianity in the year 1000 falls within the timespan, this question is of special importance because Katla is also shown performing magic, an activity disapproved by churchmen.

The question of historical veracity is unavoidably connected with the equally difficult problem of the sagas' origins and interpretation.[5] From the beginning of saga studies, when scholars imputed historicity to the oral transmission that was incorporated in all the narrative genres, the sagas of Icelanders were understood to provide accurate historical accounts of pagan Icelanders, whose political, cultural, and religious activities could be fitted into a puzzle assembled from all the sagas to form a coherent picture of ancient society.

By the middle of the nineteenth century, however, interpretive fashion began to consider these texts more literary than historical. As a result, the role of the author increased and faith in the historical veracity of oral tradition diminished. In 1914 the Swiss scholar Andreas Heusler coined the terms "free-prose" to indicate the older view that emphasized the oral tradition and "book-prose" for the newer perception that stressed the role of the author.[6] Heusler's terminology precipitated the formation of two sharply opposed camps, each of which attacked the alleged opinions of its opponents without clearly defining its own terms. Although Heusler had not included the factor of historicity in his definitions, the book-prosaists came to undermine faith in oral tradition, a necessary component of the free-prose, while they themselves fell under the spell, not so much of the author who in most cases remained anonymous, but of his literary borrowing. As scholars increasingly uncovered these elements, they further discredited the historical accuracy of oral tradition.

Book-prose theories flourished during the first half of this century, especially in the form practiced by the so-called Icelandic school, which does not deny, but minimizes as unknowable, the oral tradition behind the written saga.[7] Instead of searching for historicity, the adherents of this school have meticulously examined the individual sagas, analyzing them for literary style and borrowing (*rittengsl*), the author's milieu, and the possible influence of contemporary society on the events described. The ultimate goal was to accord to each saga its place in the development of Icelandic literature between 1100 and 1400. These efforts resulted in a series of penetrating introductions to the sagas in the editions of Íslenzk fornrit, currently the foundation of all modern saga scholarship.

In the last few decades, however, faith in oral tradition has re-emerged. The close scrutiny of different redactions of texts has demonstrated that local oral tradition about early eleventh-century events could still be tapped by sagas writers in the thirteenth century.[8] On a general level, structuralism has inspired scholars to search for universal patterns in the macro- and microstructure of the sagas.[9] Anthropologists and social historians, looking for parallels from other tribal societies, have focused attention on functions with less concern for chronology.[10] Like the practitioners of the Icelandic school who looked for European parallels, these new trends draw attention away from the island's native soil, but where the Icelandic school looked to the Christian culture of medieval Europe, formalist and anthropological studies sought connections with deep and universal human structures that preceded Christianity and persisted long after its implantation.[11]

Other scholars have been more concerned with the medieval society represented in Icelandic literature at the time of the latter's composition. Arguing that the problem of historicity of the ancient or pagan period is less important than the fact that issues in the sagas were meaningful for medieval Christian Icelanders, they have a different kind of regard for saga origins and intertextual relationships. They distill the texts' *mentalité* and obtain insights not only into the generations who told separate episodes of the sagas, but also into the authors and scribes who assembled, rearranged, and wrote the sagas, as well as those who copied and consumed the texts as readers and listeners. Particularly useful is the approach that casts the narratives as attempts by thirteenth-century authors to recapture a past culture in danger of disappearing entirely because of the loss of national independence after the Norwegian takeover.[12]

Although its results are more modest than those obtained from the long diachronic studies, they are the most secure conclusions available because of the nature of the sources. Turning to the twin problems of historicity and oral tradition, this last approach assumes that the stories and concepts have their origins in an irretrievable historical context, although one potentially not greatly altered over the centuries. Modified by succeeding generations according to societal and ideological needs and historical consciousness, narrative patterns incorporated changes in ways that modern anthropologists have identified among tribes at similar political and economic stages of development as the medieval Icelanders.

Nonetheless, I shall go one step further without returning to the naivete of the nineteenth century and read the Old Norse sources as the last and fullest evidence of a Germanic-nordic continuum that stretched back a full millennium. The Norse texts cannot be used to illuminate conditions on the Continent a millennium earlier, but the correspondences, for example, in kinship structure, marriage regulations, and articulation of grief remain striking. Indeed, medieval Icelanders themselves felt they were the last link in the Germanic continuum. In this book, however, I have read the sagas of Icelanders as evidence of a pagan-Christian continuity between Norway and Iceland.

KINGS' SAGAS

Like the sagas of Icelanders, the subject matter of the kings' sagas (*konungasǫgur*) is specified by their label.[13] The former dealt mainly with prominent Icelanders; the latter focused primarily on Norwegian kings. Whereas the sagas of Icelanders treat the limited saga age (870–1050), the kings' sagas include northern royalty from mythic times to the end of the thirteenth century.[14] Icelanders had already demonstrated their literary skills in Eddic and skaldic poetry; by the end of the tenth century they had displaced native skalds in Norway even at the court of the king. Naturally composing sagas about themselves, Icelanders also dominated the genre of the kings' sagas, although an independent Norwegian tradition may have preceded them. Whereas the authors of the sagas of Icelanders were anonymous, the historians writing the kings' sagas were named in many cases. Since they first appear in the twelfth century, the kings' sagas were composed before the sagas of Icelanders, and their vitality continued into the fourteenth century. Unlike the sagas of Icelanders, which had an almost unlimited number of subjects at their disposal, the kings' sagas were confined to a narrow circle of men, mainly Norwegian kings, whose careers were reported by subsequent generations of writers. More than the sagas of Icelanders, therefore, the kings' sagas show strong intertextual relationship, and much scholarly energy has been expended in the attempt to unravel the connections.[15]

In effect, all narratives devoted to kings belong to this category regardless of the time in which the protagonists lived and the specific theme and tenor of the individual texts. Ranging in length from dozens to more than thousands of pages, they include synopses of reigns of several kings, such as the text known as *Ágrip* (Compendium), biographies of individual kings (including hagiographies of rulers long dead, for example Oddr Snorrason's saintly description of King Óláfr Tryggvason, and Sturla Þórðarson's balanced account of his contemporary, King Hákon Hákonarson), and major compendia such as *Morkinskinna,* a genre that culminated in Snorri Sturluson's *Heimskringla.*[16]

Since the kings' sagas had long been sequestered within the custody of historians, criticism of historicity and doubts over oral tradition arrived later for this than for the other genres. The subject matter of well-known rulers verifiable from collateral sources lent a credibility to the narratives which was further reinforced by the authors' extensive use of skaldic stanzas, presumably kept alive orally since the time of their composition. By the early nineteenth century, however, when Scandinavian historians had become obsessed with German *Quellenkunde,* they dealt devastating blows both to the kings' sagas and to the Danish author Saxo Grammaticus (who wrote in Latin).[17] A simultaneous reorientation toward social and economic subjects, which were largely ignored in the kings' sagas, encouraged historians to abandon these texts; meanwhile, literary critics assimilated them into their own purview. Some historians began to use the kings' sagas not as sources for the period they purported to describe but as "remains" of the period contemporary to the authors' lives, thus contributing to the study of the mentality of the latter age.[18] The obsession with textual criticism further obscured the fact that the kings' sagas continued to tap oral tradition deep into the thirteenth century.[19] Awareness of this connection and encouragement from scholars working in the sagas of Icelanders have prompted historians to return to the kings' sagas with a renewed confidence that, with care, these texts can be used as evidence for the epochs they describe.[20]

Since the kings' sagas are concerned mainly with political history, they include women primarily as queens and consorts, and striking figures can be found, particularly from the pagan era. The Norwegian queen Gunnhildr, who was a consummate politician in *Heimskringla* and a *femme fatale* in the sagas of Icelanders, belongs in the group of politically powerful women in the royal circles of Europe during the tenth century, and I was tempted to include her in this study.[21] Her most fully developed feature, however, is that of the female inciter (or the *Hetzerin,* to use the German term preferred by scholars). Gunnhildr may well have acted as an inciter, but despite the ubiquitous presence of this figure in the sagas of Icelander, the inciter has little resonance in the everyday life of ordinary people in ancient Iceland and is totally absent from the contemporary sagas. For that reason I reserve Gunnhildr and the other inciters for my study of images.[22] In this book, the kings' sagas are useful mainly for illustrating marriage and succession among the highest circles of society. Describing the Christian world of the north, they show the slow penetration of the new religion and the concomitant social changes, thereby providing oblique glimpses of the older pagan society.[23]

CONTEMPORARY SAGAS

The term *samtíðarsǫgur,* coined by Sigurður Nordal, does not identify the genre by narrative subject matter, but by the distance between the authors and the time they describe.[24] To this group belong accounts that treat the medieval Icelandic scene, including the lay aristocracy (*Sturlunga saga*) and churchmen (the episcopal sagas, some in the form of biographical vitae).[25]

Many historians still affirm that sources written closer to the time they describe are more trustworthy than later evidence, which is deemed to be more literary. Not surprisingly, the contemporary sagas, particularly the bulky *Sturlunga saga,* have been favored by historians, and little doubt has been voiced about the genre's historical veracity.[26] The term "saga" nonetheless remains fitting, for these writings are not analytical historical works but entertaining narratives containing long passages of dialogue. In recent years literary scholars have argued that these texts are subject to the same rhetorical and narratological principles that underlie the sagas of Icelanders and therefore belong rightfully to the domain of literature.[27] In fact, as historians have begun to reclaim the sagas of Icelanders, literary critics have sought to annex not only the kings' but also the contemporary sagas, previously considered the historians' exclusive domain.

Contemporary Icelandic aristocracy is the subject matter of *Sturlunga saga.*[28] Consisting of more than a dozen separate long and short narratives, this bulky compilation was put together around 1300 and survives in two vellum manuscripts from the second half of the fourteenth century. Creating a tenuous narrative link with the sagas of Icelanders, certain Sturlung texts share individual characters with their predecessors.[29] The bulk of the collection, however, deals with the turbulent final century of political independence before internal strife forced the Icelanders to accept Norwegian overlordship in 1262. Preeminence belongs to *Sturlu saga,* and, in particular to *Íslendinga saga,* the longest text in the collection. The former is a biography of Guðný's husband Sturla Þórðarson of Hvammur, and the latter was written by her grandson of the same name, himself a participant in the events described and a well-known historian.

Composed by disparate authors, the single parts of *Sturlunga saga* must be appreciated on their individual terms. Taken as a whole, however, the collection will disappoint the reader weaned on the artistry of the sagas of Icelanders. Rich in detail and crowded with people, the Sturlung texts do not impart the same aesthetic pleasure as the leisurely pace and elegance of the sagas of Icelanders. They require repeated rereading before they yield the authors' grand narrative plan, and because of their political focus, relatively fewer women appear here than in the sagas of Icelanders;[30] nevertheless, the Sturlung texts provide sufficient information about the leaders' private lives to allow an analysis of family and household.[31]

Icelanders also wrote hagiography in Old Norse, both as translations from Latin and as original compositions. Since churchmen's role in promoting Norse literacy is clear, it is not surprising that the oldest existing manuscripts contain Latin saints' lives translated to Old Norse in a lively and entertaining style reminiscent of later sagas.[32] Individual Icelandic bishops became the object of sagas, perhaps first written in Latin but quickly translated into Old Norse, thus resulting in a genre of episcopal sagas corresponding to European vitae.[33] Particularly remarkable is a short life of Bishop Þorlákr, the first Icelandic saint, which was written a short time after his death in 1193. The importance of these texts stems from their illumination of sexual behavior among the clergy and in the population at large, as well as churchmen's attitude toward women.[34] Bishops with a reputation for sainthood, moreover, performed miracles after their deaths, which were recorded in collections composed directly in Old Norse. Often intended as salutary *exempla*, these stories resemble miracle collections on the Continent, but also recapture situations in the quotidian lives of Icelandic women and men.

LAWS

When the Continental tribes first came in contact with the Roman Empire, they presumably had customs and regulations that governed their lives and which they kept alive through oral recitation. Influenced by the written law and the language of the Roman host society, they committed their own laws to Latin beginning in the late fifth century.[35] In contrast, all the peoples in the north (including the Anglo-Saxons) wrote their laws in the vernacular. These texts—like the sagas of Icelanders—fuse old and new. Retained and disseminated orally through yearly performances by lawspeakers, the earliest secular laws were formulated before the advent of Christianity, but kings and/or churchmen quickly became instrumental in committing them to writing. In the process they undoubtedly impressed their own stamp on them, as suggested by kings who attached their names to laws or, more obviously, when churchmen introduced special legislation, clearly identified as Christian, in the text.[36]

I examine this general picture in greater detail for Iceland. During the medieval period Icelandic society was governed sequentially by three different laws, *Grágás, Járnsíða,* and *Jónsbók.*[37] *Grágás* (literally "Grey Goose") the most comprehensive of all Germanic legal texts, deserves Andreas Heusler's epithet, "the giant bird." [38] According to reliable tradition, its irretrievable core consisted of laws conveyed by Úlfljótr, one of the first settlers, from his native Norway (*Ísl* 1.2:7; *Lnd* 1:313).[39] Returning to the home country in the 920s in search of laws suitable for the colony, Úlfljótr was inspired by the Gulathing legislation from the west-coast province. No Norwegian laws are extant from the early tenth century, however, and Úlfljótr undoubtedly transported his precious cargo not in manuscripts, but in mind and memory, in the process augmenting and modifying Norwegian law to suit Icelandic conditions. He participated in the choice of the site for the alþingi, and he was most likely the first law speaker, although a continuous list starts only in 930.

Since the most important task of the law speaker was to recite the entire legal corpus during three yearly meetings of the alþingi, knowledge of the law was kept alive through oral performance for almost two hundred years. The shift from orality to text occurred abruptly in 1117 when the alþingi decided that the laws should be written down at Hafliði Másson's farm during the following winter, according to the memory of the current law speaker Bergþórr Hrafnsson. Assisted by other wise men, Hafliði and

Bergþórr were empowered to make new laws pending approval of the next meeting (*Ísl* 1.10:23–24).

The resulting text, *Hafliðaskrá* (Hafliði's scroll), no longer survives, and revisions of the law continued for generations. An important addition was the Christian law, approved sometime between 1122 and 1133, which prefaced the existing versions of the secular laws. Clearly, then, *Grágás*, as it survives today, is a compilation within which it is difficult to distinguish obsolete rules and recent enactments—with the exception of those identified as new laws (*nýmæli*)—from a larger body of legal material normally assumed applicable to the twelfth century. (Undoubtedly, many regulations were of more ancient origin and some of the nýmæli may never have been implemented.)

In contrast, the two other texts, *Járnsíða* and *Jónsbók*, are not indigenous compilations but royal codifications issued by the Norwegian king and intended to take immediate effect in Iceland. More influenced by Norwegian than Icelandic law, the former, introduced in 1271, became unpopular and was replaced by *Jónsbók*. Despite initial resistance, the latter was accepted by the alþingi in 1281 and remained in effect until modern times.[40]

The problem of historicity is even more complex for the laws than for the narratives.[41] Although the preserved legal texts can be dated more precisely than the sagas (a few fragments stem from the late twelfth century, and the two chief manuscripts, *Konungsbók* and *Staðarhólsbók*, from a century later), a serious question arises over the dating of the law itself. In Norway a royal name-tag, "the law of Óláfr," for example, might provide chronological grounding, although the common practice of repeating names from one generation to the next makes precise identification difficult. Royal authority and Christian leadership, however, raise the new issue of prescription versus description. The former mode is often associated with single or oligarchic leadership and the latter with community consensus, but both are enmeshed inextricably in the text. If laws were entirely prescriptive, they might provoke resistance, as did *Járnsíða*. In this case leaders were forced to accommodate native Icelandic tradition by adopting *Jónsbók*, a text that had more in common with *Grágás*.

It is possible to ascertain the prescriptive stance of a law by comparing its text with the current goals of political leaders, but a descriptive mode is harder to identify because of uncertainty over the period contextualized in the law. In Norway a tradition of royal legislative initiative can be traced back in saga narratives to Hálfdan the Black (*svarti*) and Hákon, foster son of the English King Aðalsteinn (*Aðalsteinsfóstri*), in the mid–tenth century (*Hkr* 26.7:91; 11:163). Kings normally would be expected to know customary law as well as the population, and they may have been content to add their prestige and name to laws already adopted by the community. Hákon had been raised in England from childhood, however, and it is possible that he was not familiar with Norwegian law. His conversion to Christianity further inspired him to formulate a program of his own, and his legislation may thus have been more prescriptive than descriptive.[42] On the other hand, in Iceland, a country without executive power, laws may be considered customary and thus descriptive of the times in which they were formulated because they tended to express communal agreement.[43] Additions to the law (*nýmæli*) may have been prescriptive at first but in fact became descriptive in due course. The etymology of *lǫg*, Old Norse for law, suggests this process. Derived from the verb "to lay down" (*leggja*) and always used in the plural form, lǫg (from *lag* [layer]) suggests a slow accumulation and laying down of individual regulations as they were approved by the alþingi; the entire body was kept alive through performance by the law speakers and eventually encrusted in layers of written text.[44]

Legislation—whether initiated by kings or the community—can be traced back to pagan times both in Iceland and Norway. Eager to find evidence of written law at this early stage but aware of the close connection between churchmen and writing, a few historians have hypothesized the existence of written versions in runes.[45] This search for pagan origins has been reinforced by a persistent belief in a Germanic *Urrecht*. It is undeniable that many regulations, concerning fines for crimes (*wergeld*) and rules for marriage, for example, exhibit striking similarities throughout the length and breadth of the Germanic world. During the nineteenth century German legal historians were eager to use nordic vernacular laws to fill out the shorter Continental Latin codes. Although postdating the latter, the former were considered as representative of a more primitive stage than the latter Latin versions.

Although they grant the similarities between the Germanic and nordic laws, most scholars today admit that it is impossible to construct an *Urrecht* from the enormous wealth of Germanic nordic legal texts that encompass almost an entire millennium between the fifth and fourteenth centuries. Taking an opposite tack, other historians, such as the Swede Else Sjöholm, deny the existence of a Germanic *Urrecht* and instead scrutinize the local texts for influence from Roman and Mosaic law.[46] Since the Swedish laws appeared later than the other Scandinavian laws, largely were issued under royal direction and nourished by local conditions different from the rest of the north, this approach is less relevant to the other nordic countries.[47] The recent turn of Old Norse scholarship toward anthropology, moreover, has encouraged the correlation between nordic laws found in texts and functions exercised by contemporary tribal societies at economic and political stages comparable to medieval Iceland.[48]

Although the legal texts raise even more complications than the narratives, both Icelandic and Norwegian laws nevertheless are important to this book. They make it possible, for example, to examine the transition from pagan to Christian regulations in marriage. The influence of churchmen can, moreover, be gauged from both content and placement of individual paragraphs in the law, as, for example, when modifications were moved from the pagan engagement section (*festa-þáttr*) in the secular laws to the Christian preambles.[49]

CHRISTIANITY, HISTORICITY, ORAL TRADITION, AND POSTSTRUCTURAL DOUBT

It is clear that the pagan-Christian transition looms large in the four genres of evidence examined here. The shift is particularly apparent in the sagas of Icelanders and in those kings' sagas that depict the pagan era. Like the Eddic poems, which had memorialized pagan Continental heroes from the fifth century, these narratives recorded the deeds of past events. The authors open their stories with descriptions of pre-Christian Norwegian ancestors who had immigrated to Iceland. Deploying these narratives as preludes to the far more important deeds of their Icelandic forebears, they focused on the so-called saga age from the early tenth to the middle of the eleventh century, a period that pivoted on the peaceful acceptance of Christianity in the year

1000, an event recorded in several of the sagas.⁵⁰ The early parts of the kings' sagas, dealing primarily with Norway, likewise bridged the pagan-Christian transition.

First encountering the new religion abroad, male Icelanders were at liberty to accept or ignore it according to personal inclination. As they pursued their habitual travels to Norway, however, they met an increasingly militant Christianity personified in the Norwegian king, who was determined to impose his new faith on his own country and persuade the distant island to accept it as well. While in Norway, they also witnessed stubborn resistance from the local population. Describing such events and figures from a multi-generational and diachronic as well as from a synchronic perspective, both the sagas of the Icelanders and the kings' sagas demonstrate increased awareness of a mounting clash between heathen and Christian culture.

This pagan-Christian conflict, however, ran deeper than mere events. Original memories recalling the oldest saga heroes were framed in a pagan consciousness. After the conversion, those memories were now in the care of Christian minds who sought to accommodate them to the deeds of their more recent ancestors, the Christian descendants of their pagan forefathers. What was considered memorable changed subtly under Christian influence and was gradually transmuted into an ethos different from the heroic mentality of the more ancient poetry. It is a mistake to think of oral tradition as a fixed and immutable legacy for prose. Indeed, not encased in poetic structure and technique, the prose tradition was even more supple and amenable to change that was poetry. During the oral phase of saga creation, when separate segments were expanded, a fusion of old and new began, reaching a culmination in the thirteenth century when the sagas were fully developed and written down by Christian authors.⁵¹

The sagas of Icelanders as well as the ancient parts of the kings' sagas thus mix pagan and Christian currents—like the Icelandic river Blanda—and it is difficult to separate the individual sources. The magnificent Icelandic landscape, barely changed today from the vivid tableaus of the sagas, and the hardships imposed by a rigorous climate on a primitive economy offered timeless features of life that the authors deployed skillfully to lend credence to other facets of their ancient stories.

The legal texts retain a similar mixture of pagan and Christian heritage. The settlers in Iceland brought with them from Norway a conception of a legal corpus agreed upon by a local community but applicable only to a small area. Once in Iceland, however, they developed the novel concept of a set of laws expanded to apply to the whole country. In both countries, the pagan community had formulated a body of early laws that included, for example, the essential social concerns of marriage and inheritance.

As churchmen gained influence, however, they made their mark on the law directly or indirectly. In Norway, where kings spearheaded Christianity's advance in a near literal sense, the names Hákon Aðalsteinsfóstri (fostered by the English King Aðalsteinn), St. Ólafr (*helgi*), and Magnús Erlingsson were attached to the provincial laws; in Iceland the country's two bishops became intimately involved in legal affairs. The Church's needs would have obviously necessitated additions and changes to the oral law already during the first century after conversion; when the law was written down in 1117, clerics were employed for the technical task of copying. A specifically Christian section was added later. Although the Christian influence in this part is self-evident, it is more difficult to separate old and new, pagan and Christian in the rest (aside from the explicitly marked "new enactments" [*nýmæli*]). The Church's influence was further enhanced when the two bishops became regular members of the law council (*Gg* 1a:211). In case of discrepancies among various written versions, the copies owned by the bishops were assigned precedence (*Gg* 1a: 213). Not all Christian ideas were readily accepted, and discrepancies between the clerical and the secular law testify to the tension.

The contemporary sagas mute this pagan-Christian clash. Devoted to the lives of bishops, the episcopal sagas obviously transmit Christian ideals, but they, and the narratives devoted to medieval Norwegian kings, also illustrate churchmen's difficulties in imposing Christian morality in sexual and marital matters both within their own ranks and among the laity. By disapproving and outlawing ancient behavior, these texts thus provide an oblique image of pagan sexuality. The secular narratives of *Sturlunga saga,* in which authors describe events within living memory in Iceland, are also largely permeated with a Christian ethos but nonetheless contain occasional reminders of the ancient mores; in 1180, for example, when the wife of an enemy of Sturla Þórðarson, Guðný's husband, who attempted to cut out one of his eyes, she claimed that she wanted to make him look like the person he would rather be, "and that is Óðinn" (*St* 1: 109).[52]

This pagan-Christian tension, however, is only the most visible part of the far more fundamental problem of historicity inherent in all sources on which I have based my study. How far should one trust narratives and legal writings allegedly describing conditions and events that were removed by several centuries from the high and later Middle Ages when the texts were written down? This question is intimately connected with the elusive issue of oral tradition. The presence in all three narrative genres of numerous skaldic stanzas at first seems to alleviate these problems. Taken from poems attributed to ancient skalds describing important events at which they had been present, the stanzas provided the most ancient warranty for the prose authors who studded their narratives with these so-called "detached stanzas" (*lausavísur*). Although these verses had not been previously inscribed, their poetic form and diction guaranteed a certain "textual" stability. If authentic, the stanzas thus vouch for a degree of historicity and corroborate the reliability of oral tradition. Recently, however, scholars have discovered that some stanzas were not the product of skalds contemporary with the events described in the stanzas and the surrounding prose, but of the prose author himself, or, in other cases, of unknown poets working in the period between the alleged poet and the prose author.[53] In other words, these stanzas do not confirm but further complicate the problems of historicity and oral tradition.

The remarkable creative energy of Icelandic writers had slackened by the end of the Middle Ages, but fortunately for modern scholarship the sagas continued to fascinate readers and listeners at home, thereby increasing the demand for copies which have survived. Outside Iceland, however, the narratives were forgotten in the late Middle Ages, with the exception of the kings' sagas, which continued to enjoy acceptance as reliable historical evidence. As the heroic sagas and the sagas of Icelanders were rediscovered by Scandinavian antiquarians during the seventeenth century, these texts at first shared a reputation for historicity.[54] Depicting heroes and mythic kings far more ancient than the protagonists of the kings' sagas, the heroic sagas eventually forced historians to consider how this material had survived between the occurrence of the events and their recording. For all but the most fantastic tales the problem was solved by postulating an oral tradition that conveyed a true picture of the events, keeping them alive for generations, until they were finally committed to writing by a person who acted more as scribe than author.

Because of their artistic merit, the sagas of Icelanders received most of the scholarly attention. By the middle of the nineteenth century, scholars began to suggest that these texts should be read as literature rather than history. As a consequence, the role of the author waxed and faith in oral tradition waned. This state of affairs has lasted for about a century. Only in the last twenty years has oral tradition again received a hearing. In slowly moving waves similar to those which eroded historicity from the successive genres of Icelandic writing, a new tide of trust in oral tradition is rising among those who study the Old Norse corpus. The present condition is turbulence produced by the tide coming in before the old waves have subsided.

The problem of historicity, moreover, has been disturbed most recently by poststructural theories that, in fact, bear special pertinence to Old Norse studies. As scholars in all fields increasingly experience poststructural doubt, the differences previously perceived between history and literature begin to collapse. Historians are asked to accept the assertion of literary critics that historical sources do not provide an objective background against which to measure literary texts. Left with language and texts not merely as the only constituents of human consciousness, but also as sole agents available for the construction of social meaning, all scholars — literary as well as historical — are likely to share comparable endeavors variously labeled New Historicism or Cultural Studies.[55]

It can be argued that these poststructural concerns are, in fact, salutary for Old Norse scholarship.[56] Because of the nature of the Icelandic saga, literature and history have always been joined in a symbiotic relationship. As historians accommodate linguistic and literary theories and critics become aware of cultural and historical concerns, many of the problems that preoccupied Old Norse scholars in the past seem less urgent. As poststructural theorists reduce everything to texts, the boundary between literature and history is constantly traversed. If texts do not reflect social reality, it is of less importance that the sagas of Icelanders, purporting to chronicle pagan society, were written two centuries after the acceptance of Christianity. If narrative devices inform all texts, not only these sagas but also the contemporary narratives and, indeed, even the laws and the charters should be scrutinized for rhetorical devices and techniques which enhance their textual meaning. In other words, although historians began to relinquish the sagas to literary scholars in the nineteenth century, historians today who have negotiated "the linguistic turn" should now be able to reclaim these priceless narratives, regardless of how they are labeled. Both sides have become increasingly accustomed to mutual interaction.

Briefly stated, after years of neglect by historians, trends within Old Norse scholarship itself combined with current critical thinking in literature and history make it unfeasible to restrict Old Norse sources to literary purposes alone. In fact, despite peculiar problems, Icelandic narrative and legal sources once again lend themselves well to an examination of Icelandic society.[57] Attenuated by the reemerging faith in oral tradition and blurred by the theoretical concerns raised by poststructuralists, the pagan-Christian conflict — although inherent in all sources — may be less significant than it appeared at first.

Finally, it is worth considering the advantages of scrutinizing the continuity of Icelandic culture rather than underscoring the temporal differences between the texts' ascription and the events they purport to describe. This continuity is suggested, in fact, by the very existence of the sagas of Icelanders and the extant copies of *Grágás*. Around the millennium Icelanders were less reluctant to accept the new Christianity than they were to acknowledge the authority of Norwegian king two and half centuries later. In the year 1000 most people had little idea of what the new religion would bring, but in 1262 many were profoundly aware of the consequences — for better and worse — of the coming Norwegian rule. At the same time they were conscious that their old political system had failed because of the absence of an executive organ. What the Post-Exilic authors did for the ancient Jews, the authors of the sagas of Icelanders sought to accomplish for their generation: they attempted to recapture the old world before it disappeared. They chose to describe their proud past as a smooth stream in which Christianity had introduced only minor, often imperceptible ripples. Not only the sagas of Icelanders, but all the evidence, should be read not merely as manifestations of medieval Christian Iceland, but also as surviving evidence of ancient pagan Iceland seen, admittedly, in the distant mirror of thirteenth-century Icelandic nostalgia.

Abbreviations

(Frequently cited texts, journals, series, and works)

ÅNOH	*Aarbøger for nordisk oldkyndighed og historie*
Áb	*Árna saga biskups*
Ad	*Adonías saga*, LMIR 3
ÆSn	*Ævi Snorra goða*, ÍF 4
Áfl	*Ála flekks saga*, ASB 17
Ág	*Ágrip*, ÍF 29
Alf	*Alfræði íslenzk*, SUGNL 37, 41, 45
ANF	*Arkiv för nordisk filologi*
APhS	*Acta Philologica Scandinavica*
ASB	Altnordische Sagabibliothek
BA	Bibliotheca Arnamagnæana
Bdm	*Bandamanna saga*, ÍF 7
Bg	*Bǫglunga sǫgur*
BHd	*Bjarnar saga Hítdœlakappa*, ÍF 3
Bkr	*Brandakrossa þáttr*, ÍF 11
BONIS	Bibliography of Old Norse-Icelandic Studies
Brð	*Bárðar saga*, ÍF 13
Bs	*Biskupa sögur*
Bsk	*Byskupa sǫgur*
DI	Diplomatarium Islandicum
DMA	Dictionary of the Middle Ages
Dpl	*Droplaugarsona saga*, ÍF 11
DSH	*Draumr Þorsteins Síðu-Hallssonar*, ÍF 11
EA	Editiones Arnamagnæanæ
Eg	*Egils saga*, ÍF 2
Erb	*Eyrbyggja saga*, ÍF 4
Erð	*Eiríks saga rauða*, ÍF 4
FB	*Flóres saga ok Blankiflúr*, RS 4

Fgs	*Fagrskinna*, ÍF 29
Flat	*Flateyjarbók*
Fld	*Fljótsdœla saga*, ÍF 11
Flm	*Flóamanna saga*, ÍF 14
Fnb	*Finnboga saga*, ÍF 14
FSN	Fornaldar sögur Norðurlanda
Ftb	*Fóstbrœðra saga*, ÍF 6
Gg	Grágás, Finsen 1852, 1879, 1883
Gí	*Gísla saga*, ÍF 6
GKd	*Gunnars saga Keldugnúpsfífls*, ÍF 14
Gn	*Grœnlendinga saga*, ÍF 4
Gnl	*Gunnlaugs saga Ormstungu*, ÍF 3
Gr	*Grettis saga*, ÍF 7
Grm	*Grímnismál*, N/K
Grn	*Grœnlendinga þáttr*, ÍF 4
Gtr	*Gautreks saga*, FSN 4
GÞb	*Gunnars þáttr Þiðrandabana*, ÍF 11
HáH	*Hálfs saga ok Hálfsrekka*, FSN 2
Hðv	*Heiðarvíga saga*, ÍF 3
Hgr	*Haralds saga gráfeldar*, ÍF 26
Hh	*Þáttr Hrómundar halta*, ÍF 8
Hhb	*Hákonar saga herðibreiðs*, ÍF 28
Hhf	*Haralds saga ins hárfagra*, ÍF 26
Hkr	*Heimskringla*, ÍF 26–28
Hld2	*Halldórs þáttr Snorrasonar inn síðari*, ÍF 5
Hlf	*Hallfreðar saga*, ÍF 8
Hn	*Hœnsa-Þóris saga*, ÍF 3
Hrð	*Harðar saga*, ÍF 13
HrF	*Hrafnkels saga Freysgoða*, ÍF 11
HrG	*Hrafns þáttr Guðrúnarsonar*, ÍF 8
HrGt	*Hrólfs saga Gautrekssonar*, FSN 4
Hrkr	*Hrólfs saga kraka*, FSN 1
HrS	*Haralds saga Sigurðarsonar*, ÍF 28
Hrþ	*Hreiðars þáttr*, ÍF 10
HsÍ	*Hávarðar saga Ísfirðings*, ÍF 6
Hss	*Haraldssona saga*, ÍF 28
Íbm 1, 2	*Íslensk bókmenntasaga 1, 2*
ÍF	*Íslenzk fornrit*
ÍS	*Íslendinga sögur* 1987
Ísl	*Íslendingabók*, ÍF 1
JEGP	*Journal of English and Germanic Philology*
JH	*Jarlamanns saga ok Hermanns*, LMIR 3, RS 6
JHS	*Journal of the History of Sexuality*
Jn	*Jónsbók*
Jms	*Jómsvíkinga saga*
K	*Konungsbók*, Gg 1 a, b

Kjn	*Kjalnesinga saga*, ÍF 14
KLNM	Kulturhistorisk leksikon for nordisk middelalder
Krm	*Kormáks saga*, ÍF 8
KrR	*Króka-Refs saga*, ÍF 14
Ljs	*Ljósvetninga saga*, ÍF 10
LMIR	Late Medieval Icelandic Romances
Lnd	*Landnámabók*, ÍF 1
Lx	*Laxdœla saga*, ÍF 5
ME	*Magnúss saga Erlingssonar*, ÍF 28
Mg	*Magnúss saga ins góða*, ÍF 28
Mgs	*Magnússona saga*, ÍF 28
MHN	*Monumenta Historica Norvegiæ*
Mj	*Mágus saga jarls*, RS 2
MM	*Maal og Minne*
Mn	*Mírmanns saga*, LMIR 3
Mr	*Maríu saga*
MS	*Mediaeval Scandinavia*
MSE	*Medieval Scandinavia: An Encyclopedia*
Msk	*Morkinskinna*
NG	*Nornagests þáttr*, FSN 1
NgL	Norges gamle Love
(N)HT	(Norwegian) *Historisk Tidsskrift*
Njála, see *Nj*	
Nj	*Njáls saga*, ÍF 12
QO	*Qrvar-Odds saga*, RSN 2
ON	Old Norse
Óh	*Óláfs saga helga*, ÍF 27
ONIL	Old Norse-Icelandic Literature
Ork	*Orkneyinga saga*, ÍF 34
OSM	Oddr Snorrason munkr
OSt	*Orms þáttr Stórólfssonar*, ÍF 13
ÓT	*Óláfs saga Tryggvasonar*, ÍF 26
ÓTm	Ólafur Halldórsson ed. 1958
Rkd	*Reykdœla saga*, ÍF 10
RS	Riddarasögur 1954
S	*Staðarhólsbók*, Gg 2
SBVS	*Saga-Book of the Viking Society*
Sf	*Sigrgarðs saga frœkna*, LMIR 5
SI	*Scripta Islandica*
SÍ	*Saga Íslands*
Skj	Finnur Jónsson 1908–15
Sl	*Sǫrla þáttr*, ÍF 10
SN	*Saulus saga ok Nikanors*, LMIR 2
SnH	*Sneglu-Halla þáttr*, ÍF 9
Sp	*Speculum*
SS	*Scandinavian Studies*

St	*Sturlunga saga*
SUGNL	Samfund til Udgivelse af Gammel Nordisk Litteratur
Sv	*Sverris saga*
Svf	*Svarfdæla saga*, ÍF 9
VB	*Viktors saga ok Blávus*
Vbr	*Vǫðu-Brands þáttr*, ÍF 10
VGl	*Víga-Glúms saga*, ÍF 9
Vgl	*Víglundar saga*, ÍF 14
VLj	*Valla-Ljóts saga*, ÍF 9
Vls	*Vǫlsunga saga*, SUGNL 36
Vp	*Vápnfirðinga saga*, ÍF 11
Vtn	*Vatnsdæla saga*, ÍF 8
Yn	*Ynglinga saga*, ÍF 26
ÞH	*Þorgils saga ok Hafliða*, St 1
Þhb	*Brot af Þórðar sögu hreðu*, ÍF 14
Þhr	*Þórðar saga hreðu*, ÍF 14
Þhv	*Þorsteins saga hvíta*, ÍF 11
Þsf	*Þorsteins þáttr Austfirðings*, IF 11
ÞSH	*Þorsteins saga Síðu-Hallssonar*, ÍF 11
Þsk	*Þorsteins þáttr skelks*, ÍS 3
Þskf	*Þorskfirðinga saga*, ÍF 13
Þss	*Þorsteins þáttr sǫgufróða*, ÍF 11
Þst	*Þorsteins þáttr stangarhǫggs*, ÍF 11
Þtv	*Þorsteins saga víkingssonar*, FSN 3
Þux	*Þorsteins þáttr uxafóts*, ÍF 13
ÞÞ	*Þiðranda þáttr ok Þórhalls*, ÓTm

Notes

PREFACE

1. By "Old Norse" I mean "Old West-nordic," the language spoken by the Norwegian immigrants who arrived in Iceland from the late ninth century. Subsequently undergoing changes in the two countries, it became Norwegian and Icelandic respectively. Throughout the medieval period "Old Norse" encompasses both languages, but the overwhelming majority of Old Norse manuscripts were written in Icelandic. Unfortunately, for reasons of brevity, "Icelandic" cannot be accommodated in the title. On these problems, see Jónas Kristjánsson 1993.

2. "The sagas of Icelanders," coined from the Icelandic *Íslendingasǫgur,* is increasingly replacing the term "family sagas" in English and will be used in this book.

3. It will be published by University of Pennsylvania Press in 1996. Henceforth, it will be referred to as *ONIW.* In this work, I shall pay particular attention to divine female figures and four vivid images of human women, the warrior, the prophetess or sorceress, the revenger, and the whetter.

4. Duby 1980, 147.

5. With the exception of physical lovemaking, the subject of love—heterosexual and homosocial bonding—will not be treated in these books, but I hope to turn to them in the future. For a preliminary version, see Jochens 1992.

6. Grønbech 1909–1912 and Grönbech 1932.

INTRODUCTION

1. The meeting may have taken place in the year 999; see Ólafía Einarsdóttir 1964.

2. The statement comes from Ari's "Book of Icelanders" (*Íslendingabók*); the text is found in the series Íslenzk fornrit vol. 1, and the passage occurs in chap. 7, p. 17. The following texts from this series will be cited by abbreviated title, volume (without series indication), chapter, and page (in this case *Ísl* 1.7:17). In Chapter 3 I return to the continuation of this law which ordered the abolition of infanticide.

3. On the conversion, see Jón Hnefill Aðalsteinsson 1978.

4. On Benjamin's use of *Geschichtsschreibung,* see his essay "The Storyteller: Reflections on the Works of Nikolai Leskov," in Benjamin 1955, 83–109, esp. 97, and his "Theses on the Philosophy of History," Benjamin 1955, 255–66.

5. The sources are discussed more fully in the Appendix.

6. Two other genres, the heroic sagas (*fornaldarsǫgur*) and the chivalric sagas (*riddarasǫgur*), are used occasionally here to test the mentality of the authors on specific issues, but their full exploitation is reserved for my study of images.

7. I am grateful to Ian Baldwin and Davíð Erlingsson for help with this paragraph.

8. Two are mentioned in *Landnámabók,* a record of four hundred of the original settlers and the land they appropriated (*landnám*); see, for example, *Lnd* 1:377 and 74. On this text, see Appendix n. 1.

9. The name is found only in the late *Hrana saga hrings,* a saga that exists only in manuscripts from the nineteenth century. For the reference to Svartá, see *Íslendinga sögur* 1949, 9:417.

10. Likewise, the third most important Christian celebration after Christmas (*Jól*) and Easter (*Páskar*) was called *Hvítasunna* (White Sunday; cf. English Whitsun).

CHAPTER ONE. GUÐNÝ BǪÐVARSDÓTTIR AND GUÐRÚN GJÚKADÓTTIR: NORDIC-GERMANIC CONTINUITY

1. The historicity of Sigurðr is questionable; his name has been associated with the Merovingian king Sigibert from the sixth century, known from Gregory of Tours, and with Arminius, leader of the Cherusci tribe in the first century and known by contemporary Roman historians.

2. Storm 1888, 24, 126, 326; *Flat* 3:525.

3. References to *Sturlunga saga* (volume and page in the 1946 edition) will henceforward appear in the text. For a more recent edition, see Appendix, n. 28.

4. Nonetheless, Bǫðvarr was among five named Icelandic chieftains singled out for special opprobrium for their sexual behavior in a letter from the Norwegian Archbishop Eysteinn in 1180 (DI 1:260–64).

5. They are listed in the following order: Þórðr, Sighvatr, Snorri, Helga, and Vigdís (1:52). When Sturla died in 1183, the boys' ages were given as eighteen (Þórðr), thirteen (Sighvatr), and five (Snorri; 1:229). Sons were almost always listed before daughters, so we cannot conclude that the girls were younger. If they were older, they would have been born during the first five years of the marriage, suggesting that Guðný was in her late teens when married and thus ready for reproduction. If Þórðr was the oldest, the infertile years would suggest that she had not yet reached menarche. Of course, the spacing of Guðný's sons would have allowed for births in the intervals. If Snorri was only three at his father's death, as suggested by other passages, the girls could still be younger than the boys.

6. On fostering, see Kreutzer 1987, 221–34, and Jochens 1996b.

7. Recently Sverrir Tómasson has suggested that by sending Snorri away, Sturla may have intended to leave a greater share of his inheritance to the two older sons, as fathers on the Continent did when they sent younger sons to a monastery; see *Íbm* 1:369. For a case in the context of the sagas of Icelanders, see Þorkell and Þiðrandi in *Fld* 11.4: 221–22.

8. On the importance for Snorri himself, see Jochens 1994b.

9. For a discussion of sources, see Appendix. The sagas of Icelanders (and the kings' sagas) are available in the series Íslenzk fornrit (ÍF) and the former also appear in *Íslendinga sögur* 1987 (*ÍS*). See Introduction, n. 2, for citation principles. Practically all these texts have been translated into English. For a comprehensive list, see Fry 1980 and Acker 1993.

10. On this episode, see Bjarni Einarsson, "Hörð höfuðbein," in Bjarni Einarsson 1987, 107–14, Heller 1984, and Helgi Þorláksson 1992. The date of Snorri's death comes from the so-called *Ævi Snorra goða* (4:185–86), thought to be written by Ari Þorgilsson, the author of *Íslendingabók;* see Einar Ól. Sveinsson's introduction (ÍF 4: xi–xiv).

11. The genealogy can be worked out from many texts; see, for example, *St* 1:64.

12. Sturla's fourteen children, evenly divided between legitimate and illegitimate, were more than matched by Snorri's nineteen legitimate and three illegitimate children.

13. The family arrived when the country was "completely settled" (*albyggt*) and had to receive land from others (*Lnd* 1:180).

14. Having received news of Gísli's death, Þórdís divorced her second husband Bǫrkr and left the farm at Helgafell (*Gí* 6.37:117). When Snorri obtained this farm as his paternal inheritance by buying out his uncle, Þórdís moved back and managed the estate for her son (*Erb* 4.15:26). Twenty years later Snorri swapped farms with Guðrún Ósvífrsdóttir and lived for the rest of his life at Sælingsdalstunga (*Lx* 5.56:169; *Nj* 12.114: 286).

15. To trace Guðný's genealogy back to Kveld-Úlfr, see, for example, *Þhb* 14.7:246–47.

16. Perhaps occurring within the author's memory, the incident may be more reliable than many other events reported in the sagas of Icelanders. Although not included in the present form of the *Ævi* (n. 10), the events may have been part of Ari's original work and would undoubtedly have been reported by Snorri's daughter Þuríðr, to whom Ari elsewhere referred as a great fountain of knowledge (*Lnd* 1.1:4). On Ari's historical production, see Ellehøj 1965, 15–84; Jakob Benediktsson's introduction in ÍF 1, passim, and Sverrir Tómasson in *Íbm* 1:292–99.

17. It is possible that Snorri Sturluson's murder in 1241 prompted the author to include Snorri's mother in his story.

18. There is a verbal echo in this stanza of stanza 40 in the Eddic poem *Guðrúnarkviða ǫnnur,* see 6.18:58, n.

19. Scholars have discussed whether the stanzas were genuinely those of a ninth-century poet Gísli, were written by the thirteenth-century prose author as embellishment for his narrative, or were composed in the intervening period; see Foote 1963, 112–23, and Turville-Petre 1944.

20. For genealogies ending in Guðný and beginning in the first colonists (*landnámsmenn*), see, for example, *Lnd* 1: 77–79, 316–18; *ÞÞ* (*Flat* 1:418–21); *Þst* 11:78–79.

21. On this issue, see Faulkes 1978–1979.

22. This is the *Sturlubók, Þórðarbók,* and *Hauksbók* versions; see *Lnd* 1:239–41. Ragnarr appeared in other genealogies in *Lnd;* see 1:214. Recently, McTurk has revived an old idea that the nickname "Furry-Breeches" (*loðbrók*) referred to a woman; see McTurk 1991, 9–10.

23. Other families also ranged themselves in this lineage, including the settlers in Greenland and in the New World; for examples, see *Erb* 4.1:4, *Nj* 12.1:6, 113:285, 114: 286–87, *Erð* 4.7:217, *Ftb* 6.2:124. In the contemporary sagas, see *St* 1:64.

24. Details are provided by *Vǫlsunga saga.*

25. See Faulkes 1978–1979, 101–4. They are found in DI 1:504–6 and 3:5–8, 10–13.

26. The date of the list can be approximated by examining which of her children were considered marriageable and therefore included.

27. A version composed about 1230 (DI 1:504–6) includes four women, one from 1290 (DI 3:5–8) had six, and one from 1310 (DI 3:10–13) arrived at twelve by including collateral lines.

28. The tree of Jesse, the visual type for these genealogies, depicts the biblical Jesse reposing like a woman after childbirth and dreaming about his male descendants, who hang like ripe fruit from the branches of a huge phallic trunk that sprouts from his loins. See Jochens 1987b, 327–29, with references (n. 6). On the proto–Indo–European roots of these ideas, see Linke 1992.

29. *Vǫlsunga saga* is only the most spectacular example of nordic authors' attempts to keep the ancient subject matter alive, efforts that also resulted in imprints in the popular imagination. See also *NG* in FSN 1:307–35 and *SnH* 9.3:267–68.

30. This is the famous Guðrún Ósvífrsdóttir. On the similarity between the poetic Brynhildr and the prose Guðrún, see Anne Heinrichs, "*Annat er várt eðli.* The type of prepatriarchal woman in Old Norse literature," in *Structure* 1986, 110–40.

31. See *Skj* 1B:303. Connoting a divine secret, Guðrún was a pan-Germanic name. Although rare in West Scandinavia, it is found on Swedish runic stones already in the eleventh century.

32. NgL 5:19–21, esp. 20. In *Gg*, including the Christian section, lawmakers referred to N. or N. N. Relatively rare in the sagas of Icelanders (16 cases), Jón had come to rival the names derived from Þórr by the middle of thirteenth century, as suggested by the registers to DI vols. 3 and 4.

33. See *Nöfn Íslendinga,* 261. Traditionally the first part of the name has been associated with the word for battle. I am grateful to James E. Knirk for runic information and to Marianne Kalinke for her scrutiny of the Reykjavík telephone book. For medieval occurrences, see Lind 1905–1915, 389–91, and 1931, 339–45.

34. Dronke 1969, 45, thinks that this poem may have been composed in Norway. See also Jón Helgason 1953, 96. For a recent treatment in English of the historiography of Eddic poetry, see Harris in *ONIL,* 68–156. See also *Íbm* 1, 75–187.

35. See Einar Ól. Sveinsson 1953, 100–101.

36. On this story, see Bergljót Kristjánsdóttir 1990, Sigurður Sigurmundsson 1963, and Preben Meulengracht Sørensen, "Guðrún Gjúkadóttir in Miðjumdalr. Zur Aktualität nordischer Heldensage im Island des 13. Jahrhunderts," in *Heldensage* 1988, 183–96. An act of revenge against Gizurr Þorvaldsson, the burning occurred the day after the wedding of his son Hallr to Sturla's daughter Ingibjǫrg, Guðný Bǫðvarsdóttir's great-granddaughter.

37. On her acquisition of this estate, see n. 14.

38. This "sibyl-grave" (*vǫluleiði*) is the first mention of a burial site of an ancient sorceress, but other cases are reported in later folktales; see *Lx* 5:224, n. 3. An Eddic reference is found in *Baldrs draumar,* str. 4.

39. See the discussion between Helgi Skúli Kjartansson and Bergljót S. Kristjánsdóttir in *Skáldskaparmál* 2 (1992):270–80.

CHAPTER TWO. MARRIAGE

1. On the Germanization of Christianity, see Russell 1994.
2. Köstler 1943, Wemple 1981, 31–50. For additional bibliography, see Jochens 1991b, 362, n. 14.
3. Vilhjálmur Finsen 1849, 236, n. 5, Maurer 1908, 541, and article "Bröllop" in KLNM 2:306–22, but compare Krause 1926, 217, who connects it with a dance; the term may refer to rituals now lost.
4. Magnús, King Óláfr *helgi*'s (St. Óláfr) only son and heir, was born by a noble woman, Álfhildr, who had been abducted from her native England and brought to Norway (Jochens 1987b, 335, n. 38). See the marriage between Ketill and Arneiðr; the latter had been abducted from the Hebrides together with her mother and brought to Norway (*Dpl* 11.1–2:138–40). In contrast, see the relationship between Leifr and the Hebridean woman whom he had impregnated but did not dare take away (*Erð* 4.5: 210, 414).
5. On Icelandic men's violent behavior toward women see Jochens 1991b.
6. For the legal aspects of nordic law the best and fullest treatment are still Vilhjálmur Finsen 1849–1850 and Maurer 1908, 473–678. See also Vilhjálmur Finsen's unpublished manuscript, AM Access 6b, in Árnastofnun in Reykjavík. For a German view, see Merschberger 1937.
7. For further discussion of these issues, see Appendix.
8. "Lawfully begotten" (*skilgetinn*) is used in Norwegian law whereas Icelandic law and the older sagas prefer the term "conceived purely" (*skírgetinn*). See, for example, *Vtn* 8.13:37, n. 4 and Maurer 1883.
9. Bigamists were outlawed and children from the second marriage were not able to inherit. The only exception concerned Icelandic men on extended trips to Norway who were allowed a wife in each country. Children born by the two women could inherit, provided both marriages had been entered into legally (*Grágás* 1a:226, 1b:240; 2:70). Henceforward *Grágás* will be abbreviated Gg. The three main manuscripts were edited by Vilhjálmur Finsen 1852 (*Gg* 1 a–b; *Konungsbók*), 1879 (*Gg* 2; *Staðarhólsbók*), and 1883 (*Gg* 3). See also Appendix, n. 37.
10. For further details, see Jochens 1987b and the section "Reproduction and Royal Succession" in Chapter 3.
11. See Vilhjálmur Finsen, 1849, 285, and article "Oäkta barn" in KLNM 13:67–76.
12. For the oldest marriage regulations in the Norwegian laws, see NgL 1:16, 27–28.
13. See, for example, NgL 1:27.
14. *Gg* 1b:29–75 and *Gg* 2:152–209.
15. The passage is controversial. The older *Konungsbók* states that a man can buy a woman "for his bodily pleasure," or "as his concubine" (*til karnaðar;* 1a:192), whereas the term in *Staðarhólsbók, til eiginkonu,* implies marriage (2:190). See also *Gg* 1b:239–40. Men may eventually have received permission to marry an unfree woman, but the innovation remained gender specific. See Vilhjálmur Finsen, 1849, 224, and Maurer 1908, 577. On gender symmetry in law, see Jochens 1993b. On the marriage of slaves, see Karras 1988, passim.
16. See, for example, Þórdís (*Hsí* 6.15:342), Ólof (*Þhr* 14.6:191), Þórdís (*Dpl* 11.6:151), Valgerðr (*Nj* 12.148:424), Spés (*Gr* 7.87:274), Vigdís (*Lx* 5.11:21), and Freydís (*Gn* 4.2: 245). Although the expression was not used about Guðrún's first marriage, it was clearly

the reason since it was stipulated that she should manage their property and own half of it regardless of how long the marriage might last (*Lx* 5.34:93). This saga contains a rare case of a man, Þórðr, who married for money (*Lx* 5.32:87).

17. The proud Dalla warned her son Kormákr that too great a "social distinction" (*mannamunr*) existed between him and Steingerðr. It was in his favor and the displeasure of Steingerðr's father was caused by Kormákr's frequent visits (*Krm* 8.3:215). Part of Kormákr's hesitation to go through with the marriage may have been that he would have married down.

18. Inability to determine which way a saddle was to be placed on a horse defined mental impairment. The child was to be maintained by the mother's family. This rule is also found in canon law but undoubtedly had native origin as well.

19. See, for example, *Gg* 2:69.

20. Guðný's great-grand-daughter, Ingibjǫrg Sturludóttir, was married in 1253 at the age of thirteen; see *St* 1:481–90. I shall return to this wedding.

21. See article "Incest" in KLNM 7:370–79. Fowler 1981.

22. Helgi Hálfdanarson's wife/daughter Yrsa left him when she discovered the truth about her parentage (*Hrkr, FSN* 1.13:25–26).

23. See the notorious case of Bjarni Ólason who in 1481 was accused of having had a long-standing relationship with his daughter, begun when she was thirteen; DI 6:371–73. The case has been treated by Einar Arnórsson 1932–1935. I am grateful to Sverrir Tómasson for these references. See also Hastrup 1990a, 161–63, and Már Jónsson 1993.

24. Transgressors would lose "property and peace" (*fé ok friði*), be outlawed, and never permitted back in the country. Among many texts, see NgL 1:149, 350; 2:302; the last passage is from King Magnús Hákonarson in the late thirteenth century. See also the reference to incest between mother and son referred to in *Postola sögur*, 321–22; for this episode see Chapter 3, n. 67.

25. In an unpublished manuscript (see n. 6) deposited in Árnastofnun in Reykjavík, Vilhjálmur Finsen wonders about this problem: "How was this in pagan times?" (*Hvorledes var dette i den hedenske tid?*; 1:334). In another passage (1:634) he expresses the hope, with resignation, that during paganism sexual crimes within the family were punished. (Quoted with permission from Árnastofnun.) On the possible Germanic origin on extensive incest restrictions, see de Jong 1989.

26. See Jochens 1996c.

27. See section "Infanticide" in Chapter 3.

28. Gaudemet 1987, 26–38. Roman sources do refer to engagement, but little is known about it and it seems to have been of a less-binding nature than the Germanic. See Treggiari 1991, 83–160. Personal conversation with Suzanne Dixon.

29. On this problem, see Jochens 1991b. A particularly good illustration is found in Kolfinna's marriage to Gríss after Hallfreðr's visits (*Hlf* 8.4:145–50). *Bkr* (11.2:189) and *Brð* (13.10:135) illustrate the unusual situation of a father who offered his daughter in marriage to a visitor who had fallen in love with her.

30. Found in *Flateyjarbók* and imbedded in its version of *Óláfs saga helga;* see *Flat* 2: 193–99, esp. 196–97.

31. In *Vǫlsunga saga* Grímhildr suggests to Gjúki that he should offer Guðrún in marriage to Sigurðr; *Vls* 28:65.

32. Some arrangements were negotiated by only two visitors and a few by the suitor

alone. In case of Guðrún's fourth marriage a party of twenty-five arrived (*Lx* 5.68:200). Engagements could also be negotiated at the þing.

33. Among many cases, see *Erb* 4.25:63; 28:71; *Rkd* 10.19:211; *Vtn* 8.18:52.

34. On the former, see Guðríðr's father's refusal of the rich Einarr because he was the son of a former slave (*Erð* 4.3:203–4). In a rare case a suitor eloped with the girl with her mother's blessing after the father had refused the match (*Fnb* 14.1:254).

35. Not substantiated in law, this distinction is equally rare in the contemporary sagas where it also appeared only once; see Ingibjǫrg, *St* 1:480. See also Oddný's three-year wait in *BHd* 6.2:114; 5:123.

36. Þorleifr's request for Helga was turned down by her brother who felt that the suitor not yet had revenged the shame he incurred when hot porridge was poured down his neck in Norway three years earlier (*Erb* 4.41:112).

37. The *Staðarhólsbók* (*Gg* 2:177) followed the marriage sequence, whereas the *Konungsbók* (*Gg* 1b:48) placed the father after the husband and before the son.

38. See, for example, NgL 1:49, 51 and *Jn* 70–77.

39. A father resented the size of his daugher's dowry of one hundred ounces of silver paid by his brother in his own prolonged absence, and he demanded restitution from his son-in-law (*Flm* 13.20:277, 29:313, 30:314).

40. See, for example, Drew 1973, 81, 90–91.

41. See Vilhjálmur Finsen 1849, 208, n. 1. On the nunneries, see Anna Sigurðardóttir 1988.

42. It is not spelled out, but one would assume that a widow also would have the option of becoming a nun.

43. This double engagement is unique in the literature.

44. Among many cases of marriages that sealed the end of feuds, see Þórhildr's in *Erb* 4.10:18 and Jórunn's in *Ljs* (10.12:137; the passage is found in *Vǫðu-Brands þáttr*).

45. An extreme case is found in *Krm* 8.7:227 where Steingerðr discovered she was being married only as the wedding guests arrived.

46. This may be no more than a romantic motif, but the law's allowance of bigamy for Icelandic men living in Norway suggests an awareness of the problem of too long absences.

47. The Norwegian laws were more lenient; see Maurer 1908, 535.

48. See Vilhjálmur Finsen and Maurer as in n. 3.

49. Vilhjálmur Finsen 1849 (236, n. 5) refers to a passage in the contemporary sagas (*St* 1:169) where the bride "jumped out of bed the first night when Hrafn was led into her" (*hljóp ór hvílu ina fyrstu nótt, er Hrafn var innar leiddr*), and Maurer 1908 (541) to a similar passage in one of the heroic sagas where it is stated about Hrólfr, who expected to marry the queen, that "after a while he was led to bed and she was already there" (*um síðir er honum fylgt til sængr ok var hún þar fyrir; Hrkr* FSN 1.7:15). Unfortunately, no passage from the sagas of Icelanders illuminates this rite, but a more detailed description involving the undressing of two brides and their grooms is found in one of the chivalric sagas (*JH,* RS 6.22–23:229–30; LMIR 3.24–25:61–63).

50. See Jochens 1993e, especially 286–88.

51. First names were sought in the lines of both the father and mother, and newborns were often named after a recently deceased ancestor. The custom continued in Christian times, also for illegitimate children; about 1205 Snorri Sturluson named his son

Órækja after his mistress's grandfather (*St* 1:242), and his nephew Þórðr remembered his mistress's father in their son Styrmir (*St* 2:85).

52. The examples are numerous; see *Eg* 2.20:49 and 77:240, *Erb* 4.57:157. See also Krause 1926, 161–65.

53. Recall Guðný's wedding at her husband's farm (Chapter 1). See also Egill Skalla-Grímsson's concession to the prestige (*metorð*) of his daughter Þorgerðr's future father-in-law, allowing her wedding to take place at his farm (*Lx* 5.23:65).

54. The dying Bárðr informed the king that he wanted Þórólfr to take over his inheritance, including his lands and property, wife and child (*Eg* 2.9:24–25). In another case Þorgils gave his wife to his companion Þorsteinn because he had noticed that Þorsteinn liked her, "although you have behaved well in this matter" (*Flm* 13.17:264).

55. On the so-called *Friedelehe*, see Ebert 1993 and Jochens 1994a.

56. For details on this and other cases, see Jochens 1987b, 333–34.

57. Þóra remained in Norway in 1066 when Haraldr left for his ill-fated expedition to conquer England, but he brought Ellisif and her two daughters with him; *Hkr* 28.82: 178.

58. Women might also be involved with several men during their lifetime, most often serially, however, a pattern also encouraged by the easy divorce.

59. DI vols. 3–5 provide numerous illustrations.

60. Also showing Christian influence, one paragraph imposed a monetary fine for a kiss obtained secretly from a woman (*kona*), but the lesser outlawry when it was done to a married woman (*manns kona; Gg* 1b:47, 2:176).

61. Providing the only illustration that the woman might have taken the initiative ("if a woman sleeps with a man"), a paragraph allowed the prosecutor to fine her (*Gg* 1b:53; 2:185). If the prosecutor was the woman's husband this rule seems self-defeating as it would deplete their common resources, but it might be of interest to a brother.

62. *Gg* 1b:242 (MS A. M. 347 fol.) contains a list of seventeen prosecutors (*aðiljar*). On the issue of gender symmetry in *Grágás*, see Jochens 1993b. Although the Icelandic law hardly refers to the sexual use of slaves, it was undoubtedly a common phenomenon. The Norwegian laws mention that if a man sells his pregnant slave, the new owner must return her and the child after birth; NgL 1:30.

63. He may have fallen in love with her as a child and his later infatuation with her is clear; see Bredsdorff 1971. His flirtation with Arnfiðr's daughter does not qualify as a relationship (*Eg* 2.48:120–21).

64. For more details on the following, see Jochens 1991b.

65. Njáll was in charge of a case of illegitimate intercourse (*legorðssǫk*) against Þorgeirr, who had impregnated one of his relatives (*Nj* 12.64:160).

66. On this passage, see n. 15.

67. See Ruth Mazo Karras, "Servitude and sexuality in medieval Iceland," in *From Sagas* 1992, 289–304. The sources are silent on men's sexual use of male slaves, a possibility not prevented by the occasional gelding (see *ÞSH* 11.321–26).

68. Grettir did not only embrace women; his sexual activities included men and animals as well; see Chapter 3, 74.

69. On this service, see Chapter 5, "Work," 125–26.

70. As an exception to this rule, note the descendants of Úlfr, the son fathered by Óspakr Ósvífrsson on a certain Aldís (*Lx* 5.50:156–57). Úlfr obtained a high position at the Norwegian court and his great-grandson became archbishop.

71. Jochens 1980 and 1991b, esp. 376–84. I return to the problem in the following chapter.

72. See bibliography in n. 28.

73. On regulation of sexuality within marriage, see article *Hreinlifnaðartíðir* (Times for Abstinence) in the encyclopedic literature (*Alf,* 37:55).

74. See *St* 1:60–63, 69, 72–73, 117, 230, 450; Björn Þórðarson 1949.

75. For further examples, see Jochens 1980.

76. The plural of the singular *lag* (layer) is *lǫg* (law). The law came into existence as several "layers" were being "laid down." For this etymology, see bibliography in Appendix n. 45. The expression *fylgja at lagi* seems to indicate a private single agreement between a man and a woman without binding consequences, similar to the English term "common-law marriage."

77. Variations such as *fylgjukona, fylgikona, lagskona, fylgjulag* can also be found; for examples, *St* 1:53, 79, 80, 82, 89, 95, 102, 201; *Bs* 1:802. Most often these expressions imply that the woman was the secondary person who followed the man, but occasionally the man is the semantic subject; see *St* 1:102. This suggests equality for the two partners, a notion also reflected in the gendered words for the partners, *friðell* (the man) and *frilla* (the woman), and may support the idea of a pre-Christian *Friedelehe;* see Jochens 1994. Formal divorce seems to occur in these relationships; see *St* 1:80. When Bishop Guðmundr's parents arranged their cohabitation (*til tók lag þeira*), his mother Úlfheiðr—earlier married against her will to another man—gave her lover Ari a large sum of money "for household expenses and management" (*til forráða ok meðferðar; St* 1:118).

78. See Jochens 1987b and Chapter 3.

79. NgL 1:123; translation (modified) in Larson 1935, 216.

80. With many alliterations, the passage in NgL 2:302 has a particularly pleasing character.

81. Guðný's father, Snorri Sturluson's maternal grandfather, was included in the list; see Chapter 1, n. 4.

82. Several versions of the ordinance are found in DI 1:423–63; for the specific rule, see 450, 453, 457, and passim.

83. In the early modern period women increasingly refused to divulge the names of their lovers, possibly because of the frequency of incest and the harsh punishment against it; see Hastrup 1990a, 164, and Már Jónsson 1993.

84. Texts from several manuscripts can be found in DI 2:12–69. For the specific rule, see 26, 31, 36.

85. Sexual crimes as well as harsher treatment of women than men for these continued into Early Modern times. No longer under the jurisdiction of the church, these crimes were treated equally severely by the Danish government. The so-called Big Verdict (*stóridómur*), ratified by royal decree in 1565, decreed that people who had committed adultery were to be punished with fines, flogging, and—when caught for the third time—execution, men by decapitation and women by drowning. Both types of punishment did take place, but no evidence remains of public decapitation. Visitors to the site of the alþingi, however, are still shown the drowning pool (*drekkingarhylur*) where adulterous women ended their lives. On these problems, see Hastrup 1990a, 149–80, and Már Jónsson 1993, 90–156.

86. The first term was used in Norway in 1277 (Archbishop Jón's Christian Law; NgL

2:369). When Bishop Árni formulated the new Icelandic Christian Law in 1275 he still used the less specific term that the priest should "sing over the couple," but a later manuscript added the formulation from the Norwegian text; see NgL 5:36–38 and n. 5. On the gendered use of this vocabulary, see Jochens 1986a, 167–69.

87. Thus, in 1224, when Gizurr Þorvaldsson was married, his father wanted "above everything else" (*fyrir hvern mun*) that his brother Bishop Magnús be present (*St* 1: 304).

88. The underlying rationale was well expressed by Auðr/Unnr—allegedly a heathen woman living in pagan Iceland—to her grandson when she arranged his marriage: "I am of the opinion that your wedding feast should be held toward the end of the summer, because that is the best time for getting all the necessary provisions" (*Lx* 5.7:11; according to *Lnd* 1:146–47 she was Christian).

89. De Jong 1989, 44. The mapping out of the prohibited network depends largely on the method of calculation. The Roman system counted each step (*gradus*) between relatives passing through a common ancestor. Using words like *generatio* or *genu* (limb), the Germanic method counted individually the number of generations separating two kinsmen from their common ancestor. A change from Roman to Germanic custom, therefore, would cut the number of degrees in half and, in reverse, the implementation of the Germanic system would clearly be impossible. Churchmen may have chosen the symbolic number of seven without realizing the implications in the Germanic system. In the Roman system the uneven number suggests that men reached down to the cohort below them for their spouses, since a couple within the same cohort would be related in an even number (sister and brother in the second, first cousins in the fourth, and second cousins in the sixth degree).

90. See Bouchard 1981, Herlihy 1990.

91. See n. 146 for an Icelandic illustration in which the discovery of a previous relationship prompted the bishop to command a couple to divorce.

92. See Lynch 1986.

93. See Vilhjálmur Finsen 1849, 213–22, and Maurer 1908, 552–82.

94. On the changes in marriage proposed at the council, see Baldwin 1970, 1:332–37.

95. Poor married people are mentioned in *Jn* 75. For the reading of banns, see, for example, DI 2:26–27 (1269), 197 (1280), 277 (1290), 364 (1309), 518 (1323), 754 (1342), 812 (1345), and NgL 3:368, 370.

96. On this problem, see Baldwin 1993 and Jochens 1986a and 1993e. Describing Bishop Gizurr, the author of *Hungrvaka*—a short history of the Icelandic bishops—expressed gender equality in the following way: "Everybody wanted to sit and stand as he [Gizurr] asked, young and old, rich and poor, women and men" (*Bsk* 1.4:85).

97. On this issue, see Appendix, 177–78.

98. For details, see Jochens 1986a, 145–50.

99. See Jochens 1986a, 142. In 1429 the bishop of Hólar granted a divorce to a woman because she had never in her heart agreed to marry her husband although a little "yes-word" had been forced out of her by other people's persuasions and by "fear and dread of her father" (DI 4:394).

100. Snorri Sturluson's treatment of his daughters is particularly illustrative; see Jochens 1994b.

101. Brundage 1987, 235–78.

102. Austin 1962 uses marriage as an illustration of a speech-act (1–24).

103. See article "Kristenrettar" KLNM 9:297–306. On the speed with which Gratian's ideas became known in Norway, see Gunnes 1970, rpt. 1983.

104. *Gnl* offers an interesting mixture of pagan and Christian engagement rules. A few years before the introduction of Christianity to Iceland, the twelve-year old Gunnlaugr was studying law with Þorkell, the father of Helga with whom he fell in love. Arguing that he had not yet learned how to conduct an engagement, he enticed Þorkell to teach him, and he demonstrated his progress by engaging Helga. The witnesses recall the pagan tradition, but the taking of Helga's hand is in conformity with the new rules; 3.4:60.

105. Text in NgL 5:36–40.

106. On this problem in the late medieval period, see Ozment 1983, 25–49. Bjarni Einarsson has suggested that the bride shown on the dust jacket and heading each chapter—an illustration in the margin of a manuscript of *Jónsbók* (Reykjabók, MS. AM 345 fol. 38v) dated circa 1600—is reluctant and perhaps even weeping. Her tears account for the large handkerchief in the left hand. With a determined face and a hand on her daughter's elbow, the mother urges the bride forward. Below this group (not shown on the dust jacket) an elderly gentleman, the bride's father, awaits the groom's party arriving on horseback. See Bjarni Einarsson 1989. This interpretation is reinforced by the fact that the bride is found at the place in the text which states that if a woman marries without the advice of her father, mother, and brother, she will lose her inheritance.

107. *ÁB* 77; *Bs* 1:718. The bishop's concern for gender equality caused him not only to envision secret marriages of women, but also "men who marry against the advice of their kin."

108. See Kalinke 1981, 182–85.

109. In this saga Snorri declared to his daughter's prospective step-father-in-law that "she shall only marry the man who pleases her" (*Lx* 5.70:206). When Flosi was negotiating with Njáll about the marriage of his niece Hildigunnr, he assured her that "it is sufficient for me to call off the negotiations if you do not want to get married" (*Nj* 12.97:241). For further illustrations, see Jochens 1986b, 38, rpt. 104.

110. Hildigunnr (previous note) consented to the proposal, provided Hǫskuldr could be provided with a chieftainship. When the demand was met, they were married (*Nj* 12.97:241–47).

111. For references, see Frank 1973 and Jochens 1986b, 48, n. 84; rpt. 122, n. 56.

112. For examples, see Jochens 1986a, especially 151–58, and 1993e.

113. A good illustration is provided by the marriages of Óláfr Tryggvason's sisters. According to the oldest version, *Historia de antiquitate regum Norwagiensium* written about 1180 by the monk Theodricus, the women were married at the behest of their brother. Snorri allowed consent for one sister and the latest biography of Óláfr written early in the fourteenth century made consent an integral part of the marriages of all four sisters. For details, see Jochens 1986a, 153–54.

114. For closer analysis and more illustrations of this subject, see Jochens 1986a, 159–67.

115. Text in Cederschiöld 1884, 85–123.

116. *Dámusta saga*; text in Tan-Haverhorst 1939, 48–198, esp. 69.

117. *HH* and *QO*.

118. *Þtv,* FSN 3.2:4.

119. See, for example, *Tristams saga ok Ísöndar,* RS 1.14:25, 24:55 and *Elis saga ok Rósamundu,* RS 4.2:5.

120. Guðbrandr Vigfússon's date of 975 was modified by Finnur Jónsson; see Einar Ól. Sveinsson's introduction to *Nj* (12:lxi).

121. The fire was mentioned briefly in almost all the Icelandic annals; see Storm 1888, 26 and seven additional places. For the detailed description of the wedding and the arson, see *St* 1:481–96. Ingibjǫrg was allowed to leave the burning farm, but Hallr was wounded as he tried to escape and died later.

122. See Dronke 1981.

123. The case, known as the *Jóreiðar-mál,* became notorious; see *St* 1:309–11.

124. On this issue, see Jochens 1993a.

125. This was according to law since Þorgerðr had none of the four male relatives (son, son-in-law, father, or brother) who would have preceded her mother as guardian. It is more surprising that while he was still alive, Þorgerðr's father had ceded the privilege of naming her to Hallgerðr (12.14:46).

126. Neither the bride nor the groom were mentioned at their wedding in Reykjahólar in 1119; on this event, see Chapter 4, 105. In heroic poetry women held prominent place. Although W. P. Ker 1987 does not single out women, his notion of the continuity of the heroic ideals from heroic poetry to the sagas of Icelanders is well illustrated by the prominence of women in general and specifically at Hallgerðr's celebration. Likewise, the decline of heroic ideals and the fading of women in the contemporary sagas is exemplified at Ingibjǫrg's wedding.

127. See Jochens 1986b and Schwerin 1930. The law passages can be identified from Vilhjálmur Finsen's glossary, 3:670–71 (under *skilnaðr* [divorce]).

128. On the different gender treatment in the poor laws, see Jochens 1993b.

129. A wealthy spouse should say to the other: "I wish to be divorced from my partner (*felaga minn*) because I do not wish to let my partner's needy relations waste my property" (*láta eyða fé mínu; Gg* 1b:40). If the couple was not able to support their children, a new child was prosecuted as a case of illegitimate intercourse (*legorð; Gg* 1b: 41; 2:169).

130. The few cases of female violence in the narrative sources are treated in *ONIW.*

131. The only case of Christian influence on divorce in the sagas of Icelanders is found in the late epilogue to *Grettis saga.* The Byzantine Spes was forced to prove her innocence on charges of adultery by appealing to the bishop and swearing a deceptive oath, a theme obviously borrowed from the Tristan and Iseut story (*Gr* 7.87–89:276–85). On other Christian influence in this narrative, see Jochens 1996b.

132. Inappropriate clothing was also a legal justification for a man to divorce his wife (*Gg* 1b:203), as also illustrated by Þórðr's subsequent divorce of Auðr (*Lx* 5.34–35:93–96). On the gender aspect of clothing in these scenes, see Jochens 1991a and 1993c. Reported both in *Gí* and *Erb,* Þórdís's divorce is told more fully in the former (4.14:26; see also 6.37:116–17).

133. On the two divorces of this man, Barði Guðmundarson, see Bjarni Guðnason 1993, 148–49. Auðr tried to kill her husband after he had divorced her (*Lx* 5.35:97–98).

134. Men whose wives divorced them because of their violence might consider themselves lucky, however, because — according to the literary evidence — a wife could repay

her husband for a slap by arranging his murder, as Hallgerðr did no less than three times; *Nj* 12.11:33–35; 16–17:48–49; 48:124; 77:189.

135. The female inciter (the *Hetzerin*) is treated in *ONIW*.

136. The first statement is from *BHd* 3.18:158 and the second from *Gí* 6.9:33. See also *Lx* 5.48:150 and *Gn* 4.8:266. The couples in *Nj* 12.150:429 and *Flm* 11.21:287 were not in bed.

137. One case involved the rare situation where the woman urged her husband *not* to get involved in revenge (*Flm* 11.21:287). In a reversal of gender, a single case illustrates the opposite situation where the husband suggested that his marriage might end unless his wife was able to handle to his satisfaction a difficult and delicate task during his absence, but in contrast to the sexual and monetary terms used by the women, he referred to their relationship as their "friendship" (*vinfengi; GÞb* 11.5:208).

138. In addition to the cases mentioned, see *Hsí* 6.7:314; *Rkd* 10.25:230 (Skúta and Þorlaug); 10.11:176; 15:194; 16:197 (Háls and Helga). On the latter saga, see Baetke 1958. When another Helga returned to her father without declaring her divorce formally she was fetched back by her husband who "was searching for what belongs to him" (*sœkir eptir sínu; Flm* 13.30:316).

139. *Vp* 11.6:36. No evidence exists for the author's assertion that this was customary behavior.

140. Personal honor was also behind Vigdís's wish to divorce Þórðr. The case demonstrates male opposition. When she returns to her uncle, he is upset and lets it be known that he demands her share of the property. Her husband allies himself with the astute Hǫskuldr, who declares that Vigdís has no "reason for going away" (*brautgangssǫk; Lx* 5.16:37–38).

141. "Þórðr . . . went to the Law Rock, called witnesses and declared himself divorced from Auðr, on the ground that she wore pants with inserts (*setgeirabrœkr*) like masculine women"; *Lx* 5.35:96. On this passage, see Jochens 1991a.

142. In *Bkr* Droplaug enters marriage with her "treasures" (*gripir*) in a trunk (11.3: 190), and in *Lx* Vigdís leaves her husband, taking only her "personal belongings (*gripir*) with her (5.16:37).

143. In a rare case a father expressed unhappiness when his daughter was returned (*VGl* 9.16:50).

144. For other examples, see *St* 1:102 and 186. Not all stressful marriages ended in divorce. Recall the sexual career of Yngvildr Þorgilsdóttir. Before her escapades she "did not love her husband Halldórr, but they managed while her father Þorgils was alive. But afterwards they could not endure it." A divorce was avoided when Halldórr went on a pilgrimage and died (*St* 1:69).

145. Guðmundr refused his daughter Ingibjǫrg to Þorfinnr "because it was according neither to the law of God nor the law of the land" (*St* 1:175).

146. See the amusing story of the priest Hǫgni who refused to let his daughter Snælaug separate from her husband Þórðr after it was discovered that her husband was related to the father of her illegitimate child (*Bs* 1:284–8). The story is retold in Jochens 1980, n. 14. Archbishop Guttormr gave Þorvaldr Gizurarson and Jóra Klængsdóttir, nicknamed *biskupsdóttir* from her father Bishop Klængr, permission to stay together for ten years. Her death at the end of the period alleviated the pain Þorvaldr felt at the impending separation (*St* 1:62).

147. Unfortunately, information from pre-Christian Norway is too scanty to test this hypothesis.

148. I return to this in the Conclusion. See also Clover 1993.

149. This information is conveyed at a moment when she was spotted on her way to the mountain pastures (*til sels*), where, as I shall show, women spent most of the summer performing dairy work. Her forceful, masculine aspects are highlighted by the fact that she was the only one in her party "in colored clothing" (*í litklæðum*), normally a prerogative of men (see "Foreign Cloth" in Chapter 6). The story is also told in *Ftb* 6.1:121.

150. See *Lx* 5.69:202–4 and *Gþb* 11.7:209–11.

151. According to the internal chronology of the saga, she would have been forty-eight at the birth; see introduction to the ÍF edition.

152. The phenomenon is not limited to the north; see Shahar 1983, 93–98 and passim.

153. *Lx* 5.4:7. Translation (modified) from Magnusson and Pálsson 1969, 51–52.

154. Limited to the wealth that could be brought on small ships, the first colonists abandoned the social stratification that prevailed in Norway. Initially each settler was allowed to grab as much land as he was capable of, but these large land claims (*landnám*) caused problems for people who arrived later. Eventually the Norwegian king Haraldr Fairhair (*hárfagri*) decided that: "No man was allowed to claim more land than he and his crew could mark off in a single day by the use of fire. They were to kindle the first fire when the sun was in the East, and then other fires should be built so that the smoke from one might be seen from the next. Those kindled while the sun was in the East must be kept burning until night-fall. Then they should walk until the sun was in the West and then make other fires" (*Lnd* 1:337, 339). Special restrictions applied to women: "It was decreed that a woman could not claim any more land than she could [walk around] leading a two-year old, well-fed heifer between dawn and sunset on a spring day" (*Lnd* 1:321). For Auðr's land claim, see *Lnd* 1:139.

155. Like the female inciter in *Njála*, the number may suggest a literary topos; this subject is treated further in *ONIW*.

156. The two heroes thanked her for her "valiant behavior" (*slíkr drengskapr*), using an expression from the gender-blurring category (6.5:141).

157. Gríma went to unusual lengths to protect her daughter against unwelcome visits from Þormóðr (10:162–64). From *Ljs* comes the story of the widow Þorgerðr in Miklabœ. In charge of her estate, she invited a hundred men for dinner and offered them tents, timber, and provisions (10.16[26]: 85–87). Gróa, who had arrived in Iceland after her husband's death, managing her own ship, became very wealthy and was sought in marriage by many men, but she refused them politely with the excuse that she so missed her husband that she did not intend to marry again (*Fld* 11.10:237–38).

158. Jóreiðr Hallsdóttir should not be confused with the young dreamer Jóreiðr Hermundardóttir.

CHAPTER THREE. REPRODUCTION

1. The earlier assumption of Trobriand Islanders' denial of biological paternity (Malinowski 1929, 179–86) has been modified by anthropologists' understanding of the difference between the roles of genitor, the biological father, and pater, the sociological

father; see Leach 1966 and Paige and Paige 1981. For a historical overview, see Ross 1994, 144–52.

2. For views common in Europe around 1200, see Baldwin 1993.

3. Medical knowledge was assembled in *Læknisfræði; see Alf* 37:61–77.

4. For construction of reproductive theories based on nordic mythology, see Ull Linke, "The Theft of Blood, the Birth of Men: Cultural Constructions of Gender in Medieval Iceland," *From Sagas* 1992, 265–88.

5. For a human/animal comparison, see the story of the man who was cured by praying to Bishop Guðmundr; his "testicles had become so enlarged that they looked like those of a two-year-old bull" (*Bs* 1:615).

6. For Hrafn's medical training, see the introduction in Tjomsland 1951.

7. The practice of gelding was not limited to men, as suggested by the name of Hlíf *hestageldir,* a Shetland woman nicknamed for her profession of gelding horses (*Lnd* 1.S72/H60:102–3). Done at the age of three weeks, gelding of sheep was easily accomplished by women; see article "Kastration af husdyr," KLNM 9:596–99. Horses were more difficult, and the process occasionally caused problems even for men; see *Bs* 1: 121, 345. Gelding and castration may have promoted perceptions of a greater male than female role in reproduction.

8. Nevertheless, the couple separated later and Órækja was not known to have fathered children. Gade (1994) has suggested that the episode is purely fictional; her arguments are intriguing but not convincing.

9. See Krause, 234–35. When used about women, *ala* implied both conception, gestation, and birth. Unusual concern for expressing dual responsibility is articulated in the case of the king and queen who "between them had conceived a young son" (*hofdu getit sin a medal einn son iungan; SN,* LMIR 2.2:5).

10. See Chapter 1. The concept was found throughout Scandinavia; for its use in Sweden, see *Óh* 27.78:111.

11. On this problem, see Jochens 1987b.

12. For specific texts, see *Sv* 112:119; *HH* 4:9, 12:18, 88:77–78.

13. Mulvey (1975) coined the term "the male gaze." On the entry of this stance into Norse literature, see Jochens 1993c.

14. See Jochens 1991a.

15. See Helga Kress 1991.

16. Likewise, the old Bjǫrgólfr became so aroused by the young Hildiríðr at a feast that he married her immediately after (*Eg* 2.7:16–18). The sight of Steingerðr's ankles became the *coup de foudre* that signaled Kormákr's lifelong infatuation with her (*Krm* 8.3:207).

17. Helga and Helgi were "excited by talk, kisses, and embraces in affection and love" (*Hh* 8.2:307–8). See also the first meeting between Gunnarr and Hallgerðr at the alþingi, so fueled by good looks, splendid clothing, and exciting conversation that their relationship was described as a "match dominated by lusty desire" (*girndarráð; Nj* 12.33: 87).

18. See, for example, Þórdís's reference to the sunshine that appeared when her lover rode into the yard (*Sl* 10.1[5]:110) and the conversation between Óláfr and Sigríðr (*Hsí* 6.4:304–7).

19. On this issue, see Jochens 1991b and 1996a. I am grateful to Garland Press for

allowing me to reprint part of the latter essay published in *Handbook on Medieval Sexuality.*

20. The term *gaman,* with a similar semantic spread, is often used for sexual intercourse in Eddic poetry in the expression *geð ok gaman.* In this sense the latter part of the expression is used at least once in the sagas of Icelanders (*Gr* 7.61:200).

21. For further examples, see the long version of *Gí,* found in *Tvær sögur* 1849, 98, and *Svf* 9.20:186. Sexual intercourse is also implied in expressions such as "to bed down" (*rekkja; Lx* 5.12:24), "go to bed" (*koma í sæng; Hlf* 8.9:181), and "lie next to" (*liggja hjá; Nj* 12.61:154), used almost exclusively about mistresses. The result of illegal sexual activity was sometimes referred to by the verb "to get with child" (*barna*); see *Nj* 12.64: 160 and *Fnb* 14.40:327.

22. Used in this way about mythical creatures, *faðmlag* is found in *Ftb* 6.3:135 and *faðm* in 6.4:138.

23. In another scene a young couple walked down the road holding hands; *St* 1:233.

24. On the connection between drinking and sexual arousal, see Jochens 1993a.

25. She was "nubile" (*vel frumvaxta*) and "walked about and flirted (*skemmti sér*)." A couple would continue to find pleasure in drinking *tvímenningr,* as did Kormákr and Steingerðr in Norway long into their troubled relationship (*Krm* 8.25:295).

26. For examples, see *Hlf* 8.4:145, *Krm* 8.19:272, and *Hn* 3.16:42. The formulaic character of the expression is particularly evident in the last case in which a young man visited a woman who lived in a tent.

27. On this saga, see Bergljót S. Kristjánsdóttir 1992. Female sexual initiative used for deception is foreign to Old Norse and may be due to Christian influence in this late saga. On women's use of sex for more innocent purposes, see below.

28. Unable to consummate their relationship, Kormákr continued to kiss Steingerðr (*Krm* 8.24:291–93).

29. The first word is used about Kormákr (*Krm* 8.24:293) and the second about Hallfreðr (*Hlf* 8.4:145).

30. Kisses were a sign not only of erotic love but also of parental affection. Having presented his young and beautiful daughter Hallgerðr to his brother, Hǫskuldr "tilted her chin and kissed her" (*Nj* 12.1:7).

31. In a gesture of general leave-taking, Gunnarr "embraces everybody" (*hverfr til allra manna; Nj* 12.75:182).

32. For examples, see *Nj* 12.147:421; 149:427; 159:463; *Lx* 5.45:135. The old Hávarðr "kissed" (*minntisk við*) his wife before embarking on his revenge (*Hsí* 6.9:321). This was also the way in which Hrútr parted from Queen Gunnhildr after their two-week love tryst (*Nj* 12.3:15).

33. For a new edition and commentary, see Sveinbjörn Rafnsson 1983a.

34. The technical term was "to inspect his head" (*skoða í hǫfði honum; Lx* 5.24:109).

35. For illustrations, see *Hǫv* 3.20:273 (the washing was done by the woman mentioned above who was supposed to have resisted kissing her lover after his face had been smashed); see also *Ljs* 10.14(24):77 and *Vgl* 14.18:98. The last case involved not only a wash but also a haircut with the added promise that the hero would not let anyone but his beloved Ketilríðr perform these services, in a vow similar to the one the Norwegian king Haraldr Fairhair (*hárfagri*) gave to Gyða; (*Hhf* 26.3–4:96–97). For further details on hair washing, see Chapter 5, 125.

36. The author may have used the request as a pretext to goad Auðr. The fullest elaboration of the shirt as a love token is found in *QO, FSN* 2.11–12:238–44.

37. Wide sleeves were a normal feature of male clothing. They needed to be narrowed to enable the man to work, and scarcity of buttons made this a daily chore; for additional illustration, see Chapter 5, 126. Even when buttons were available they may have been sewn on every morning; see KLNM 3:282; see also article "Knap" in KLNM 21: 236–37.

38. Known to have taken pleasure in Óláfr's company, Sigríðr was accused of having put her arms around his neck, an inappropriate gesture for unmarried people (*Hsí* 6.2: 296). A man in Greenland complained that his permanent companion, interested in another man, did not put her arms around him as often as before (*Ftb* 6.21:226, n. 1).

39. Likewise, Þuríðr "put her arms around his neck" (*lagði . . . hendr yfir háls honum*) to persuade her husband not to burn Þórgunna's bed linen as he had promised the dying woman (*Erb* 4.51:143). See also Grimhildr in *Vls* 28:65. However, Yngvildr's similar gesture expressed neither love nor ulterior motives, but gratitude over having been bought out of slavery (*Svf* 9.27:204).

40. Another wife provided the basic need of warming her cold husband in bed (*Hsí* 6.15:342–5).

41. Translation (modified) from Preben Meulengracht Sørensen, "Murder in Marital Bed," *Structure and Meaning,* 249–50, quoting the M text from *Tvær sögur,* 29. The passage is almost identical to the S version used in the ÍF edition (6.16:53–54). The episode has engendered a large literature; for the purpose of the argument developed here, see Andersson 1969.

42. See Andersson 1969, 37–38, for examples.

43. An almost identical scene is found in *Dpl* 11.13:170–71. Scholars do not agree on the relationship between the two episodes, but most assume that the author of *Gí* borrowed from *Dpl;* see the overview in Andersson 1969, 28–39. The erotic overtones are clearer in *Gí* than in *Dpl.* An echo—albeit ironic—of an erotic scene is also noticeable in Þórðr's reaction as he "turned on his side" (*snerisk a hliðina*), only to be pierced by his former wife's sword (*Lx* 5.35:98).

44. On this passage, see Jochens 1987b, esp. 338–39.

45. The expression "they rested that night" (*hvíldu þau þá nótt*) is another euphemism.

46. Queen Semerana "turned toward the count," thinking it was her royal husband, and became pregnant (*Ad,* LMIR 3.7:87); in the same text, see also 3.7:86.

47. With reference to the apostle Paul, it is used in the *Homiliu-bók* as a term for sexual desire (*munoþ síns licama; Wisén* 1872, 117 line 8).

48. *Hjúskaparfar,* from *hjú-skapr* (the *hjún* [marital couple and/or household]).

49. See Chapter 2, 59. In the interval before Unnr's departure "their relationship (*samfarar*) was good," but *samfǫr* here carries a general meaning (*Nj* 12.7:26).

50. Despite the presence of a little girl and the fact that Unnr—instructed by her father—had initiated the proceedings herself, the girl played no role in the game.

51. See Dronke 1981, 10.

52. See P. M. Sørensen 1983, Jochens 1996a.

53. *Gg* 2:392, NgL 1:57. On this issue, see Jochens 1992.

54. For narrative use of the latter word, see King Haraldr's question to Halli whether

he would be willing to let himself be "screwed" (*serðask*) to obtain a beautiful axe (*SnH* 9.10:294). The same story contains the innuendo that the king had played the passive role in a sexual encounter with a horse; see Minkov 1988.

55. Edited and commented by Ólafur Halldórsson 1990, 19–50.

56. A generation separated her and Hrútr, and she was even older when "she found pleasure in talking with" (*skemmtan at tala við*) his nephew Óláfr (*Lx* 5.21:52). The author added that people said she would have enjoyed it whether or not he had been Hrútr's nephew.

57. In her fifties and "a large woman, both tall and broad, and getting stout," Þórgunna was smitten by a young boy then aged thirteen or fourteen whom she "loved dearly" (*elskaði . . . mjǫk;* a rare expression). The boy was "both large of size and manly to look at," but her attention "made him keep his distance," a behavior that caused her to become "irritable" (*skapstygg; Erb* 4.50:139). On this episode, see Jochens 1991a.

58. Her competitor Geirríðr grouped her among "witches in beautiful skin" (*flǫgð í fǫgru skinni; Erb* 4.16:29). On the difference between authorial interest in men and in women, see Jochens 1991a.

59. According to another account, he died from his wounds (*Lnd* 1.S79:112).

60. A similar expression is used collectively by a group of men, boasting that they proved their manhood better by going against enemies than by "stroking their wives' belly" (*klappa um maga konum sínum; Ftb* 6.17:208). This saga contains a rare reference to a man who feared wasting his strength through lovemaking; see the description of Þorgrímr as "a man little interested in women" (*lítill kvennamaðr; Ftb* 6.3:128).

61. For a comparable interpretation of a few crucial stanzas in *Gí,* see Sørensen 1983. On the use in *Krm* of the expression *kaupa um knífa* (exchange knives, or penises) as a sexual metaphor for divorce in a case of impotence, see Jochens 1991b, n. 91. See also Clover 1993.

62. Inspired by Andreas Heusler who referred to *Grágás,* the Icelandic law, as "the giant bird" among Germanic laws, modern scholars often consider *Grágás* an honorable term. *Gás* (goose), however, was also a vulgar expression for female genitalia, as suggested by a story in which King Haraldr requested the use of a man's daughter and her *gás* (*Jómsvíkinga saga* 1882, 8:43; the detail is not found in the version used in *Jms*). The nickname *Tregagás* (literally, a slow goose) may have indicated female frigidity; see Fritzner 1886, 3:564.

63. On the language in this saga, see Amory 1988. On the interpretation of geographic features in sexual terms, see Ross 1973 and Margaret Clunies Ross, "An interpretation of the myth of Þórr's encounter with Geirrøðr and his daughters." in *Specvlvm Norroenvm,* 370–91. On the almost pornographic description of intercourse in *Bósa saga,* see Jochens 1991a, 380–81, and Sverrir Tómasson 1989.

64. This is the woman who had been in love with a young boy (see n. 57).

65. On the passage, see Lecouteux 1986, 71–72. For a general medieval context for this phenomenon, see Schmitt 1994.

66. See Chapter 2, 41.

67. An interesting illustration is found in the translation of the life of the apostle Andrew, in which a certain Sostratus complains to the apostle that his mother desired him because of his beauty: "She often encourages (*eggjar*) me to have intercourse with

her" (*Postola sögur* 322). The text reveals the ancient problem of incest within the family as well as the new issue of blaming women for sexual transgressions.

68. This expression is used consistently in the topos of the illicit love visit; the connection between *fífla* (seduce) and *fífl* (fool) suggests the contempt in which the female partner was held.

69. One of the secular leaders praised him for his "chastity" (*hreinlífi; St* 1:157).

70. The vision was Irish in origin. For text of the translation known as *Duggals leizla*, see Cahill 1983. See article "Tundalus," KLNM 19: 53–56, and "Visionsdiktning," KLNM 20:171–86.

71. The most recent edition of the text is in Stefán Karlsson 1983, 92–99. See also *Bs* 1:451–55 and 2:9–11. For a recent treatment of the full vision and its illustrations, see Kren and Wieck 1990.

72. For further treatment, see Jochens 1980 and 1991b.

73. See Sørensen 1983 and Jochens 1996a.

74. See Kreutzer 1987, 86–107. For a specific case, see Queen Semerana's careful planning of conception according to the stars (*Ad, LMIR* 3.3:77–79). The mothers of Flóres and Blankiflur claimed that their children were conceived on the same day; this story is useful because it supplies the technical term for conception, *taka við hǫfn* (literally, "take possession" [*FB, RS* 4.2:141]).

75. See also NgL 1:48.

76. For examples, see Krause 1926, 229–30. The term *maðr* is also used, making it obvious that its meaning is not "man" but "person."

77. The translated *Bevers saga* has a richly detailed description of a birth in a forest, but since the original is not known, it is unclear whether the scene was translated or added to provide local color; text in RS 1.24:357–58; see Kreutzer 1987, 109–10.

78. See article "Barsel" in KLNM 1:354–65; Krause 1926, 229–36, Kreutzer 1987, 134–45; Weiser-Aall 1968; Jacobsen 1984.

79. See the make-believe birth scene in *Áfl*, RS 5.2:127. Ásta, the mother of Óláfr *helgi*, was lying on the floor unable to give birth to the future royal saint. She was helped when the magical belt of one of his ancestors, Óláfr *Geirstaðaálfr* (the Elf of Geirstaðir), was placed around her (*Flat* 2:8–9); on this story, see Heinrichs 1989. Gélis (1991) has assembled useful information from France from a later period. See also Shahar 1990.

80. Two very similar stories are told in *Bs* 2:166–68 and *Mr* 156–57, in which a pregnant woman, so large that she was unable to walk, was helped by Mary and Bishop Guðmundr. With the bishop at the woman's shoulders, Mary stroked her body so firmly that the child was forced out. See Kreutzer 1987, 123–27.

81. *Margrétar saga* is found in *Heilagra manna sögur* 1:474–81 (the quoted passage 480). See also KLNM 11:347–48. Manuscripts containing *Dorotheu saga* may have been used in the same way. One saga text suggest that other women brought food to a new mother (*Dpl* 11.3:143).

82. On this ceremony, see Shahar 1990, 275–76, n. 106.

83. If her husband wanted her to stop sooner and she did not obey, she was fined (NgL 1:340). Suggesting awareness of the need for physical recovery, a Norwegian law makes a slave owner responsible for his pregnant slave from the time she starts parturating until she is able to carry two pails of water from the well; NgL 1:30.

84. See Eggert Ólafsson 1772, 240. Hastrup 1990b (184–200) suggests that a connection may exist between the cultural deconstruction of the period and lack of breastfeeding. If her theory is correct, it is difficult to imagine a more poignant symbol of a nation in decline questioning its own identity than mothers who deem their own milk unsuitable for their babies. See also Benedictow 1985.

85. See Jochens 1985, 104, for the Sturlung age.

86. The information about his long illness is found in *Lx* 5.78:226.

87. In recent years the history of motherhood has been investigated; see Atkinson 1991. Norse mothers were often closer to sons than fathers, but little intimacy is recorded between mothers and daughters; for further details, see Jochens 1996b.

88. The statement is repeated in King Sverrir's Christian Law; see NgL 1:419.

89. For an analysis of the father's role, see Grönbech 1931, 1:291–300.

90. See also *QO*, FSN 2.1:202.

91. See Perkow 1972.

92. The term has, mistakenly, been interpreted as referring to cesarian section; see Halldór Halldórsson 1958, 93–110. When the slave Myrgjol "took care of the queen's unborn (*óborit*) child while she was in the bath," the baby had not yet been brought to its father (*Lnd* 1.S96/H83:138); see discussion in Kreutzer 1987, 111–13.

93. See Maurer 1880, esp. 202–3. The well-known story of the Frisian Liafburg, whose pagan grandmother tried to kill her before she had taken food, is not helpful in clarifying the problem, since the father is not mentioned. For the latest treatment of this story, see Boswell 1988, 211.

94. My conclusion is different from Kreutzer's (1987, 154). See also Benedictow 1985.

95. See the illegitimate Kjartan in *Erb* 4.40:107–8 and Kolli in *Bhd* 3.32:202. The former was the focus of the aging Þórgunna's attention; see n. 57.

96. On Þórdís's career, see *St* 1:242, 302, 304, 322–3, 358, 360, 361, 363, and Jochens 1994b. In 1242 and in 1243 Þórdís was reported to be living on a farm at Æðey with her legitimate son. This was undoubtedly the property that had belonged to Óláfr Æðeyingr, one of her earlier lovers, who had been forced by her father to hand the farm over to him as a fine for having impregnated her. Óláfr's relatives were allowed to redeem it, but since information is lacking, it is not possible to determine whether Þórdís had received the farm from her father or her former lover; see *St* 1:360, 2:28, 65.

97. On the dating of the Christian laws, see article "Kristenretter" in KLNM 9:297–306. For later versions, see NgL 1:130–46, 2:294–386.

98. *Gg* 1b:25, 49, 216; 2:58, 149, 178, 182, 206; 3:20, 146, 419, 456. See Vilhjálmur Finsen's glossary to *skírsla* (3:671–72).

99. This stipulation may have been caused by men who escaped with a favorable outcome. In Norway the ordeal was used in case of a woman who claimed a dead or absent man as her impregnator. If she succeeded, the man or his family became responsible for the child, but if she was hurt or injured, the child remained her problem (NgL 1:130).

100. Historians have normally assumed that infanticide was practiced in all non-Christian societies, but recently Boswell (1988) has provoked a discussion. Claiming that infanticide has been conflated with *expositio* (abandonment), he argues that the latter is conveyed by the Old Norse "carrying out of children" (*barna útburðr*), and that the purpose was not to expose the children but to make them available for others.

Clover (1988; rpt. 1990), defends the traditional point of view, arguing for preferential female infanticide. Although it is true that the child was found in all eight cases of exposure in the narratives, it is hard to disagree with Clover that the nordic climate would have prevented what she calls Boswell's "open-air adoption service" (1988, 156). Citing the case from *Rkd* 10.7:169, both scholars suggest that the proposed killing of old people and children should be interpreted as ritual sacrifice (Clover, 152; Boswell, 286; disconcertingly, Boswell refers to the Icelandic "city" and its "townsmen"). As pointed out in the introduction to the ÍF edition of the saga (lxviii–lxix), this chapter is inspired by *Svaða þáttr ok Arnórs kerlingarnefs,* in which the same hunger is treated. The two heroes of the *þáttr* proposed the killing of old men, but children are not mentioned; the text can thus not be used to argue for infanticide (*Flat* 1:435–39; *ÍS* 3:2249–53).

101. For a listing of the cases, see Clover 1988.

102. Boswell 1988 and Shahar 1990 do not focus on this aspect.

103. The figures have been worked out by Jesch 1991, 81.

104. See Guttentag and Secord 1983, 13–33.

105. For more details on the following, see Jochens 1996c.

106. The two manuscripts of *Erð* use slightly different formulations.

107. See also the case of Helgi's wife Þórunn who gave birth to a daughter on an island in Eyjafjörður before her husband had found suitable land on which to settle (*Lnd* 1:252, 253). The comment in *Fld* that a couple "had four daughters among whom not one lived beyond childhood, but later they had a son," sounds more like genuine regret over the loss of baby girls than female infanticide, but the late date of the text makes it less valuable than the other illustrations (*Fld* 11.1:216).

108. The new Christian policy against infanticide further improved chances of survival. It is significant that it was a baby girl who was saved by a miracle performed by Bishop Þorlákr after having survived birth during winter in the wilderness and subsequent serious damage by weather (*Bs* 1:327–28).

109. The most important study of the female component in *Lnd* is Grethe Jacobsen's unpublished manuscript completed several years ago but still awaiting publication in *MS.* See the comments in her review of Karras 1988 (*Sp* 66[1991]:650–52). I am grateful to her for allowing me to read her work.

110. In addition to Clover and Boswell, see Pentikäinen 1968 and (criticism by) Almqvist 1971.

111. For an overview of the sources, see Jón Hnefill Aðalsteinsson 1978, 55–62. The other versions of the conversion are dependent on this passage. According to the author of *Njála,* exposure of children and the eating of horse meat were allowed only in secret (*Nj* 12.105:272). The best modern treatment is Jón Jóhannesson 1974, 124–38.

112. See Jochens 1991c. On the historical emergence of Óláfr Tryggvason's role, see Lönnroth 1963.

113. Boswell 1988, 220–21.

114. See Taranger 1890.

115. See Boswell 1988, 285–86. It is possible that Gizurr's second wife, Þórdís *eyverska* (from the Orkneys), was a Christian; see Jón Hnefill Aðalsteinsson 1978, 67, n. 35 with references. On the eating of horse meat, see "Hästkött," KLNM 7:280–81.

116. As indicated in several sources, the secular laws were introduced by Óláfr's predecessor, Hákon Aðalsteinsfóstri. Having encountered trouble in his efforts to impose

Christianity, he was not able to include Christian laws in his legislation. This was now remedied by Óláfr in a movement similar to the one through which the Christian Law was added to *Grágás* in 1122.

117. A text from the early fourteenth century makes the law speaker argue for a connection between the two conditions (*ÓTm* 2:196–97): "But because those who have most vigorously opposed Christianity can hardly fathom how it would be possible to raise all children who are born from poor and rich alike, if it is denied and forbidden to use as human food those things that the public at large earlier had as their mainstay, they shall have their way in this that the old law shall remain with respect to the exposure of children and the eating of horseflesh." Logically it would seem that if the inexpensive meat was allowed, children need not be exposed.

118. On these issues the king and the Icelanders apparently worked together, and the king continued to feel warmly toward Skapti, even entrusting him with his arch-rival, the old Hrœrekr whom the king had blinded but did not want to kill (*Óh* 27.85: 127). Later, however, animosity developed between them when the Icelanders refused to hand over to the king a small island off the northern coast of Iceland and likewise refused to pay taxes. When Óláfr demanded that Skapti and the other leaders come to Norway to discuss the situation, they sent their sons instead, among whom was Skapti's son Steinn. Skapti's previous clinging to the old ways on the issue of infanticide receives a faint echo in his son's career in Norway. Finding himself in a position in which he had to assist in the birth and baptism of a child, Steinn declared after the ceremony that "he was not going to hold any more baby girls (*meybǫrn*) over baptism" (*Óh* 27.138:245).

119. In one manuscript the last passage contains the year 1122. The phrasing of the passage in the first two versions still carries its oral origin. On the age of the existing versions, see article "Kristenrettar, Island," KLNM 9:304–6. The importance of the law can be gauged from the fact that more copies exist of the Christian Law than of any other part of the law; see *Gg* 3: 1–376.

120. See also *Gg* 2:1, 3:1, 55, 97, 193, 231, 292.

121. The difference between the north and Rome on this issue is striking. Since infant baptism was not generally accepted until the sixth century, conversion in the Mediterranean world was a conscious decision for adults. This may explain why Rome did not foster a single intellectual willing to defend the pagan religion there the way Snorri Sturluson championed heathenism in the north.

122. See article "Gulatingsloven" in KLNM 5:559–65. Most of the crucial passages are quoted and translated in Pentikäinen 1968, 76–86 (but see criticism by Almqvist 1971).

123. See, for example, the treatment of church maintenance and burial (NgL 1:6–7, 14). Magnús added marital restrictions (1:15–16), included castration among the already severe punishments for bestiality (1:18), and attempted to limit male violence against women (1:19).

124. Translation (modified) from Larson 1935, 49. See also the fragment of an un-mixed Óláfr text in NgL 4:5.

125. In the same chronological group, the Frostathing Law stated that every child born with a human head must be raised, thus allowing the exposure of children who did not meet the qualification (NgL 1:130). For later evidence of deformities, see Liliequist 1991. The right to expose deformed infants is also assumed in the Christian section of the old Bjarkö Law (NgL 1:303).

126. See Clover's spirited arguments (1988, 150–72). Her article has not received the attention it deserves.

127. This is the Borgarthing version; for the almost identical Gulathing version, see NgL 2:310, 327. The same formulation is also found in Archbishop Jón's Christian Law (NgL 2:341) and retained in the last medieval Christian Law from 1360 (NgL 4:161). The less bold version from the so-called King Sverrir's Christian Law ("every child must be raised . . . if it has a human head;" NgL 1:419) probably belongs to the same period; see KLNM 9:301.

128. This version was also brought to Iceland by Bishop Árni Þorláksson and accepted by the alþingi in 1275 for the southern diocese of Skálholt (NgL 5:19–20).

129. The Icelandic Poor Laws obligated parents to raise their children, but the passages do not deal with newborns (*Gg* 1b:1, 5; 2:103, 106). The problem is not included in Iceland's only penitential issued by Bishop Þorlákr in 1178.

130. The expressions *bera út* (NgL 1:13) and *slá út* denote exposure and not previous killing; see Pentikäinen 1968, 82; Boswell 1988, 292–93; and Kreutzer 1987, 245. A hundred years later the fine had been reduced by half (NgL 2:343–44), suggesting that the problem had become minor.

131. See Weiser-Aall 1968 and Grøn 1912. The latter points to Augustine, *De civitate* 16.8.

132. Kreutzer 1987 (175) calls the longest description of a deformity (NgL 1:339) an *Unmöglichkeitstopos.* I am grateful to Ian Baldwin for advice on this section.

133. See Jochens 1996c.

134. This is a common topos in Continental literature, particularly concerning pregnant nuns; see Boswell 1988, 372–73.

135. See Lynch 1986.

136. On the problem of lay people's knowledge of prayers in Latin versus Old Norse, see Stefán Karlsson 1990.

137. See Diplomatarium Norvegicum 1: 26, 6: 10. This ordinance excluded spittle. NgL: 2:293 also excluded dew.

138. For more details on this problem, see Jochens 1987b.

139. See Geary 1988, 179–220.

140. As late as the fourteenth century two brothers shared the rule.

141. It is worth noticing that Ingi's physical condition — he limped and was a hunchback, handicaps incurred when he, as a two-year-old, was carried into battle — might have prevented him from retaining his position as king in the pagan world.

142. For references, see Jochens 1987b, n. 50.

143. There is a rich literature on this subject; for the Norse context, see Miller 1988a.

144. For other cases, see Jochens 1987b, 342–43.

145. Sverrir himself seems to have doubted his story since he did not dare undergo the ordeal. He replaced his original justification of his right to the monarchy through blood by claiming a special spiritual and intellectual kinship with Óláfr *helgi;* see Aron Gurevich, "From Saga to Personality: *Sverris saga,*" *From Sagas* 1992, 77–87.

CHAPTER FOUR. LEISURE

1. For a definition of the sex ratio, see Chapter 3, 86.

2. For cessation of slavery in Iceland, see Karras 1988, 142–45. See the description of Guðmundr the Rich (*inn ríki*), who enjoyed the company of young men so much that he let them stay with him without doing any work (*Sl* 11.1[5]:109). This undefined privilege could be lost even in the world of contemporary sagas; see the story of Þórhallr Svartsson, who at his marriage moved in with his parents-in-law, bringing with him his considerable property in the form of livestock and other movables. When his previous sexual indiscretions were discovered, his father-in-law took his property under his own administration and Þórhallr "was forced to work" (*St* 1:97–98).

3. See also the description of Skalla-Grímr as a "hard-working man" (*iðjumaðr mikill; Eg* 2.29:75). This attitude has not changed; see Finnur Magnússon, "Work and the Identity of the Poor: Work Load, Work Discipline, and Self-Respect," in Durrenberger and Pálsson 1989, 140–56.

4. The growing of grain on Flatey is mentioned as exceptional (*Þks* 13.10:198). See also the description of the unusual yield of grain in Reykjahólar in 1119 (*St* 1:27). The grain gathered was wild, rather than harvested from sown fields; this observation is probable in *BHd* 3.12:139 and certain in *St* 2:100. On the Icelandic *melur* grasses, see Griffin and Rowlett 1981. (I owe this reference to Margaret Clunies Ross.)

5. References to a "summer without grass" (*grasleysusumar*) preceded or followed by a "winter of illness" (*sóttarvetr*) are frequent; see *St* 1:130, 136.

6. The most striking exception concerns the role of the female inciter (the *Hetzerin*). This figure does contain a social component, but since I consider her more as an image, she is treated in *ONIW*.

7. Concerning the father's move to Laugaból, see 6:123, n. 4, and 142, n. 1.

8. On the revelations at Ásgerðr and Auðr's sewing scene that led to the death of all the men in the saga, see Chapter 3, 71–72.

9. When Gísli comes a second time, Þorkell refuses to open the door and responds only when his brother had thrown into the house a stick with a message written in runes. By saying that Þorkell "got up," the text suggests that he had been in bed (*Gí* 6.24:77).

10. A case of teenage laziness is that of Glúmr, who regularly slept until midmorning despite his mother's urging that he get up and work (*VGl* 9.5:15; 7:24; 8:26).

11. It seems to be exceptional that Einarr "was used to rise early in the morning," but even he was summoned from his bed by his shepherd (*Ljs* 10.6[14]: 29–30).

12. In another case a female farm manager gets help from her male colleague brewing beer during the night after the farmer and his numerous male guests have gone to sleep (*St* 2:129).

13. This gender difference does not seem to have changed over time in the north as elsewhere; see Avdem and Melby 1985.

14. When Bjǫrn comes home late at night, badly wounded, the housewife and a servant woman take care of him before notifying his father (*Erb* 4.29:79).

15. See also *St* 1:91.

16. Among numerous examples, see *HrF* 11.8:126, *Gn* 4.8:265–66, *Lx* 5.48:149–50, *Þhv* 11.6:12, *Þst* 11:70, 71, *Fld* 11.1:215.

17. A husband claimed that his wife is so "bad in bed" (*rekkjuilla*) that he is forced to sleep elsewhere (*Rkd* 10.4:161).

18. Unable to sleep because she was concerned about her wounded son, Auðbjǫrg got out of bed and went outside (*Gí* 6.18:59). Although everybody was asleep and Ásdís herself in bed, she was awake when her son Grettir came home (*Gr* 7.47:152). For exceptions, see *Þst* 11:74 and *Nj* 12.112:282.

19. The most spectacular swimming feat was Grettir's crossing from the island of Drangey, his last refuge, to the mainland, a distance of almost five miles (*Gr* 7.38:130; 76: 238–39). For men escaping danger by swimming, see *HsÍ* 6.10–11:325–27. For swimming in icy water on 26 January 1250, see *St* 2:93. See also *Gr* 7.38:130, 56:182, 59:193; *Hrð* 13.17:47. Stuck on an island with two young sons, Helga escaped by "throwing herself in the water" (*kastar sér til sunds*) at night, ferrying her four-year-old son and returning for her eight-year-old sibling who was drowning (*Hrð* 13.38:89). Gunnarr was said to "be able to swim like a seal" (*var syndr sem selr; Nj* 12.19:53), but he never demonstrated this ability. Two brothers, Þorgils and Sighvatr Bǫðvarsson, were also praised as good swimmers (*St* 2:104). In the kings' sagas, see the pretender Sigurðr Sham-Deacon (*slembidjákn*) who escaped his captors by swimming ashore; on the importance of this episode for male clothing, see Jochens 1991a, 12.

20. This game was, most likely, the same one (*skemmtan*) enjoyed by a group of young men in the Laxá river (*Lx* 5.33:91–92).

21. Among numerous examples, see Hrafn and Kálfr in *HrG* 8.2:321–22. A particularly detailed description is found in *Gr* 7.72:235–36.

22. In the latter case the games were started as soon as the fjord froze over.

23. For a detailed description, see *Erb* 4.43:115–18. Night games also occurred; see *Flm* 13.22:283.

24. Gísli's troubles started after violence at two ball games (*Gí* 6.15:49–50, 18:57–58). In another case six men died during the games and another from his wounds immediately after (*Hrð* 13.23:62).

25. For good illustrations, see *Gr* 7.29:99–100, *Rkd* 10.12:181–83, and *St* 2:272–73. For analysis, see Bjarni Vilhjálmsson 1990.

26. In this saga complex the fights often took place on Sunday; *St* 1:101, 322, 420.

27. See *BHd* 3.23:174–75. Only the ironic titles of two poems that Þórðr and Bjǫrn composed about each other's wives have been preserved. As confirmed by Þórðr's son's reaction and the subsequent violent behavior of the protagonists, the poems belonged to the forbidden genre of *mansǫngr* in which a man praised a woman over whom he had no sexual rights or boasted about his conquest of her; see Jochens 1992.

28. See also *Yn* 26.24:63–64 and *Eg* 2.40:98–99. See Björn Bjarnason 1905. A late saga provides a rare glimpse of boys and girls in their teens who competed in an ice game (*Brð* 13.5:114).

29. Among many examples, see *Vtn* 8.25:65 and *Hǫv* 3.28:297.

30. See Jochens 1989. On the four complete sets of chess pieces probably of Icelandic origin found in the Hebrides in 1831, see Taylor 1978.

31. For other fights in connection with games, see *St* 1:398 and 2:105.

32. According to the Icelandic annals, Þuríðr died at the age of eighty-eight in 1112 or 1113 (Storm 1888, 19, 59, 111, 320). Her marriage was recorded in *Lnd* (1.S81/H69: 118/119).

33. See the notice about Bishop Þorlákr's mother Halla who had taught him "historical and genealogical information" (*ættvísi ok mannfræði; Bsk* 2:181).

34. The most detailed description concerns Þorbjǫrg *lítil-vǫlva* (the little sibyl) who performed in Greenland. The text is found in *Erð* 4.4:206–9. This scene and the role of the *vǫlva* is treated in *ONIW.*

35. Also seated on a chair, Gunnarr Lambason told the story of the burning of Njáll and his sons to an audience in the Orkneys consisting of the Irish king and two earls (*Nj* 12.154:442).

36. Although this story is plausible in general terms, it is unlikely that Þorsteinn told the king's adventures in his presence; see Jónas Kristjánsson 1988, 306.

37. Among the most important literature, see Hermann Pálsson 1962; Peter Foote, "Sagnaskemtan: Reykjahólar 1119," in Foote 1984, 65–83; and Torfi Tulinius 1995, 45–52.

38. Although lost in prose, their subject matter has been preserved in fifteenth-century rhymed narratives (*rímur*). See Ursula Brown 1952.

39. The story is told in *Sturlu þáttr, St* 2.2:231–35. On *Huldar saga*, see Úlfar Bragason 1990.

40. On gender and drinking, see Jochens 1993a.

41. Toward the end of the pagan era the old feasts lost their spiritual content, but the celebrations continued; see the statement about Gísli who no longer sacrificed after he had been to Vébjǫrg (Viborg) in Denmark but still celebrated mid-winter with a big party (*Gí* 6.10:36).

42. See Árni Björnsson 1981.

43. Unnr (*Lx* 5.7:13). For cases involving men, see *Lx* 5.26:73; *Eg* 2.78:257; *Erb* 4.54: 148; *Þhr* 14.1:164.

44. The word *festarǫl* is rare. It refers to the wedding and not—as suggested by the word—the engagement, an event that did not call for toasts. The word is occasionally found in charters and may have been more common in Norway; see "Festermål," KLNM 4:233–41.

45. See Helga in *Flm* 13.2:235 and Hildiguðr in *Yn* 26.37:68.

46. Thus, Þorkell was laughed at when he was serving at a wedding (*Vtn* 8.44:117).

47. At Hallgerðr's third wedding set in the 970s two married women considered guests served the others, whereas at Ingibjǫrg's wedding in 1253 the servers were all men (*Nj* 12.34:89; *St* 1:483). A good case of a male server is found in the late *Vgl* where the setting is Norway and the king is present (14.5:69).

48. When Earl Arnfiðr of Halland (Sweden) was assured that Egill and his brother had not come to loot, he invited them to a feast (*veizla*) at which the earl's daughter was allotted to drink with Egill (*Eg* 2.47–48:119–21). Earlier in the same saga, the *tvímenningr*, in which the young Hildiríðr shared a horn with the old Bjǫrgólfr, took place in Hálogaland in Norway (7:16).

49. See, for example, Ingigerðr (*Óh* 27.72:95) and Skjaldvǫr Óláfsdóttir (*Msk* 52:367).

50. One of the few times when drinking is specifically mentioned in *Njála*, it takes place on board a ship that has just arrived from Norway and that therefore has plenty of supplies (12.2:10). For a similar situation, see *Lx* 5.68:199.

51. The most graphic examples are found in *Eg* 2.43:107–11; 71:222–27. On the possible ritual significance of the second purging episode, see Dronke 1992, 664, and North 1990, esp. 156.

52. See, for example, *St* 1:452–53, 2:274. By this time the imported *bjórr* was preferred to *ǫl*, the local home brew. When Gizurr returned from Norway in 1258 he brought with him "large drinking supplies" (*mikil drykkjarfǫng*) and as a result "there was a lot of drinking during the winter" (*St* 1:525).

53. See Þorvaldr in *Nj* 12.11:33–34, Arnórr in *VGl* 9.11:38, and Askell in *Rkd* 10.7:170–71. A husband struck his wife because she had taken flour from a sack hanging from the ceiling (*Brð* 13.9:130).

54. See also *Þhr* 14.12:221, where the drink was so plentiful that Skeggja, in a rare deviation from normal behavior in Iceland, fell asleep under the table. In this case a man (Eiðr) arranged the seating. At a wedding where important verbal vows (*heitstrenging*) were exchanged, drinking was not mentioned, however, although both the ceremony and the vows would vouch for its presence (*Hn* 3.12:33–35).

55. Even when two queens, as Guðrún and Brynhildr, met under festive circumstances they did not drink, although Brynhildr had offered Sigurðr a cup immediately prior to this episode (*Vls* 25:59; 26:61–62).

56. On the first activity, see the episode of Auðr and Ásgerðr busy with their sewing (*Gí* 6.9:30), on the second the women assembled in Hallgerðr's room (*dyngja*) with only two men present (*Nj* 12.44:113).

57. See *Hld2* 5.2–3:267–73.

58. Children, at least boys, also drank. Egill's father had prohibited him from going to this party because "you do not know how to behave in company when there is lots of drink and you are not easy to handle even if you are sober" (*ódrukkinn;* cf. Danish *ædru; Eg* 2.31:81). In this case the author may have wanted to provide an early indication of Egill as a great drinker (as saints' lives often showed pious behavior of the hero as a baby). It is worth noticing, however, that in the Eddic poem *Atlakviða* Guðrún used the term "merry from beer" (*ǫlreifr*) to describe the regular state of her two young sons (str. 38).

59. For bibliography on the passage, see n. 37.

60. The best example is found in *QO*, FSN 2.27:310–21. See Jochens 1993a, 169–70.

61. See Queen Ingigerðr (*HrGt*, FSN 4.8–9:75–83) and Ástríðr (*Jms*, SUGNL 7.27: 96–97). Hrútr and Queen Gunnhildr drank, but neither became inebriated (*Nj* 12.3:15).

62. I am using Dronke's translation. The chivalric sagas provide a few cases of queens who remained sober while they gave their suitors drinks laced with sleeping potion; see Fulgida in *VB* (12:37) and the unnamed maiden king (*meykonungr*) in *Sf* (LMIR 5.5: 57).

63. See Silverman 1988. The theories of Irigaray (1985a, 1985b) are of interest in this connection.

64. On female silence, see Österberg 1991, 9–30. On female mourning in Old Norse, see Carol Clover, "Hildigunnr's lament," in *Structure and Meaning* 1986, 141–83. See also the story of the slave Melkorka, who, while pretending to be mute, in secret taught her son her native Irish (*Lx* 5.13:27; 20:51). Women's share in the saga dialogues may have been greater than men's; see Krause 1926, 53.

65. Þráinn's wife Þorhildr, known as a big-mouthed poetess, had provoked her husband by expressing her displeasure at his visible infatuation with the daughter of the bride at a wedding, resulting in Þráinn's divorcing her. Although Þorhildr had been serving food before drink appeared, no indication suggests that she had been imbibing.

Nevertheless, this is the only case where a woman expressed feelings during a feast that she otherwise might have held back (*Nj* 12.34:87–90). See the loud-mouthed Álfdís, whose torrent of words saved Gísli's life (*Gí* 6.27:86–88).

66. According to the text, only the lonely host was drinking, but the behavior of the other men strongly suggests that they also were imbibing. More important, however, is the fact that the women did not participate in the game but were working. The rare male nickname *leikgoði*, implying the existence of a role as *goði* in a game or drama, suggests another area of entertainment for men (*Vtn* 8.47:127).

67. The word *syrpa* was occasionally used as a proper name; see *Fnb* 14.3:256.

68. See Clover 1986, n. 64, and Miller 1984.

69. *The Vandal Wars*, 2.6.534. Tacitus's *Germania* ch. 27 may also contain an oblique reference to men's elegies.

70. On the *Männerbund*, see Harris 1992.

71. See Jochens 1992. I hope to treat the subject more fully in a later work.

72. Among the rich literature on this poem, see Krömmelbein 1983, 130–69, Richard North, "The Pagan Inheritance of *Sonatorrek*," in *Poetry* 1988, 147–67, A. C. Bouman 1962, 17–40, and Harris 1994.

73. For comment and translation, see Turville-Petre 1976, 24–41.

74. For examples, see *Fld* 11.18:267 and *GKd* 14.8:374.

75. For further details on the following, see Jochens 1993b.

76. The four heroes in *Gí* 6.6:20. See also *St* 1:112.

77. See *Gg* 1a:170; 1b:44, 184; 2:172, 176, 199–200, 364, 392–93.

78. The position as leader (*goði*) of a chieftaincy (*goðorð*) could be inherited, but if it fell to a woman she was obliged to consign the position to a male within her district (*Gg* 1a:141–42).

79. They remained at home managing the farm in the husband's absence or were occupied with the transhumance. The examples abound in the narratives. For example, Hallgerðr was present at the alþingi in her marriageable state of second widowhood. Once remarried to Gunnarr, however, she stayed at home on the farm during his numerous trips, as did her rival Bergþóra (*Nj* 12.33:85; 36:92–96 and subsequent chapters).

CHAPTER FIVE. WORK

1. Anna Sigurðardóttir (1985) treats women's work over the entire span of Icelandic history.

2. For examples, see *Erb* 4.11:19; *Hǫv* 3.16:264–65; *St* 1:139, 140, 171. In 1119 the widow Yngvildr moved in with the priest Ingimundr (*St* 1:23). In 1222 Ingibjǫrg Guðmundardóttir, widowed since 1212, lived with her son at a farm managed by a certain Hafr (*St* 1:288–89).

3. The only indication that Guðrún's mother had died is Kjartan's refusal to let her join him on his trip abroad because her brothers were unmarried (*óráðnir*) and her father old; if she left they would be "deprived of all care" (*Lx* 5.40:115).

4. *St* 1:407. Most often employed by unmarried or widowed men (*Ljs* 10.5[13]:17, *Fld* 11.10:240, *St* 1:161), a *matselja* was occasionally also found when a wife was in charge (*Erb* 4.20:51, *Eg* 2.85:295, and *Nj* 12.39:103). The translation is not "laundress," as suggested by Cleasby and Vigfusson 1975, 414. Sometimes the position is hidden in the

expression that the woman was *fyrir bui,* as in the case of Helga who managed her brother's farm after her sister-in-law's death (*Krm* 8.7:224). Men with several farms and, increasingly, those who became heavily involved in politics took on female managers; for examples, see *Nj* 12.90:225, n. 5; *St* 1:230, 2:152.

5. In a letter of 1202 the bishop-elect Guðmundr invited Sigurðr and his wife Þuríðr to manage his "estate and financial affairs" (*staðarforráða ok fjárvarðveizlu*). Stipulating that their own capital not diminish during their tenure, they accepted (*St* 1:155–57, 239). In this case the woman had a formal position, but on the large farm Kirkjubær where Illugi was the bailiff (*bryti*), his untitled wife Bergljót was busy helping him boil meat at night (1250; *St* 2:91). For other cases of the position of bailiff, see *St* 1:154, 488, 492; 2:125. Þorgils's dealings first with a *ráðskona* (a variant term) and later a *bryti* suggest a change in gender and a simultaneous increase in prestige (*St* 2:122, 125). In the late *Flm,* *ráðsmaðr* and *bryti* were used interchangeably (13.20:276 and 24:298).

6. Herdís's household consisted of over one hundred people including seventy or eighty workers (*Bs* 1:131–32). For household management of the few unmarried bishops, see *St* 2:200; *Bs* 1:203, 239, 839.

7. For further details, see Jochens 1985 and Miller 1988b. I fail to understand Miller's criticism of my argument, especially since we arrive at similar results. Dealing with a more limited subject, he provides richer details on the issue of household size. Titled "A la recherche de la famille nucléaire," my article does not argue for the universal existence of the nuclear family any more than Miller wishes to "prove that Iceland had a joint-household system" (321).

8. In the same story Þórðr's rival Bjǫrn picked up a newborn calf from the barn floor and placed it in a stall, a task his workman refused to do. When Þórðr heard this, he commented that Bjǫrn had "enough men and women to look after such matters and there was no need for him to attend to a cow," suggesting both a social and gendered hierarchy of work (*BHd* 3.16:152–53). On the attitude toward animals, see Teuscher 1990.

9. For a specific statement of male obligations in the narratives, in this case prompted by the absence of a man, see *Svf* 9.23:193.

10. Hallgerðr did not manage the farm in her second marriage until after her brother-in-law left, but after the celebration of her third marriage, when she and her fourteen-year-old daughter were wedded simultaneously, both women took over the management of their respective farms (*Nj* 12.14:45–46, 34:90).

11. On women in this narrative, see Guðrún Ingólfsdóttir 1992.

12. In a similar way, Dalla, the mother of Bishop Gizurr, was in charge of the episcopal household in Skálaholt (*fyrir innan stokk*); she was eventually replaced by Steinunn Þorgrimsdóttir, his wife (*Bs* 1:66, 68, 69).

13. The significance of Hǫskuldr's cape is treated in *ONIW.*

14. *Lǫg* (law) is the plural of *lag* (layer); see See 1964, 73–102, and Kirsten Hastrup, "Text and Context," in Hastrup 1990b, 139–53. See also the Appendix.

15. The formula, including the same expression, is found also in *Gr* 7.72:233 and *Hǫv* 3.33:313. Atli referred to himself as a ploughman (*akrgerðarmaðr; Nj* 12.36:95). The two descriptions in *Nj* mentioned earlier of men sowing are exceptional.

16. Cf. Hallgerðr's insult to the beardless Njáll whom she accuses of not having manured his chin (*hann ók eigi í skegg sér*); as a consequence she wants to call him "the beardless" and his sons "dungbeards" (*taðskegglinga*) (*Nj* 12.44:113).

17. See chaps. 181, 188, 205, 206 in *K*. (*Gg* 1b). See the amusing story of Arnórr (also named Þorljótr), who led a calf home in "long and strong rope," one loop tied around the calf and the other around his own neck. Arnórr lifted the calf to the top of a fence and slipped down on the other side himself, but the calf fell backward. Since the distance was greater on Arnórr's side, both man and calf were strangled; *SnH* 9.6: 279–80.

18. See Kirsten Hastrup, "Male and Female in Icelandic Culture: A Preliminary Sketch," Hastrup 1990b, 269–82, for a contemporary description of the male dominance of the ram exhibition (*hrútasýning*) at the collecting of sheep from the mountains in the fall.

19. See Bjargey in *Hsí* 6.5:308, 7:315.

20. In one case "both men and women" helped to extinguish a fire (*Kjn* 14.4:13).

21. Only the manuscript A.M. 158 B does not identify these tasks as specifically female (*Gg* 3:211). The version in A.M. 181 includes a particularly detailed list (*Gg* 3:332–40).

22. The reference at this place to cloth (*vara*) is not a permission to trade, as suggested by the translators (Dennis et al. 1980, 40). The word belongs to the previous term for cloth (*fǫt*, often used in the expression *stórfǫt*) which it is permitted to dry "if men are in need," supposedly because of inclement weather.

23. An obstreperous bull prevented women from milking the cows (*Fnb* 14.7:263). It took miraculous help from Bishop Þorlákr before a woman succeeded in getting the upper hand in a fight with a bull (*Bs* 1:319, 345).

24. The woman in *Lx* 5.38:108 seems to be herding and not milking the sheep. See also *Hrð* 13.22:60.

25. Another *meystelpa* died in a fire next to her employer; *St* 1:323.

26. *Nj* 12.78:192; *Gí* 6.12:41.

27. *Gg* 1b:70–72; *Flm* 13.32:319.

28. A particularly detailed description is found in *Erb* 4.51:139–40. See also *Gr* 7.48:153–55 and *OSt* 13.2:400. One would assume that differences in physical strength caused the gender division between cutting and raking; it is therefore surprising that modern Icelandic women consider the former less strenuous than the latter (Anna Sigurðardóttir 1985, 392).

29. For this or similar expressions, see *Lx* 5.11:22, 29:77; *Vtn* 8.16:44; *Eg* 2.59:177; *Rkd* 10.13:187–88. *Gí* 6.7:26 may suggest a connection between a wife's paternal share of the farm managed by her husband and her supervision during his absence. A male assistant occasionally helped the wife. Unfortunately, the narratives do not illustrate the case discussed in the law that a married woman could remain as full owner of the farm; see *Gg* 1a:161; 2:322.

30. This seems to be the conclusion of the stipulation that allowed the picking of small amounts on Sundays ("no more than can be carried in the picker's hands;" *Gg* 2: 29). *Gg* 1b:94 allows a person to eat berries and seaweed on another man's property but not to carry the produce away.

31. In Norway angelica was sold at markets; see the story—found in many versions— of Óláfr Tryggvason bringing a stalk to his wife; see, for example, *Hkr* 26.82:343. On this episode and the use of the plant (for cleaning teeth), see Sverrir Tómasson 1984.

32. For seaweed, see *St* 1:22, 65. The berries known as *krækiber* were abundant enough to be used for wine (*Bs* 1:135). A woman eager to live the hermetic life (*ein-*

setulíf) of an anchorite nun told berry-picking women that she could survive in nature by herself by eating berries (*Bs* 1:203–4, 255–57). Men collected eggs from an island and young boys were involved in picking eggs and birds out of nests on steep rocks (*St* 1:84). This activity was so lucrative that the owner of a mountain would demand a mountain toll (*bergtollr*; *St* 2:167). Whaling episodes in the narratives are frequent and the law contains numerous references to jetsam, including a special "wreckage section" (*reka þáttr*; *Gg* 3:379–407).

33. On the transhumance, see Hitzler 1979. Not requiring milking, animals reserved for slaughtering were kept on islands; see *Gr* 7.69:225.

34. See *Vtn* 8.40:105–6, *Lx* 5.55:165–66.

35. See *Eg* 2.85:297, *Lx* 5.35:97, *Hlf* 8.9:180–81.

36. *Í selí.* Some years later this woman, Þórdís, was in the mountains with two other sons, finding time to wash her hair in a lake (*Brð* 13.11–12:140–41). Apparently assuming that the word *sel* (shieling) comes from *selr* (seal), the translators (*Bárðar saga* 1984, 63, 67) wrongly place the passages in the context of a fishing outpost; the context is entirely pastoral.

37. For another scene involving women and a young girl *í selí*, see *Bs* 1:189.

38. Einarr "had driven the ewes into the pen. He was lying on the fence, counting them while the women were milking" (*HrF* 11.3:104). See also *Hn* 3.17:43. Milking was one of the chores that got women up early in the morning, as seen by the exceptionality of the case in *Gr* 7.33:115.

39. *Búalög* 1966, 18. In addition to the milking, one of the women was responsible for cooking in the shieling, and the two others were to return and work on the main farm in the afternoon. I am grateful to Stefán Karlsson for having provided me with this edition of *Búalög*, a great improvement over the previous edition (1915–1933). A collection of prices and wages beginning in the fifteenth century, the *Búalög* exists in many versions. A satisfactory edition is still lacking and many problems concerning dating are unresolved; see KLNM 21:131–32 and Helgi Þorláksson 1991, 517–22.

40. Having gone to the shieling to get food (*matr*), Auðunn returned with *skyr* carried on horseback in skin sacks called *skyrkyllir* (*Gr* 7.28:96).

41. At one farm, apparently, laundry was normally done by a home-well (*heima-brunnr*), but because its water was bad (*vándr*), the chore was temporarily moved close to a stream (*VGl* 9.26:88).

42. See, for example, *HrF* 11.8:126, *Þhr* 14.3:176; 5:185, 188.

43. One of the miracles attributed to Bishop Þorlákr involved a woman who fell into a hot spring (*hverr*) as she was carrying home a large kettle of hot water. She burned herself so badly that skin and flesh came off her legs as people removed her shoes and socks (*Bs* 1:120, 322–23). For the later evidence, see Anna Sigurðardóttir 1985, 73.

44. On the importance of the weather, see *Sl* (*Ljs*) 10.1[5]:110, *Þhr* 14.5:188, and *Bs* 1:307 (a miracle produced by a prayer to Bishop Þorlákr). Drying poles or beams (*váðmeiðr* or *váðáss*) are mentioned in *Rkd* 10.22:219–20, *VGl* 9.26:88 (for drying the large pieces of cloth [*stórfǫt*]), and *HrF* 11.5:119–20 (to string eight men hung through holes pierced in their heels). In an unusual crossing of gender lines, Bjǫrn, who had just returned from abroad, helped his mother dry the linen spread on the ground (*BHd* 3.11:137).

45. A bathtub (*kerlaug*) is also mentioned in *Svf* 9.2:131, but, again, the setting was

Norway (*pace* Magnús Már Lárusson, KLNM 1:297). In Iceland a bathtub was used only to wash wounds (*Þhr* 14.7:197, 199). An Icelander, Aron Hjǫrleifsson, introduced large communal bathing in Norway; see *St* 2:271–72.

46. The sagas of Icelanders occasionally refer to men riding to the baths. In addition to cases already mentioned, see *Þhr* 14.12:219, 4:185; *Gr* 7.50:162; *Ljs* 10.8(18):45, 46, 58; *Bdm* 7.7:327. In *Vtn* 8.44:117 Glæðir was merely washing hands, as were Flosi and his men in *Nj* 12.116:290. The scene in *Lx* 5.33:91–92 involves swimming rather than bathing.

47. About Ásbjǫrn, the first suitor, the author states that he often went to the bath "to amuse himself" (*at skemmta sér*) a term often containing sexual connotations. See also *St* 2:152–53 where the same expression is used about Þorgils, who demonstrated his intentions by joking with (*glensa*) and grabbing the hand of Jóreiðr, a beautiful woman who was at the bath washing clothes.

48. Only in this generation have Icelanders begun to exploit fully the seemingly inexhaustible supply of hot water that boils out of the ground in many places. Funneled through pipes, it is used to heat entire cities; see Rosenblad 1990, 353–71.

49. For examples of the former, see *St* 1:72, 82, 87, 350; 2:152, 258. There are a few exceptions to this distinction; in 2:135 two men "walked to the bath (*gengu . . . til laugar*), because their horses were not ready. Snorri, who had "been in the bath" (*sat í laugu*), was being led back to the house by the man who had kept watch (*St* 1:319–20). A particularly clear case of the bath on the premises is found in *St* 1:336: "At night when the bishop had gone to bed and those who wanted to, had gone to the baths, a dance was held in the hall." Returning from the bath, a man came into the hall dressed in a bathrobe. See also *St* 2:97, 148, 254.

50. See the touching story of Þorkatla, who went to the bath during the winter with a big load of laundry. While working, she hid her shoes under a stone, and a raven stole them. Knowing she would not be able to return barefoot in the snow, she finished her work but did not dare to stay, "because some tramps had died in the bathhouse" earlier. After she had taken a bath and prayed to Bishop Jón, the raven returned her shoes (*Bs* 1:209–10). The story is full of interesting details of which the most pertinent here is the fact that Þorkatla was said to be working for the housewife on the farm, not her husband (both named), and that the laundry belonged to the wife.

51. See article "Bastu" in KLNM 1:384–90 and Jón Jóhannesson 1974, 337–44. In *St* 2:33 a certain Símon was in his *baðstofa* and had made *reykr* (smoke), suggesting a steam bath.

52. The most famous steam bath in the sagas of Icelanders is the underground *baðstofa* in which two berserks were killed (*Erb* 4.28:72–74).

53. For a different interpretation, see Nanna Ólafsdóttir 1973.

54. For cases of politicking and socializing, see *St* 1:72, 87, 319, 329; 2:135–36. For wounding and killing, see *St* 1:382, 510; 2:33.

55. The neutral plural pronoun *þau* (they), included Guðný and her male guests as "they" rode to the *laug* (*St* 1:232). The reason for the presence at a bath of two unnamed women hiding a man with their bodies is not clear (*St* 1:498); that they are unnamed suggest that they were doing laundry and not bathing.

56. For an example of a woman combining laundry and hair wash in the sagas of Icelanders, see *Dpl* 11.1:138.

57. For after-dinner bathing, see *St* 1:336; 2:40, 254.

58. The ominous import of the itch was revealed later. A story concerning the Jóms-vikings assumed that a woman would serve a man in the bath (*Flat* 1:202). In the professionalized world of late thirteenth-century Bergen, the law provided wage tariffs for a bath woman (*baðkona;* NgL 3:15). In passing it is worth noticing that this passage was followed by rules for the female baker (*bakstur kona*), suggesting that the need for heat grouped the two professions in the same building.

59. When Hallgerðr paid so much attention to the visiting Sigmundr that she "gave him money and served (*þjónaði*) him no less than she did her own husband, so people began to talk and wondered what was behind it," the reader is prepared for her later affair with Hrappr that earned her the designation of a "harlot or prostitute" (*hornkerling eða púta; Nj* 12.41;106, 88:220, 91:228).

60. See Þuríðr in *Höv* 3.22:276–77.

61. The couple Þórðr and Oddný slept in the same room as the workwoman who "dressed and undressed them" (*togaði af þeim klæði; BHd* 3.14:149). The institution continued to puzzle travelers until the nineteenth century; see illustration in *Úr Íslandsferð J. Ross Browne 1862* (Reykjavik, 1976), reproduced in Anna Sigurðardóttir 1985, 65.

62. A similar warming of a cold and shivering man was done by Þórdís for her husband Atli (*Hsl* 6.16:344–45). See Gunnar Benediktsson 1980, for the sexual connotations of this passage.

63. The custom historian Michelle A. Nordtorp-Madson is working on "the style of 1340." I have borrowed from her the idea that the inserted sleeve may have been adopted from plate armor. It is not the bishop, as indicated by Falk 1919, 151, but Gizurr Þorvaldsson. See also *Vls,* SUGNL 36.7:14.

64. Among numerous examples, see *Ftb* 6.9:164, *Fld* 11.19:279–80, *Krm* 8.16:260, *Svf* 9.19:176, *St* 1:383, 394–95, 421, 494, 507.

65. See Jón Jóhannesson 1974, 288–328, Gelsinger 1981, 3–16.

66. The scene in which "bread and butter" was served to Egill and his companions naturally took place in Norway (*Eg* 2.43:107). Bread continued to be scarce; see Sveinbjörn Rafnsson 1983b.

67. The scarcity of the raw material is evident when a bishop requires that land rent be paid in flour (*St* 1:269). See also "Bakning," KLNM 1:307–10.

68. At the king's court the fare was meat, and when Sneglu-Halli resorted to his familiar buttered porridge he was ridiculed (*SnH* 9.4:269–74). Concerning elderly people, see description of Bersi, *Krm* 8.16:260.

69. See articles "Kvarn" and "Kvinnearbeid" in KLNM 9:536–45, 565–71. Among the poetic sources it is mentioned in the Eddic *Grottasǫngr* and *Helgakviða Hundingsbana ǫnnor.*

70. Nordland 1969, 58. In all-male institutions, however, the monks undoubtedly took over the task, as suggested by the nickname *ǫlgerðarmaðr* (brewer) of an Icelandic monk (*St* 1:483–91). On this issue, see Jochens 1993a.

71. "The housewife on whom all the responsibility rested" (. . . *hvsfreyian. es alt abyrgþesc í; Bs* 1:339). For other brewing miracles, see *Bs* 1:63–64, 316, 340.

72. It was considered particularly offensive to pour out the beer during an attack on an enemy, as it happened at Sturla Sighvatsson's farm in 1229 (*St* 1:329).

73. See Þórhallr nicknamed *Ǫlkofri* (Ale-Hood) in the *þáttr* by this name (11:83–94).

The alþingi had a house for brewing (*heituhús*) and a male brewer (*heitumaðr*) who used a large fireproof kettle (*hituketill*) to produce his brew which was served in an ale-booth (*ǫlbúð*); see *OSt* 13.4:403–04 and *St* 1:267, 343. In contrast to Norwegian laws, *Grágás* carried no prohibition against drinking at the meetings.

74. For a particularly detailed description of lenten food, see *St* 1:379–80.

75. At the farm Fróðá supplies were stored in cupboards stuffed so tightly that the door could not be closed and people had to use a ladder to get to the top of the pile; *Erb* 4.52–54:147–50. See also *St* 1:312.

76. For a man fishing, see *Ftb* 6.11:169, 171. The most sustained attention to fishing concerns the woman Bjargey. Her and her husband Hávarðr's household depended on the usual number of animals, and no mention was made of fishing as long as Hávarðr was active, except that he expected his share of a whale stranded on his property. Grieving over the killing of his son, he took to his bed for three years, and during this time his wife fished, assisted by a man (*HsÍ* 6.3:300–2, 5:308, 8:315).

77. See Hastrup 1985, chap. 5; Hastrup 1990a chap. 3; and Gísli Ágúst Gunnlaugsson 1988. For a disparaging remark about fishermen, see *St* 2:29. Admitting that he would rather do anything else but steal, Grettir reluctantly decided to fish (*Gr* 7.55:178). Þórir found it preferable to break into a burial mound rather than to go fishing (*Þsk* 13.3:183).

78. As often noticed by scholars, Óddr Ófeigsson had earned his wealth through fishing and trading, but, characteristically, he eventually invested his fortune in animals and land; see *Bdm* 7.1–2:295–98.

79. On fishing, see, for example, *Bs* 1:350 (ice fishing), 360, 365.

80. See the dispute on board Óláfr's ship in fog concerning the correct direction to Ireland (*Lx* 5.21:53), and the lottery used to determine how the limited spaces on the lifeboat were to be distributed (*Erð* 4.13:235, 433–34). For the need to stay peaceful on board ship, see also *Ftb* 6.20:23.

81. For similar modern perceptions of the "skipper effect" in fishing, see E. Paul Durrenberger and Gísli Pálsson, "Forms of Production and Fishing Expertise," in Durrenberger and Pálsson 1989, 3–18.

82. Among the numerous examples of division of whales, see *HsÍ* 6.3:300, *Ftb* 6.7: 148–49, *Gr* 7.12:29–30; on boat launches, see *Flm* 13.32:319. Whales were important not only because they were an unexpected bonanza from the ocean, but also because the church allowed the consumption of whale meat (but not walrus and seal) during Lent (*Gg* 1a:34, 2:43). The most comprehensive list is found in NgL 5:33–47, 50–51. On one occasion a stranded whale—predicted by Bishop Guðmundr—served to feed the multitude of people who followed him (*St* 1:144).

83. After a shipwreck the crew survived by softening the walrus hide used for tackle with the contents of a casket of butter (*St* 1:474).

84. See DI 2:194–95 for the monastery on Viðey.

85. See "Smörhandel," KLNM 16:322–36, esp. 334.

86. A young boy fell in a whey container (*sýruker*) and a woman thought the body was a piece of meat; *Bs* 1:318. Cheese and curds were often served for supper; see *Erb* 4.45:130 and *BHd* 3.27:185. Whey was occasionally used to extinguish fires; see *Gí* 6.3: 12 and *Nj* 12.129:328.

87. Scarcity of "food and hay" is mentioned in 1252 as causing a great famine (*St* 2: 97).

88. On this episode, see Andersson 1984, esp. 503–4.

89. For examples, see *St* 1:389, 421, 510, 513; 2:32. When Þórðr the Stammerer (*kakali*) and his men were outlawed, he contemptuously called the sentence a "milk sentence" (*flautasekt*) because they had been served a supper of only cream or whipped milk (*flautir; St* 2:30).

90. The title of Brahe's work was "Oeconomia or Household Book for Young Noble People"; see "Kvinnearbeid," KLNM 9:565–71. The work was reissued in 1971. The precise dating of the Oseberg burial is possible through dendrochronology; see Bonde 1994.

91. Fire is merely implied in *Krm* 8.4:216 (it is not clear whether Steingerðr or Narfi was doing the cooking). In *Erb* 4.51:144 the expression *at matseld* is probably not *matseld* (suggesting fire), but *mat-seld*, the equivalent of *matreiða;* both expressions refer to the arranging and preparing of (cold) food for serving. For a different view, see Anna Sigurðardóttir 1985, 90–91. Viga-Glúmr was being chided for having spent too much time near the pantry shelf (*búrhilla*), discussing cooking (*matargerðr*) with his mother (*VGl* 9.18:62).

92. For examples, see *Erb* 4.43:117 (games); 39:104–6 (on board ship), *Nj* 12.145:407 (at the alþingi), *Þtf* 11:331 (on foreign shores). A scene in Greenland shows a husband cooking while his wife is engaged in (more important) magical activities (*Ftb* 6.23:245). Named *Gamli* (old), he may have joined other old men in female occupations. It was considered a special honor when Kolbeinn himself "served the food and spread the tablecloth" for Bishop Guðmundr, who was related to his wife (*St* 1:153).

93. For examples, see *Bs* 1:351, 368.

94. On insurance and the arrangement of the house, see Jón Jóhannesson 1974, 337–44.

95. On the former term, see *Krm* 8.4:216, *Bs* 1:357 (the scene is England); on the latter, *Nj* 12.145:407.

96. A house with a fire (*eldahús*) in Norway was said to be located "a short distance from the other houses" (*Eg* 2.43:106). Óláfr built a similar house (*eldhús*) at Hjarðarholt "larger and better than men had seen before" (*Lx* 5.29:79).

97. A story describing a woman who "went out of the hall . . . into the house with the fire" (*eldhús*) suggests that the latter was a separate building (*Bs* 1:354).

98. See *St* 1:185, 199 for illustrations. Jón Jóhannesson 1956, 405, identifies the pantry (*matbúr*) as the earliest extension built on to the main house. Haraldur Bessason's translation of this term as "the pantry" (Jón Jóhannesson 1974, 340) does not suggest a fire. On the medieval house, see also Björn Þorsteinsson, 1966, 106–12.

99. No information is given about the source of the famous fire in *Njála*. When Qnundr was burned (1197) the attackers found no fire on the spot and had to search for ember at neighboring farms (*St* 1:189). Likewise, the fire at Þorvaldr's farm (1228) was started with embers from elsewhere (*St* 1:322). Intending to burn Sturla's farm (1229) in retaliation for their father's burning, Þorvaldr's sons fashioned "many torches" (*log-brandar*) on their last stop on the journey. Kept alive during the next twenty-four hours, they were put to use on Sturla's farm, although the burners also found fire locally (in the *eldhús; St* 1:325–26). At the fire at Flugumýrr (1253) the burners used fire found on the farm, but they brought a tar-pin (*tjǫrupinnr*) from which they smeared tar on sheepskin to make them burn more easily (*St* 1:489).

100. See also the *langeldar* in *Krm* 8.15:258 (for warmth) and the "great fire" in *St* 1: 325 (for drying out).

101. See the scene in *Ljs* where the housewife reheats hot milk by taking the stone out and heating it again (10.11:61).

102. On this episode, see Kjartan G. Ottósson 1983.

103. An expression used metaphorically, "to break up the fire" (*raufa seyðinn*) suggests the existence of buried ovens from which smoke was not supposed to emerge; see Guðrún's statement: "There you are stirring up a fire, Kjartan, that should not be allowed to smoke" (*Þann seyði raufar þú, Kjartan, at betr væri, at eigi ryki; Lx* 5.46:144). Although not in evidence in Iceland, buried ovens have been used almost universally and were known from archaeological discoveries in Greenland.

104. The kettle used by two women to carry hot water from a spring was large and heavy and was undoubtedly also used for cooking (*Bs* 1:342).

105. See the story of the "large and beautiful kettle" (*ketill mikill ok góðr*) in *ÞSH* 11.2: 303.

106. For *gervibúr*, see *Vp* 11.4:29, *OSt* 13.3:402; for *útibúr*, *Vp* 11.4:30, *Fld* 11.16:264, *VGl* 9.1:5, *Hn* 3.9:26, *Flm* 13.25:303, *Erð* 4.3:203, 7:219 (the last three cases occur in Greenland).

107. *HrF* 11.5:119–20; *St* 1:487, *Vtn* 8.44:117; *Dpl* 11.11:166.

108. In *St* 1:195 women ferreted a man out of the pantry (*matbúr*) through the window (*vindauga*); see also *St* 1:199.

109. For the "southern room" (*suðrbúr*), see *St* 1:71. See also the "large curd containers" (*skyraskar stórir*) in which Egill and his men were served the ubiquitous nourishment which here was so thin that it was drunk (*Eg* 2.43:107).

110. During the legal proceedings Gunnarr referred to the room as a house (*hús; Nj* 12.51:132).

111. For examples, see *Hsí* 6.11:329, *St* 1:370, 513.

112. Roussell 1941, 230.

113. Flour and probably whale meat were also stored in these rooms; see *St* 1:213, 240.

114. A couple and a servant woman also slept in their pantry (*útibúr; BHd* 3.14:149).

115. Among many examples, see *Vp* 11.4:29–30, *GÞb* 11.6:209, *Fld* 11.20:283 on the two first methods, and *HrF* 11.5:120, *Hrð* 13.27:68, *St* 1:166 on the last.

116. Keys as part of female equipment is found in Eddic poetry; see *Þrymskviða* str. 16, 19 and *Rígsþula* str. 23. This image may strengthen the argument for the late date of these poems.

117. See the trunk keys (*kistuluklar*) given by a Norwegian to his colleague when he had premonitions of his own death (*Nj* 12.63:155). Keys were also needed for Sturla's weapon trunk (*vápnkista*) and Solveig's jewelry box (*gullhús*) although both were opened by force on this occasion (*St* 1:327–28). See also *Ftb* 6.13:188. Vigdís secured a pantry with a lock (*láss*) without evidence of keys (*Lx* 5.14:31). The precious headdress (*motr*) disappeared despite double protection; it was kept in Hrefna's locked chest (*kista*) placed inside Guðrún's pantry (*útibúr; Lx* 5.46:140). On archaeological evidence of keys, see Else Roesdahl, "On Keys," in *Twenty-Eight Papers* 1993, 217–24.

118. For examples, see *Lx* 5.33:88, 45:136, *St* 1:102. Sturla suggested that his wife arrange a ring game (*hringleikr; St* 1:89). See also Anna Sigurðardóttir 1985, 91. Celebrating her daughter's wedding, Yngvildr did not dare to ask an obstreperous guest

to leave but deferred to the most prestigious man present (*St* 1:26). The Eddic poem *Hávamál* does not mention women in connection with the basic features of hospitality offered to a guest: warmth, food, dry clothes, water, and towel (str. 2–4).

119. See *St* 1:167, 273, 312.

120. For my purposes the two most important narratives are *Gþb* and *Fld*. Both texts are found in vol. 11 of ÍF. Henceforth, only page reference to this volume will be given in the text.

121. Guðrún had accepted Gunnarr during her husband's absence, and despite his objections she kept him as long as he needed it. According to another version, Gunnarr came to her farm under an assumed name before her last wedding; she risked her new marriage by insisting on keeping him; see *Lx* 5.69:202–4. See also Chapter 2, 61–62. Geirmundr kept Hrolleifr in his storage room (*Vtn* 8.25:66). In Greenland Þormóðr was kept safe an entire winter in a similar place (*Ftb* 6.24:248).

122. Þórdís kept her cousin Gestr in her pantry overnight (*Hðv* 3.10:236), as did Þorbjǫrg with her sister-in-law Helga and her two children (*Hrð* 13.38:89).

123. See *VGl* 9.14:44–45; it was used to keep a man safe. The variant to *Ftb* 6.24:248, n. 2, does not seem plausible since the setting is Greenland. A particularly impressive log cabin (*stokkabúr*) with ingenious iron locks was built by Gísli in the Y version (*Gí* 6.9:29–30). A "very strong house" (*allsterkt hús*) in Norway was called both an *útibúr* and a *fatabúr* (*Gr* 7.19:66; 68 provides a plan of the building). One man identifies his *stokkabúr* together with his purse and axe as his "trusted friends or patrons" (*fulltrúar*, *VGl* 9.14:44–45; in the singular *fulltrúi* was used when addressing a pagan god; in the same narrative, see 9.9:34). See also "Bur" in KLNM 2:366–67.

124. On this episode, see *Íbm* 1:336–39.

125. The bishop's storage room, known as *biskupsbúr*, was used as a place of safety for Tumi Kolbeinsson (*St* 1:288). Julia McGrew's translation as "the bishop's quarters" (*Sturlunga saga* 1970, 1:183) does not convey the specificity of the place.

126. For examples, see *St* 1:196, 349, 478, 497, 498; 2:36, 37, 178.

127. The most thorough treatment of this subject is Helgi Þorláksson 1991. His study is not yet available commercially, and I am grateful to Helgi for providing me with a copy.

128. On the farm management necessary for the production of surplus wool, see Jón Haukur Ingimundarson, "Spinning goods and tales: market, subsistence and literary productions," in *From Sagas* 1992, 217–30.

129. *Vaðmálsreikningur;* the expression was coined by Jón Jóhannesson 1974, 331 (Icelandic version 1956, 394). See also Þorkell Jóhannesson 1933, 25–45, and Gelsinger 1981, 17–44.

130. In contrast, when the absence of women forced men to engage in the female task of cooking, they easily got into trouble; see *Ftb* 6.15:197–200.

131. The story concerned Steinuðr the Old (*en gamla*) and the first settler Ingólfr; see *Lnd* 1.S394:392. The incident is also mentioned in *Gr* 7.12:32. It is a typical case of *don* and *contredon*. On gift giving, see Grönbech 1931, 54–76 and Miller 1986b.

132. When sheep farming was reintroduced in Greenland in the early twentieth century, the pastures—unused for five centuries—were so rich that it took less than half the acreage needed in Iceland to support the animals (Krogh 1982, 69). Similar conditions may have obtained in Iceland when the settlers first arrived.

133. Þórir sold both "wool and skin" (*ull ok klippingar*) in return for linen (*Ljs* 10.5[13]:22–23).

134. On the following, see Anna Sigurðardóttir 1985, 325–46.

135. It is possible that the urine pit (*hlandgróf*) into which Rannveig threw her husband's clothes before leaving him was kept for this purpose (*Dpl* 11.9:158).

136. While growing up Grettir underwent an interesting transition from performing children's work—tending geese—to women's work—rubbing his father's back (part of "service" [*þjóna*])—before being allowed the male task of taking care of a horse. When his father complained that he did not massage his back hard enough, Grettir picked up a comb left by women who had been "working the wool (*tó*) during the day" (*Gr* 7.14: 38). The father's subsequent pain was not only caused by Grettir's strength but by the comb's metal teeth, assuming that Grettir's comb was like the wool comb (*ullkambr*) on which the bishop of Greenland used a hammer to put back a tooth; *Grn* 4.1:275). See also the wool comb used for torture in *Heilagra manna søgur* 1:262. From *tó* comes the modern Icelandic verb *tæta;* hairdressers—and literary scholars—of this generation have given new life to the related English "tease."

137. Meager at best, a single spinning scene depicts the sorceress Katla working her distaff (*rokkr*), but, as it turned out, it was her son in disguise (*Erb* 4.20:51–53). Confirming the impression of the simple distaff, the text states that Katla "spun thread off the distaff" (*spann garn af rokki*) and left it on the bench when she went on to another task. The spinning wheel, invented in Germany in the late sixteenth century, did not appear in Iceland for another two centuries.

138. For the following, see Falk 1919, 9–18; "Oppstadsvev," KLNM 12:621–29; Hoffmann 1964; Poole 1991, 116–56.

139. Large farms, such as Bergþórshváll, had a special weaving room (*vefjarstofa*), perhaps equipped with several looms (*Nj* 12.132:344). Not all farms had a loom, however, and poor women had to send yarn out to have it woven into cloth, as did Gríma (*Ftb* 6.9:162).

140. Guðrún probably was referring to the warp when she told Bolli that she had spun *garn* sufficient for twelve ells of cloth while he had killed Kjartan (*Lx* 5.49:154). On this problem, see Helgi Þorláksson 1991, 309–11. The soap stone with a man-made hole found in Lance-aux-Meadows is one of the most important pieces of evidence for Norse presence in North America. Used either as a spindle in the spinning process or as a weight on a loom, Ingstad referred to it as a spindle-whorl (1969, 213–14). Spindleheads and loom weights are among the most common artifacts in ancient farm sites in Iceland; see Jón Jóhannesson 1974, 310.

141. Poole gives the most satisfactory description of this process (1991, 132–36).

142. A poor woman who had made an extravagant purchase of wax for a candle to honor Bishop Þorlákr was pleasantly surprised to discover, when "her loom was taken down," that "the homespun was four ells longer than she had expected" (*Bs* 1:367).

143. The only description of the distaff (*rokkr*) contained an element of magic; see n. 137. *Darraðarljóð* is inscribed in *Njála* (12.157:454–58). Ingibjǫrg's dream in found in *Jms* 8:10.

144. This fundamental assumption is corroborated only by two other brief references. I return to the first; the other is mentioned in n. 157.

145. The contradictions between the prose and the poetry has engendered a rich lit-

erature; see, for example, Holtsmark, 1939; KLNM 2:667–68; See (1959) 1981, 329–43; Poole 1991, 120–25.

146. The subject is treated in greater detail in *ONIW*.

147. Their identity cannot be doubted. Referred to as valkyries (str. 6, 7), they call themselves "Óðinn's friends" (str. 1); six were mentioned by name, including three well-known valkyrie names (str. 3).

148. In addition to Holtsmark 1939, see Damsholt 1984 and See (1959) 1981, 329–43.

149. Among Eddic poems, *Vǫluspá* mentioned the names of six valkyries (str. 30) and *Grímnismál* thirteen (str. 36).

150. Also referred to as beaters, *sverðum* in str. 3 is plural.

151. See the episode in *Flm* 13.32:318–19.

152. See "Arbeidssanger," KLNM 1:201–3. This argument does not preclude the possibility that women might be singing by themselves while working, as done, for example, so enticingly by the beautiful Þóra working "by the mill," that King Hákon took her to bed immediately (*Hss* 28.18:325–26), nor does it deny that a rhythmic song occasionally might facilitate women's work, as in the Eddic *Grottasǫngr*.

153. The loom Ingibjǫrg saw in her dream also used men's heads as weights, in one case a recognizable person; *Jms* 8:10.

154. They do not ride to the battle, as Carol Clover suggests, since the battle must be coterminous with the weaving (DMA 4:106). The division in two groups may reflect a pagan-Christian conflict, as proffered by the wise Þórhallr when he was asked to explain the appearance of nine female riders dressed in black arriving from the north and nine white ones from the south (*Þþ*; text in *ÍS* 3:2253–55, *Flat* 1:419–21, and *ÓTm* 2:145–50).

155. See "the threads of fate" (*ǫrlǫgþáttu*) in *Helgakviða Hundingsbana in fyrri*, str. 3–4, and the "lines of fate" (*ǫrlǫgsímu*) in *Reginsmál*, str. 14. For a prose elaboration of this theme, also in a martial context, see *Ad*, LMIR 3.33:140.

156. This is treated in more detail in *ONIW*.

157. The only other statement about women weaving concerns Þórgunna, who refused *vásverk* (work that made a person tired or wet) but "worked at the loom (*vann váðverk*) every day when there was no hay work" (*Erb* 4.50:138).

158. *Búalög* 1966, 18, 43. On the issue of the weaver's wages, see Helgi Þorláksson, "Arbeidskvinnens, særlig veverskens, økonomiske stilling på Island i middelalderen," in *Kvinnans* 1981, 50–65.

159. See Anna Sigurðardóttir 1985, 343–46.

160. The method of using clay for fulling known among the Romans and their immediate neighbors was unknown in northern Europe, but the close affinity between the words "clay" and "cloth" is more than accidental; Falk 1919, 37–38. Old Norse *klæði*, the cognate to cloth, almost without exceptions denotes foreign textiles, while *vaðmál* identifies the indigenous homespun.

161. Anna Sigurðardóttir 1985, 322–25. In the sagas of Icelanders procuring of magical clothing was one of the few gender differences in the performance of magic.

162. Preparing for battle in 1211 but without protection for their bodies (*bolhlíf*), men cut felt coats (*stakka ór þófum;* see Guðrún P. Helgadóttir 1987, 17:35; the passage is omitted in the *St* version of the saga [2:221]). Davidson provides references to various ways in which cloth was made impenetrable (Davidson and Fisher 1980, 2:152–53).

163. See *Búalög* 1966, 16. Hoffmann assumes that it refers to twenty ells of cloth,

which seems little for a day's work. It is more likely that it is twenty pieces of the standard measure of six ells a piece, making it 120 ells; see KLNM 19:466.

164. Two boys were sent out by their mother to collect *litgrǫs* (plants for dye), keeping it in a *baggi* or *belgr* (*Svf* 9.18:172). Treating the same episode, another text identified the plant as *jafni*, used until modern times as yellow dye (*Lnd* 1:254); see also Falk 1919, 42.

CHAPTER SIX. THE ECONOMICS OF HOMESPUN

1. Largely imported, linen was also produced locally in small amounts; see Anna Sigurðardóttir 1985, 316–20. Used for underwear among wealthy people, it was woven in the same way as wool. Because of its importance as exchange and export, wool forms the focus of this chapter.

2. See Óttarr's *Hǫfuðlausn* str. 20 (*Skj* 1B, 272).

3. Such sails could be put to other uses than the obvious. Another Norwegian king was able to extinguish a fire in Bergen in 1248 by soaking a "long-ship sail" in water and throwing it on the flames (*St* 2:113). This specimen need not be of Icelandic provenance, but its appearance in a story glorifying the Icelander Þorgils Harelip (*skarði*) makes it likely.

4. Among the rich literature on the ship burials, see Marstrander 1986 for a recent popular treatment.

5. Among many examples, see *Nj* 12.116:289, *Gí* 6.15:51, *St* 1:494, *Jms*, SUGNL 7.3:14, *Bs* 1:877, *DI* 1:251, 255, 267. The tapestries were often acquired abroad, as was the case in *Gí*; on these, see Elsa E. Guðjónsson 1991.

6. Grettir benefited from the transparency of the cloth when he covered the entrance to his cave with "gray homespun" (*Gr* 7.58:187).

7. For table cloths and towels, see *Nj* 12.116:290, *St* 1:153. A woman can appreciate the outrage of the housewife who scolded Sveinn Úlfsson, the disguised Danish king, when he used an entire towel to dry his hands (*HrS* 28.64:153). Left without clothes, a man wrapped himself in the "homespun from the bed" (*rekkjuvaðmál; Dpl* 11.9:158). On clothes or cloth with downs or feathers (*dúnklæði*), see *St* 1:494, 2:95, 255; *Bs* 1:802.

8. A rare mention of female outerwear is the precious cape made of homespun from Greenland (*vaðmálsmǫttull grœnlenzkr*) included among Leifr's presents to his pregnant girl friend Þorgunna (*Erð* 4.5:210, 414; most likely the same as in *Eyr*).

9. Undoubtedly of poor quality, it would match his "worn shoes."

10. Another man appeared in a white cape (*í hvítri heklu; Ftb* 6.14:195).

11. Without criminal intent Skúta used a black and white cloak (*vesl . . . tvískipt; VGl* 9.16:52 and *Rkd* 10.26:233).

12. See Guðrún P. Helgadóttir 1987, 11:23, 20:43–44. The "browning herb" (*brúngras*) that Syrpa sent her husband to find was undoubtedly used for this purpose (*Fnb* 14.3: 256).

13. Known on the Continent from the late fourteenth century, knitting was not found in Iceland until the late sixteenth century; see Anna Sigurðardóttir 1985, 346–51.

14. For illustrations, see *Nj* 12.22:59, *Lx* 5.62:185.

15. *Þsk ÍS* 3:2291–92. This coat was used not only against cold but also as protection against a tremendous noise produced by a devil whom Þorsteinn encountered in the

privy. In another case a pile coat (*loðkápa*) was later referred to simply as a *kápa* and a *feldr* (*Gr* 7.21:75).

16. See Falk 1919, 174–78 and Elsa E. Guðjónsson 1962. Jón Jóhannesson seems to have been the first to understand the unique character of these coats; see his *Íslendinga saga* 1956, 368–70 (Eng. trans. 1974, 310–12). Occasionally *vararfeldir* are still translated as "sheepskins"; see Hermann Pálsson and Paul Edwards 1972, 39:103.

17. See the many references to the gray fur (*grávara*) the Norwegian king expected from the Finns as their contribution to the royal treasury; (*Eg* 2.13:34, 17:42–43).

18. Regardless of how the Thorslunda bronze plates are interpreted, their seventh-century provenance and the shaggy pants worn by a man vouches for an ancient origin of fur clothing; see Arent 1969, 133–39 (with illustration) and McTurk 1991, 10.

19. The preference for woolen coats may have been a fashion; Adam of Bremen remarked that the Prussians offered precious martens' skins in exchange for woolen coats known as *faldones*; Schmeidler 1917, 245–46. The woven shaggy cloth was invented in many cultures; see illustrations in Elsa E. Guðjónsson 1962.

20. When Bersi and Halldórr killed Váli they used his own coat (*vararfeldr*) to cover his body (*Krm* 8.16:263).

21. *Hðv* 3.11:242 (on board ship) and *VGl* 9.2:7, 3:9. For other examples, see *Kjn* 14.8: 21. The fashion also reached the Orkneys, but it is impossible to determine the origin of the furry coat (*loðkápa*) worn by Sveinn Ásleifarson on board ship (*Ork* 34.93:251).

22. See Falk 1919, 188–89 for a discussion of the cloak (*ólpa*). It seems desirable to reverse the terms in the most commonly used translation of *Eg*; see Hermann Pálsson and Edwards 1976, 193.

23. It is likely that the Icelander Hrafn Guðrúnarson brought his pile coat (*loðkápa*) from home and that it was not part of the clothes (*klæði*) he received from Signý and Helga (*HrG* 8.34:324–27). The Norwegian merchant Þórólfr returned and gave his brother Þorsteinn an entire new outfit of clothes, including a pile coat (*loðkápa*), undoubtedly acquired abroad, perhaps in Iceland (*Svf* 9.2:132).

24. The best description is Elsa E. Guðjónsson 1962 (see the English summary, 65–71). A somewhat similar technique is used in the *rya* rugs still popular in northern Europe; see article "Rya," KLNM 14:513–15. A hint that the loops were "laid" or "pushed" is suggested by Refr's enigmatic speech, examined in connection with weaving (*KrR* 14.16–17:153–55). Invented by mistake, terry cloth is produced in a similar way.

25. For illustration, see Björn Þorsteinsson and Bergsteinn Jónsson 1991, 45. These authors have understood the nature of the cloth and coats (see 47).

26. Likewise, the pile coat (*loðkápa*) worn by the same hero while he was waiting for a ghost was torn only after a lengthy pulling at each end by the notoriously strong Grettir and the equally strong ghost (*Gr* 7.35:119–20).

27. The same expression is used in *KrR* 14.17:155.

28. Scholars have pointed out that the events mentioned in the poetry do not match the saga narrative. In the case of str. 14 and 15 the transactions between the two men occurred only in the poetry; see the introduction in ÍF 3:lxxi and Vogt 1921, 31, 42. Bjarni Einarsson, the defender of the unity between prose and poetry in the skalds' sagas, deals briefly with this stanza; see Bjarni Einarsson 1961, 239 (not included in the translation [Bjarni Einarsson 1976]).

29. Receiving the payment in a bag at the last minute before departing, Helgi dis-

covered only later that "the coats were bad and many torn." He returned to shore and asked a friend to prosecute the case. Þórir was outlawed and forced to leave the country. In the A version Þórir is known as Þorgils Akrakarl. See Andersson on the importance of this difference (Andersson and Miller 1989, 70–74).

30. This posture—moody, perhaps meditating or murmuring, the head buried in the cloak—was not uncommon for saga heroes. Egill also assumes this stance when he is in the throes of unrequited love (*Eg* 2.56:148). Its authenticity is vouched for by an early-eleventh-century skaldic stanza: "it is a sign of danger when men at the þing deeply droop their heads and bury their noses in the depths of their cloaks; silence has seized the thanes" (*Greypt es, þat's hǫfðum hneppta / heldr ok niðr í feldi / slegit hefr þǫgn á þegna / þingmenn nǫsum stinga; Ág* 29.34:33; see also *Mg* 28.16:30; str. 32 of Sigvatr's *Bergsǫglisvísur*). The prose author of the first text used the stanza to explain that "everybody buried their faces in their cloaks and remained silent, offering no reply" (*stungu allir nefi í skinnfeld ok veittu allir þǫgn, en engi ansvǫr*). See also Poole 1991, 8–10. A technical term, "meditate in one's coat" (*þylja í feld sinn*), identified the ritual body language of a man meditating in his coat; two old men assumed this stance (Geitir *þuldi í feld sinn* [*Þux* 13.5:350] and Bragi [*St* 1:6]). Without the privacy of the coat, Njáll "often went away from other men and meditated (*þuldi*) alone" (*Nj* 12.100:255). Þórir used the cup formed by his hands for meditation (*þuldi í gaupnir sér; HrG*, FSN 4.20: 123).

31. See *Ftb* 6.23:231, *Fnb* 14.39:326, 40:329.

32. Mentioned in several sources, the event is described most fully by Ari (*Ísl* 1.7: 16–17). The texts are conveniently assembled and analyzed in Jón Hnefill Aðalsteinsson 1978, 55–62.

33. Jón Hnefill Aðalsteinsson (1978) goes too far in ascribing shamanistic absence to Þorgeirr during this time (103–23). For an evaluation of the alleged shamanism in Iceland, see Dillmann 1993.

34. See Chapter 3, 71.

35. The knife with strap (*tygilknífr*) she gave the boy may well have been the one with which she cut the cloth (*Fnb* 14.35:316). Men seem to have been responsible for making shoes; see *Hrð* 13.23:61–62, 39:94.

36. See, for example, Hildiguðr (*Nj* 12.95:238), Þuríðr (*Hrð* 13.1:4), and Oddný, who gave her son newly made clothes (*klæði nýskorin; Þux* 13.2:343, 5:350). The word *hagr* is used about a woman on a Norwegian runic inscription; see KLNM 14:487.

37. See Sveinbjörn Rafnsson 1993, 123–27. On women's embroidery, see Elsa E. Guðjónsson, "Islandske broderier og broderersker i middelalderen," in Silja Aðalsteinsdóttir and Helgi Þorláksson 1983, 127–58.

38. The following discussion will be limited to literary sources pertaining to Iceland. The archaeological evidence and scholarship on Scandinavian coinage is prodigious; for an introduction and bibliography, see *MSE*, 101–4 and the many articles beginning with *Mynt-* (coin) in KLNM 12:38–86.

39. When Steingrímr swapped one horse for two oxen he had to pay an additional "half mark of silver in order to reach the price" (*Rkd* 10.11:177).

40. Even people in authority could not continue as Earl Sigurðr Hlǫðvésson who "was mostly paid in burnt silver" (*Erb* 4.29:76).

41. In Frisia the cloth known as *Wede* or *pallium* functioned for a short time in the same way as homespun in Iceland; see Hoffmann 1964, 227–29.

42. It is worth noticing that although the prodigious writing activity in medieval Iceland doubtlessly was done mostly by men, women's domestic work provided the prerequisite—abundant supplies of parchment from calves and sheep.

43. On the application of modern anthropological theories to early Icelandic trade, see Helgi Þorláksson 1991, 31–84, and his "Social ideals and the concept of profit in thirteenth-century Iceland," in *From Sagas* 1992, 231–45.

44. One important reason for the settlers to leave was the increasing demands of the royal government.

45. *Gg* 1a:159. See also the glossary in *Gg* 3:701–3, and Jón Jóhannesson 1974, 60–62.

46. For a discussion of the changes in class and gender as a productive tribal society is made to support an unproductive bureaucracy, see Gailey 1987.

47. The Icelandic Annals give the date as 1096 (Storm 1888, 59, 110, 251, 319, 472), whereas manuscripts of the law vary between 1096, 1097 and 1098 (DI 1:70–162). Most scholars accept 1096, but see Jón Jóhannesson 1974, 149, n. 72. The text is found also in *Gg* 1b:205–15, 2:46–57, 3:43–54, where it may have been inscribed as part of the first writing of the laws in 1117–1118. As usual in Icelandic history, however, none of the documents mentioned above is contemporary with the events.

48. Notice the elaborate oath involving book or cross mentioned in paragraph 9 in some of the versions of the tithing law; for examples, see DI 1:78, 102, 110–11, 134–35, 144.

49. The tithe was divided into four parts intended for the priest, the bishop, the local church, and the poor of the area, respectively. One of the manuscripts specified that the quarter of the tithe intended for the church could be paid in "wax, lumber, incense, tar, or new linen suitable for church use available in the area and obtainable for homespun, although the entire amount can also be paid in this cloth" (DI 1: 147, paragraph 22), thus suggesting the fungibility of the new medium. The tithe was accepted earlier in Iceland than in the other nordic countries; see article "Tiend" in KLNM 18:280–300. *St* 1:158 shows Bishop Guðmundr ready to carry his "tithing cloth" on board ship.

50. See Helgi Þorláksson 1991, 337–84.

51. For a short introduction, see "Vadmål" in KLNM 19:409–16. See also Helgi Þorláksson 1991, 205–334, and Hoffmann 1964, 194–226. For equivalencies in Norway, see chap. 235 in the Gulathing Law in NgL 1:78–79. See also "Eyrir" in NgL 5:165–71.

52. Gelsinger 1981, 33–44; Jón Jóhannesson 1984, 331; Þorkell Jóhannesson 1933, 39; Helgi Þorláksson 1991, 124–44. The second author assumes that the rule went back to Úlfljótr's law of 930 or even beyond, whereas the third is more careful. The crucial text is *Gg* 1b:192, 3:462: "At the time when Christianity first arrived in Iceland silver was used as payment for all large debts . . . one hundred in silver was counted the same as four hundred in homespun (*vaðmál*), thus one ounce (*eyrir* [of silver]) was worth half a mark (*mǫrk*) of homespun (*vaðmál*)," allowing for a ratio of 1:4. The former text has 420 instead of 400, but as Vilhjálmur Finsen suggests (*Gg* 3:668–69), it is undoubtedly a mistake that should be corrected from *Gg* 3:462.

53. DI 1:162–67; *Gg* 1b:192–95. The date of this enactment has been discussed. Jón Sigurðsson, the editor of this volume of DI, placed it in 1100 (1857, 162–64), whereas Jón Jóhannesson (1984) dates it a few years earlier (334). See also Gelsinger 1981, 40–42, where a translation is provided. The ratio was repeated around 1300; see DI 2:168; on the dating of this document, see Gelsinger 1981, 266, n. 16.

54. For examples, see DI 1:203 (1150), 250–51 (1179), 265 (1180), 278 (1185), 342 (1203). The dates are approximate.

55. DI 1:65–66, *Gg* 1b:195.

56. See *HrS* 28.36:119, *Fgs* 29.56:261, and *Flat* 3:343; the first two indicate the price as "four hundred homespun" and the last "three mark homespun" (144 ells). On this passage, see Helgi Þorláksson 1991, 89–90, 115.

57. On this problem, see Reuter 1933 and Ulff-Møller 1991 and 1993–1994.

58. For examples, see *Nj* 12.2:8–9, *Svf* 9.13:158, 14:159, *Hrð* 13.19:51, *Flm* 13.20:277, 29:313.

59. For examples, *Lx* 5.88:247, *Flm* 13.20:277, *Hrð* 13.10:27.

60. The distinction between the two types of payment concerning fines is pointed out by Lúðvík Ingvarsson 1970, 349.

61. On the ell, see Gísli Gestsson 1968. On the changing price of fish, see Gelsinger 1981, 181–94.

62. Discussing the price for killing Bjǫrn, Þórðr and his party agreed to merge their resources (*fé*) to pay for the fines (*fébœtr*) they would incur (*BHd* 3.30:194). In this case the vagueness of the expression might be excused since the protagonists were talking about a future eventuality, but the term is also used in cases where fines had already been paid. Thus Þórir paid fines (*fé*) on behalf of Egill (*Eg* 2.45:114) and Ásbjǫrn rendered fines (*fébœtr*) for his son Bjǫrn (*Erb* 4.29:80).

63. A complete mixing of metaphors is found in the term "movable ounces: (*flytjandi eyrir; Gr* 7.13:34). Another curious term in the same saga is the redundant "money payment" (*fégjǫld;* 45:146).

64. Among the many illustrations of "one hundred silver," see *VLj* 9.5:246. At the end of this chapter is a reference to "two hundred silver," followed in the next chapter by a purchase of "six hundreds worth," in this case undoubtedly in homespun. Hǫskuldr paid "two hundred silver" for the murder of his son-in-law to this man's father (*Nj* 12.12:39–40). The reference to "three marks silver" is found in *Gr* 7.51:165. The notes in the ÍF editions are studded with reference to the problem; see, for example, 7:165, n. 1, 7:324, n.1, 10:92, n. 4, 11:44, n. 3, and 12:40, n. 1.

65. This reading combines the two versions, but the statements were made by two different chieftains.

66. This was the case of the "thirteen ounces" imposed on Oddr in *Bdm*. It consisted of "pieces of rings and hard things" (K text), or "old shields, bits of rings, and the cheapest trash" (M text; 7.10:352). See Jón Jóhannesson 1974, 405, for illustration of hack silver.

67. Although fewer than in other nordic countries, foreign silver coins (English, Irish, German, and Arabic) have been found in Iceland; see *Saga Íslands* 2:19–20. It is more puzzling how a few Roman coins from the third century had reached the island; see *Saga Íslands* 1:123–24.

68. An outline of these occurrences is found in Miller 1990, 183.

69. Although not stated specifically in the first case, Skarpheðinn's immediate admiration of the "great and beautiful silver" (*fé it mikla ok it góða*) involved in the third payment shows that Gunnarr must have paid up immediately.

70. On the former expression, see *Erb* 4.14:25, *Gí* 6.19:63, *BHd* 3.34:208; on the latter, see *Ftb* 6.5:141, *Hsí* 6.7:314, *Bdm* 7.8:335, *Hrð* 13.10:26. Uniform visible silver was probably involved when Jófríðr asked her shepherd to bring her newborn baby girl in safety to avoid its exposure, saying "here are three marks silver" (*Gnl* 3.3:56).

71. When Snorri had vowed to make the killing of Hǫskuldr the most expensive case in the country, he set a fine of six hundred silver to be paid at once. Njáll came up with one hundred, his sons and sons-in-law with another hundred, and the rest was collected on the spot from friends and relatives. The huge sum formed such an enormous pile (*hrúga*) that Flosi could kick it apart (*hratt*) when he rescinded the agreement (*Nj* 12.123:311–14).

72. In the same saga the identical amount contained in a purse was handed over by Snorri for a similar crime (*Erb* 4.31:86).

73. The same theme is found in *Lx* 5.15:36.

74. Snorri bought his uncle's share of his paternal inheritance with sixty ounces of silver contained in a purse (*Erb* 4.14:25). Koðrán showed Þórdís the Prophetess (*spákona*) no less than three purses before she "weighed" three mark from the last one to use for Þorvaldr (*ÓTm* 1:281); on this passage, see Jochens 1991e. See also *Ftb* 6.10:168.

75. *Bdm* 7.7–8:329–35. Used once in the K text when Ófeigr talked to a group of chieftains, the theme is repeated in the M text during his negotiations with Egill. On a similar note, see *Flm* 13.19:273 and 32:320.

76. See *Bdm* 7.8:335–36, *HsÍ* 6.7:314, *Ftb* 6.5:141.

77. For examples, see *Gr* 7.22:80, 24:84. Visible silver also appeared in *BHd* 3.24: 175–76 and *Rkd* 10.27:236.

78. Later in the saga Gísli asked Þorkell for "three hundred homespun;" his brother complied by giving him "some cloth and some silver" (*Gí* 6.23:74).

79. Apparently not understanding the term *þriggja álna aura* (the devalued "three ells ounce"), McGrew and Thomas translate "eighty hundreds and three alna in aurar" (*Sturlunga saga* 1974, 2:68).

80. See *St* 1:307, 341, 415, 480, 2:225.

81. Recall the sail given to the Norwegian king in *Egils saga* (2.41:104). In the contemporary accounts, see *St* 2:206, 207.

82. The expression is extremely common; see, for example, *Gr* 7.17:49, *Eg* 2.35:89, 40: 102, *Hrð* 13.12:33, *Þux* 13.8:356.

83. Part of Hǫrðr's supplies consisted of russet homespun (*Hrð* 13.12:33–35).

84. Óláfr approached Þorbjǫrn for a loan of homespun and promised that he would "get a high price" or "pay a high interest" (*taka vǫru af honum at láni ok gera mikit at*); the translation as "a big loan" as in the most popular translation (Magnusson and Hermann Pálsson 1969, 87) is too simple.

85. As part of a settlement in 1245, Kolbeinn was to give Þórðr "sixty hundreds homespun as travel supplies" (*St* 2:68).

86. Feelings of female solidarity concerning textile work may be behind the reaction of another Guðrún, wife of the head of the raiding party, as she refused to house the stolen goods (*ránsfé*), although she had urged revenge a few hours earlier (*St* 1:195–96).

87. See also *St* 2:128.

88. Writing toward the end of the twelfth century, Oddr *munkr* (monk) reported that during the reign of Óláfr Tryggvason Icelandic men came to Norway to sell "both homespun (*vaðmál*) and shaggy coats" (*vararfeldir*; OSM 40:122).

89. Hagland 1988. Several inscriptions refer to "sacks" and one to "thread." See the criticism by Seim and Nedkvitne in (N)*HT* 1989, Hagland's reply in 1990, as well his article in *ANF* 104 (1989):89–102.

90. Falk 1919, 50–51. See also Helgi Þorláksson 1991, 205–66. See, for example, the "everyday clothes" worn by Helgi and Grímr that included a homespun coat (*sǫluvaðmálskufl; Fld* 11.11:243) and the homespun cape (*vǫruváðarkufl*) worn by the slave Bolli (*Hrð* 13.27:69).

91. The Norwegian Frostathing Law knew a thumb ell (*þumalǫln;* NgL 1:246). When a person measured the cloth he placed his thumb after each measurement, perhaps adding to the length; see "Alen," KLNM 1:71–75. The longer ell, extending to the finger-tips, is illustrated in a *Jónsbók* manuscript where men and women controlled their measuring sticks; see KLNM 8:47.

92. Written shortly after Bishop Páll's death in 1211, his vita may be considered a reliable source. The additional information from the documents in the DI collection are likewise not open to doubt, and the assignment by the editor to "about 1200" for the alþingi's enactment seems reasonable (DI 1:306).

93. See Jón Jóhannesson 1974, 317–18. The fullest treatment is by Gelsinger 1981, 124–29, with notes 253–54. See also Helgi Þorláksson 1991, 215–22.

94. Among the entries in the income accounts from the duke of Normandy from 1198 is the revenue from the sale of "the seventeen remaining sacks of wool from an Icelandic ship," suggesting direct sale to Rouen; see Gelsinger 1981, 138–39.

95. This problem is also encountered by modern weavers working on reproductions of medieval loom; see Hoffmann 1964, 135.

96. *Gg* 1b:250. This passage also indicates that when homespun was measured for length it had to be done in the middle and not at the selvages since they tended to pucker and thus shorten the cloth. Gelsinger 1981, 219, n. 65, has computed the amount of cloth produced by changing the width.

97. Outlawry was imposed on a certain Þórhallr for having used a wrong yardstick (*St* 1:99). Correct measurements was also defined in *Jónsbók* (see *Jn* 214).

98. The description of Finnbogi (*Fnb* 14.38:324). Among other cases, see the two men named Bolli, father and son, in *Lx* 5.28:77 and 77:224–25, Einarr in *Erð* 4.3:203, and Helgi in *Fld* 11.19:276. Only one woman is characterized as a "clothes conscious woman" (*skartskona;* Þuríðr in *Erb* 4.50:137), although Helga on one occasion "adorned herself a lot" (*skartaði . . . allmikið; GKd* 14.2:346).

99. The difference between dress clothes (*skrúðklæði*) and ordinary clothes made of homespun is well illustrated in *Hrþ* (10:253).

100. The crimson dress clothes (*skrúðklæði*) that Dalla "cut" for her foster son were undoubtedly made of imported material (*Fnb* 14.35:315), as well as the green cloak (*kyrtill*) of "new cloth" which Gróa ordered for her young visitor Þorgils in Iceland (*St* 2:106). Later in Norway the same Þorgils undoubtedly turned over to a competent tailor the six ells of scarlet cloth he received from Queen Margrét when she noticed his clothes had been badly burned because of his bravery during a fire the previous night (*St* 2:114). Earlier, the king had given him fourteen ells of "leaf green cloth" that he may well have brought back to Iceland (*St* 2:113). As other evidence of fancy cloth being turned into clothes in Norway, see the story of the priest Ingimundr who recognized the sixteen ells of excellent red-brown cloth, bought by him in England but later stolen, on the backs of some of the king's retainers in Bergen (*St* 1:136–37).

101. A boastful merchant named Gísli was enlisted in the efforts to get the outlawed Grettir down from his mountain hideout. Planning an encounter with Grettir, Gísli

convinced his two companions that they should wear dressy clothes (*litklæði*) and "let the outlaw see that we are not like the common tramps you normally meet around here." Seeing their fancy clothing (*skrúðklæði*) from his hideaway, Grettir did succumb to their appeal. Rushing down the mountainside, he grabbed a sack of clothes tied to the back of Gísli's saddle. Protesting that he would rather lose "thirty hundreds" than the sack, Gísli attacked, but was pursued by Grettir. He escaped by taking off one piece of clothing after the other, arriving at a river in his underwear (*Gr* 7.59:188–93).

102. Intense interest in clothes cost a certain Dagstyggr his life; see *St* 1:343.

103. *Jónsbók* contains a chapter with rules against men who wore dress clothes (*skrúðklæði; Jn* 115–16).

104. The examples are numerous; see, for example, *Lx* 5.62:185, 187; *Ljs* 10.1(6):119 (*Ófeigs þáttr*); *VGl* 9.8:27. In *VLj* 9.1:235 the victim is dressed in blue.

105. Trying to scare off a would-be rapist, Ólof donned blue male clothing and a sword (*Vgl* 14.8:78).

106. See also the crimson sleeves appearing under the two layers of homespun that disguised Gunnarr when he presented Hrútr with summons to retrieve Unnr's dowry (*Nj* 12.22–23:59, 64). The issue is worth a comprehensive study, but it is beyond the scope of this investigation. See Valtýr Guðmundsson 1893 and additional bibliography in Harris 1975, n. 21.

107. Other manuscripts substitute "harrying work" (*hernadar verkinn*) or "work of revenge" (*hefndarverkin*). For the first, see text in Kålund's edition in *Altnordische Saga-Bibliothek* 4 (158) and SUGNL 19. See Ólafur Halldórsson, "Morgunverk Guðrúnar Ósvífursdóttur," in Ólafur Halldórsson 1990, 271–74.

108. Most recently Ólafur Halldórsson's interpretation has gained support from Jonna Louis-Jensen, "A Good Day's Work," in *Twenty-Eight Papers* 1993, 267–81.

CONCLUSION

1. See Chapter 1, 14–15. Translators and commentators often (wrongly) translate *vinar míns* in the plural. For the argument advanced here — the intimacy between the two individual women — the correct form in the singular is important.

2. See section "Widowhood," in Chapter 4, 61–64.

3. Clover 1993, 380; rpt. 78.

4. The expressions include terms such as "valiant" (*drengr*), "forceful" (*skǫrungr*), and "overpowering" (*mikill fyrir sér*).

5. The young Hildiguðr (Hildigunnr), unmarried and living at home, was characterized as both "very valiant" (*skǫrungr mikill*) and "full of courage" (*drengr mikill; Nj* 12.95:238–39).

6. Published by C. R. Unger in 1871. For a brief overview, see "Maríu saga," *MSE* 407–8. The poetry was composed in the form of a *drápa*, a *flokkr*, a *grátr*, a *kvæði*, and *vísur*.

7. See Anna Sigurðardóttir 1988.

8. Recall the story of Hildr, who declared that berries and clear water would sustain her in the wilderness; *Bs* 1:203–4, 254–56. See also *Bs* 1:478.

9. This subject is treated in *ONIW*.

10. The church even offered a few women opportunities to study. A charming

vignette shows a certain Ingunn who studied (*var í frœðinœmi*) at the cathedral school in Hólar where Latin books were read to her "while she sewed or played games" (*Bs* 1: 241).

11. Although ordinary men often allowed illegitimate children to inherit, legitimate birth was becoming a prerequisite for the royal succession in Norway; see Chapter 3, 94–97.

12. On the possible influence of Christianity on the development and articulation of feelings of motherhood, see Jochens 1996b.

APPENDIX

1. I leave out of consideration the remarkable "Book of Settlement" (*Landnámabók; Lnd*), although I have used it to search for Guðný Bǫðvarsdóttir's ancestors. Listing more than four hundred of the original settlers, their background in Norway and their descendants in Iceland, the work is embellished with colorful vignettes, some of which provided material for saga narratives. By recording thousands of names, this work makes possible a demographic study of the early settlers and their descendants. Text in ÍF 1. Sveinbjörn Rafnsson 1974 has dealt with the purpose of the lineages after the settlement and I have utilized Grethe Jacobsen's analysis of the female component; see Chapter 3, 86–87.

2. For texts and translations, see Chapter 1, n. 9.

3. The only parallel is the reports by inquisitorial interrogators from Albigensian heretics operating at Montaillou in the south of France during the early fourteenth century. Recorded verbatim by stenographers, these testimonies have been used by Emmanuel Le Roy Ladurie in his reconstruction of the *histoire totale* of this small village; see Ladurie 1975.

4. On the narrative style, see Jónas Kristjánsson, "The Roots of the Sagas," in *Sagnaskemmtan* 1986, 182–200, esp. 192–200, and his "Learned style or saga style," in *Specvlvm Norroenvm*, 260–92.

5. On the following, see Andersson 1964, Einar Ól. Sveinsson 1958, Carol J. Clover, "Icelandic Family Sagas (*Íslendingasögur*)," in *ONIL* 1985 239–315, *Íbm* 2: 39–79, and Sørensen 1993, 17–120. For a brief overview, see Jónas Kristjánsson, "Roots," (previous note) and Vésteinn Ólason, "Norrøn litteratur som historisk kildemateriale," in *Kilderne* 1987, 30–47, and his "Sagas of Icelanders," in *Viking Revaluations* 1993, 26–42.

6. Heusler 1914. For an annotated selection of the most important documents pertaining to the debate, see Mundal 1977.

7. The first to identify "the Icelandic school" was Dag Strömbäck (1935) and Hallvard Lie (1939); for references see Oskar Halldórsson 1978 and Jón Hnefill Aðalsteinsson 1991.

8. For an illustration, see Theodore M. Andersson in Andersson and Miller 1989, 70–72.

9. Andersson (1967) suggests a general structure encompassing whole sagas, and Clover (1974) identifies smaller narrative components. Joseph Harris has identified structure in the short stories (*þættir*) in several articles; see Harris 1972, 1976. See also his "Saga as Historical Novel," in *Structure* 1986, 187–219. For criticism of the structural approach, see Jónas Kristjánsson 1986, "Roots" (n. 4).

10. See Miller 1984, 1986a, and 1986b; Bagge 1986 (esp. p. 148, n. 8); and Jón Viðar Sigurðsson 1993.

11. Clover 1982.

12. See Sørensen 1977 (trans. 1992) and 1993, Byock 1982, Hastrup 1985 and 1990a, Jochens 1993e. The most important part of Sørensen 1993 is in this context the first chapter, which is available in English in *From Sagas,* 27–41.

13. For a recent survey in English, see Diana Whaley, "The Kings' Sagas," in *Viking Revaluations* 1993, 43–64.

14. In this classification considerations of chronology are ignored.

15. For an overview in English of these problems, see Theodore M. Andersson, "Kings' Sagas (*Konungasögur*)," *ONIL* 1985, 197–238, with bibliography for editions of the texts. For a briefer introduction, see *MSE* 362–66. See also Jónas Kristjánsson in *Saga Íslands* 2:222–41.

16. For a more detailed classification, see *Íbm* 1:358–401; 451–58.

17. See, for example, Weibull 1911.

18. English lacks a technical term for this concept that plays such a large role in European historiography; cf. German *Überreste,* Swedish *kvarlevor,* and Danish *levninger.*

19. This is evident, for example, in *Morkinskinna* composed around 1220. See Andersson in *ONIL,* esp. 217–19, and his "Snorri Sturluson and the Saga School at Munkaþverá," in *Snorri Sturluson* 1993, 9–25.

20. For *Heimskringla* in particular, see Sverre Bagge, "From sagas to society: the case of *Heimskringla,*" in *From Sagas,* 61–75, further elaborated by Bagge 1991.

21. For this type of woman, see Stafford 1983.

22. The fullest portrait of Gunnhildr is Sigurður Nordal 1941; I have treated her inciter aspect in Jochens 1987a, esp. 116–19.

23. See Jochens 1986a and 1987b.

24. Sigurður Nordal 1953, 180–288, esp. 181. His other groups include "the sagas of ancient times" that deal with the period before 850 on a larger Scandinavian or even European scale. Grouping together the heroic sagas (*fornaldarsǫgur*), chivalric sagas (*riddarasǫgur*) and some of the kings' sagas, including the most remote parts of Snorri's *Heimskringla,* these stories are the furthest removed from the events they describe. Less distant is a middle group, "the sagas of the past," that focus on the nordic world in the period from 850 to 1100 and encompass most of the (mainly Norwegian) kings' sagas and all the sagas of Icelanders.

25. Sigurður Nordal included the contemporary kings' sagas, such as *Sverris saga, Bǫglunga sǫgur,* and *Hákonar saga Hákonarson,* in this group, but I have grouped them within the other royal narratives.

26. The historians of the fifties relied almost entirely on *Sturlunga saga* and the law; see, for example, Jón Jóhannesson 1956, Engl. trs. 1974.

27. Úlfar Bragason has been particularly vocal on this subject; among his works, see 1981, 1992. See also Tranter 1987. For the emergence of a medieval style, see Pizarro 1989.

28. Until recently, the most available edition was *Sturlunga Saga* 1946. A new edition appeared in 1988 edited by Örnólfur Thorsson; it contains a valuable third volume of information and studies (*Skýringar og fræði*). McGrew's English translation (*Sturlunga Saga* 1970–1974) should be used with care.

29. This is the case, for example, with Geirmundr the Darkskinned (*heljarskinn*) and Bishop Ketill. See also the introduction to the 1988 edition.

30. The male-female ratio in *Lx* and *Erb* is about 3:1, but in *St* 5:1. See Jochens 1986b, 46, n. 69.

31. See Jochens 1985, Miller 1988b.

32. See Jónas Kristjánsson 1988, 135–46 and his "The Roots" (n. 4). Although beyond the scope of this study, the translated saints' lives are also of interest. The original choice of texts and modifications in translation can reveal clues concerning the intended audience; see, for example, Carlé 1985.

33. For a more precise classification of this literature, see *Íbm* 1:421–79.

34. The standard edition is *Biskupa sögur* 1858–1878. New editions are appearing in Iceland and Denmark; see, for example, *Byskupa sǫgur,* ed. Jón Helgason, and *Árna saga biskups,* ed. Þorleifur Hauksson.

35. See Drew's introduction in *The Laws of the Salian Franks,* 1991, 1–27.

36. The Norwegian laws can be found in NgL. I am grateful to Grethe Autén Blom and Norsk Historisk Kjeldeskrift-Institutt for providing me with a copy of this work, especially since it is not available in libraries in my area. Some of these laws are translated to English; see Larson 1935.

37. The three main manuscripts of *Grágás* were edited by Vilhjálmur Finsen 1852, 1879, 1883; all rpt. 1974. A new edition appeared in 1992 (*Grágás* 1992). References will be to Vilhjálmur Finsen's editions. Parts of the law have appeared in English translation; see Dennis et als. 1980. *Járnsíða* is available in NgL 1:259–300; 5:13–15 and *Jónsbók* in Ólafur Halldórsson 1904, rpt. 1970.

38. *Grágás* was not used about the Icelandic law until the sixteenth century; see *Grágás* 1992, xxiv. The translation "Grey Goose" may be deceptive since *gás* (goose) can also refer to female genitalia; see Fritzner 1:564; see also Chapter 3, n. 62 (204).

39. On this, see Sigurður Líndal 1969.

40. Some parts, for example chap. 60, "The wreckage section" (*rekabálkr*), are still valid.

41. On this issue, see Per Norseng, "Lovmaterialet som kilde til tidlig nordisk middelalder," in *Kilderne* 48–77.

42. On the depiction of Hákon's Christianity in the various sources, see Jón Hnefill Aðalsteinsson, "A Piece of Horse-Liver and the Ratification of Law," in *Snorrastefna,* 81–98.

43. See Foote 1977, Peter Foote, "Some lines in Lǫgréttuþáttr," in Foote 1984, 155–64, and "Reflections on Landabrigðisþáttr and Rekaþáttr in Grágás," in *Tradition,* 53–69.

44. See Kirsten Hastrup, "Text and context: continuity and change in medieval Icelandic history as 'said' and 'laid down,'" in Hastrup 1990b, 139–53. For a full discussion of the word *lǫg,* see See 1964, 174–95. It is sobering to notice that the singular *lag* also can be used about a sword strike; *lǫgðir* is thus a poetic word for sword and Saxo names a sword *Lǫgthi;* see Alexander Jóhannesson 1956, 750.

45. For Norway, see Robberstad 1970, and for Iceland Bjorn Magnússon Olsen 1883. Around 1300 the provincial law for Scania (Skåne) was transcribed in runes.

46. See Sjöholm 1976 and 1988; the latter is largely a Swedish version of the earlier work in German.

47. See Sverre Bagge's review of Sjöholm's 1986 work in (N)*HT* 1989:500–507. For Iceland, see Sveinbjörn Rafnsson 1985 and 1990 and his article "Grágás og Digesta Iustiniani," in *Sjötíu ritgerðir,* 720–32.

48. See Miller 1990, esp. Chapter 7, "Law and the Legal Process."

49. In addition to serving as the written legal language, Old Norse was also used

in charters in Iceland and Norway, (whereas Latin was preferred in Sweden and Denmark). Such charters furnish the first reflections of the new marriage legislation proposed by the Church. Icelandic and Norwegian charters are collected in the series Diplomatarium Islandicum and Diplomatarium Norwegicum respectively. For further information, see article "Diplomatarium," in KLNM 3:82–86, and "Diplomatics," *MSE* 137–38.

50. The conversion may have taken place in 999; see Ólafía Einarsdóttir 1964. At least one saga, *Ftb*, was placed entirely in the Christian era; see Preben Meulengracht Sørensen, "On Humour, Heroes, Morality, and Anatomy in Fóstbrœðra saga," in *Twenty-Eight Papers*, 395–418.

51. See Clover 1982 and 1986.

52. It is also worth noticing that Sturla's grandson, Sturla Sighvatsson (1199–1238), was nicknamed Dala-Freyr after one of the ancient gods; *St* 1: 326, 327, 353.

53. For illustrations of these problems, see Poole 1991. In other cases prose authors did not fully understand the stanzas they used.

54. Reception history is becoming an important endeavor among Old Norse scholars; see Ross 1994 and Wawn 1994. Sarah M. Anderson is preparing a study of the reception of Icelandic texts in pre-modern Denmark and Sweden.

55. For an overview of these problems as they relate to medieval history, see Spiegel 1990.

56. See Jochens 1993c.

57. For examples of this approach, see Miller 1990 and Jón Viðar Sigurðsson 1993.

Bibliography

Note: To save space, essay collections from which several articles have been used are listed here and titles of individual essays only are given in the Notes. Icelandic authors are listed by surname.

Acker, Paul. 1993. Norse Sagas Translated into English. A Supplement. *SS* 65:66–102.

Aðalsteinsdóttir, Silja, see Silja Aðalsteinsdóttir.

Aðalsteinsson, Jón Hnefill, see Jón Hnefill Aðalsteinsson.

Alexander Jóhannesson. 1956. *Isländisches etymologisches Wörterbuch.* Bern: Francke.

Almqvist, Bo. 1971. Some Thoughts Evoked by Juha Pentikäinen's Thesis The Nordic Dead-Child Tradition. *Arv* 27:69–95.

Amory, Frederic. 1988. Pseudoarchaism and fiction in *Króka-Refs saga. MS* 12:7–23.

Andersson, Theodore M. 1964. *The Problem of Icelandic Saga Origins: A Historical Survey.* New Haven: Yale University Press.

——. 1967. *The Icelandic Family Saga: An Analytic Reading.* Harvard Studies in Comparative Literature, 28. Cambridge, MA: Harvard University Press.

——. 1969. Some Ambiguities in *Gísla saga:* A Balance Sheet. *BONIS:* 7–42.

——. 1980. *The Legend of Brynhild.* Islandica 43. Ithaca, N.Y.: Cornell University Press.

——. 1984. The Thief in Beowulf. *Sp* 59:493–508.

Andersson, Theodore M., and William Ian Miller. 1989. *Law and Literature in Medieval Iceland: "Ljósvetninga Saga" and "Valla-Ljóts Saga."* Stanford: Stanford University Press.

Anna Sigurðardóttir. 1985. *Vinna kvenna á Íslandi í 1100 ár.* Reykjavík: Kvennasögusafn Íslands.

——. 1988. *Allt hafði annan róm áður í páfadóm: Nunnuklaustrin tvö á Íslandi á miðöldum og brot úr kristnisögu.* Reykjavík: Kvennasögusafn Íslands.

The Anthropology of Iceland. Ed. E. Paul Durrenberger and Gísli Pálsson. 1989. Iowa City: University of Iowa Press.

Arent, A. Margaret. 1969. The Heroic Pattern: Old Germanic Helmets, *Beowulf* and *Grettis Saga.* In *Old Norse Literature and Mythology: A Symposium,* ed. Edgar C. Polomé, 130–99. Austin: University of Texas Press.

Árna saga biskups. Ed. Þorleifur Hauksson. 1972. Reykjavík: Stofnun Árna Magnússonar.

Árni Björnsson. 1981. Barnsöl og sængurbiti. In *Afmæliskveðja til Halldórs Halldórssonar, 13. júli 1981*, ed. Guðrún Kvaran, 5–23. Reykjavík: Íslenska Málfræðifélag.

Arnórsson, Einar, see Einar Arnórsson.

Atkinson, Clarissa W. 1991. *The Oldest Vocation: Christian Motherhood in the Middle Ages*. Ithaca, N.Y.: Cornell University Press.

Austin, J. L. 1962. *How to Do Things with Words*. 2d ed. J. O. Urmson and Marina Sbisà. Cambridge: Harvard University Press.

Avdem, Anna Jorunn, and Kari Melby. 1985. *Oppe först og sist i seng: Husarbeid i Norge fra 1850 til i dag*. Oslo: Universitetsforlaget.

Bachman, W. Bryan, Jr. 1985. *Four Old Icelandic Sagas and Other Tales*. Lanham, Md.: University Press of America.

Baetke, Walter. 1958. Die Víga-Glum-Episode in der Reykdœla-Saga. In *Beiträge zur deutschen und nordischen Literatur. Festgabe für Leopold Magon zum 70. Geburtstag 3. April 1957*, ed. Hans Werner Seiffert, 5–21. Berlin: Akademie-Verlag.

Bagge, Sverre. 1986. Borgerkrig og statsudvikling i Norge i middelalderen. (N)*HT* 65: 145–97.

———. 1991. *Society and Politics in Snorri Sturluson's "Heimskringla."* Berkeley: University of California Press.

Baldwin, John W. 1970. *Masters Princes and Merchants: The Social View of Peter the Chanter and His Circle*. Princeton, N.J.: Princeton University Press.

———. 1993. Consent and the Marital Debt: Five Discourses in Northern France around 1200. In *Consent and Coercion to Sex and Marriage in Ancient and Medieval Societies*, ed. Angeliki Laiou, 257–70. Washington D.C.

———. 1994. *The Language of Sex: Five Voices from Northern France around 1200*. Chicago: University of Chicago Press.

Bárðar Saga. Ed. and trans. Jón Skaptason and Phillip Pulsiano. 1984. Garland Library of Medieval Literature 8 A. New York: Garland.

Benedictow, Ole Jørgen. 1985. The Milky Way in History: Breast Feeding, Antagonism between the Sexes, and Infant Mortality in Medieval Norway. *Scandinavian Journal of History* 10:19–53.

Benediktsson, Gunnar, see Gunnar Benediktsson.

Benjamin, Walter. 1955. *Illuminationen. Ausgewählte Schriften*. Frankfurt a/M: Suhrkampf.

———. 1968. *Illuminations*. Trans. and ed. Hannah Arendt and Harry Zohn. New York: Harcourt, Brace and World.

Benveniste, Émile. 1966–1974. *Le vocabulaire des institutions indo-européennes*, 2 vols. Paris: Éditions de Minuit.

Bergljót S. Kristjánsdóttir. 1992. Skarðið í vör Skíða: Um hjónabönd og samfarir í Íslendingasögum. *Skáldskaparmál* 2:135–47.

Biskupa sögur. 1858–1878. 2 vols. Copenhagen: Hið íslenzka bókmenntafélag.

Bjarnason, Björn, see Björn Bjarnason.

Bjarni Einarsson. 1961. *Skáldasögur*. Reykjavík: Bókaútgáfa Menningarsjóðs.

———. 1976. *To skjaldesagaer: En analyse af Kormáks saga og Hallfreðar saga*. Oslo: Universitetsforlaget.

———. 1987. *Mælt mál og forn fræði*. Reykjavík: Stofnun Árna Magnússonar.

241

Bibliography

—. 1989. Döpur brúður í Jónsbókarhandriti. In *Orðlokarr sendur Svavari Sigmund-syni fimmtugum, 7–8.* Reykjavík.

Bjarni Guðnason. 1993. *Túlkun Heiðarvígasögu.* Studia Islandica 50. Reykjavík: Bók-menntafræðistofnun Háskola Íslands.

Bjarni Vilhjálmsson. 1990. Postulínsgerð og hestavíg. *Gripla* 7:7–50.

Björn Bjarnason. 1905. *Nordboernes legemlige Uddannelse i Oldtiden.* Copenhagen: Prior.

Björn Magnússon Ólsen. 1883. *Runerne i den oldislandske Literatur.* Copenhagen: Gyldendal.

Björn Þórðarson. 1949. Móðir Jóru biskups dóttur. *Saga* 1: 289–346.

Björn Þorsteinsson. 1966. *Ný Íslandssaga.* Reykjavík: Heimskringla.

Björn Þorsteinsson and Bergsteinn Jónsson. 1991. *Íslands saga til okkar daga.* Reykjavik: Sögufélag.

Björnsson, Árni, see Árni Björnsson.

Bǫglunga sǫgur: Soga om Birkebeinar og Baglar. Ed. Hallvard Magerøy. 1988. 2 vols. Norrøne tekster nr. 5. Norsk Historisk Kjeldeskrift-Institut. Oslo: Solum.

Boer, R.C., ed. 1888. *Qrvar-Odds saga.* Leiden: Brill.

Bonde, Niels. 1994. De norske vikingskibsgraves alder: Et vellykket norsk-dansk forskningsprojekt. Nationalmuseets Arbejdsmark 1994, 128–48. Copenhagen: Nationalmuseet.

Boserup, Ester. 1970. *Woman's Role in Economic Development.* New York: St. Martin's Press.

Boswell, John Eastburn. 1988. *Kindness to Strangers: The Abandonment of Children in Western Europe from Late Antiquity to the Renaissance.* New York: Pantheon.

Bouchard, Constance B. 1981. Consanguinity and Noble Marriages in the Tenth and Eleventh Centuries. *Sp* 56:268–87.

Bouman, A. C. 1962. *Patterns in Old English and Old Icelandic Literature.* Leiden: University of Leiden.

Boyer, Régis. 1978. *Les sagas islandaises.* Paris: Payot.

Bragason, Úlfar, see Úlfar Bragason.

Brahe, Per. (1585). *Oeconomia.* Ed. John Granlund and Gösta Holm. 1971. Nordiska museets Handlingar 78. Lund.

Bredsdorff, Thomas. 1971. *Kaos og kærlighed: en studie i islændingesagaers livsbillede.* Copenhagen: Gyldendal.

Brenner, Oscar, ed. 1881. *Speculum regale.* Munich: Kaiser.

Brown, Ursula, ed. 1952. *Þorgils saga ok Hafliða.* Oxford: Oxford English Monographs.

Brundage, James A. 1987. *Law, Sex, and Christian Society in Medieval Europe.* Chicago: University of Chicago Press.

Búalög: verðlag á Íslandi á 12.-19. öld. Ed. Arnór Sigurjónsson. 1966. Reykjavík: Fram-leiðsluráð Landbúnaðarins.

Byock, Jesse L. 1982. *Feud in the Icelandic Saga.* Berkeley: University of California Press.

—. 1988. *Medieval Iceland: Society, Sagas, and Power.* Berkeley: University of California Press.

Byskupa sǫgur. Ed. Jón Helgason. 1938–1978. 2 vols. Copenhagen: Munksgaard/Reitzel.

Cadden, Joan. 1993. *Meanings of Sex Difference in the Middle Ages: Medicine, Science, and Culture.* Cambridge: Cambridge University Press.

Cahill, Peter, ed. 1983. *Duggals leiðsla.* Rit 25. Reykjavík: Stofnun Árna Magnússonar.

Carlé, Birte. 1985. *Jomfru-Fortællingen: Et bidrag til genrehistorien.* Odense: Odense University Press.

Cederschiöld, Gustav. Ed. 1884. *Fornsögur Suðrlanda.* Lund: Berling.

Cleasby, Richard, and Gudbrand Vigfusson. 1957. *An Icelandic-English Dictionary.* 2d ed. Rpt. 1975. Oxford: Clarendon.

Clover, Carol J. 1974. Scene in Saga Composition. *ANF* 89:57–83.

——. 1982. *The Medieval Saga.* Ithaca, N.Y.: Cornell University Press.

——. 1986. The Long Prose Form. *ANF* 101:10–39.

——. 1988. The Politics of Scarcity: Notes on the Sex Ratio in Old Norse Society. *SS* 60:147–88. Rpt. 1990. *New Readings on Women in Old English Literature,* ed. Helen Damico and Alexandra Hennessey Olsen, 100–34. Bloomington: Indiana University Press.

——. 1993. Regardless of Sex: Men, Women, and Power in Early Northern Europe. *Sp* 68:363–87. Rpt. 1993. *Studying Medieval Women,* ed. Nancy F. Partner, 61–85. A Speculum Book. Cambridge: Medieval Academy of America.

Codex Frisianus. Ed. C. R. Unger. 1871. Christiania: Malling.

Cook, Robert. 1992. Women and Men in *Laxdœla saga. Skáldskaparmál* 2:34–59.

Damsholt, Nanna. 1984. The Role of Icelandic Women in the Sagas and in the Production of Homespun Cloth. *Scandinavian Journal of History* 9:75–90.

Davidson, Hilda Ellis, and Peter Fisher. 1979–1980. *Saxo Grammaticus: The History of the Danes Books I–IX.* Vol. 2: *Commentary.* Cambridge: D. S. Brewer.

Davíðsdóttir, Sigrún, see Sigrún Davíðsdóttir.

Dennis, Andrew, Peter Foote, and Richard Perkins, trans. 1980. *Laws of Early Iceland: Grágás I.* Winnipeg: University of Manitoba Press.

Dictionary of the Middle Ages. Ed. Joseph Strayer. 1982–1989. 13 vols. New York: Scribner's.

Dillmann, François-Xavier. 1993. Seiður og shamanismi í Íslendingasögum. *Skáldskaparmál* 2:20–33.

Diplomatarium Islandicum. Íslenzkt fornbréfasafn. 1857–72. 16 vols. Hið íslenzka bókmenntafélag: Copenhagen and Reykjavík.

Diplomatarium Norvegicum. 1846–1934. 20 vols. Oslo: Universitetsforlaget.

Drew, Katherine Fischer, trans. 1973. *The Lombard Laws.* Philadelphia: University of Pennsylvania Press.

——, trans. 1991. *The Laws of the Salian Franks.* Philadelphia: University of Pennsylvania Press.

Dronke, Ursula, ed. 1969. *The Poetic Edda.* Vol. 1: *Heroic Poems.* Oxford: Clarendon.

——. 1981. *The Role of Sexual Themes in Njáls Saga.* The Dorothea Coke Memorial Lecture in Northern Studies. London: Viking Society for Northern Research.

——. 1992. Eddic Poetry as a Source for the History of Germanic Religion. In *Germanische Religionsgeschichte: Quellen und Quellenprobleme,* ed. Heinrich Beck et al., 656–84. Ergänzungsbände zum Reallexikon der Germanischen Altertumskunde 5. Berlin: de Gruyter.

Duby, Georges. 1980. *The Three Orders: Feudal Society Imagined.* Trans. Arthur Goldhammer. Chicago: University of Chicago Press.

Durrenberger, Paul E., and Gísli Pálsson, eds. 1989. *The Anthropology of Iceland.* Iowa City: University of Iowa Press.

Ebert, Else. 1993. *Der Konkubinat nach westnordischen Quellen.* Ergänzungsbände zum Reallexikon der germanischen Altertumskunde 8. Berlin: de Gruyter.

Eggert Ólafsson. 1772. *Reise igiennem Island.* Sorø: Det Kongelige Videnskabsakademi.

Einar Arnórsson. 1932–1935. Þáttur Bjarna Ólasonar í Hvassafelli. *Blanda* 5:343–87; 6: 37–49.

Einar Ól. Sveinsson. 1953. *The Age of the Sturlungs: Icelandic Civilization in the Thirteenth Century.* Trans. Jóhann S. Hannesson. Islandica 36. Ithaca N.Y.: Cornell University Press.

——. 1958. *Dating the Icelandic Sagas.* London: Viking Society.

——. 1962. *Íslenzkar bókmenntir í fornöld.* Reykjavík: Almenna bókafélagið.

Einarsdóttir, Ólafía, see Ólafía Einarsdóttir.

Einarsson, Bjarni, see Bjarni Einarsson.

Ellehøj, Svend. 1965. *Studier over den ældste norrøne historieskrivning.* BA 26. Copenhagen: Munksgaard.

Elsa E. Guðjónsson. 1962. Forn röggvarvefnaður. *Árbók hins íslenzka fornleifafélags,* 12–71.

——. 1991. *Reflar í íslenskum miðaldaheimildum fram til 1569.* Reykjavík: Elsa E. Guðjónsson.

Falk, Hjalmar. 1919. *Altwestnordische Kleiderkunde.* Kristiania [Oslo]: Dybwad.

Faulkes, Anthony, ed. 1967; rpt. 1978. *Two Icelandic Stories: Hreiðars þáttr Orms þáttr.* London: Viking Society.

——. 1978–1979. Descent from the Gods. *MS* 11:91–124.

Finnur Jónsson, ed. 1932. *Morkinskinna.* SUGNL 53. Copenhagen.

Finsen, Vilhjálmur, see Vilhjálmur Finsen.

Flateyjarbók. 3 vols. 1860. Ed. Guðbrandur Vigfússon and C. R. Unger. Christiania [Oslo]: Malling.

Foote, P. G., and D. M. Wilson. 1970. *The Viking Achievement.* London: Sidgwick and Jackson.

Foote, Peter. 1963. An Essay on the Saga of Gisli and Its Icelandic Background. In *The Saga of Gisli,* trans. George Johnston, 93–134. Toronto: University of Toronto Press.

——. 1977. Oral and Literary Tradition in Early Scandinavian Law. In *Oral Tradition, Literary Tradition,* ed. H. Bekker-Nielsen, 46–55. Odense: Odense University Press.

——. 1984. *Aurvandilstá: Norse Studies.* Odense: Odense University Press.

Fornaldar sögur Norðurlanda. Ed. Guðni Jónsson. 4 vols. 1954. Íslendingasagnaútgáfan. Rpt. 1981. Reykjavík.

Fowler, John Howard. 1981. The Development of Incest Regulations in the Early Middle Ages: Family, Nurturance, and Aggression in the Making of the Medieval West. Ph.D. diss. Rice University.

Frank, Roberta. 1973. Marriage in Twelfth- and Thirteenth-Century Iceland. *Viator* 4: 473–84.

Fritzner, Johan. 1886. *Ordbog over det gamle norske sprog.* 3 vols. Kristiania: Den norske forlagsforening.

From Sagas to Society: Comparative Approaches to Early Iceland. Ed. Gísli Pálsson. 1992. Enfield Lock: Hisarlik Press.

Fry, Donald. 1980. *Norse Sagas Translated into English: A Bibliography.* New York: AMS Press.

Gade, Kari Ellen. 1994. *1236: Orækia meiddr ok heill gerr. Samtíðarsögur: The Contemporary Sagas*. Forprent 2 vols. Níunda alþjóðlega fornsagnaþingið, 194–207.

Gailey, Christine Ward. 1987. *Kinship to Kingship: Gender Hierarchy and State Formation in the Tongan Island*. Austin: Texas University Press.

Gaudemet, Jean. 1987. *Le mariage en Occident*. Paris: Cerf.

Geary, Patrick J. 1988. *Before France and Germany: The Creation and Transformation of the Merovingian World*. New York: Oxford University Press.

Gélis, Jacques. 1991. *History of Childbirth: Fertility, Pregnancy and Birth in Early Modern Europe*, trans. Rosemary Morris. Boston: Northeastern University Press.

Gelsinger, Bruce E. 1981. *Icelandic Enterprise: Commerce and Economy in the Middle Ages*. Columbia: University of South Carolina Press.

Gestsson, Gísli, see Gísli Gestsson.

Gísli Ágúst Gunnlaugsson. 1988. *Family and Household in Iceland 1801–1930*. Uppsala: Almqvist.

Gísli Gestsson. 1968. Álnir og kvarðar. *Árbók hins íslenzka fornleifafélag*, 45–78.

Gísli Sigurðsson. 1986. Ástir og útsaumur. *Skírnir* 160:126–51.

Grágás: Lagasafn íslenska þjóðveldisins. 1992. Ed. Gunnar Karlsson, Kristján Sveinsson, Mörður Árnason. Reykjavík: Mál og menning.

Griffin, Lisa Carson, and Ralph M. Rowlett. 1981. A "Lost" Viking Cereal Grain. *Journal of Ethnobiology* 1(2):200–207.

Grøn, Frederik. 1912. Om misfostrene i de gamle norske love: en retshistorisk-teratologisk skitse. *ÅNOH* 3R2:264–99.

Grønbech, Vilhelm. 1909–1912. *Vor Folkeæt i Oldtiden*. 4 vols. Copenhagen: V. Pio.

Grönbech, Vilhelm. 1931. *The Culture of the Teutons*, trans. W. Worster. 3 vols. London: Oxford University Press.

Guðjónsson, Elsa E., see Elsa E. Guðjónsson.

Guðmundsson, Valtýr, see Valtýr Guðmundsson.

Guðrún Ingólfsdóttir. 1992. Að utan: Um búandi konur í Íslendinga sögum. *Skáldskaparmál* 2:124–34.

Guðrún P. Helgadóttir, ed. 1987. *Hrafns saga Sveinbjarnarsonar*. Oxford: Clarendon.

Gunnar Benediktsson. 1980. "Mikla gersemi á ég". Nokkur orð um kynlífsfrásagnir í Íslendingasögum. *Saga* 19:171–76.

Gunnar Karlsson. 1986. Kenningin um fornt kvenfrelsi á Íslandi. *Saga* 24:45–77.

Gunnes, Erik. 1970. Erkebiskop Øystein som lovgiver. *Lumen* 13: 127–49. Rpt. *Nye middelalderstudier: Kongedømme, kirke, state*. Norske historikere i utvalg VI, 94–109. Ed. Claus Krag and Jørn Sandnes. Oslo: Universitetsforlaget.

Gunnlaugsson, Gísli Ágúst, see Gísli Ágúst Gunnlaugsson.

Guttentag, Marcia, and Paul F. Secord. 1983. *Too Many Women? The Sex Ratio Question*. Beverly Hills: Sage Publications.

Hagland, Jan Ragnar. 1988. Runematerialet frå gravingane i Trondheim og Bergen som kjelder til islandshandelens historie i mellomalderen. (N)*HT* 67:145–56.

Hákonar saga Hákonarsonar. Ed. Guðbrandur Vigfússon. 1887. Rerum Medii Aevi Scriptores. 88:2. London: Her Majesty's Stationery Office.

Hallberg, Peter. 1962. *The Icelandic Saga*, trans. Paul Schach. Lincoln: University of Nebraska Press.

Halldór Halldórsson. 1958. *Orlög orðanna*. Akureyri: Bókaforlag Odds Björnssonar.

———, ed. 1958. *Óláfs saga Tryggvasonar en mesta*. EA A. 2 vols. Copenhagen: Munksgaard.

Halldórsson, Halldór, see Halldór Halldórsson.

Halldórsson, Ólafur, see Ólafur Halldórsson.

Hanawalt, Barbara A. 1986. *Women and Work in Preindustrial Europe*. Bloomington: University of Indiana Press.

Harris, Joseph. 1972. Genre and Narrative Structure in Some *Íslendinga Þættir*. *SS* 44: 1–27.

———. 1975. Qgmundar þáttr dytts ok Gunnars helmings. Unity and Literary Relations. *ANF* 90:156–82.

———. 1976. Theme and Genre in Some *Íslendinga þættir*. *SS* 48:1–28.

———. 1992. Love and Death in the *Männerbund*: The *Bjarkamál* and the *Battle of Maldon*. In *Heroic Poetry in the Anglo-Saxon Period. Studies in Honor of Jess B. Bessinger, Jr.*, ed. Helen Damico and John Leyerle, 77–114. Kalamazoo, Mich.: Medieval Institute Publications.

———. 1994. Sacrifice and Guilt in *Sonatorrek*. In *Studien zum Altgermanischen. Festschrift für Heinrich Beck*, ed. Heiko Uecker, 173–95. Ergänzungsbände zum Reallexikon der Germanischen Altertumskunde. 11. Berlin: de Gruyter.

Hastrup, Kirsten. 1985. *Culture and History in Medieval Iceland*. Oxford: Clarendon.

———. 1990a. *Nature and Policy in Iceland, 1400–1800*. Oxford: Clarendon.

———. 1990b. *Island of Anthropology: Studies in Past and Present Iceland*. Odense: Odense University Press.

Hauksbók. 1892–1896. Copenhagen: Det kongelige nordiske oldskrift-selskab.

Heilagra manna søgur. Ed. C. R. Unger. 1877. 2 vols. Christiania [Oslo]: Universitetsprogram.

Heinrichs, Anne. 1989. *Der "Óláfs Þáttr Geirstaðaálfs": Eine Variantenstudie*. Heidelberg: Carl Winter.

Heldensage und Heldendichtung im Germanischen, ed. Heinrich Beck. 1988. Ergänzungsbände zum Reallexikon der Germanischen Altertumskunde. 2. Berlin: de Gruyter.

Helgadóttir, Guðrún P., see Guðrún P. Helgadóttir.

Helga Kress. 1980. Meget samstavet må det tykkes deg: Om kvinneopprör og genretvang i Sagaen om Laksdölene. (N)*HT* 59:266–80.

———. 1991. Gægur er þér í augum: konur í sjónmáli Íslendingasagna. In *Yfir Íslandsála: Afmælisrit til heiðurs Magnúsi Stefánssyni*, 77–94. Reykjavík: Sögufræðslusjóður.

Helgi Þorláksson. 1991. *Vaðmál og verðlag: Vaðmál í utanlandsviðskiptum og búskab Íslendinga á 13. og 14. öld*. Reykjavík: Fjölföldun Sigurjóns.

———. 1992. Snorri goði og Snorri Sturluson. *Skírnir* 166:295–320.

Heller, Rolf. 1958. *Die literarische Darstellung der Frau in den Isländersagas*. Halle: Max Niemeyer.

———. 1984. Die Gebeine des Goden Snorri. *ANF* 99:95–106.

Herlihy, David. 1990. Making Sense of Incest: Women and the Marriage Rules of the Early Middle Ages. In *Law, Custom, and the Social Fabric in Medieval Europe: Essays in Honor of Bryce Lyon*, ed. Bernard S. Bachrach and David Nicholas, 1–16. Studies in Medieval Culture 28. Kalamazoo, Mich.: Medieval Institute Publications.

Bibliography

Hermann Pálsson. 1962. *Sagnaskemmtun Íslendinga.* Reykjavík: Mál og menning.

Hermann Pálsson and Paul Edwards, trans. 1972. *Eyrbyggja saga.* London: Penguin.

——, trans. 1976. *Egils saga.* London: Penguin.

Heusler, Andreas. 1914. *Die Anfänge der isländischen Saga.* Abhandl. der königl. preuss. Akademie der Wissenschaften, philos.-hist. Cl. 1913. Berlin.

Hill, Joyce. 1983. From Rome to Jerusalem: An Icelandic Itinerary of the mid-Twelfth Century. *Harvard Theological Review* 76:175–203.

Hitzler, Egon. 1979. *Sel-Untersuchungen zur Geschichte des isländischen Sennwesens seit der Landnahmezeit.* Oslo: Universitetsforlaget.

Hoffmann, Martha. 1964. *The Warp-weighted Loom: Studies in the History and Technology of an Ancient Implement.* Studia Norvegica 14. Oslo: Universitetsforlaget. Rpt. 1974.

Holtsmark, Anne. 1939. Vefr Darraðar. *MM.* Rpt. 1956 *Studier i norrøn diktning.* Oslo: Universitetsforlaget.

Ingólfsdóttir, Guðrún, see Guðrún Ingólfsdóttir.

Ingstad, Helge. 1969. *Westward to Vinland: The Discovery of Pre-Columbian Norse House-Sites in North America,* trans. Erik J. Friis. Rpt. 1972. New York: Harper & Row.

Ingvarsson, Lúðvík, see Lúðvík Ingvarsson.

Irigaray, Luce. 1985a. *This Sex Which Is Not One,* trans. Catherine Porter and Carolyn Burke. Ithaca, N.Y.: Cornell University Press.

——. 1985b. *Speculum of the Other Woman,* trans. Gillian C. Gill. Ithaca N.Y.: Cornell University Press.

Íslendinga sögur. Ed. Guðni Jónsson. 1949. 12 vols. Reykjavík: Íslendingasagnaútgáfan.

Íslendinga sögur. Ed. Bragi Halldórsson et al. 1987. 3 vols. Reykjavík: Svart á Hvítu.

Íslensk bókmenntasaga 1. Ed. Guðrún Nordal, Sverrir Tómasson, and Vésteinn Ólason. 1992. Reykjavík: Mál og menning.

Íslensk bókmenntasaga 2. Ed. Böðvar Guðmundsson, Sverrir Tómasson, Torfi H. Tulinius and Vésteinn Ólason. 1993. Reykjavík: Mál og menning.

Íslenzk fornrit. 1939–1991. 20 vols. Reykjavík: Hið íslenzka fornritafélag.

Jacobsen, Grethe. N.d. The Celtic Element in the Icelandic Population and the Position of Women. Unpublished manuscript.

——. 1984. Pregnancy and Childbirth in the Medieval North: A Typology of Sources and a Preliminary Study. *Scandinavian Journal of History* 9:91–111.

Jesch, Judith. 1991. *Women in the Viking Age.* Woodbridge: Boydell.

Jochens, Jenny. 1980. The Church and Sexuality in Medieval Iceland. *Journal of Medieval History* 6:377–92.

——. 1985. En Islande médiévale: à la recherche de la famille nucléaire. *Annales: ÉSC* 40:95–112.

——. 1986a. Consent in Marriage: Old Norse Law, Life, and Literature. *SS* 58:142–76.

——. 1986b. The Medieval Icelandic Heroine: Fact or Fiction? *Viator* 17:35–50. Rpt. 1989 *Sagas of the Icelanders,* ed. John Tucker, 99–125. New York: Garland.

——. 1987a. The Female Inciter in the Kings' Sagas. *ANF* 102:100–119.

——. 1987b. The Politics of Reproduction: Medieval Norwegian Kingship. *American Historical Review* 92:327–49.

——. 1989. *Vǫluspá:* Matrix of Norse Womanhood. *JEGP* 88:344–62. Rpt. *Poetry,* 257–77.

——. 1990. Old Norse Sources on Women. In *Medieval Women and the Sources of Medieval History,* ed. Joel T. Rosenthal, 155–88. Athens: University of Georgia Press.

——. 1991a. Before the Male Gaze: The Absence of the Female Body in Old Norse. In *Sex in the Middle Ages,* ed. Joyce E. Salisbury, 3–29. New York: Garland.

——. 1991b. The Illicit Love Visit: An Archaeology of Old Norse Sexuality. *JHS* 1: 357–92.

——. 1991c. Old Norse Magic and Gender: Þáttr Þorvalds ens víðfǫrla. *SS* 63:305–17.

——. 1992. From Libel to Lament: Male Manifestations of Love in Old Norse. In *From Sagas,* 247–64.

——. 1993a. Gender and Drinking in the World of the Icelandic Sagas. In *A Special Brew: Essays in Honour of Kristof Glamann,* 155–81. Odense: Odense University Press.

——. 1993b. Gender Symmetry in Law?: The Case of Medieval Iceland. *ANF* 108: 46–67.

——. 1993c. Lexicons of Love: Native and Imported Perceptions of the Body and Sexuality in Thirteenth-Century Iceland. Paper delivered at the Ninth Berkshire Conference on the History of Women, at Vassar College.

——. 1993d. Marching to a Different Drummer: New Trends in Medieval Icelandic Scholarship. A Review Article. *Comparative Studies in Society and History* 35:197–207.

——. 1993e. "Med Jákvæði Hennar Sjálfrar:" Consent as Signifier in the Old Norse World. In *Consent and Coercion to Sex and Marriage in Ancient and Medieval Societies,* ed. Angeliki Laiou, 271–89. Washington, D.C.

——. 1994a. Review of Else Ebel, *Der Konkubinat nach altwestnordischen Quellen: Philologische Studien zur sogenannten "Friedelehe".* alvíssmál 3:101–5.

——. 1994b. Wealth and Women in Snorri's Life. In *Afmælisrit Jónas Kristjánsson,* 455–63. Reykjavík: Hið íslenska bókmenntafélag.

——. 1996a. Men, Women, and Beasts: Old Norse Sexuality. In *Handbook in Sexuality,* ed. Vern Bullough. New York: Garland. In press.

——. 1996b. Old Norse Motherhood. In *Medieval Mothering,* ed. Bonnie Wheeler and John C. Parson. Feminea Medievalia 3. New York: Garland. In press.

——. 1996c. Vikings Westward to Vínland: Problems of Women and Sexuality. In *Cold Counsel: The Women of Old Norse Literature and Myth,* ed. Karen Swenson and Sarah May Anderson. New York: Garland. In press.

——. 1996d. *Old Norse Images of Women.* Philadelphia: University of Pennsylvania Press.

Jóhannesson, Alexander, see Alexander Jóhannesson.

Jóhannesson, Jón, see Jón Jóhannesson.

Jóhannesson, Þorkell, see Þorkell Jóhannesson.

Jómsvíkinga saga. 1882. Ed. Carl af Petersen. Copenhagen: SUGNL 7.

Jómsvíkinga Saga, The Saga of the Jomsvikings. Ed. and trans. N. F. Blake. 1962. London: Thomas Nelson.

Jón Helgason. 1953. Norges og Islands digtning. In *Litteraturhistorie B: Norge og Island,* ed. Sigurður Nordal, 3–179. Nordisk kultur, 8B. Stockholm: Bonniers.

Jón Hnefill Aðalsteinsson. 1978. *Under the Cloak.* Uppsala: Almqvist & Wiksell.

——. 1991. Íslenski skólinn. *Skírnir* 165:103–29.

Jón Jóhannesson. 1956. *Íslendinga saga I.* Reykjavík: Almenna Bókafélag.

———. 1974. *A History of the Old Icelandic Commonwealth.* Trans. Haraldur Bessason. Manitoba: University of Manitoba Press.

Jón Viðar Sigurðsson. 1993. *Goder og maktforhold på Island i fristatstiden.* Bergen: Historisk Institut.

Jónas Kristjánsson. 1981. *Heimkoma handritanna.* Reykjavík: Fylgir Árbók Háskóla Íslands 1976–1979.

———. 1988. *Eddas and Sagas: Iceland's Medieval Literature.* Trans. Peter Foote. Reykjavík: Hið íslenska bókmenntafélag.

———. 1990. Var Snorri Sturluson upphafsmaður Íslendingasagna? *Andvari* 115:85–105.

———. 1993. Er Egilssaga "Norse"? *Skáldskaparmál* 3:216–31.

Jong, Mayke de. 1989. To the limits of kinship: anti-incest legislation in the early medieval west (500–900). In *From Sappho to de Sade: Moments in the History of Sexuality,*" ed. Jan Bremmer. 36–59. London: Routledge.

Jónsson, Finnur, see Finnur Jónsson.

Jónsson, Már, see Már Jónsson.

Kalinke, Marianne E. 1981. *King Arthur North-by-Northwest.* BA 37. Copenhagen: Reitzels.

Karlsson, Gunnar, see Gunnar Karlsson.

Karlsson, Stefán, see Stefán Karlsson.

Karras, Ruth Mazo. 1988. *Slavery and Society in Medieval Scandinavia.* New Haven: Yale University Press.

Ker, W. P. 1897. *Epic and Romance: Essays on Medieval Literature.* Rpt. 1957. New York: Dover.

Kilderne til den tidlige middelalders historie. Rapporter til den XX nordiske historikerkongress, Reykjavík 1987. Vol. 1. Ed. Gunnar Karlsson. 1987. Reykjavík: Sagnfræðistofnun Háskóla Íslands.

Kjartan G. Ottósson. 1983. *Fróðárundur í Eyrbyggju.* Studia Islandica 42. Reykjavík.

Klose, Olaf. 1929. *Die Familienverhältnisse auf Island vor der Bekehrung zum Christentum auf Grund der Islendingasǫgur.* Nordische Studien 10. Braunschweig: Georg Westermann.

Köstler, K. 1943. Raub-, Kauf-, und Friedelehe bei den Germanen. *Zeitschrift der Savigny-Stiftung für Rechtsgeschichte; germ. Abt.* 63:92–136.

Krag, Claus. 1991. *Ynglingatal og Ynglingesaga: En studie i historiske kilder.* Studia Humaniora 2. Oslo: Universitetsforlaget.

Krause, Wolfgang. 1926. *Die Frau in der Sprache der altisländischen Familiengeschichten.* Göttingen: Vandenhoeck & Ruprecht.

Kren, Thomas, and Roger S. Wieck. 1990. *The Visions of Tondal from the Library of Margaret of York.* Malibu, Calif.: Getty.

Kress, Helga, see Helga Kress.

Kreutzer, Gert. 1987. *Kindheit und Jugend in der altnordischen Literatur. Teil I: Schwangerschaft, Geburt und früheste Kindheit.* Münster: Kleinheinrich.

Kristjánsdóttir, Bergljót S., see Bergljót S. Kristjánsdóttir.

Kristjánsson, Jónas, see Jónas Kristjánsson.

Krömmelbein, Thomas. 1983. *Skaldische Metaphorik. Studien zur Funktion der Kenningsprache in skaldischen Dichtungen des 9. und 10. Jahrhunderts.* Freiburg: Burg.

Krogh, Knud J. 1982. *Qallunaatsiaaqarfik Grønland. Erik den Rødes Grønland.* Copenhagen: Nationalmuseet.

Kulturhistorisk Leksikon for Nordisk Middelalder. 22 vols. 1957–1978. Copenhagen: Rosenkilde & Bagger.

Kvinnans ekonomiska ställning under nordisk medeltid. Ed. Hedda Gunneng and Birgit Strand. 1981. Lindome: Kompendiet.

Ladurie, Emmanuel Le Roy. 1975. *Montaillou, village occitan de 1294 à 1324.* Paris: Gallimard.

———. *Montaillou: The Promised Land of Error.* 1979. Trans. Barbara Bray. New York: Random House.

Larson, Laurence M., trans. 1935. *The Earliest Norwegian Laws.* New York: Columbia University Press.

Late Medieval Icelandic Romances. Ed. Agnete Loth. 1962–1965. 5 vols. EA B, 20–24. Copenhagen: Munksgaard.

Leach, Edmund. 1966. Virgin Birth. *Journal of the Royal Anthropological Institute of Great Britain and Ireland* 96:39–49.

Lecouteux, Claude. 1986. *Fantômes et revenants.* Paris: Imago.

Liliequist, Jonas. 1991. Peasants against Nature: Crossing the Boundaries between Man and Animal in Seventeenth- and Eighteenth-Century Sweden. *JHS* 1:393–423.

Lind, Erik Henrik. 1905–1915. *Norsk-Isländska dopnamn och fingerade namn från medeltiden.* Uppsala: Lundequistska bokhandeln.

———. 1931. *Norsk-Isländska dopnamn och fingerade namn från medeltiden. Supplementsband.* Oslo: Det norske videnskaps-akademi i Oslo.

Líndal, Sigurður, see Sigurður Líndal.

Linke, Ull. 1992. Manhood, Femaleness, and Power: A Cultural Analysis of Prehistoric Images of Reproduction. *Comparative Studies in Society and History* 34:579–620.

Lönnroth, Lars. 1963. Studier i Olaf Tryggvasons saga. *Samlaren* 84:54–94.

———. 1990. *Two Norse-Icelandic Studies.* Litteraturvetenskapliga institutionen, Göteborgs Universitet, Meddelanden nr. 7.

Lúðvík Ingvarsson. 1970. *Refsingar á Íslandi á þjóðveldistímanum.* Reykjavík: Bókaútgáfa Menningarsjóðs.

Lynch, Joseph H. 1986. *Godparents and Kinship in Early Medieval Europe.* Princeton, N.J.: Princeton University Press.

McTurk, Rory. 1991. *Studies in "Ragnars Saga Loðbrókar" and its Major Scandinavian Analogues.* Medium Ævum Monographs New Series 15. Oxford: Society for the Study of Mediæval Languages and Literature.

Magnusson, Magnus, and Hermann Pálsson, trans. 1969. *Laxdœla saga.* Harmondsworth: Penguin.

Magoun, Francis P., Jr. 1944. The Pilgrim-Diary of Nikulás of Munkathverá: the Road to Rome. *Mediaeval Studies* 6:314–54.

Malinowski, Bronislaw. 1929. *The Sexual Life of Savages.* New York: Harcourt, Brace and World.

Már Jónsson. 1993. *Blóðskömm á Íslandi 1270–1870.* Reykjavík: Háskóli Íslands.

Maríu saga: Legender om Jomfru Maria og hendes Jertegn. Ed. C. R. Unger. 1871. Christiania [Oslo]: Brögger & Christie.

Marstrander, Sverre. 1986. *De skjulte skipene: Tuneskipet, Gokstadskipet og Osebergskipet.* Oslo: Gyldendal.

Maurer, Konrad. 1881. *Über die Wasserweihe des germanischen Heidenthumes.* Abhandlungen der Philos.-phil. Classe der Kgl. Bayer. Akademie der Wiss. Ab.724, 15.3: 175–253.

——. 1883. *Die unechte Geburt nach altnordischem Rechte*. Abhandlungen der Philos.-phil. Classe der Kgl. Bayer. Akademie der Wiss.

——. 1908. *Vorlesungen über Altnordische Rechtsgeschichte*. Vol. 2: *Über Altnordische Kirchenverfassung und Eherecht*. Leipzig: H. Deichert.

Medieval Scandinavia: An Encyclopedia. 1993. Ed. Philip Pulsiano. New York: Garland.

Merschberger, Gerda. 1937. *Die Stellung der Frau im Eherecht und Erbrecht nach den deutschen Volksrechten (unter Berücksichtigung der nordischen Quellen)*. Leipzig.

Miller, William Ian. 1984. Choosing the Avenger: Some Aspects of the Bloodfeud in Medieval Iceland and England. *Law and History Review* 1:159–204.

——. 1986a. Dreams, Prophesy, and Sorcery: Blaming the Secret Offender in Medieval Iceland. *SS* 58:102–23.

——. 1986b. Gift, Sale, Payment, Raid: Case Studies in the Negotiation and Classification of Exchange in Medieval Iceland. *Sp* 91:18–50.

——. 1988a. Ordeal in Iceland. *SS* 60:189–218.

——. 1988b. Some Aspects of Householding in the Medieval Icelandic commonwealth. *Continuity and Change* 3:321–55.

——. 1990. *Bloodtaking and Peacemaking: Feud, Law, and Society in Saga Iceland*. Chicago: University of Chicago Press.

Minkov, Michael. 1988. Sneglu-Halli, 2:11: *Dróttinserðr*. *SBVS* 22:285–86.

Monumenta Historica Norvegiæ. Ed. Gustav Storm. 1880. Kristiania (Oslo): A. W. Brøgger.

Mulvey, Laura. 1975. Visual Pleasure and Narrative Cinema. *Screen*. Rpt. Laura Mulvey. 1989. *Visual and Other Pleasures*. Bloomington: Indiana University Press.

Mundal, Else. 1977. *Sagadebatt*. Oslo: Universitetsforlaget.

——. 1982. Kvinnebiletet i nokre mellomaldergenrar: Eitt opposisjonelt kvinnesyn. *Edda* 6:241–371.

Nanna Ólafsdóttir. 1973. Baðstofan og böð að fornu. *Árbók Hins íslenzka fornleifafélags*, 62–86.

Neckel, Gustav, ed., rev. Hans Kuhn. 1962. *Edda: Die Lieder des Codex Regius nebst verwandten Denkmälern*. 4th ed. Heidelberg: Winter.

Das Nibelungenlied. Ed. Karl Bartsch. 1931. 9th ed. Leipzig: Brockhaus.

Nöfn Íslendinga. Ed. Guðrún Kvaran and Sigurður Jónsson frá Arnarvatni. 1991. Reykjavík: Heimskringla.

Nordal, Sigurður, see Sigurður Nordal.

Nordland, Odd. 1969. *Brewing and Beer Traditions in Norway: The Social Anthropological Background of the Brewing Industry*. Oslo: Universitetsforlaget.

Norges gamle Love. Ed. R. Keyser and P. A. Munch. 5 vols. 1846–1895. Christiania [Oslo]: Det kongelige norske Videnskabernes Selskab.

North, Richard. 1990. The Pagan Inheritance of Egill's *Sonatorrek*. In *Poetry*, 147–67.

Oddr Snorrason munkr. 1932. *Saga Óláfs Tryggvasonar*. Ed. Finnur Jónsson. Copenhagen: Gad.

Ólafía Einarsdóttir. 1964. *Studier i kronologisk metode i tidlig islandsk historieskrivning*. Bibliotheca Historica Lundendis, 13. Lund: Gleerup.

——. 1983. Kvindens stilling i Fristatstidens Island: Sociale og økonomiske betragtninger. *Studia Historica Jyväskyläensia* 27:227–38.

Ólafsdóttir, Nanna, see Nanna Ólafsdóttir.

Ólafsson, Eggert, see Eggert Ólafsson.

Ólafur Halldórsson. 1990. *Grettisfœrsla*. Reykjavík: Stofnun Árna Magnússonar.

Ólafur Halldórsson, ed. 1904. *Jónsbók . . . og Réttarbœtr*. Copenhagen. Rpt. 1970. Odense: Odense University Press.

Old Norse-Icelandic Literature: A Critical Guide. Ed. Carol J. Clover and John Lindow. 1985. Islandica 45. Ithaca, N.Y.: Cornell University Press.

Ólsen, Björn Magnússon, see Björn Magnússon Ólsen.

Österberg, Eva. 1991. *Mentalities and Other Realities: Essays in Medieval and Early Modern Scandinavian History*. Lund: Lund University Press.

Ottósson, Kjartan G., see Kjartan G. Ottósson.

Ozment, Steven. 1983. *When Fathers Ruled: Family Life in Reformation Europe*. Cambridge: Harvard University Press.

Paige, Karen Ericksen, and Jeffery M. Paige. 1981. *The Politics of Reproductive Ritual*. Berkeley: University of California Press.

Pálsson, Hermann, see Hermann Pálsson.

Pentikäinen, Juha. 1968. *The Nordic Dead-Child Tradition: Nordic Dead-Child Beings: A Study in Comparative Religion*. Folklore Fellows Communications 202. Helsinki: Suomalainen Tiedeakatemia.

——. 1990. Child Abandonment as an Indicator of Christianization in the Nordic Countries. In *Old Norse and Finnish Religions and Celtic Place-Names*, ed. Tore Ahlbäck, 72–91. Åbo: Donner Institute for Research.

Perkow, Ursula. 1972. Wasserweihe, Taufe und Patenschaft bei den Nordgermanen. Ph.D. diss. Hamburg.

Pizarro, Joaquín Martínez. 1989. *A Rhetoric of the Scene: Dramatic Narrative in the Early Middle Ages*. Toronto: University of Toronto Press.

Poetry in the Scandinavian Middle Ages. 1990. Ed. Teresa Pàroli. Seventh International Saga Conference, Spoleto, 4–10 September 1988. Spoleto.

Poole, R. G. 1991. *Viking Poems on War and Peace: A Study in Skaldic Narrative*. Toronto: University of Toronto Press.

Postola sögur. 1874. Ed. C. R. Unger. Christiania [Oslo].

Rafnsson, Sveinbjörn, see Sveinbjörn Rafnsson.

Reuter, Sigfrid. 1933. Zur Bedeutungsgeschichte des *hundrað* im Altwestnordischen. *ANF* 49:36–67.

Riddarasögur. Ed. Bjarni Vilhjálmsson. 1944. 6 vols. Reykjavík: Íslendingasagnaútgáfan, Haukadalsútgáfan.

Rittershaus, Adeline. 1917. *Altnordische Frauen*. Frauenfeld: Huber.

Robberstad, Knut. 1970. *Rettssoga*. 1. Oslo: Universitetsforlaget.

Rosenblad, Esbjörn. 1990. *Island i saga och nutid*. Stockholm: Norstedts.

Ross, Margaret Clunies. 1973. Hildr's Ring: a Problem in the Ragnarsdrápa, Strophes 8–12. *MS* 6:75–92.

——. 1994. *Prolonged Echoes: Old North Myth in Medieval Northern Society*. Vol. 1: *The Myths*. Odense: Odense University Press.

Roussell, Aage. 1941. *Farms and Churches in the Medieval Norse Settlements of Greenland*. Copenhagen: Reitzel.

Russell, James C. 1994. *The Germanization of Early Medieval Christianity: A Sociohistorical Approach to Religious Transformation*. New York: Oxford University Press.

Ruthström, Bo. 1993. *Öre*—förslag till en alternative etymologi. *ANF* 108:93–121.

Saga Íslands. Ed. Sigurður Líndal. 1974–1991. 5 vols. Reykjavík: Hið íslenzka bók-menntafélag.

Sagnaskemmtun: Studies in Honour of Hermann Pálsson. Ed. Rudolf Simek et al. 1986. Vienna: Hermann Böhlaus Nachf.

Sanday, Peggy Reeves. 1981. *Female Power and Male Dominance: On the Origins of Sexual Inequality.* Cambridge: Cambridge University Press.

Sawyer, Birgit. 1988. *Property and Inheritance in Viking Scandinavia: The Runic Evidence.* Occasional Papers on Medieval Topics 2. Alingsås: Viktoria.

Schach, Paul. 1984. *Icelandic Sagas.* Boston: Twayne.

Schmeidler, Hermann. 1917. *Adam von Bremen, Hamburgische Kirchengeschichte.* 3d ed. Hannover: Hahnsche.

Schmitt, Jean-Claude. 1994. *Les revenants: Les vivants et les morts dans la société médiévale.* Paris: Gallimard.

Schwerin, Claudius von. 1930. Die Ehesheidung im älteren Isländischen Recht. *Deutsche Islandforschung* 1:283–99.

Schweringen, Grace Fleming von. 1909. Women in the Germanic Hero-Sagas. *JEGP* 8: 501–12.

Scott, Joan Wallach. 1986. Gender: A Useful Category of Historical Analysis. *American Historical Review* 91:1053–75.

See, Klaus von. 1964. *Altnordische Rechtswörter: Philologische Studien zur Rechtsauffassung und Rechtsgesinning der Germanen.* Tübingen: Max Niemeyer.

———. 1981. *Edda, Saga, Skaldendichtung: Aufsätze zur skandinavischen Literatur des Mittelalters.* Heidelberg: Winter.

Shahar, Shulamith. 1983. *The Fourth Estate: A History of Women in the Middle Ages.* Trans. Chaya Galai. London: Methuen.

———. 1990. *Childhood in the Middle Ages.* New York: Routledge.

Sigrún Davíðsdóttir. *Sagastriden: Håndskriftssagen i politisk belysning.* Odense: Odense University Press. In press.

Sigurðardóttir, Anna, see Anna Sigurðardóttir.

Sigurður Líndal. 1969. Sendiför Úlfljóts. *Skírnir* 143:5–26.

———. 1984. Lög og lagasetning í íslenzka þjóðveldinu. *Skírnir* 158:121–58.

Sigurður Nordal. 1941. Gunnhildur konungamóðir. *Samtíð og saga* 1:135–55.

———. 1953. Sagalitteraturen. In *Litteraturhistorie B: Norge og Island,* ed. Sigurður Nordal, 180–288. Nordisk kultur, 8B. Stockholm: Bonnier.

Sigurðsson, Gísli, see Gísli Sigurðsson.

Sigurðsson, Jón Viðar, see Jón Viðar Sigurðsson.

Sigurður Sigurmundsson. 1963. Draumar Jóreiðar. *Andvari* 5: 33–38.

Sigurmundsson, Sigurður, see Sigurður Sigurmundsson.

Silja Aðalsteinsdóttir and Helgi Þorláksson. 1983. *Förändringar i kvinnors villkor under medeltiden.* Reykjavik: Sagnfræðistofnun Háskóla Íslands.

Silverman, Kaja. 1988. *The Acoustic Mirror: The Female Voice in Psychoanalysis and Cinema.* Bloomington: Indiana University Press.

Simpson, Jacqueline. 1961. Advocacy and Art in *Guðmundar saga dýra. SBVS* 15: 327–45.

Sjöholm, Elsa. 1976. *Gesetze als Quellen mittelalterliche Geschichte des Nordens.* Stockholm: Almqvist & Wicksell.

——. 1988. *Sveriges Medeltidslagar: Europeisk rättstradition i politisk omvandling.* Stockholm: A.-B. Nordiska Bokhandeln.

Sjötíu ritgerðir helgaðar Jakobi Benediktssyni. Ed. Einar G. Pétursson and Jónas Kristjánsson. 1977. Reykjavík: Stofnun Árna Magnússonar.

Snorrastefna. Ed. Úlfar Bragason. 1992. Reykjavik: Stofnun Sigurðar Nordals.

Snorri Sturluson: Kolloquium anlässlich der 750. Wiederkehr seines Todestages. Ed. Alois Wolf. 1993. Tübingen: Gunter Narr.

Sørensen, Preben Meulengracht. 1977. *Saga og samfund: en indføring i oldislandsk litteratur.* Copenhagen: Berlingske forlag.

——. 1983. *The Unmanly Man: Concepts of Sexual Defamation in Early Northern Society.* Trans. Joan Turville-Petre. Viking Collection 1. Odense: Odense University Press.

——. 1993. *Fortælling og ære: Studier i islændingesagaerne.* Aarhus: Aarhus Universitetsforlag.

——. 1993. *Saga and Society: An Introduction to Old Norse Literature.* Trans. John Tucker. Odense: Odense University Press.

Specvlvm Norroenvm: Norse Studies in Memory of Gabriel Turville-Petre. Ed. Ursula Dronke et al. 1981. Odense: Odense University Press.

Spiegel, Gabrielle M. 1990. History, Historicism, and the Social Logic of the Text in the Middle Ages. *Sp* 65:59–86.

Stafford, Pauline. 1983. *Queens, Concubines, and Dowagers: The King's Wife in the Early Middle Ages.* Athens: University of Georgia Press.

Steenstrup, Johannes. 1876. Rpt. 1972. Normannerne. 4 vols. Copenhagen.

Stefán Karlsson. Ed. 1983. *Guðmundar sögur biskups I.* EA B 6. Copenhagen: Reitzel.

——. 1990. Drottinleg bæn á móðurmáli. *Biblíuþýðingar í sögu og samtíð.* Studia theologica Islandica. Reykjavík: Háskóli Íslands. 145–74.

Storm, Gustav, ed. 1888. *Islandske Annaler indtil 1578.* Christiania [Oslo]: Gröndahl.

Structure and Meaning in Old Norse Literature: New Approaches to Textual Analysis and Literary Criticism. Ed. John Lindow, Lars Lönnroth, and Gerd Wolfgang Weber. 1986. Odense: Odense University Press.

Sturlunga saga. Ed. Jón Jóhannesson, Magnús Finnbogason, and Kristján Eldjárn. 2 vols. 1946. Reykjavik.

Sturlunga Saga. Trans. Julia H. McGrew, and R. George Thomas. 1970–1974. 2 vols. New York: Twayne / American-Scandinavian Foundation.

Sturlunga saga. Ed. Örnólfur Thorsson. 1988. 3 vols. Reykjavík: Svart á Hvítu.

Sveinbjörn Rafnsson. 1974. *Studier i Landnámabok: Kritiska bidrag till den isländska fristatstidens historia.* Bibliotheca Historica Lundensis 31. Lund: Blom.

——. 1983a. Skriftaboð Þorláks biskups. *Gripla* 5:77–114.

——. 1983b. Um mataræði Íslendinga á 18. öld. *Saga* 21:73–87.

——. 1985. The Penitential of St Þorlákur in its Icelandic context. *Bulletin of Medieval Canon Law.* New series. 15:19–30.

——. 1990. Forn hrossreiðalög og heimildir þeirra. *Saga* 28:131–48.

——. 1993. *Páll Jónsson Skálholtsbiskup: nokkrar athuganir á sögu hans og kirkjustjórn.* Ritsafn sagnfræðistofnunar 33. Reykjavík: Sagnfræðistofnun Háskóla Íslands.

Sverrir Tómasson. 1975. Tækilig vitni. In *Afmælisrit Björns Sigfússonar,* ed. Björn Teitsson et al., 251–87. Reykjavík: Sögufélag.

——. 1984. Hvönnin í Olafs sögum Tryggvasonar. *Gripla* 6:202–17.

———. 1988. *Formálar íslenskra sagnaritara á miðöldum.* Reykjavík: Stofnun Árna Magnússonar.

———. 1989. Hugleiðingar um horfna bókmenntagrein. *Tímarit Máls og menningar* 50: 211–26.

Sverris saga. Ed. Gustav Indrebø. 1920. Kristiania [Oslo]: J. Dybwad.

Tan-Haverhorst, Louisa Fredrika, ed. 1939. *Þjalar Jóns saga. Dámusta saga.* Leiden, Haarlem: H. D. Tjeenk Willink & Zoon.

Taranger, Absalon. 1890. *Den Angelsaksiske Kirkes Indflydelse paa den norske.* Kristiania: Den norske historiske Forening.

Taylor, Michael. 1978. *The Lewis Chessmen.* London: British Museum Publications.

Teuscher, Simon H. 1990. Islendingenes forhold til dyr i høymiddelalderen: en mentalitetshistorisk analyse av noen ættesagaer. (N)*HT* 69:311–37.

Tjomsland, Anne. 1951. *The Saga of Hrafn Sveinbjarnarson: The Life of an Icelandic Physician of the Thirteenth Century.* Islandica 35. Ithaca, N.Y.: Cornell University Press.

Torfi H. Tulinius. 1995. *La "Matière du Nord": Sagas légendaires et fiction dans la littérature islandaise en prose du XIIIe siècle.* Paris: Presses de l'Université de Paris-Sorbonne.

Tradition og historieskrivning: Kilderne til Nordens ældste historie. Ed. Kirsten Hastrup and Preben Meulengracht Sørensen 1987. Acta Jutlandica 53:2. Aarhus: Aarhus universitetsforlag.

Tranter, Stephen Norman. 1987. *Sturlunga saga: The Rôle of the Creative Compiler.* Frankfurt a/M: Peter Lang.

Treggiari, Susan. 1991. *Roman Marriage: "Iusti Coniuges" from the Time of Cicero to the Time of Ulpian.* Oxford: Clarendon.

Tulinius, Torfi H., see Torfi H. Tulinius.

Turville-Petre, E. O. G. 1944. Gísli Súrsson and his Poetry: Traditions and Influences. *Modern Languages Review* 39:374–91.

———. 1976. *Scaldic Poetry.* Oxford: Clarendon Press.

Tvær sögur af Gísla Súrssyni. Ed. Konráð Gíslason. 1849. Nordiske Oldskrifter 8. Copenhagen: Det nordiske literatur-samfund.

Twenty-Eight Papers Presented to Hans Bekker-Nielsen on the Occasion of His Sixtieth Birthday, 28 April 1991. 1993. Odense: Odense University Press.

Úlfar Bragason. 1981. Frásagnarmynstur í Þorgils sögu skarða. *Skírnir* 155:161–70.

———. 1990. Um hvað fjallaði Huldar saga? *Tímarit Máls og menningar* 51:76–81.

———. 1992. Sturlunga saga: Textar og rannsóknir. *Skáldskaparmál* 2:176–206.

Ulff-Møller, Jens. 1991. The Higher Numerals in Early Nordic Texts, and the Duodecimal System of Calculation. *The Audience of the Sagas.* The Eighth International Saga Conference, Gothenburg. Preprints. 2 vols. 2:323–30.

———. 1993–1994. Systems of Calculation in "Long Hundreds" and Their Employment within Weight and Measurement Systems. *Cahiers de Métrologie.* Ed. Jean-Claude Hocquet. Éditions du Lys. 11–12:501–18.

Valtýr Guðmundsson. 1893. Litklæði. *ANF* 9:171–98.

Vandvik, Eirik. 1959. *Latinske dokument til Norsk Historie.* Oslo: Universitetsforlaget.

Viking Revaluations: Viking Society Centenary Symposium, 14–15 May 1992. 1993. Ed.

Anthony Faulkes and Richard Perkins. London: Viking Society for Northern Research.

Viktors saga ok Blávus. Ed. Jónas Kristjánsson. 1984. Riddarasögur 2. Reykjavík: Handritastofnun Íslands.

Vilhjálmsson, Bjarni, see Bjarni Vilhjálmsson.

Vilhjálmur Finsen. 1849–1850. Fremstilling af den islandske Familieret efter Grágás. *ÅNOH* 1849:150–331, 1850: 121–272.

——. Den islandske Retshistorie indtil Fristatens Undergang. Unpubl. ms., AM Access 6b. Árnastofnun, Reykjavík.

——, ed. 1852. *Grágás: Islændernes Lovbog i Fristatens Tid.* Copenhagen: Gyldendal. Rpt. 1974. Odense: Odense University Press.

——, ed. 1879. *Grágás efter det Arnamagnæanske Haandskrift Nr. 334 fol., Staðarhólsbók.* Copenhagen: Gyldendal. Rpt. 1974. Odense: Odense University Press.

——, ed. 1883. *Grágás. Stykker* . . . . Copenhagen: Gyldendal. Rpt. 1974. Odense: Odense University Press.

Vogt, Walther Heinrich. 1921. Die Bjarnar saga hítdœlakappa: Lausavísur, frásagnir, saga. *ANF* 33:27–79.

Vries, Jan de. 1941–1942. *Altnordische Literaturgeschichte.* 2 vols. Grundriss der germanischen Philologie, 15–16. Berlin: de Gruyter. Rpt. 1964–1967.

——. 1977. *Altnordisches etymologisches Wörterbuch.* Leiden: E. J. Brill.

Vǫlsunga saga ok Ragnars saga loðbrókar. 1906–1908. Ed. Magnus Olsen. SUGNL 36. Copenhagen: S. L. Møller.

Wawn, Andrew, ed. 1994. *Northern Antiquity: The Post-Medieval Reception of Edda and Saga.* Enfield Lock: Hisarlik Press.

Weibull, Lauritz. 1911. *Kritiska undersökningar i Nordens historia omkring år 1000.* Lund. Rpt. 1948. *Nordisk Historia: Forskningar och undersökningar. 1: Forntid och vikingatid,* 310–22. Stockholm: Natur och Kultur.

Weiser-Aall, Lily. 1968. *Svangerskap og fødsel i nyere norsk tradition.* Oslo: Norsk Folkemuseum.

Wemple, Suzanne Fonay. 1981. *Women in Frankish Society: Marriage and the Cloister, 500–900.* Philadelphia: University of Pennsylvania Press.

Wisén, Theodor, ed. 1872. *Homiliu-bók.* Lund: Gleerup.

Wolf, Kirsten. 1991. On the Authorship of *Hrafnkels saga. ANF* 106:104–24.

Þórðarson, Björn, see Björn Þórðarson.

Þorkell Jóhannesson. 1933. *Die Stellung der Freien Arbeiter in Island.* Copenhagen: Levin and Munksgaard.

Þorláksson, Helgi, see Helgi Þorláksson.

Þorsteinsson, Björn, see Björn Þorsteinsson.

Index

Although the index contains only the most important men, I have attempted to include all the women. Whenever possible, both first names and patronymics have been indicated. If only the former is available, the women are identified by husband or profession. Those not named in the text have been identified in the index, their names followed by *. The Icelandic letters have been alphabetized in the following way: no distinction between accented and unaccented vowels; æ is placed after ae, ð after d, œ and ǫ after oe, and þ at the end.

Atli (Attila), leader of Huns, 7, 11, 13–14, 107
Auðbjǫrg, housewife, 211n18
Auðr (Bróka-Auðr), wife of Þórðr
  Ingunnarson, 101, 198nn132,133, 199n141,
  203n43
Auðr Snorradóttir*, divorce, 58
Auðr/Unnr Ketilsdóttir, 62, 196n88, 200n154,
  212n43
Auðr Vésteinsdóttir, 71, 108–9, 146–47, 203n36,
  210n8, 213n56

Bæsingr (child of the stall). *See* Children:
  illegitimate, terminology for
Baker, female (bakstur kona), 219
Bandamanna saga, 25–26, 151–52
Banns, reading of, 6, 43, 46, 196n95. *See also*
  Marriage
Baptism, 43, 93–94, 209n137
Barðar saga Snæfellsáss, 14
Barna útburðr (exposure of children). *See*
  Children.
Barsel. *See* Birth
Barter, 147, 150, 228n39
Bath attendant, female (baðkona), 219n58
Bath room (baðstofa), 124
Bathing, 123–24, 168–69; laugarfǫr (bath
  travel), 124
Beer brewing, 127
Benjamin, Walter, 3, 188n4
Bergljót, wife of Illugi, 215n5
Bergþóra Skarpheðinsdóttir, 34, 214n79
Bestiality, 78
Bigamy (tvíkvenni), 20, 191n9. *See also* Mar-
  riage
Birth, 5, 80, 106, 205n79; skilgetinn (lawfully
  conceived), 20
Bishop Árni's New Christian Law. *See* Árni
  Þorláksson, bishop: New Christian Law
Bjargey Valbrandsdóttir, 112, 202n32, 216n19,
  220n76
Bjargrýgr. *See* Midwife
Blanda (mixed river), 4–5, 63, 179
Blankiflur, 205n74
Board games, 103–4
Bǫðvarr Þórðarson, father of Guðný, 8, 188n4,
  195n81
Bǫrkr Þorsteinsson, 11
Borgarthing Law, 4, 82, 90; Older Christian
  Law, 45, 168

Borinn (carried). *See* Children: carried to
  father
Bride price (mundr), 20, 26–27, 82
Brúð(h)laup. *See* Wedding
Brynhildr, ix, 13, 107, 213n55
Búalög (household laws), 139–40, 217n39,
  225nn158,163
Búr. *See* Storage room
Butter, 127–28, 220nn83,85

Castration, 22
Cecilía Sigurðardóttir, 44
Celibacy, 6, 36, 77–78, 205n69. *See also* Mar-
  riage
Children, 81, 83, 213n58; baptism of, 15; carried
  to father (borinn), 82; exposure of (barna
  útburðr), 85; illegitimate, terminology of,
  79; naming of, 30, 82; sprinkling of, 82
Chivalric sagas (riddarasǫgur), 49–50, 188n6
Chrétien de Troyes, 49
Christian mediation of sources, 4–5, 19
Churching of women, 41, 80, 165
Cloth/clothes making, 146–47; foreign, 158–
  60, 232n100; fulled cloth (þófi), 143; fulling
  (þæfa), 140; litklæði (colored cloth), 140
Clover, Carol, 162
Coats, 142–46; export of, 154–56; shaggy
  (vararfeldir), 144–47, 155; þylja (meditate in)
  146, 228n30
Codex Regius, 13
Coins, 151–52
Conception, 65–67, 201n9, 205n74
Concubinage, 18, 20–21, 37, 39, 41, 48; frilla, 31;
  fylgikona 31, 195n77; fylgja at lagi, 35, 39. *See
  also* marriage
Confirmation, 43
Consanguinity, 42–44. *See also* Marriage
Consent, 5–6, 17, 27, 37, 44–52, 167–68. *See also*
  Marriage
Contemporary sagas (samtíðarsǫgur), 4, 19,
  175–76
Continuity, Germanic-nordic and pagan-
  Christian, 5–6, 161–70
Cooking, 129–31
Couple drinking (tvímenningr), 69, 107–8
Curds (skyr), 128, 131

Dairy products and meat, 128–29
Dairy work, 120, 122–23

Grágás, (law code), 4, 176–77; on baptism, 93–94; on berry picking, 216n30; on bigamy, 191n9; and Christian Law, 88; debarring women from politics, 113–14; on divorce, 55–57, 198n129; on the ell, 157; on engagement, 25–27; on incest, 43; on inheritance, 26–27; on marriage, 21; name of, 236n38; on poverty, 83, 99; on regulation of work, 42; on responsibility for illegitimate children, 83; on sexuality, 31–33; on shaggy coats, 155–56; on slaves for sex, 35; on the wedding, 30; on work, 117, 119–20
Gratian, *Decretum*, 37
Gratiana, Greek princess, 50
Grettisfœrsla, 74
Gríma í Ǫgri, mother of Þórdís, 200n157
Gríma in Greenland, performing magic, 221n92
Grimhildr, mother of Guðrún Gjúkadóttir, 192n31, 203n39
Gripir. See Women: gripir (personal treasures of)
Gróa Álfsdóttir, 131, 232n100
Gróa Gizurardóttir, 77
Gróa, widow, 200n157
Grønbech, Vilhelm, xi
Guardian (fastnandi), 25
Guðmundr Arason, bishop of Hólar (1203–1237), 78, 205n69
Guðný Bǫðvarsdóttir, 5, 7–13, 63, 175, 180; at bath, 218n55; children of, 30, 188n5, 190n26; genealogy of, 189nn15,20, 234n1; wedding of, 8, 194n53
Guðríðr, name, 13
Guðríðr Þorbjarnardóttir, 193n34
Guðrún Bjarnardóttir, 59
Guðrún Gjúkadóttir, ix, xi, 5, 7–8, 11–16, 107, 110, 161, 170; and drinking, 213n55; in *Nibelungenlied*, 11
Guðrún Járn-Skeggjadóttir, 58
Guðrún, name, 13, 190n33
Guðrún Ósvífrsdóttir, 15–16, 69, 101, 159–60, 189n14, 190n30, 214n3, 222n103; age of, at marriages, 47, 62, 200n151; and consent to marry, 47; divorce of, 58–59; fourth wedding of, 158–59, 193n32; headdress of, 222n117; marriage for money, 191n16; and protection of Gunnarr, 133, 199n137, 223n121, 133; and spinning, 224n140, 233n107; as widow, 61–62
Guðrún Ǫnundardóttir, 231n86
Guðrún Þórðardóttir, 39, 154

Guðrún Þorkelsdóttir háks*, washing husband's hair, 125
Guðrún, wife of Þorgils Þórðarson ǫrrabeinsstjúpr*, given by husband to other man, 194n54
Gulathing Law, 65, 89–90, 176, 229n51
Gundaharius (Gunnarr), 7
Gunnarr Þiðrandabani, 61, 133
Gunnhildr, mother of King Sverrir, 97
Gunnhildr, queen of Norway, 70–71, 174–75, 235n24; affair with Hrútr, 73–75; and drinking, 213n61; and kiss, 202n32; and young men, 204n56
Gunnlaugs saga, 25
Gyða Eiríksdóttir, 202n35

Haflidaskrá, 177
Hagiography, 175–76
Hákon Aðalsteinsfóstri, king of Norway, 82, 179, 207n116
Hákon Hákonarson, king of Norway, 40, 67, 95
Halla Lýtingsdóttir, 59
Halla, mother of Bishop Þorlákr Þórhallsson, 212n33
Hallbera Snorradóttir, 60
Halldóra Gunnsteinsdóttir*, discusses food with son, 221n91
Halldóra Skegg-Brandsdóttir, wife of Jon Loftsson, 38
Halldóra Tumadóttir, daughter-in-law of Guðný Bǫðvarsdóttir, 9
Hallfríðr Einarsdóttir, 81
Hallfríðr garðafylja, 126
Hallgerðr Hǫskuldsdóttir, 71, 75–76; at alþingi, 214n79; consent to marry, 47, 53; and gossiping, 213n56; infatuation of, 201n17; insults of, 215n16; kiss by father, 202n30; management of and household, 215n10; murder of husbands, 199n134; naming of daughter, 198n125; and stealing, 128–29, 132, 168; third wedding of, 52–54, 198n126, 212n47; and þjóna, 219n59
Haraldr Eiríksson gráfeldr, king of Norway, 155
Haraldr harðráði, king, 76, 95, 105, 203n54; bigamy of, 20, 31; ships sent to Iceland by, 149
Haraldr hárfagri, king, 31, 82, 200n154
Heimanfylgja. See Dowry
Heimskringla, 4, 88, 104, 174
Heitkona (promised woman). See Engagement
Helga Arnardóttir, 212n45